COMMUNION AND OTHERNESS

COMMUNION AND OTHERNESS

Further Studies in Personhood and the Church

JOHN D. ZIZIOULAS

EDITED BY
PAUL McPARTLAN

t&t clark

Published by T&T Clark

A Continuum imprint

The Tower Building, 11 York Road, London SE1 7NX

80 Maiden Lane, Suite 704, New York, NY 10038

www.continuumbooks.com

British Library Cataloguing-in-Publication Data

A catalogue record for this book is available from the British Library

Typeset by CA Typesetting, www.sheffieldtypesetting.com

Printed on acid-free paper in the U.S.A.

ISBN 0567031470   (hardback)

ISBN 0567031489   (paperback)

To the memory
of Father Georges Florovsky
and Professor Colin E. Gunton

CONTENTS

FOREWORD
by the Archbishop of Canterbury

Metropolitan John Zizioulas' earlier work, *Being as Communion*, has a fair claim to be one of the most influential theological books of the later twentieth century; it had a lasting effect on ecumenical discussion and on the vocabulary and assumptions of many churches as they sought to clarify their self-understanding and indeed their understanding of ordained ministry. But what Zizioulas had to say about the Church was firmly anchored in a set of arguments about what we meant by the word 'God', and how our understanding of being itself had to be wholly informed by our understanding of God. In the following pages, these reflections are worked out at greater and greater depth, producing finally a comprehensive model for the whole of Christian theology.

This book is, in effect, a systematic theology, though it is not structured like one. But it is also a work of apologetics in its way. Zizioulas mounts a formidable challenge to atheism by affirming very simply that it is meaningless to discuss 'whether or not' God exists in abstraction from the question of 'how' God exists. To ask whether God exists is really to ask about what the relations are that you can recognize yourself as involved in – because God is irreducibly a living complex of relation, Father, Son and Holy Spirit. But this 'complex' is not just a given plurality, it is the work of freedom – the Father's personal liberty and love generate the inseparable Other, the eternal Son, and 'breathe out' the eternal Spirit. The Father is never alone, nor is the Father simply one among three divine beings alongside each other; it is his absolute freedom to be completely for and in the Other that is the root and rationale of Trinitarian life. And this utter freedom for the Other becomes the insight that allows us to make sense of the freedom of creation, with all that this implies.

Apart from the application of this to Church and sacramental life, there are consequences for ethics and for our understanding

of life and death. Christian ethics is not essentially about awarding
merit points on the grounds of someone's behaviour or habits; it
is founded upon the basic respect for and joy in the otherness of
the world and, above all, of the *personal* other, free and mysterious,
which is drawn out by the indwelling of the Spirit within the communion of Christ's people.

On page after page of this outstanding book, our assumptions
are challenged and our minds led back to the most deeply significant aspects of Christian faith, and to the conceptual and practical
map drawn not only in Scripture but in the Greek Fathers, including
the Fathers of the desert and their teaching on practice and prayer.
The discussion of what is implied in classical Christological statements is of special note; so is the chapter on the Spirit. But insights
abound, into death and sexuality, individualism and postmodernity,
prayer and ecology. Zizioulas engages boldly with different strands
of modern philosophy, refuting most effectively the idea that he is
simply recycling some kind of existentialism or secular personalism,
and offering a deeply suggestive reading and correction of Levinas
on the Other as fundamental for ethics.

Few will read this book without sensing that they have been invited
to rediscover Christianity itself in its richest traditional form. There
are passages where they will have to work hard; some may wonder
whether he always does justice to the Augustinian legacy in its
varied implications as he diagnoses the failures of Western Christian thinking; and the outworking of his ethical structure remains a
tantalising agenda with a great deal of specific application to be followed through. But there can be no doubt that this is a major work
which will be discussed and quarried even more extensively than the
author's earlier writing. A great book and a converting one, which
reintroduces us to the essential Christian conviction that there is no
life without relation with God, as God is himself eternally alive in and
only in the relations initiated by the free love of God the Father, generating the everlasting Son in whom and for whom all things exist,
growing into their fullest possible connectedness with God through
the gift of the Spirit's presence.

Rowan Cantuar
Lambeth Palace, July 2006

PREFACE

The reception accorded to my book, *Being as Communion*, has encouraged me to proceed with the publication of the present volume. This volume contains a number of essays on personhood and the Church along the lines of a relational ontology in which communion constitutes the key idea for ecclesiology as well as anthropology. But whereas in *Being as Communion* the emphasis is on the importance of relationality and communion for *unity*, the present essays lay stress on the aspect of *otherness*. In this sense, the present book must be read as an attempt to complement and balance the previous one.

Certain parts of this book have already appeared elsewhere. Many of them, however, including the first and longest of the essays, are published for the first time here. In both cases, the text has undergone special revision in view of the present edition.

I should like to express my warmest thanks to the Reverend Dr Paul McPartlan, now the Carl J. Peter Professor of Systematic Theology and Ecumenism at the Catholic University of America, for his invaluable assistance in editing this book. Father Paul has been an excellent interpreter of my thought to the English-speaking theological world through his important work, *The Eucharist Makes the Church: Henri de Lubac and John Zizioulas in Dialogue* (Edinburgh: T&T Clark, 1993)[1], and a number of significant articles. It has been a pleasure and a rewarding experience for me to have had many discussions of the contents of this book with him during the process of putting it together. I am also grateful to him for translating from the French Chapter 7 of the book. My thanks are also due to Dr Norman Russell for his excellent translation of the Appendix to Chapter 7 from the Greek. I would also like to express my thanks to Professor R.J. Berry of University College, London, for his kindness in reading and commenting on the part of my manuscript of Chapter 1 relating to biology.

---

[1] A new edition is forthcoming from Eastern Christian Publications, Fairfax, Virginia, USA.

This book is dedicated to the blessed memory of two theologians who have been especially dear to me. Father Georges Florovsky, the great Orthodox theologian of last century, was my teacher and exercised a profound influence on my thought. Professor Colin E. Gunton, a precious friend and colleague at King's College, London, with whom I shared so much in theology over more than two decades, and whose premature death was a great loss to systematic theology, will always be remembered with affection and gratitude. May the Lord grant to both of them eternal rest and a place in his Kingdom.

INTRODUCTION:
Communion and Otherness

Communion and otherness: how can these be reconciled? Are they not mutually exclusive and incompatible with each other? Is it not true that, by definition, the other is my enemy and my 'original sin', to recall the words of the French philosopher, J.P. Sartre?[1] Our Western culture seems to subscribe to this view in many ways. Individualism is present in the very foundation of this culture. Ever since Boethius in the fifth century identified the person with the individual ('person is an individual substance of a rational nature'),[2] and St Augustine at about the same time emphasized the importance of consciousness and self-consciousness in the understanding of personhood,[3] Western thought has never ceased to build itself and its culture on this basis. In our culture protection from the other is a fundamental necessity. We feel more and more threatened by the presence of the other. We are forced and even encouraged to consider the other as our enemy before we can treat him or her as our friend. Communion with the other is not spontaneous; it is built upon fences which protect us from the dangers implicit in the other's presence. We accept the other only in so far as he or she does not threaten our privacy or in so far as he or she is useful for our individual happiness.

There is no doubt that this is a direct result of what in theological language we call the 'Fall of man'. There is a pathology built into the very roots of our existence, inherited through our birth, and that is the *fear of the other*.

This is a result of the rejection of the Other *par excellence*, our Creator, by the first man, Adam — and before him by the demonic powers that revolted against God. The essence of sin is fear of the

---

[1] J.P. Sartre, *L'être et le néant*, 1949, p. 251.
[2] Boethius, *Con. Eutych. et Nest.* 3.
[3] Augustine was the first Christian to write *Confessions* as an exercise in the Christian self-consciousness of the believer.

other, which is part of this rejection. Once the affirmation of the *'self'* is realized through the rejection and not the acceptance of the Other — this is what Adam chose in his freedom to do — it is only natural and inevitable for the other to become an enemy and a threat. Reconciliation with God is a necessary pre-condition for reconciliation with any 'other'.

The fact that the fear of the other is pathologically inherent in our existence results in the fear not only of the other but of *all otherness*. This is a delicate point which, I think, requires serious consideration. For it shows how deep and how widespread the fear of the other is: we are not afraid simply of a certain other or others, but, even if we accept certain others, we accept them on condition that they somehow are like ourselves. Radical otherness is anathema. Difference itself is a threat. That this is universal and pathological is to be seen in the fact that even when difference does not in actual fact constitute a threat for us, we reject it simply because we have distaste, or dislike it. To take an example, even if a person of another colour is not threatening us in any way, we reject him or her on the basis of sheer difference. This is an extreme example, as we would all tend to agree nowadays. But there are so many more subtle examples that show how the fear of the other is in fact nothing but the fear of the different; we all want somehow to project into the other the model of our own selves, which shows how deeply rooted in our existence the fear of the other is.

When the fear of the other is shown to be the fear of otherness we come to the point of identifying difference with division. This complicates and obscures human thinking and behaviour to an alarming degree. The moral consequences in this case are very serious. We divide our lives and human beings according to difference. We organize clubs, fraternities, even churches on the basis of difference. When difference becomes division, communion is nothing but an arrangement for peaceful co-existence. It lasts as long as mutual interests last, and may easily be turned into conflict and confrontation as soon as those interests cease to coincide. Our societies and our world situation as a whole so amply witness to this today.

Now, if this confusion between difference and division were simply a moral problem, ethics would suffice to solve it. But it is not. St Maximus the Confessor recognized in this not only universal but even cosmic dimensions.[4] The entire cosmos is divided on account

---

[4] Maximus Conf., *Theol. Pol.* 20 (PG 91, 249C); *Amb.* 67 (PG 91, 1400C).

of difference, and it is different in its parts on the basis of its divisions. This makes the problem of communion and otherness a matter organically bound up with the problem of death. Death exists because communion and otherness cannot coincide in creation. Different beings become distant beings: because difference becomes division, distinction becomes distance. St Maximus made use of these terms to express this universal and cosmic situation. Διαφορὰ (difference) must be maintained, for it is good. Διαίρεσις (division) is a perversion of διαφορὰ, and is bad.[5] The same is true of διάσπασις (decomposition), and hence death. All this is due, as St Gregory of Nyssa had already observed, to the διάστημα (space; in the sense of both space and time) that characterizes creation *ex nihilo*.[6] Mortality is tied up with createdness out of nothing, and it is this that the rejection of the Other — God — and of the other in any sense amounts to. By turning difference into division through the rejection of the other, we die. Hell, eternal death, is nothing but isolation from the other, as the desert Fathers put it.[7] We cannot solve this problem through ethics. We need a new birth. This leads us to ecclesiology.

*

How is the relation between communion and otherness realized? What is the place of the other in ecclesial communion?

The Church is a community that lives within history, and therefore within the fallen state of existence. All our observations concerning the difficulty of reconciling communion with otherness in our culture are applicable also to the life of the Church. Sin as fear and rejection of the other is a reality experienced also within the Church. The Church is made up of sinners, and she shares fully the ontological

---

[5] Maximus Conf., *Ep.* 12 (PG 91, 469AB).

[6] Gregory Nys., *In Eccl.*, Homily 7 (PG 44, 729C).

[7] See the striking words attributed to St Macarius the Great (the Egyptian) in one of his *Apophthegmata* (PG 34, 229-264): 'Walking in the desert one day, I found the skull of a dead man, lying on the ground. As I was moving it with my stick, the skull spoke to me. I said to it, "Who are you?" The skull replied, "I was a high priest of the idols and of the pagans who dwelt in this place; but you are Macarius, the Spirit-bearer. Whenever you take pity on those who are in torments, and pray for them, they feel a little respite." The old man said to him, "What is this alleviation, and what is this torment?" He said to him, "As far as the sky is removed from the earth, so great is the fire beneath us; we are ourselves standing in the midst of the fire, from the feet up to the head. *It is not possible to see anyone face to face* [πρόσωπον πρός πρόσωπον], *but the face of one is fixed to the back of another. Yet when you pray for us, each of us can see the other's face a little.* Such is our respite." The old man in tears said, "Alas the day when that man was born" ' (trans. B. Ward, *The Sayings of the Desert Fathers*, 1975, p. 136f.).

and cosmic dimension of sin which is death, the break of communion and final *diastasis* (separation and decomposition) of beings. And
yet, we insist that in her essence the Church is holy and sinless. On
this, Orthodox theologians differ from those of other confessions,
particularly from those of the Protestant family. What does this tell
us about the subject of communion and otherness?

The first thing that is implied in this position of the Orthodox
is the very opposite of triumphalism, namely that the essence of
Christian existence in the Church is *metanoia* (repentance). By being
rejected, or simply feared by us, the other challenges and provokes
us to repent. Even the existence of pain and death in the natural
world, which is not caused by any one of us individually, should lead
to *metanoia*. For we all share in the fall of Adam, and we all must feel
the sorrow of failing to bring creation to communion with God and
the overcoming of death. Holiness in the Church passes through sin-
cere and deep *metanoia*. All the saints weep for the sufferings of innocent creation.[8]

The second implication of the Orthodox position concerning the
holiness of the Church is that repentance can only be true and genuine if the Church and her members are aware of the *true nature* of
the Church. We need a model by which to measure our existence.
And the higher the model the deeper the repentance. That is why
we need a maximal ecclesiology and a maximal anthropology — and
even cosmology — resulting from it. Orthodox ecclesiology, by stressing the holiness of the Church, does not and should not lead to triumphalism but to a deep sense of compassion and *metanoia*.

What is the model of such a maximal ecclesiology for the purpose
of understanding and living communion with the other properly?
From where can we receive guidance and illumination in order to live
our communion with the Other and with others in the Church?

*

There is no model for the proper relation between communion
and otherness either for the Church or for the human being other
than the Trinitarian God. If the Church wants to be faithful to her
true self, she must try to mirror the communion and otherness that

[8] 'The heart that has learned to love is sorry for all created things', said St Silouan
the Athonite, who 'bewailed his own harshness in "unnecessarily" killing a fly, or
pouring boiling water on a bat that had settled on the balcony of his store', and
told 'how sorry he felt for every living thing, all creation, when he saw a dead snake
hacked to bits', Archimandrite Sophrony (Sakharov), *St Silouan the Athonite*, 1991,
p. 94f.

exists in the triune God. The same is true of the human being as the 'image of God'. The relation between communion and otherness in God is the model both for ecclesiology and for anthropology. What can we learn about communion and otherness from the doctrine of the Trinity?

The first thing that emerges from a study of the doctrine of the Trinity is that otherness is *constitutive* of unity, and not consequent upon it. God is not first one and then three, but simultaneously one and three. His oneness or unity is safeguarded not by the unity of substance, as St Augustine and other Western theologians have argued, but by the *monarchia* of the Father, who himself is one of the Trinity. It is also expressed through the unbreakable *koinonia* that exists between the three persons, which means that otherness is not a threat to unity but a *sine qua non* condition of it.

Secondly, a study of the Trinity reveals that otherness is *absolute*. The Father, the Son and the Spirit are absolutely different (*diaphora*),[9] none of them being subject to confusion with the other two.

Thirdly, and most significantly, otherness is not moral or psychological but *ontological*. We cannot tell *what* each person is; we can only say *who* he is. Each person in the holy Trinity is different not by way of difference of natural qualities (such qualities are all common to the three persons), but by way of the simple affirmation of being who he is.

As a result, finally, otherness is inconceivable apart from *relationship*. Father, Son and Spirit are all names indicating relationship. No person can be different unless he is related. Communion does not threaten otherness; it generates it.

*

We cannot be the 'image of God', either at the ecclesiological or the anthropological level, unless we are incorporated in the original and only authentic image of the Father, which is the Son of God incarnate. This implies the following for our subject:

(a) Communion with the other requires the experience of the *Cross*. Unless we sacrifice our own will and subject it to the will of the other, repeating in ourselves what our Lord did in Gethsemane in relation to the will of his Father, we cannot reflect properly in history the communion and otherness that we see in the triune God. Since the Son of God moved to meet the other, his creation, by emptying himself

---

[9] Cf. Basil, *Adv. Eun.* 1.19 (PG 29, 556B), and Maximus Conf., *Ep.* 15 (PG 91, 553D): διαφορὰ προσωπική.

through the *kenosis* of the Incarnation, the 'kenotic' way is the only one that befits the Christian in his or her communion with the other — be it God or one's 'neighbour'.

(b) In this 'kenotic' approach to the other, communion is not determined in any way by the qualities that he or she might or might not possess. In accepting the sinner, Christ applied to communion the Trinitarian model, as we described it above: the other is not to be identified by his or her qualities, but by the sheer fact that he or she is, and is *himself* or *herself*. We cannot discriminate between those who are and those who are not 'worthy' of our acceptance. This is what the Christological model of communion with the other requires.

*

The Holy Spirit is associated, among other things, with *koinonia* (2 Cor. 13.13), and the entrance of the last days into history (Acts 2.17-18), that is, *eschatology*. When the Holy Spirit blows, he creates not good individual Christians, individual 'saints', but an event of communion, which transforms everything the Spirit touches into a *relational* being. In that case the other becomes an ontological part of one's own identity. The Spirit de-individualizes and personalizes beings wherever he operates.

On the other hand, the eschatological dimension of the presence and activity of the Spirit deeply affects the identity of the other: it is on the basis not of someone's past or present that we should identify and accept him or her, but on the basis of their *future*. And since the future lies only in the hands of God, our approach to the other must be free from passing judgement on him or her. Every 'other' is in the Spirit a potential saint, even if he or she appears to have been or continues to be a sinner.

*

All the observations we have made so far concerning faith in the Trinity, in Christ and in the Spirit take their concrete form in the Church. It is there that communion with the other fully reflects the relation between communion and otherness in the holy Trinity, in Christ and in the Spirit. Let us consider some concrete forms of ecclesial communion that reflect this.

(a) *Baptism*. This sacrament is associated with forgiveness. Every baptized person by being forgiven ceases to be identified by his or her past, and becomes a citizen of the city to come, that is, of the Kingdom. What we said earlier about forgiveness receives its concrete application in the Church through Baptism.

(b) *Eucharist*. This is the heart of the Church, where communion and otherness are realized *par excellence*. If the Eucharist is not celebrated properly, the Church ceases to be the Church.

It is not by accident that the Church has given to the Eucharist the name of 'Communion'. For in the Eucharist we can find all the dimensions of communion: God communicates himself to us, we enter into communion with him, the participants of the sacrament enter into communion with one another, and creation as a whole enters through man into communion with God. All this takes place in Christ and the Spirit, who brings the last days into history and offers to the world a foretaste of the Kingdom.

But the Eucharist not only affirms and sanctifies communion; it also sanctifies otherness. It is the place where difference ceases to be divisive and becomes good. *Diaphora* does not lead to *diairesis*, and unity or communion does not destroy but rather affirms diversity and otherness in the Eucharist. Whenever this does not happen, the Eucharist is destroyed and even invalidated, even if all the other requirements for a 'valid' Eucharist are met and satisfied. Thus, a Eucharist which excludes in one way or another those of a different race or sex or age or profession is a false Eucharist. A Eucharist celebrated specially for children or young people or blacks or whites or students, and so on, is a false one. The Eucharist must include all of these, for it is there that otherness of a natural or social kind can be transcended. A Church which does not celebrate the Eucharist in this inclusive way risks losing her catholicity.

Are there no limits to otherness in the eucharistic communion? Is the Eucharist not a 'closed' community in some sense? Do we not have such a thing as exclusion from eucharistic communion? These questions must be answered in the affirmative. There is, indeed, exclusion from communion in the Eucharist, and the 'doors' of the synaxis are indeed shut at some point in the Liturgy. How are we to understand this exclusion of the other?

The answer to this question is that there is only one kind of exclusion that eucharistic communion permits, and that is the exclusion of exclusion itself, that is, of those things that involve rejection and division. Such are the things that *in principle* and by *an act of faith* — not by way of failure to apply the true faith — lead to a kind of communion that disturbs Trinitarian, Christological, Pneumatological and ecclesiological faith, as we described it earlier. Heresy with regard to these matters involves a disturbed faith that has inevitable practical consequences concerning communion and otherness. If, for example, one denies the Trinitarian being of God, one inevitably denies the existential consequences with regard to communion and otherness. The same is true about Christology, Pneumatology and ecclesiology: heretical views on these matters entail different existential attitudes to the 'other'. Schism is also an act of exclusion. When schism occurs, eucharistic communion inevitably becomes exclusive. In both cases, heresy and schism, we cannot pretend that we are in communion with the other when in fact we are not. This is the case with 'intercommunion'. In disagreeing with its practice, we do not preach exclusiveness and exclusion of the other; we simply acknowledge that such an exclusion does exist, and until the causes of it are removed, communion with the 'other' suffers.

(c) *Ministry*. Perhaps there is no area of Church life where communion and otherness co-exist so deeply as in the case of the Church's ministry. Ministry involves *charismata* of the Spirit, and charisms involve variety and diversity. 'Are all apostles? Are all prophets? Are all teachers? Do all…have the charism of healing?' (1 Cor. 12.29). Such questions are posed by St Paul and he gives them a blunt negative answer. The body of Christ consists of many members, and these members represent different gifts and ministries. No member can say to the other 'I have no need of you' (1 Cor. 12.21). There is an absolute *interdependence* among the members-ministries of the Church: no ministry can be isolated and conceived apart from the 'other'. Otherness is of the essence of the ministry.

Having said that, we must add that otherness is acceptable only when it leads to communion and unity — not if it leads to division. When *diaphora* becomes *diairesis*, to recall St Maximus' terminology to which we referred earlier, we immediately encounter the 'fallen' state of existence. In order to avoid this, the Church needs a ministry of unity, someone who would himself be needful of the 'others' and yet capable of protecting difference from falling into division. This is the office or ministry of the *bishop*.

It is not accidental that there can be no Church without a bishop. And it is not accidental either that there can be only one bishop in a Church (canon 8 of Nicaea). A Church without a bishop risks allowing difference to fall into division. And more than one bishop in a Church leads to difference becoming a divisive factor. The present-day situation of the Orthodox diaspora is such an unfortunate, dangerous and totally unacceptable phenomenon. It allows ethnic and cultural differences to become grounds of ecclesial communion centred on different bishops. A bishop who does not in himself transcend ethnic and cultural differences becomes a minister of division and not of unity. This is something that the Orthodox should consider very seriously indeed, if distortion of the very nature of the Church is to be avoided.

*

All these observations lead to important *anthropological* consequences. Theology and Church life involve a certain conception of the human being. This conception can be summed up in one word: *personhood*. This term, sanctified through its use in connection with the very being of God and of Christ, is so rich in implications for the theme of communion and otherness that it becomes imperative to reflect on it, even if briefly.

(a) *The Person is otherness in communion and communion in otherness.* The person is an identity that emerges through relationship (*schesis*, in the terminology of the Greek Fathers); it is an 'I' that can exist only as long as it relates to a 'thou' which affirms its existence and its otherness. If we isolate the 'I' from the 'thou' we lose not only its otherness but also its very being; it simply cannot be without the other. This is what distinguishes a person from an individual. The orthodox understanding of the holy Trinity is the only way to arrive at this notion of personhood: the Father cannot be conceived for a single moment without the Son and the Spirit, and the same applies to the other two persons in their relation with the Father and with each other. At the same time, each of these persons is so unique that their hypostatic or personal properties are totally incommunicable from one person to the other.

(b) *Personhood is freedom.* In its anthropological significance, as well as in its theological significance, personhood is inconceivable without freedom; it is the freedom of being other. I hesitate to say 'different' instead of 'other', because 'different' can be understood in the sense of qualities (clever, beautiful, holy, etc.), which is not what the person is about. It is noteworthy that in God all such qualities are common to all three persons. Person implies not simply the freedom to have different qualities, but mainly the freedom simply to be yourself. This means that a person is not subject to norms and stereotypes; a person cannot be classified in any way; a person's uniqueness is absolute. This finally means that only a person is free in the true sense.

And yet because, as we have already observed, one person is no person, this freedom is not freedom *from* the other but freedom *for* the other. Freedom thus becomes identical with *love*. God is love because he is Trinity. We can love only if we are persons, that is, if we allow the other to be truly other, and yet to be in communion with us. If we love the other not only in spite of his or her being different from us but *because* he or she is different from us, or rather *other* than ourselves, we live in freedom as love and in love as freedom.

(c) *Personhood is creativity.* This applies to the human person and is a consequence of the understanding of freedom as love and of love as freedom. Freedom is not *from* but *for* someone or something other than ourselves. This makes the person *ec-static*, that is, going outside and beyond the boundaries of the 'self'. But this *ecstasis* is not to be understood as a movement towards the unknown and the infinite; it is a movement of *affirmation of the other*.

This drive of personhood towards the affirmation of the other is so strong that it is not limited to the 'other' that already exists, but wants to affirm an 'other' which is the totally free grace of the person. Just as God created the world totally as free grace, so the person wants to create its own 'other'. This is what happens in art; and it is only the person that can be an artist in the true sense, that is, a creator that brings about a totally other identity as an act of freedom and communion. Living in the Church in communion with the other means, therefore, creating a *culture*.

This leads me to a point that may appear to have little to do with our subject, and yet it is totally relevant to our consideration of communion and otherness. I am referring to the *ecological* problem. What does this have to do with our subject?

To put it briefly, for that is all that I can do here, the ecological problem which is becoming so threatening for God's creation is due to a crisis between the human being and the *otherness of the rest of creation*. Man does not respect the otherness of what is not human; he tends to absorb it into himself. This is the cause of the ecological problem.

Now the tragedy of the matter is that in a desperate attempt to correct this, man may easily fall today into the pagan alternative of absorbing man into nature. We have to be very careful. Theology is particularly called to offer the right Christian answer to the problem out of its own tradition. Nature is the 'other' that man is called to bring into communion with himself, affirming it as 'very good' through personal creativity. This is what happens in the Eucharist, where the natural elements of bread and wine are so affirmed that they acquire *personal* qualities (the body and blood of Christ) in the event of the communion of the Spirit. Similarly, in a para-eucharistic way, all forms of true culture and art, for example the icon or music or architecture, are ways of treating nature as otherness in communion, and these are real antidotes to the present ecological illness.

*

The chapters contained in this volume aim at tackling the subject of communion and otherness in different ways.

In the first chapter, the subject of otherness is raised in its absolute ontological significance. Otherness is not secondary to unity; it is primary and constitutive of the very idea of being. Respect for otherness is a matter not of ethics but of ontology: if otherness disappears, beings simply cease to be. In Christian theology there is simply no room for ontological totalitarianism. All communion must involve otherness as a primary and constitutive ingredient. It is this that makes freedom part of the notion of being. Freedom is not simply 'freedom of will'; it is the freedom to be other in an absolute ontological sense.

This is followed and applied to the notion of the person in the next chapters. With the help of the Trinitarian theology of the Greek Fathers, particularly the Cappadocians, and their understanding of what it means to be a person, first in God and then in the human being, communion and otherness are shown to be fundamental parts of the doctrine of the holy Trinity. God is not, logically or ontologically speaking, first one and then many; he is one in being many. Otherness, the Trinity, is built into the very oneness of divine being. Even when we look for what accounts for (i.e. causes) divine being, we are confronted with otherness, that is, with a particular person, the Father. Ontological causation is thereby tied up with personal freedom, that is, with the freedom to be other.

In Chapters 6 and 7, we move to the realm of the divine Economy. The doctrine of creation presents the subject of otherness not so much as that of personal alterity, as is the case with the doctrine of the Trinity, but as otherness at the level of natures, that is, as natural otherness. This is crucial in terms of the relation between Greek and biblical faith, and shows how otherness at the level of natures, with its absolute radicality and its serious consequences for the existence of man and creation, needs to be bridged by communion in order to acquire ontological content, that is, to avoid and transcend mortality. For the act of creation *ex nihilo* involves the emergence of so absolute and radical an otherness between God and the world that unless otherness is bridged by communion the world would ontologically collapse. This bridge is provided in Christ through the hypostatic union, that is, through the intermediary of personal otherness, and in the Holy Spirit who extends this communion and otherness to all humanity and nature. Personal otherness thus saves and redeems natural otherness without destroying it.

All this is finally applied to ecclesial experience in the concluding chapter, where the subject of ecclesial mysticism is used in order to illustrate the problems relating to the accommodation of otherness in the reality of communion. This is intended to demonstrate that the inseparable unity of communion with otherness is of crucial importance for the understanding of mysticism in an ecclesiological way.

Chapter 1

ON BEING OTHER:
Towards an Ontology of Otherness

INTRODUCTION

The theme of otherness is a fundamental aspect of theology. Being 'other' is part of what it means to be oneself, and therefore to be at all, whether reference is made to God or to humanity or to anything that is said to exist. Connected with this is the subject of freedom. Freedom is not to be restricted to the psychological and moral sense traditionally attributed to it, that is, to the idea of the 'freedom of the will' and of making moral decisions; it should be related to the fundamental question of *being*. Being other and being free in an ontological sense, that is, in the sense of being free to be yourself, and not someone or something else, are two aspects of one and the same reality.

The problem of the Other has been central to philosophy in our time.[1] In the twentieth century, it particularly preoccupied the philosophical schools of phenomenology and existentialism, culminating in the thought of philosophers such as M. Buber and E. Levinas, who made the idea of the Other a key subject of philosophical discourse. It is, in fact, a subject as old as Greek philosophy itself, as is evident from the place it occupied in the Platonic dialogues, particularly *Parmenides*, in Aristotle and even in the Pre-Socratics. There can hardly be any philosophy worthy of the name that does not involve, directly or indirectly, a discussion of this subject.

Theology cannot remain indifferent to the subject of otherness. As I shall try to show in this essay, Patristic theology is penetrated

---

[1] M. Theunissen, *The Other* (English trans. by C. Macann), 1986, p. 1: 'The problem of the Other has certainly never penetrated as deeply as today into the foundations of philosophical thought'.

by it, and so is Christian doctrine in general. What is even more significant, the subject of otherness is present today, implicitly or explicitly, in many areas of Christian, or religious in general, experience and discourse. In the first place, it is an intra-Christian problem, as it appears when we consider the issue of the balance between communion or community and the individual, or between the one Church and the many Churches.[2] Communion seems to strike a sensitive chord in a Christian world fed up with individualism and institutional rigidity. Yet if the idea of communion is not qualified by that of otherness, it can lead to many problems. The task of working out an understanding of communion linked organically with an understanding of otherness appears to be imperative in theology today.

The same significance of the subject of otherness is evident at the cultural level. Respect for otherness is becoming a central ethical principle in civilized societies today. This clashes very often with traditional norms which have enjoyed authority for centuries. It also becomes problematic in so far as it can lead to individualism, with which modern man is not totally happy. If otherness is not somehow qualified with communion, it can hardly produce a satisfactory culture. In any case, neither otherness nor communion can be valid solely on ethical grounds; they have to be related to the truth of existence. The crucial question has to be not simply whether otherness is acceptable or desirable in our society — the ethical principles of societies are usually transient — but whether it is a *sine qua non* condition for one's very being and for the being of all that exists. This is what an ontology of otherness is about. And this is what an existentially relevant theology cannot but be concerned with.

In the lines that follow, the problem of otherness will be approached from different angles, all of them corresponding to fundamental aspects of the Christian faith. In all these aspects, the 'other' will be shown to be ontologically constitutive for the being of God, both in his immanent and in his 'economic' existence, including the person and work of Christ and the Spirit, as well as for the being of creation and the human being in their actual condition and their eschatological destiny.

I. OTHERNESS AND THE BEING OF CREATION

1. *The Gulf between Uncreated and Created Being*

The assumptions on which ancient Greek philosophy rested created serious difficulties to the Christian theologians of the first centuries,

---

[2] I have dealt extensively with this in my *Being as Communion*, 1985, *passim*.

who had to reconcile them with their biblical faith. Thus, the assumption that nothing can come out of nothing,[3] which accounted for the priority of unity and the One over against otherness and the Many in ancient Greek thought,[4] clashed with the Christian view that the world did not always exist but came into being out of a free act of the free and transcendent God. The doctrine of creation was, therefore, the first occasion for a drastic revision of Greek ontology by Christian theology. That this revision involved the introduction of the dimension of otherness and freedom into the concept of being is what concerns us directly here.

Is the being of the world real? Or is it a φαινόμενον, a disclosure of the only truly real being, which is God? If the world is real only by virtue of its participation in the true being (in this case, God),[5] it

---

[3] This is a view shared by all ancient Greek philosophers. 'Nothing could have come to be out of what is not, for there must be something present as a substrate'; Aristotle, *Phys.* 191Λ, 23, in basic agreement with Parmenides as to the principle that everything comes from something. If we do not observe this Parmenidean principle, we generate being from non-being. See his *De Gen. et Corrupt.* 317Λ, 34; 319Λ, 12f. Cf. J. Rist, *The Mind of Aristotle*, 1989, p. 208; and F.M. Cornford, *Plato and Parmenides*, 1939, p. 31: All Greeks would agree that nothing can come out of nothing, and 'no advance can be made from the premiss that all that exists was once in a state of non-existence or that non-entity can exist'.

[4] That the real is ultimately one had been assumed from the very beginning of Greek philosophy. The extreme view of Parmenides (*Fig.* 8.36) that 'there is and shall be no other (ἄλλο) besides what is (πάρεξ ἐόντος)' was questioned by Plato, who argued that the many or 'other' exist, yet only as dependent on the One. Thus Plato, *Parm.* 165Ef., in his last of eight hypotheses concludes that, 'if there is no One, but only things other than one, what must follow? The others will not be one; but neither will they be many. For if they are to be many, there must be a one among them; since, if none of them is one thing (ἕν), they will all be no-thing (οὐδέν), and so not many either... Therefore, if there is no One, the others neither are, nor can be imagined to be one or many... If there is no One, there is nothing at all'. Cf. F.M. Cornford, *Plato and Parmenides*, and R.E. Allen, *Plato's Parmenides*, 1997, pp. 64 and 338. Aristotle, too, would insist on the reality of the many, yet what survives their destruction is ultimately the substrate from which they are generated. *De Gen. et Corr.* 320A2f. Cf. A. Edel, *Aristotle and his Philosophy*, 1982, p. 48. For Aristotle, too, 'whatever *is* is one, and whatever is one is... Being and unity are terms standing above the distinction of categories and applicable to every category'; W.D. Ross, *Aristotle*, 1959, p. 154. This ontological ultimacy of the One survives in ancient Greek philosophy well into the time of Neoplatonism. See K. Kremer, *Die neuplatonische Seinsphilosophie und ihre Wirkung auf Thomas v. Aquin*, 1971, p. 79f.

[5] In the case of Plato, one could speak of 'degrees of reality' (see G. Vlastos, *Platonic Studies*, 1973, p. 58f.), in accordance with the doctrine of participation in the ideas: only the ideas are ὄντως ὄντα; the world's beings are μᾶλλον ὄντα. This would not agree with the Christian understanding of reality, since according to this understanding the world is *totally* other, having come out of nothing. The Platonic doc-

must follow that God and the world are somehow joined together with an ontological affinity (συγγένεια). This would make God a Creator by necessity and the world not ultimately other than God. *The absence, therefore, of freedom in the act of creation would amount automatically to the loss of ontological otherness, for both the Creator and his creation.* Otherness as an ontological category for both the Creator and his creation emerges as a logical imperative when creation is conceived as an act of freedom, that is, as an act that cannot be explained by being itself; it cannot be attributed axiomatically to being itself, but to a factor other than being itself which causes being to be. Creation *ex nihilo* implies that being does not come from being, which would make it necessary being. This, therefore, is the reason why otherness and freedom are interwoven in ontology with regard, in the case under consideration, to the being of creation. Otherness in this case has to be ontological in character or else freedom in the ontological sense disappears: the Creator would be bound up ontologically with his creation.

That the question of ontological freedom is tied up with ontological otherness in any doctrine of creation is illustrated well by Plato's idea of creation, as expressed in the *Timaeus*. In this work, Plato professes faith in God the Creator and even goes as far as to attribute the act of creation to God's 'free will'. This has led many people, including early Christian theologians such as Justin,[6] fully to endorse the *Timaeus* from the Christian viewpoint. But Plato's Creator acted according to his will (θελήσει),[7] in a way that was not ontologically free: the Demiurge had to create out of pre-existing matter and to do so with absolute respect for the ideas of Beauty and Goodness, while a pre-existing space (χώρα) dictated to him the circumstances and conditions under which the world he created ought to exist.[8] In this case, therefore, creation was an ontologically constrained and unfree act. This was so because there was no absolute otherness between the Creator and his creation, in an ontological sense, or, vice-versa, there was no absolute otherness because there was no ontological freedom; the two things, freedom and otherness, are interdependent.

The Christian theologians of the patristic era had to cope with this problem. Origen, following the alterations applied to the platonic

trine of degrees of reality would not do for Christian ontology, precisely because of the ontological primacy attached by the latter to otherness.

[6] Justin, *Apol.* I, 20 (PG 6, 357C); 60 (PG 6, 417A); *Dial.* 5 (PG 6, 488B).
[7] Plato, *Tim.* 29.
[8] Plato, *Tim.* 29.

doctrine of creation by Philo, Albinus and other Middle Platonists,[9] rejected the restrictions imposed on the Creator by the pre-existence of matter and the ideas, but together with these philosophers he understood these ideas as the thoughts of God, eternally existing in him, in unity with his eternal Logos.[10] Thus, in a subtle way, God's freedom was taken away from his act of creation,[11] and so was the radical ontological otherness of the world. As a consequence, Origen had to assume that there was something eternal in creation, expressing a certain affinity between God and the world.[12] The eternity of the soul and of the intelligible world contained in the Logos, which had no beginning in time and will have no end,[13] was in reality nothing but a way of removing both otherness and ontological freedom from the act of the creation of the world.

It was not until St Athanasius and Nicaea stepped in that the position of the Church on this matter was clarified. Between God and the world there is total ontological otherness: God's being is uncreated, while that of the world is created, that is, contingent.[14] Does this make the world's being somehow less real? Does otherness amount

[9] See R.M. Jones, 'The Ideas as Thoughts of God', *Classical Philology* 21 (1926), pp. 317-26. H.A. Wolfson, *The Philosophy of the Church Fathers*, 1976, p. 258f., distinguishes this view from, on the one hand, Aristotle's understanding of the Platonic ideas as self-subsistent real incorporeal beings, among which is the idea of the Good, which is identified with God, and, on the other hand, Philo's view that the ideas contained in the divine Logos exist first as thoughts of God and then as real beings created by him.

[10] Origen, *In Joan* I.22 (PG 14, 56CD); XIX.5 (PG 14, 568BC), etc. H. Crouzel, *Origène et Plotin*, 1991, p. 53, sums up Origen's position in the following words: 'cette création coéternelle à Dieu, ce κόσμος νοητός, qui s'identifie au Fils, est constitué par les idées, au sens platonicien, et les raisons, au sens stoïcien, contenues dans le Fils en tant qu'il est la Sagesse'.

[11] Cf. G. Florovsky, *Creation and Redemption* (vol. 3 of Collected Works), 1976, p. 52ff. 'Origen had to admit the necessity of a conjointly ever-existent and beginningless "not-I" as a corresponding prerequisite to and correlative of the Divine completeness and life... If...God creates out of necessity, for the sake of the completeness of His Being, then the world must exist; then it is not possible that the world might not have existed' (p. 54).

[12] Origen, *De Princ.* I.2.10 (PG 11, 138-9); II.3.3 (PG 11,191); *Exhor. mart.* 47 (PG 11, 629); *C. Cels.* 3.30 (PG 11, 972). Cf. H. Crouzel, *Origène et Plotin*, p. 40: 'Toute la création intellectuelle participe à la nature même du Père, du Fils et du Saint Esprit; il y a une certaine parenté entre l'homme et Dieu...'

[13] See H. Crouzel, *Origène et Plotin*, p. 340. For a different interpretation, more sympathetic to Origen, see J. Rebecca Lyman, *Christology and Cosmology*, 1993, p. 55ff.

[14] Cf. Athanasius, *C. Arian.* 1.20-21 (PG 26, 53); 2.2 (PG 26, 152); 3.60 (PG 26, 448f.).

to ontological diminution? The answer would be 'Yes' in the context of Greek philosophy, but it is not so in the case of patristic thought. A totally *other* being *can* exist side by side with God's being, because being does not necessarily come out of being itself; rather, it results from freedom. Since something *can* come out of nothing, *ex nihilo*, it can be both real and other in the absolute sense. The doctrine of creation out of nothing was about otherness and freedom in ontology.

Now, for the Fathers, the world's being was fully and truly being, but it was, of its nature, a perishable being: having come out of nothing, it could return to nothing and perish.[15] Such a position would be scandalous to the ancient Greeks, who could never conceive of being as ultimately perishable; even in the Platonic idea of non-being (μὴ εἶναι), there is eternal survival of being thanks to participation in the being of the One. Did the Greek Fathers depart from this principle entirely? Had they done so, they would have ceased to be Greek, since the hallmark of Greek thought is concern with the survival of being. The world's being is, for them, perishable by nature. However, since being does not emerge from being naturally but rather through the intervention of personal freedom, it is not logically *bound to be* ultimately perishable. Contrary to what the Greeks believed, what has had a beginning does not *necessarily* have an end.[16] So the world's being can be eternal *in the end* without having been eternal in the beginning, that is, in its nature. Nature does not determine being. By the logic of the possibility of having a being emerge not from being by necessity but by a free act, the beginning of being does not dictate its end; the end can be more than the beginning.[17]

It is in this way that otherness and contingency can be conceived as true being. The world is a reality in the ultimate ontological sense not because of a natural necessity of some kind, but because being does not depend on nature but on freedom, having truly come out of a free act of a free person. If the world is based simply on its own nature, it is bound to perish, for it is part of its nature to be perishable, having come out of nothing (Athanasius). Had it been imperishable by nature, (a) it would have come not out of nothing but out of an imperishable something; (b) its being would be due to necessity, not freedom; and

---

[15] Athanasius, *De Incarn.* 4-5 (PG 25, 104).

[16] Cf. G. Florovsky, *Creation and Redemption*, p. 216: For the Greeks 'only that which had no beginning could last for ever. Christians could not comply with this "philosophical" assumption'.

[17] G. Florovsky, *Creation and Redemption*, p. 219: 'the world has a *contingent beginning*, yet *no end*. It stands by the immutable will of God'.

(c) it would not be ontologically 'other', since its being would be essentially and ultimately identical with the nature from which it has come forth. Its end would have been like the beginning by necessity, and, if the beginning was nothing, it would return by necessity to nothing, whereas if its beginning was 'something', it would return by necessity to that 'something' from which it came forth. Being would then have to be cyclical if it were to survive, as was in fact conceived by the ancient Greeks. In that case, ontology would be 'totalitarian', recalling Levinas' accusation against Greek philosophy.

Once being was liberated from itself, as the Christian doctrine of creation implies, being could survive eternally in spite of its perishable *nature*. The truth of the world's being would be located not in nature but in personhood. Contingency does not logically imply a false ontology, an untrue being, once the axiom of necessary being is removed or abolished.

It can therefore be concluded that one of the fundamental consequences of the doctrine of creation *ex nihilo* has been the logical possibility of making the 'other' a true being without linking it up with its cause *through nature*, that is, by necessity. God's nature and the world's nature could never coincide; there is absolute 'abysmal' otherness between these two.[18] In this way, otherness acquires full ontological status, thanks to the intervention of freedom in ontology — something the ancient Greeks had never thought of. By freely granting being to something naturally other than himself, God sanctified otherness and raised it to full ontological status.

2. *Bridging the Gulf of Otherness*

Otherness is necessary for freedom to exist: if there is no absolute, ontological otherness between God and the world, there is no ontological freedom allowing each of these two 'beings' to be *themselves* and thus to be at all. But if this were all we could say about otherness, *separateness* and *distance* would be a *sine qua non* condition for otherness. Christian doctrine, however, does not seem to imply or accept such a condition. The very fact of the Incarnation precludes a philosophy of otherness that would regard separateness as a condition of otherness. But how can otherness retain its absolute ontological character if separateness is not its constitutive element? How can God and the world be, as we have pointed out,

---

[18] According to St Maximus, between God and creation there is a real gulf (χάσμα). See H.U. von Balthasar, *Kosmische Liturgie*, 1961², pp. 89 and 161. Cf. Maximus, *Amb.* 41 (PG 91, 1305A).

abysmally other ontologically, and yet remain unseparated? This question lies at the heart of the problem of reconciling otherness with communion.

We have already ruled out any ontological connection between God and the world on the basis of nature or substance, for this would amount to a necessary unity between the two and would contradict the idea of creation *ex nihilo*. Those who hold a substantialist ontology and identify being with substance would find it difficult to call God's relationship with the world 'ontological'.[19] It is no wonder that, ever since Christianity influenced philosophy, particularly in the West, the gap between God and creation has been filled mainly not through ontology but through ethics or psychology: communion between the Creator and creation has been conceived either in terms of obedience to God's commandments or through some kind of 'religion of the heart'.[20] Whenever mysticism was used as a form of communion between God and the world, this was either rejected outright or accepted at the expense of otherness. And yet, there is a possibility of working out an *ontological* way of relating God to the world without denying their ontological otherness and returning to the monism of ancient Greek thought. This is so because ontology does not have to be substantialistic in order to be true ontology. The Greek Fathers witness precisely to such a possibility.

A careful study of the history of patristic thought would reveal that the problem of relating God and the world ontologically occupied a central place in the creative theology of that time. Leaving aside the liturgical or 'symbolic' approach to the relation between created and uncreated being – an approach mainly to be found in the Areopagetic writings – we may depict three ways in which Greek patristic theology tried to solve this problem:

---

[19] L. Thunberg, in his excellent study of St Maximus, *Microcosm and Mediator*, 1995[2], pp. 406, 435, and elsewhere, assumes such a definition of ontology when he writes that for Maximus the relation between God and the world is not ontological. He apparently contrasts 'ontological' to 'existential' (e.g., p. 416), as if existence were not an ontological category. This, however, would rule out of ontology the *tropos* of being, which would contradict the Cappadocians and Maximus.

The medieval scholastic *analogia entis* naturally causes concern about God's otherness for theologians such as K. Barth, P. Tillich, etc. However, a more satisfactory explanation of the ontological relation of God to creation is necessary than the alternative of the *analogia fidei* proposed by Barth (*Church Dogmatics* I.1; 1975; p. 243f.). This alternative would appear to be problematic for a Greek patristic view on two counts: because of the idea of analogy and because of its non-ontological nature.

[20] One may observe tendencies to the former in Calvinism, and to the latter in Lutheranism (Schleiermacher, Pietism, etc.).

(a) Through the concept of the *Logos* and the *Mind* (νοῦς) as an *intellectual principle*. According to this principle, the world is sustained through the Logos — an ancient Greek philosophical notion available to the Greek Fathers mainly in the form worked out by the Stoics — 'through whom' and 'in whom' the world was made (John 1) and who is present in the world and unites all things, thus bringing creation into communion with the Creator. This idea was found to be extremely useful, because the *logos* concept indicates at once both unity and otherness, particularly since in its cosmological application it is to be found also in the plural, as *logoi*. The employment of the same term to indicate both plurality and unity, otherness and communion, naturally made this term a key notion in theology.

Now, the primary meaning of *logos*, and perhaps the most obvious one, had to do with *intelligence*. Ever since Parmenides, Greek philosophy ceaselessly associated being with thought, and *logos* with *nous* or mind.[21] In employing this term, many theologians of the patristic period followed the same line. This was particularly the case with Origen, Evagrius,[22] and to some extent Maximus the Confessor, who however modified the *logos* idea in a fundamental way.[23]

The basic idea behind this approach is that the world can be brought into communion with God through *contemplation* by the human mind, purified from whatever prevents it from *seeing* God. In this case, ontology is *contemplative*: the mind brings together the various *logoi* of creation and makes them part of the one divine *Logos*, thus bridging the gap between Creator and creation through contemplation, illumination, and 'knowledge' (γνῶσις). In the Evagrian tradition, the *vita contemplativa* belongs to the 'mind' and is the ultimate reality of man's unity with God.

[21] Parmenides, *Fragm.* 5d, 7; cf. Plato, *Parmen.* 128b.
[22] Following Origen, Evagrius considered the mind as embodied for purification in the flesh, and therefore as in need of a departure from the body (*Cent. Gnost.* 2.6; W. Frakenberg's edition, *Evagrius Ponticus*, 1912, p. 133) so that it may contemplate God, although not grasp him, as the 'naked' mind (*Cent. Gnost.* 3.6; Frakenberg, p. 193), i.e., free from all worldly representations, in which nothing is left but the divine reflection itself. In this way, the mind becomes the divine element in man, and it is the ultimate link of affinity between God and the human being. Knowledge is the light of the mind (*Cent. Gnost.* 1.81; Frakenberg, p. 119) through which contemplation, not only of the holy Trinity, but also of all intelligible beings, is experienced (*Cent. Gnost.* 3.6; Frakenberg, p. 193).
[23] For a fuller discussion of the fundamental differences between Maximus and Evagrius in this respect, see P. Sherwood, *St Maximus the Confessor: The Ascetic Life. The Four Centuries on Charity*, 1955, esp. pp. 92 and 237f.; also L. Thunberg, *Microcosm and Mediator*, esp. pp. 404ff.

There are difficulties with this attempt to reconcile communion with otherness. One such difficulty has to do with the gnoseological and contemplative character of this ontology. As Levinas demonstrated in an impressive way in his *Totalité et Infini*, a gnoseological ontology is inevitably a 'totalitarian' ontology (hence his rejection of all ontology on the — wrong — assumption that ontology cannot but be gnoseological).[24] The case of Origen and Evagrius proves this point, since with both of them the affinity between the divine and the human intellect or *nous* is such that the end result of communion between God and man is the elimination of otherness: the world differs essentially from God only in its materiality, which in any case is temporary and destined to disappear.[25] This means — and this is a second difficulty — that such a way of relating the world to God leaves the material world with no place in the relation between the Creator and creation and deprives it of all ontological content, as if it did not *truly* exist.[26]

(b) Through the *Logos* as a *personal principle*. It was the merit of Maximus the Confessor to modify the *logos* idea in a way that could serve as the basis of an ontology of communion and otherness. Maximus shares with Origen and Evagrius the contemplative dimension of the *logos* idea, but does not base his ontology on this. Fundamental to his cosmology is the idea of the *logoi* of beings, which account for the otherness of beings in creation and which unite in the person of the divine *Logos* so as to be involved in communion with each other and with God. This unity does not abolish otherness but exists simultaneously with it.

Maximus is keen to distinguish between *diaphora* (difference) and *diairesis* (division).[27] For him, *diaphora* is an ontological characteristic because each being has its *logos* which gives it its particular identity, without which it would cease to be itself and thus to be at all. Without *diaphora* there is no being, for there is no being apart from beings.[28]

---

[24] See below, n. 86.

[25] On Origen, cf. nn. 10 to 13, above. On Evagrius, cf. n. 22 above. For both of these authors, the material world will, in the end, disappear.

[26] Another important difficulty with uniting God and the world through the mind (νοῦς) relates to the freedom of God: if the link between God and the world is to be found in God's *logoi* as his 'thoughts', the intelligent world at least must be conceived as co-existing with him. Cf. nn. 10-11, above.

[27] For a very good discussion of this aspect of St Maximus' theology, see L. Thunberg, *Microcosm and Mediator*, pp. 51ff.

[28] Διαφορὰ is *constitutive* of beings (συστατικὴ). See *Theol. Polem.* 21 (PG 91, 249C) and *Amb.* 67 (PG 91, 1400C).

This is an ontology applied also to Trinitarian theology,[29] as well as to Christology and to cosmology. How does Maximus manage to avoid a 'totalitarian' or monistic ontology, so deeply feared by Levinas, in God's relation with creation? How can communion and otherness coincide in ontology?

The following aspects of Maximus' theology relate directly to this question:

(i) The *logoi* of creation are *providential* (προνοητικοί); they are not part of God's intelligence but of his *will* and *love*.[30]

(ii) The *Logos* that unites the *logoi* of creation is a *Person*, not intelligence or *nous*, but the *Son* of the Father. In being united with the *Logos*, the *logoi* of creation do not become part of God's substance but retain their creaturely nature.[31]

(iii) The fact that the *Logos* unites in himself the *logoi* of creation *as a Person* and not as divine *nous* or intelligence or any similar *natural* quality of God, means that it is *through the Incarnation* that the *logoi* are truly united to God.[32] In other words, the gulf of otherness between God and the world is bridged in a personal or hypostatic manner (ὑποστατικῶς). In Chalcedonian terminology, the unity between God and the world takes place while the divine and the human natures unite *in a Person* 'without confusion', that is, through a communion that preserves otherness.[33]

(iv) Bridging the gulf of otherness between God and the world through 'hypostatic union', that is, *through a Person* (the Son of the Trinity), and not through nature, requires, philosophically speaking, an ontology which is conceived not on the basis of *what* things are (their nature), but of *how* they are (their 'way of being', or hypostasis). Maximus uses for that purpose a distinction between *logos* and *tropos*:[34]

---

[29] Maximus, *Ep.* 15 (PG 91, 553D): διαφορὰ προσωπική. Cf. Basil, *Adv. Eun.* 1.19 (PG 29, 556B).

[30] *Amb.* 7 (PG 91, 1081A-C); 42 (PG 91, 1329C).

[31] *Quaest. Thal.* 35 (PG 90, 377C); *Cap. theol. econ.* 2,10 (PG 90, 1129A).

[32] See esp. *Amb.* 33 (PG 91, 1285C-1288A).

[33] The key idea of Maximus is the idea of the ultimate union of all creatures in the Incarnate Word, without, however, an absorption of the diversity of creation by the union. See the important observations of L. Thunberg, *Microcosm and Mediator,* pp. 434-35.

[34] This distinction goes back to the Cappadocian Fathers, but it is Maximus who makes of it a key concept in theology. For a full discussion, see P. Sherwood, *The Earlier Ambigua of St Maximus the Confessor,* 1955, pp. 155-66. Cf. A. Louth, *Maximus the Confessor,* 1996, p. 51. Since Maximus clearly and categorically equates the terms 'mode of existence' (τρόπος ὑπάρξεως), the 'how' beings exist (πῶς εἶναι), and *hypos-*

in every being there is a permanent and unchangeable aspect and an adjustable one. In the Incarnation, the *logos physeos* remains fixed, but the *tropos* adjusts being to an intention or purpose or manner of communion. In other words, the love of God bridges the gulf of otherness by affecting the changeable and adjustable aspect of being, and this applies equally to God and to the world: God bridges the gulf by adjusting his own *tropos*,[35] that is, the *how he is*, while created existence also undergoes adjustments not of its *logos physeos* but of its *tropos*.[36] This amounts to a 'tropic identity', that is, to an ontology of

---

tasis/person (see *Amb.* 67, PG 91, 1400f.; *Amb.* 5, PG 91, 1053B; *Myst.* 23, PG 91, 701A; *Amb.* 1, PG 91, 1036C; etc.), it is difficult to follow J.-C. Larchet's argument (*La divinisation de l'homme selon s.Maxime le Confesseur*, 1996, p. 267f.) against the association of the 'innovation of nature' according to its *tropos* with the hypostatic way of existence (which association is nevertheless admitted by Larchet in Maximus' Trinitarian theology, Christology and anthropology, p. 269). This is of crucial significance because, without an association of the innovation of natures with the hypostatic way of existence, we would be forced to apply the innovation of divine nature in the Incarnation also to the Father and the Spirit, who share the same nature with the Logos. If, in the Incarnation, the 'innovation of natures' according to their *tropos* does not refer to the hypostatic way of existence but to the natures as such, or to their *energeia* (Larchet, p. 271f.) in a sense which is not hypostatically qualified, Maximus' intention in using the *logos-tropos* distinction in Christology would be fundamentally misunderstood. Cf. n. 35.

[35] It is of special significance for our thesis here that, according to Maximus, the Incarnation affects the mode (τρόπος) not only of created beings but also of God himself. See *Amb.* 5 (PG 91, 1056) and 41 (PG 91, 1308C; esp. 1313C). In the Incarnation, the Logos 'showed the innovation of *tropos* with regard to both natures (divine and human) in the fixity of the natural *logoi* which are preserved, [and] without which none of the beings is what it is' (*Amb.* 6; PG 91, 1052A). In the Incarnation, 'natures are innovated (καινοτομοῦνται) and paradoxically in a supernatural manner the naturally totally unmoved moves immovably (ἀκινήτως κινεῖται) around the naturally moving (φύσει κινούμενον), and thus God becomes man' (*Amb.* 41; PG 91, 1308CD). This great mystery of the Incarnation would have been totally inconceivable (at least in Chalcedonian terms) had it not been for the fact that both the divine and the human being exist not only as natures but also as hypostases — not only as *logos* but also as *tropos* (cf. *Amb.* 42; PG 91, 1341D). This leads St John of Damascus to speak of the Incarnation as a 'mode of second being' (τρόπος δευτέρας ὑπάρξεως) of the Logos (*C. Jacob.* 52; PG 94, 1464A).

[36] Every creature possesses a *tropos hyparxeos*. Maximus is even prepared to apply the term, *hypostasis*, to everything that exists, not only to human beings (*Ep.* 15; PG 91, 549BC). This is sometimes used as an argument against the interpretation of the patristic idea of person in the sense of freedom of transcendence — what is labelled rather disapprovingly as 'modern personalism' imposed on the Fathers! Since the Fathers, the argument goes, use the term, *hypostasis* (which they identify with person) to describe non-humans as well, such a personalism cannot be found in them. This criticism, based mainly on a literalistic treatment of the patristic sources, entirely misses the theological point, emphasized particularly by St Maximus, that

tropos, of the 'how' things are. This *is* a matter of ontology, because the *tropos* of being is an inseparable aspect of being, as primary ontologically as substance or nature. God, therefore, relates to the world with a change not of *what* each of these identities are, but of *how* they are. Given the fact that no being exists as a 'naked' nature, but always in a particular 'mode' or *tropos*, the relation of God to the world is not 'ethical' or 'psychological' or anything other than *ontological*, that is, a relation allowing for communion with each other's very being, albeit without a change of *what* each of them is.

We are dealing here with two kinds of identity. The first one implies natural otherness, and in itself and by itself, that is, as substance or nature *per se*, allows for no possibility of communion. The second one concerns not nature *per se*, its *logos*, but the way it relates, its *tropos*, and it is this that makes communion possible. Had it been conceivable without its *tropos*, no ontological unity between God and the world would have been possible. It is because of and through their *tropos* that the divine and the creaturely natures can unite, since it is the *tropos* that is capable of adjustment. Substance is relational not in itself but in and through and because of the 'mode of being' it possesses.[37]

---

all created beings exist as different *hypostases* only by virtue of their relation to, and dependence upon (see *Amb.* 41), the free *hypostasis* of the human being, and ultimately of Christ, who 'always and *in all* wills to effect the mystery of his embodiment (ἐνσωμάτωσις)' (*Amb.* 7; PG 91, 1084CD). In the Maximian view of creation, there is no true *hypostasis* of any being which is not embodied in a free *hypostasis*. As L. Thunberg puts it so well, with reference to St Maximus, 'Existence includes more than being, but *hypostasis* too as the principle of *personal* being, related particularly to the aspect of the realisation of what belongs to nature, is a reality which seems to transcend the strict limits of nature... This aspect of transcendence cannot be grasped by any automatism of nature as such; rather it is an expression of *personal existence, of decisive freedom* [my italics]... We must conclude with von Balthasar, that a new perspective is opened up, where personal existence and the mystery of union in infinity are brought together on the basis of Christological insights into what was felt as *the deepest secrets of created life*' (*Microcosm and Mediator*, p. 89f.). The 'personalist' interpretation, therefore, of the patristic idea of *hypostasis* remains valid and more faithful to patristic theology than a literalistic treatment of the sources which fails to place its findings in the broader theological context of the patristic texts.

[37] We become θείας κοινωνοὶ φύσεως (2 Pet. 1.4) not by a direct communion of our nature with divine nature, but only in and through the person of the Logos. In this way, Maximus clarifies Athanasius' idea of divine nature as being generative or 'fruit-bearing' (καρπογόνος) by giving it a personalist nuance, thus rescuing it from the accusation of implying an involuntary generation. This ingenious interpretation of the *homoousios* by Maximus means that the Son belongs to the realm of divine substance not because God is *active* (an idea favoured by R. Williams, *Arius:*

Such an ontology based on the distinction between *logos* and *tropos* — a distinction characteristic of Maximus' thought — is dictated by the faith, so fundamental to the Christian Gospel, in a God who remains transcendent and therefore ontologically other and free, without his transcendence, freedom and otherness preventing him from reaching outside himself and establishing communion with his creation.[38] In other words, an ontology of this kind allows freedom to be not freedom *from* the other but freedom *for* the other without a loss or depletion of otherness. It is an ontology which permits communion and otherness to coincide thanks to the intervention of personhood between God and creation.

We shall deal below with the implications of this ontology for human existence. At the present stage, which concerns the relation between God and the world, our commenting on Maximus' thought may suffice to show that patristic theology provides us with the philosophical tools to work out an *ontology of love* in which freedom and otherness can be conceived as indispensable and fundamental existential realities without the intervention of separateness, distance or even nothingness, or a rejection of ontology, as so much of so-called post-modernity[39] assumes to be necessary in dealing with the subject of otherness.

(c) To this Maximian ontology, which in my view is philosophically the best and most satisfying way of working out an ontology of communion and otherness, we should add, mainly for historical reasons, another way of relating God's being and the being of the world in patristic thought, namely through the *energies* of God. Knowing God through his energies and not his totally unknowable *ousia* is an idea encountered already in the Cappadocian Fathers,[40] but it was mainly St Gregory Palamas in the fourteenth century who developed and promoted it against the background of the controversy with Barlaam and the experience of Hesychasm.

Heresy and Tradition, 1987, pp. 229, 231, 238, 243, and other theologians), which would involve the risk of understanding generation in terms of *energeia*, but because being is *tropical*, i.e., hypostatic and personal.

[38] God, in Christ, moves out of himself in love, and this makes all true love ecstatic (Dionysius Areop., *De div. nom.* 4.13; PG 3, 712AB). This, according to St Maximus, makes God, who is by nature unmovable, to be moved as ἔρως and ἀγάπη towards creation, moving at the same time towards himself those who are capable of receiving this divine movement and responding to it (notably the creatures that possess freedom). All this takes place at the level of the *tropos* of existence (*Amb.* 23; PG 91, 1260CD).

[39] See below.

[40] E.g., Basil, *Ep.* 234.1 (PG 32, 868-869).

The issue at stake was again the way in which God relates with his creation: does he communicate his own uncreated being to the world or not? In other words, is the communion which relates God to the world *ontological*? Palamas would answer this question in the affirmative. Paraphrasing Maximus, he would write that 'God in all fulness comes to dwell in *the complete being* (ὅλοις) of those who are worthy of it, and the saints fully dwell with their *complete being* in the *whole* (ὅλῳ) *God* by drawing to themselves the *whole God*'.[41] This, however, immediately raises the question of otherness: in what sense does God remain ontologically other with regard to creation, if he dwells with his whole being in the complete being of the saints? There is no way of answering this question satisfactorily according to Palamas, except by, on the one hand, distinguishing between essence and energy, and, at the same time, applying the notion of being not only to essence but also to energy: energy, too, is an *ontological* notion.[42] Divine essence cannot be known or communicated — this safeguards the otherness of God. It is only through the energies that communion between God and creation is realized. Since the energies are an aspect of God's being, communion is ontological in character, but it is so while respecting and maintaining otherness, by means of the distinction between essence and energy.

The similarities with Maximus in this case are obvious: in both Fathers, the gulf between created and uncreated being is bridged ontologically, and not ethically or psychologically, and it is bridged in such a way as to respect otherness and communion at the same time. But there are nuances which distinguish the two theologians and which are philosophically noteworthy.

In the first place, Maximus' ontology is grounded in the distinction between the *logos* of nature and the mode or *tropos* of being, whereas Gregory seeks to preserve the otherness of God and creation in communion by using the distinction between nature and energy. In this respect, Maximus seems to root the ontology of otherness and communion, more directly than Gregory, in the personalism of Trinitarian theology, and eventually in the Incarnation of the *person* of the *Logos* (ὑποστατικῶς). For Maximus, the gulf between divine and

---

[41] Gregory Palamas, *Triad.* III.1.27 (ed. P. Chrestou, *Gregory Palamas Works [Συγγράμματα]*, vol. 1, 1962, p. 639); Maximus, *Amb.* 7 (PG 91; 1088). Cf. J. Meyendorff, *A Study of Gregory Palamas*, 1964, p. 213.

[42] Gregory Palamas, *C. Akindynos* III.10 (ed. P. Chrestou, vol. 3, p. 184): 'The essence is necessarily being, but being is not necessarily essence'. Cf. *Triad.* III.2.7 (ed. P. Chrestou, vol. 1, p. 661).

human nature is bridged because God's nature is hypostatic or personal, that is, because it possesses a 'mode of being' which enables or allows it to relate to another nature ontologically without losing its otherness. This makes it almost inevitable to connect this bridging of the gulf with a person of the Trinity, that is, with the *Incarnation*: without the Incarnation of the Logos, the ontological distance between God and the world cannot be overcome, since it is only through the adjustment of a divine 'mode of being', that is, a person, that communion and otherness can coincide.[43]

Such a personalist solution to the problem of communion and otherness does not seem to emerge *directly* from the theology of Palamas.[44] Filling the gap between created and uncreated being through the energies of God does not necessarily and immediately require the Incarnation, since the energies of God operate as links between God and creation in any case from the beginning of creation, and are common to all three persons, being manifestations of the divine *nature* (the 'what', not the 'how', of God).

The concept of energy not being in itself a personalist concept ontologically, as it is clearly distinct from *hypostasis* and common to all the Trinity, offers itself for a bridging of the gulf between uncreated and created nature *primarily* via a communion of *natural* properties, and only indirectly hypostatically. Yet the fact that Gregory Palamas clearly understands the divine energies to be enhypostatic[45] places him *essentially* in the same line as Maximus concerning the relationship between God and creation.

As a conclusion, drawn mainly from Maximus' theology, we can say that the only way to maintain both otherness and communion in

---

[43] We noted above (cf. nn. 34 and 35) that Maximus, following the Cappadocians, identifies the *tropos hyparxeos* with the ὅπως εἶναι (the 'how' of being) and with *hypostasis*. The divine energies (τὰ περὶ τὴν οὐσίαν) which are operative in creation reveal *only that God exists*, and nothing more. See *Amb.* 34 (PG 91, 1288BC). In this sense, the energies cannot be regarded as forming the basis of communion except in so far as they are enhypostatic.

[44] For Gregory, the unity of the saints with God takes place with respect neither to God's essence nor to the hypostatic union, since the latter is fulfilled only in the case of the incarnate Logos. It is realized as they are united to God with respect to this energy (*One Hundred and Fifty Chapters*, 75, ed. Sinkewicz, p. 170; PG 150, 1173BC). Yet it must also be underlined that Gregory is very keen to stress that without the Incarnation we would be left with no more than the divine energies simply revealing God in creation (*Hom.* 16.19).

[45] See S. Yagazoglou, *Communion of Theosis: The Synthesis of Christology and Pneumatology in the Work of St Gregory Palamas*, 2001, p. 155f. (in Greek).

an ontological sense between God and creation is through *an ontology of love understood in a personal way*. Only by understanding personhood as a mode or *tropos* of being can we work out a unity which does not end up in totality but allows for otherness to be equally primary ontologically. It is for this reason that Maximus allows himself to speak of God as 'moving unmovably' towards creation. It is as *eros* and *agape* that God can be at once unmovable and 'ecstatic',[46] that is, other in communion. This divine movement is one of divine *persons*, not of divine substance and energy as such. God is not a physical object radiating loving energy. It is as *persons* that he 'emigrates' with his ἔρως and fills the gulf of otherness with his love. A non-personalist theology would turn God into a natural object and would have nothing to do with the living God of the Bible and the worshipping Church.

God and the world are united without losing their otherness only in the person of the divine *Logos*, that is, only *in Christ*. It is a *person* that makes this possible, because it is only a person that can express communion and otherness simultaneously, thanks to its being a *mode* of being, that is, an identity which, unlike substance or energy, is capable of 'modifying' its being without losing its ontological uniqueness and otherness. All other, that is, non-personalist, ways of uniting God and the world, while safeguarding otherness, involve either a non-ontological relationship between God and the world (e.g., ethics, psychology, religiosity, etc.) or an undermining of the Incarnation, that is, of the 'hypostatic (= personal) union' between created and uncreated being.

This is precisely the danger in 'maximizing' the energies in the God-world relationship. To make the divine energies into the 'personal presence and activity outside the divine nature itself'[47] is to obscure the difference between person and energy. The divine energies *qua* energies never express God's *personal* presence, since they belong to the level of *nature* and to *all three persons* of the Trinity. If the world and God were to be united through the divine energies *qua* energies, the unity would have been one with *all three persons* simultaneously, and not via the Son — it would not have been a *hypostatic* union.[48]

[46] See above, n. 38.

[47] N.V. Harrison, 'Zizioulas on Communion and Otherness', *St Vladimir's Theological Quarterly* 42 (1998), p. 283.

[48] J. Polkinghorne, *Science and the Trinity*, 2004, p. 98 n. 15, is correct in writing that some forms of the discourse on divine energies in Orthodox theology 'may seem to be in danger of verging on a form of emanationism'.

The description of the energies as the 'media in which the divine persons enter into interpersonal communion with created beings',[49] although an idea absent, as far as I know, in patristic thought, can be a helpful one. It can be accepted, however, only if it means that it is ultimately *personhood*, the *hypostasis* of the *Logos*, and not divine energies, that bridges the gulf between God and the world. Therefore, 'maximizing' the role of divine energies may obscure the decisive significance of personhood for the God-world relationship — and this is, in fact, the case with many modern Orthodox theologians.[50] It is extremely important not to forget or overlook the fact that the God-world relationship is primarily *hypostatic*, that is, in and through *one person* of the Trinity, and not through an aspect of God's being that belongs to all three of the Trinitarian Persons, such as the divine energies.[51]

[49] N.V. Harrison, 'Zizioulas on Communion and Otherness', p. 287.

[50] Such a 'maximizing' of divine energies allows N.V. Harrison to endorse the view that we should 'kiss the trees, the flowers, the grass, and everything else, since within them flows the energy of God' ('Zizioulas on Communion and Otherness', p. 282). In the Orthodox Church, we venerate *persons*, not natures or energies. Even in venerating and kissing the icons we do so only because they *explicitly* carry with them the representation of a person or persons. See Theodore the Studite, *Antir.* III.1 (PG 99, 405AB): the veneration of an icon goes not to the substance (οὐσία) but to the person (ὑπόστασις) of the icon. Given the fact that, according to the well-known canon 82 of the Council of Trullo, only *historical* facts can be depicted in icons, to venerate any object which is not related to an historical person associated with our salvation in Christ, such as trees, flowers, etc., is to be in danger of falling into some form of paganism. It is noteworthy and quite revealing that neither John of Damascus nor any of the defenders of the icons during the iconoclastic controversy made much reference to divine energies in connection with the icons. Instead, and this is significant, they defend the icons strictly on the basis of the Incarnation and of the distinction between essence and person, attaching veneration exclusively to the latter.

[51] It is noteworthy that Maximus emphasizes that the gulf between created and uncreated being is bridged only by the Incarnation (see *Amb.* 5; PG 91, 1057C). As L. Thunberg (*Microcosm and Mediator*, p. 426) observes, it is *'in the field of mode of existence'* that deification takes place, according to Maximus. As he puts it with emphasis, deification is realized *'through a process of interpenetration* (between God and man), *which maintains the gulf of the fixity of natures but communicates the mode of existence'* (*Microcosm and Mediator*, his italics). Gregory Palamas is also categorical that it is ultimately the Incarnation and not the energies that unite God and the world. It is his modern Orthodox interpreters who maximize his teaching about the divine energies to the point of obscuring this truth.

Thus, the view that union between God and the human being — what is called *theosis* in the Orthodox tradition — is not realized at the level of *hypostasis* but only at that of *energeia*, appears to be questionable. Such a view, if accepted, would make it difficult to identify *theosis* with υἱοθεσία (filial adoption) — an identification with

Now, because the world was created in a person and is sustained in and through a person ('in Christ'), it exists in and through a being capable of modifying itself (person as mode of being) so as to unite with other beings while remaining other. This makes creation reflect in its very constitution the coincidence between communion and otherness. In a striking way, St Maximus preceded modern science in describing the universe as a dynamic interaction between unity and difference, substance and event, that is, as a relational reality made up of particulars tending to modify themselves constantly so as to sustain or obtain otherness through communion and communion through otherness.[52]

Maximus insists so much on this point that he calls otherness *constitutive* (συστατικὴ) of the entire universe,[53] which means that otherness is ontological in cosmology. But this cosmological otherness is, for Maximus, grounded in *Christology*.[54] This means that the same

deep roots in the Bible (e.g., Ps. 82.6; Hos. 1.10; Rom. 8.12-17, 23; Gal. 4.5f.; Eph. 1.5; Heb. 12.5; etc.) and in the Fathers, particularly Irenaeus (e.g., *Adv. Haer.* 3.19.1; 4.38.4. PG 7, 939; 1109), the Alexandrian tradition (e.g., Clement, *Str.* 5.12. PG 9, 337; *Paed.* 1.6. PG 8, 281; Athanasius, *C. Ar.* 1.39; 2.59. PG 26, 92; 273; Cyril, *Quod unus sit Chr.*, PG 75, 1293; *Dial. Trin.* 5 and 7, PG 75, 976 and 1097; *In Jo.* 1.9; 4.1; 5.5; etc. PG 73, 528; 549; 864; etc.), and even Maximus (e.g., *Quest. Thal.* 6. PG 90, 280f.; 63. PG 90, 685: τὴν πρὸς θέωσιν χάριν τῆς υἱοθεσίας; *Or. Dom.* 1, PG 90, 876f.; *Amb.* 42, PG 91, 1348: υἱοθεσία = *theosis*: θεοποιὸν γέννησιν, τὴν εἰς υἱοθεσίαν γέννησιν). *Theosis* is not simply a matter of participating in God's glory and other *natural* qualities, *common to all three persons of the Trinity*; it is also, or rather above all, our recognition and acceptance by the Father as his *sons* by grace, *in and through our incorporation into his only-begotten Son by nature* (thus Athanasius, *C. Ar.* 2.59. PG 26, 273; cf. Irenaeus, *Haer.* 3.19.1; 3.20.2-5. PG 7, 939; 1035). It is, therefore, precisely at the hypostatic level — the *hypostasis* of the Son — that *theosis* is realized through our adoption *by grace* (= in the Spirit) as sons in the Son: τῇ πρὸς τὸν Υἱὸν συμμορφίᾳ (Cyril of Alex., *Dial. Trin.* 5; PG 75, 976; cf. Athanasius, *C.Ar.* 2.59; PG 26, 273). As to the fear, expressed by certain authors, that this may lead to the absorption of our personal particularities by the *hypostasis* of the Son, this is totally excluded in an understanding of personhood as *communion in otherness*, according to which, as I insist throughout this essay, personal union does not preclude, but on the contrary generates, otherness and particularity. This allows us to speak of Christ as *one* and *many* at the same time (*polyhypostasity*), i.e., of Christ not as an individual but as a *body*, the Church, in which alone *theosis* can be realized, since it is there, and especially in the Eucharist, that υἱοθεσία is ἐνυπόστατος (Maximus, *Myst.* 20; PG 91, 696), thanks to the privilege of calling God 'our Father' and thus becoming 'gods' (θεοὺς) by grace through worthy eucharistic communion (Maximus, *Myst.* 20; PG 91, 697).

[52] On this relational character of the universe in science, see J. Polkinghorne, *Science and the Trinity*, pp. 60-87.

[53] Maximus, *Theol. Pol.* 21 (PG 91, 249C); *Amb.* 67 (PG 91, 1400C).

[54] Maximus, *Amb.* 33 (PG 91, 1285C-1288A). Cf. I.-H. Dalmais, 'La théorie des "logoi" des créatures chez saint Maxime le Confesseur', *Revue des sciences philosophiques et théologiques* 36 (1952), p. 249.

principle of 'modification' that enables Christ's person as 'a mode of being' to be incarnate must be used to unlock the mystery of the universe, too. The divine *Logos* is present everywhere in creation[55] through the particular *logoi* of beings, Maximus would add. A 'panentheistic' conception of the world would seem to result from such a teaching. It would, however, have to be expressed not in substantialist but in personalist categories. This means that, in its deeper being, the world is what it is, namely a whole of particulars constantly undergoing modification so as to become relational and at the same time other, not by virtue of an interaction of substances in a sort of quasi-chemical manner, but in and through the presence and involvement of a Person who lends *his mode of being*, his hypostasis, so as to 'effect the mystery of his embodiment in everything',[56] enabling everything in creation to undergo the modification necessary for its being relational and particular or other at the same time.

Creation is not a person, but unless it is constituted and sustained in and through personhood, unless it is permeated by a personal presence and 'hypostasized' in it, it cannot be simultaneously communion and otherness. What the scientist sees today as a relational, indeterminate, 'chaotic' universe does not call simply for a creator God, but for a God who is so personal as to be capable of self-modification to the point of lending his very 'mode of being' to constitute and sustain the being of creation. By pervading the world through the person of the divine *Logos*, God not only unites it to himself while maintaining his otherness, but at the same time brings about and sustains a world existing as simultaneously communion and otherness in all its parts, from the greatest to the smallest, from the galaxies to the simplest particle of matter.

II. Otherness and the Being of God

One could perhaps easily accept the notion of otherness with regard to the doctrine of creation and the being of the world, but what about the being of God himself? Can otherness be ontologically ultimate in the case of God's being? Would it not threaten the unity of God? This is precisely what the doctrine of the Holy Trinity is about.

---

[55] Athanasius, *De Incarn.* 8 (PG 25, 109A).
[56] Maximus, *Amb.* 7 (PG 91, 1084CD): 'The Logos of God and God wills always and in everything the realization of the mystery of his embodiment'.

The logical difficulties entailed in the doctrine of the Trinity have to do with the ontological ultimacy of otherness. This has been the stumbling block of Trinitarian theology since its inception. Classical Greek ontology, to which I referred extensively at the beginning, has interfered continuously with this doctrine, and it has succeeded in influencing it several times and in various ways.

In the first place, Greek ontology was an acute influence in the case of Sabellianism. There, otherness almost disappeared from the being of God. The three persons became three manifestations of the one God. No wonder it provoked the reaction that it did in the early Church.

Secondly, the influence of the same Greek ontology was to be seen in the case of Arianism, particularly in its extreme form with the Anomeans, or Eunomianism. Arianism could not tolerate otherness or multiplicity in the divine being.[57] In the case of Eunomianism, the notion of substance, employed already in an official way by Nicaea, was used to show that it was logically impossible to introduce otherness in God: by identifying divine substance with the ungenerated Father, the Anomeans applied a strictly monistic ontology to God; one cannot go beyond substance, that is all there is in ontology.

The third instance of an indirect, though essential, influence of Greek ontology came with St Augustine and his Trinitarian theology. In this case, otherness was not excluded from the being of God but was made secondary to oneness expressed through the idea of substance. Scholars have detected a platonic influence in Augustine's theology,[58] but our interest here is limited to a particular aspect of this influence, namely to what concerns the ontology of otherness. There can be no doubt that Augustine makes otherness secondary to unity in God's being. God *is* one and *relates* as three. There is an ontological priority of substance over against personal relations in God in Augustine's Trinitarian theology.[59] This was followed faithfully by

[57] Cf. R. Williams, *Arius, Heresy and Tradition*, p. 231.

[58] See, e.g., H. Chadwick, *Saint Augustine. Confessions*, 1991, p. xxiii; *Augustine*, 1986, pp. 8f., 18-24, etc.

[59] '[I]n contrast to the tradition which made the Father its starting-point, he [Augustine] begins with the divine nature Itself', J.N.D. Kelly, *Early Christian Doctrines*, 1977[5], p. 272. Thus, Augustine, *De Trin.* 5, 3 & 7f. Cf. H.A. Wolfson, *The Philosophy of the Church Fathers*, 1956, p. 326f.: Augustine 'identifies the substratum (of the Trinity) not with the Father but with something underlying both the Father and the Son', i.e., divine substance.

medieval Western theology, which treated *De Deo uno* before the Trinity. On the whole, Reformation theology followed the same course, and the result has been an inability of Western theology to accommodate the doctrine of the Trinity in its devotion and logic.[60] The fact, well-known as an observation of historians, that the West always started with the one God and then moved to the Trinity, whereas the East followed the opposite course,[61] quite often has amounted to the West's beginning and ending up with the one God and never actually arriving at the Trinity (cf. the case of Deism and the ontological assumptions underlying modern atheism).[62]

There is, in our time, a growing uneasiness about making the Trinity secondary to the one God. Barth, Rahner and others have raised their voices against this. But the problem will remain for as long as otherness is not made into a primary ontological category, even with regard to God. This, I think, is what the Cappadocian Fathers succeeded in doing, and by taking them as our guides we can arrive at a clearer view of the elevation of otherness to a primary ontological status. It is no accident that they were anxious to make the three *hypostaseis* their starting point, thereby indicating that otherness is crucial in ontology.[63]

The decisive point in Cappadocian theology concerning our subject is the association of divine *monarchia* in its ontological sense with the person of the Father *and not with divine substance*. Equally decisive was their attachment of the notion of ontological causality to divine personhood *and their rejection of causality at the level of substance*. I shall argue more extensively for the importance of this in a subsequent chapter.[64] I can only mention here that the above views of the Cappadocians are of crucial importance for the ontology of otherness. If otherness is to be ontologically primary, the one in God has to be a person and not substance, for substance is a *monistic* category by definition (there can only be *one* substance and

---

[60] See K. Rahner, *The Trinity*, 1970, *passim*, and esp. p. 58ff.

[61] Since Th. de Régnon, *Etudes de théologie positive sur la sainte Trinité*, vol. 1, 1898.

[62] Atheism, in its modern form, is based on the assumption that something can simply *be or not be* regardless of any consideration of *how* it is. The ultimate and decisive question in the case of God, which precludes any further discussion about him, is for atheism a substantialist one.

[63] Cf. Gregory Naz., *Theol. Or.* 5, 14 (PG 36, 149): the Trinity is 'three suns', one light. As J.N.D. Kelly (*Early Christian Doctrines*, p. 264) observes, the Cappadocian Fathers made 'the three hypostases, rather than the one divine substance, their starting point'.

[64] See below, Chapter 3.

no other in God), while a person, such as the Father, is inconceivable without relationship to other persons. By making the person of the Father the expression of the one ontological ἀρχὴ in God, we make otherness ontologically constitutive in divine being. Equally, by attributing divine being to a personal cause rather than substance, we elevate particularity and otherness to a primary ontological status. Finally, by attaching primary ontological causation to only *one* person of the Trinity, we affirm that the 'One' of platonic and Greek ontology does not ontologically precede the 'Many' but is itself 'One' of the 'Many'. In other words, had the Three been simultaneously the ontological ἀρχὴ of divine being, there would be no 'One' in God, but ultimately only 'Many' — unless a unitive concept such as 'Triunity' is introduced,[65] which would imply something like a fourth principle in divine being. Equally, if the One were not one of the Three, this would not allow for the Many to be constitutive of being. The ontological monarchy of the Father, that is, of a *relational* being, and the attachment of ontological causation to him, serve to safeguard the coincidence of the One and the Many in divine being, a coincidence that raises otherness to the primary state of being without destroying its unity and oneness. That is what makes Cappadocian theology capable of responding to the demands of Greek ontology in a Christian way, that is, by turning divine being from a necessary being to a being attributable to personal freedom.

Thus, Cappadocian Trinitarian theology leads to an ontology of freedom analogous to the one we observed in connection with the doctrine of creation. Not only is the being of creation to be attributed to an act of freedom, but divine being itself is inconceivable without freedom. When the Arians challenged Athanasius to prove that his *homoousios* did not in fact imply a necessary generation of the Son, he simply stated categorically that it did not, and that this generation was free. However, it was only when the Cappadocians worked out their Trinitarian theology, particularly their view of the Father as the personal cause of divine being, that it became clear how and why the generation of the Son (and the procession of the Spirit) could not be conceived as necessary aspects of God's being.[66]

---

[65] See below, Chapter 3.

[66] The divine will is 'concurrent with divine nature' (Cyril of Alexandria, *De Trin.* 2; PG 75, 780B) but there is no will without the 'willing one' (ὁ θέλων) who is a *person*, Gregory Nazianzen explained (*Theol. Or.* 3.6-7; PG 36, 80f.). Thus, although the Son does not derive his being from the divine will, his generation is not unwilled. See

Divine being is not an uncaused, that is, self-explicable and thus a logically necessary, being. Its explanation lies in a free person; it is attributed to a particular person who is himself One of the Many and at the same time *the* One of the Many who, in his capacity as a *radically other person*, yet inconceivable without the other radically other persons, causes otherness and its ontological content. Had it not been for their idea of the Father as cause, divine being would have to be a logically necessary and self-explicable being in which neither otherness nor freedom would have any primary role to play.

God is not a logically 'necessary being'. His being is constituted freely thanks to its being caused by a person, the Father. Contingency is not the logical alternative to necessity. The fact that God's being is not contingent does not automatically mean that it is not attributable to freedom. By not absorbing and appropriating the Cappadocian idea of the Father as cause, Western theology, both medieval and modern, is in danger of failing to appreciate the constitutive role that freedom and otherness play in the oneness of God.

III. OTHERNESS AND THE BEING OF CHRIST

If we now come to Christology, we shall see how otherness and freedom meet in the constitution of the being of the Saviour. Chalcedon defined Christ's being as being made up of two natures, divine and human, united 'without division and without confusion'. The issue of otherness is central to this definition. We noted above, in connection with the doctrine of creation, that the being of God and the being of the world are by definition totally other, owing to the intervention of freedom in the event of creation. We also noted at the same point that owing to its having come out of nothing — and not being an extension of God's being — creation is *by nature* perishable although not necessarily perishable, since its being is ultimately explicable not by reference to its own nature — which *is* perishable — but by reference to the freedom of God who can grant it eternal existence through free communion with him. As we have already shown, the survival of creation is the ontological content of Christology. If salvation concerns anything less than eternal survival, that is, liberation from the natural 'mortality' of creation, it has no ontological relevance.

Now, the final overcoming of creation's mortality and its eternal survival is not to be realized through a loss of otherness. Creation must always remain ontologically other than God. The idea of *theosis* does not involve the absorption of creation by divine nature, that is, the loss of its otherness. Christ as the *locus* of salvation should not be understood as bringing about a *theosis* in which God would cease to be totally other than creation. Chalcedon safeguards divine and human otherness by insisting that the two natures in Christ remained always 'without confusion'. Thus, Christology sanctions otherness in a fundamental way.

The same must be said about freedom. God and man remain other, and thus ontologically free, by virtue of the fact that they are united in a *hypostatic* way, that is, in and through the free person of the Logos. Just as divine nature escapes ontological necessity by being constituted or 'hypostasized' through the person of the Father, the oneness of Christ's being is realized in freedom by being a matter of unity in and through a person, the hypostasis of the Son. Again, just as in the case of divine being, the ἀρχὴ of being is a person, so that oneness may be maintained through personal uniqueness, Christ's oneness is a personal unity involving *one* person (against Nestorianism). Christ's being has to be one, and this oneness could be based either on one substance (Monophysitism) or on one person. The hypostatic manner of Christ's oneness safeguards the role freedom plays in Christ's being.

The role of freedom and otherness in Christology is evident also in the involvement of the Holy Spirit in Christ's being.[67] The fact that Christ was 'born of the Holy Spirit and the Virgin Mary', according to the Creed, implies (a) that the event of the Incarnation took place in freedom on both the divine and the human side,[68] and (b) that Christ's unity with us was a unity in otherness. The Spirit is, by definition, connected with freedom and with the distribution or 'division' of gifts in a personal way.[69] The unity that the Spirit brings about in constituting Christ's body fully respects both freedom and other-

[67] Mt. 1.18-20; 3.16-17; Lk. 1.35; 3.22; 4.1; etc.
[68] This indicates the crucial importance of Mary's role in the Incarnation. Without her free 'yes' on behalf of humanity, the Incarnation would not have taken place. This is part of what it means to say that Christ was born 'of the Holy Spirit'.
[69] 2 Cor. 3.17; Acts 2.3: 'He [the Spirit] rested on each one of them'.

ness. In fact, it is thanks to the Spirit that the Incarnation results in Christ's becoming 'of countless hypostases'.[70] This leads us to a brief look at the idea of the Church.

IV. OTHERNESS AND THE BEING OF THE CHURCH

The Church is the place where the freedom to be other becomes crucial. K. Rahner and J. Ratzinger together published a book some years ago dealing with the relation of the local to the universal Church.[71] What is interesting in this book is the philosophical reasoning it employs in order to justify the ontological priority of the universal Church over against the local: it is, in effect, nothing other than the argument that the 'one' precedes the 'many' and that substance has priority over existence. Indeed, the problem of the one and the many that we encountered in our glance at Greek philosophy is fully operative in ecclesiology in this case. Is it unity or oneness that gives being to the many local churches? Roman Catholic ecclesiology, as represented in the above authors, would say that the one Church precedes and 'subsists' in each local church.[72] Protestant ecclesiology would tend to be more 'congregationalist' and to give priority to the local community, sometimes not even bothering about the one Church, at least in its visible form.[73] It is clear that in both cases the question of otherness is at stake.

If we take as our basis a pneumatologically constituted Christology, the ontological question regarding the Church can only be answered properly by taking into account what has been said throughout this chapter. The Church's being cannot be given *a priori* as a necessary datum. The one cannot precede the many, and otherness cannot be secondary to unity. The 'many' must have a constitutive and not a derivative role in the Church's being; local and universal must somehow coincide. This is not the place to show how this can be achieved (I have tried to do this elsewhere[74]), but it is certainly important to

---

[70] See below, n. 168.

[71] K. Rahner, J. Ratzinger, *Episkopat und Primat*, 1962.

[72] For an excellent discussion of the problem, see P. McPartlan, *The Eucharist Makes the Church: Henri de Lubac and John Zizioulas in Dialogue*, 1993. The discussion within Roman Catholicism was revived recently in a dialogue between Cardinals J. Ratzinger and W. Kasper. See P. McPartlan, 'The Local Church and the Universal Church: Zizioulas and the Ratzinger-Kasper Debate', *International Journal for the Study of the Christian Church* 4.1 (2004), pp. 21-33.

[73] See, e.g., M. Volf, *After Our Likeness: The Church as the Image of the Trinity*, 1998.

[74] See my *Being as Communion*, 1985, *passim* and esp. pp. 123-42.

maintain the same ontological principles in ecclesiology as we have applied to the other doctrines. The Church in its very structure and ministry must express and realize the freedom of otherness.

V. OTHERNESS AND THE HUMAN BEING

1. *Otherness as Constitutive of the Human Being*

(a) The human being is *defined* through otherness. It is a being whose identity emerges only in relation to other beings, God, the animals and the rest of creation. It is almost impossible to define the human being substantially. Attempts to locate human identity in rationality have failed to survive the criticism of Darwin, who showed that rationality can be found also in the animals.[75] Equally, biology fails to point out an element in the human body that does not ultimately connect it with the animals.[76] The Fathers define the human being with the help of the *imago Dei*, and speak of its capacity to be λογικός (rational) as its distinctive characteristic. But they qualify rationality with freedom: the human being is distinguished from the animals by his or her freedom to take a distance from nature and even from his or her own nature.[77] Freedom, the αὐτεξούσιον, is not for the Fathers a psychological faculty, but relates to the acceptance or rejection of everything *given*, including one's own being, and of course God himself. This is what accounts for the Fall and the ontological consequences it has had. There would have been no such consequences had freedom not been an ontological matter. Freedom means the drive to ontological otherness, to the ἴδιον, the particular, in all respects: with regard to God, to the animals and to other human beings.

Freedom as otherness, however, is not only a negative thing; its ontological character involves a positive aspect expressed as a drive

[75] C. Darwin, *The Descent of Man*, vol. 1, 1898, p. 193.

[76] It is estimated that the genetic difference between a chimpanzee and a human being (*homo sapiens*) is very slight (approximately 1.2 to 1.8%). Cf. E. Mayr, *What Evolution Is*, 2002, p. 236: 'The similarity (between man and chimpanzee) is so great (in terms of molecules) that certain enzymes and other proteins of man and chimpanzee are still virtually identical, for instance haemoglobin. Others differ slightly, but the difference is less than that between chimpanzees and monkeys'.

[77] St John of Damascus interprets the term 'rational' (λογικόν) by identifying it with freedom (αὐτεξούσιον): The non-rational (ἄλογα) beings are not free, because they are led by nature rather than leading it... Man, being rational (λογικός), leads nature rather than being led by it' (*De fide orth.* 27; PG 94, 960D-961A). It is noteworthy that freedom is not identified as conformity with nature but in contrast with it. (Influence of modern existentialism, some modern critics would say!)

towards *love* and *creativity*. The freedom to be other involves the tendency to create a world other than the given one, that is, to bring
about otherness in the radically ontological sense of the emergence
of new identities bearing the seal of the lover's or the creator's personhood. This is expressed in art, when it is not a mere copy of reality,
and it is a distinctive characteristic of the human beings in creation.[78]
It is also expressed in *eros* as we shall see later. Creativity, therefore,
and *eros* are the positive exercise of human freedom, as they 'image'
God's will and capacity freely to bring about beings other than himself which bear his personal seal, albeit, in the case of human being,
not out of nothing but out of a given world. This is possible thanks
to the fact that being possesses also a *tropos*, the capacity of modification and innovation, to recall St Maximus once again.

At the social level, this freedom for otherness is strongly expressed
whenever the human being refuses to be identified as part of a class
or group, or even a category or stereotype of natural or moral qualities. Classes or qualities of any kind lack ontological otherness, as
they can be applied to more than one being. If free, the human
being resists classification. What the human being aspires to achieve
through otherness is not simply difference but uniqueness.[79] This is
also a distinctive mark of humanity related to the *imago Dei*.

However, perhaps implied in all this is the most important specificity of the human being, that is his or her tendency to be free
from death and to acquire immortality. All creatures detest death
and strive to avoid it; the drive towards life is implanted in all of creation. But it is only the human being that refuses to accept the finality of death, inventing ways of prolonging the existence of loved ones
for ever.[80] As we shall see later, this is what makes human existence

[78] We must distinguish between creative art and manufacturing. Certain animals
can make tools in order to satisfy needs, but only the human being can create works
of art as personal representations of the existing world. Cf. below, Chapter 6. Many of
the impressive technological achievements of which human beings boast today indicate only a difference of *degree* not of *kind* between humanity and the animals. The
difference of kind arises only where there is the freedom to bring about new identities through sounds or words or colours, etc., i.e. to bring about a new world.

[79] Otherness and difference are not exactly the same. The latter can be expressed
in terms of qualities, whereas the former cannot. See below, section 3 (b).

[80] It is not only religions and philosophies that have proposed beliefs or ideas
of immortality. Anthropologists — and biologists with their help — seem to locate
the earliest evidence of the species *homo* in customs such as the burial of the dead
and the placing of personal items in their tombs, clear indications of the refusal to
accept the finality of death.

tragic. Death is the worst enemy of otherness. No human being can *really* ignore it.[81]

(b) The drive of the human being towards otherness is rooted in the divine *call* to Adam. The call simultaneously implies three things: *relationship*, *freedom*, and *otherness*, all of them being interdependent. A call involves, indeed establishes, a relationship, but it is not a call unless it implies otherness — the recipient who cannot be the same as the calling one — and the invitation to respond with a 'yes' or a 'no', not in a verbal or in a moral sense (freedom of the will) but in an ontological sense, that is, by the sheer acknowledgement, recognition and affirmation of the calling one as *other*, as an identity other than one's own, and at the same time as one granting the called one an identity in the form of a *Thou* (or a name: Adam).

Through the call, Adam is constituted, therefore, as a being other than God and the rest of creation. This otherness is not the result of self-affirmation; it is an otherness *granted* and is not self-existent, but a particularity which is a gift of the Other. Thus, while the rest of creation is other than God and other creatures only in the form of species (God created the plants, the animals, etc. without addressing them with a call), the human being is singled out, not merely as a species, but as a particular partner in a relationship, as a respondent to a call.

This is the constitutive event of humanity. Outside this event of divine call, humanity is part of the animal species. In the patristic period, it was commonplace to speak of humanity in terms of nature (human nature) with objectively (substantially) defined characteristics and elements (body, soul, etc.) — that was the prevailing anthropology of the time. But in our time, when human *nature* is, as we have seen, hardly distinguishable from the rest of mammals by biological science,[82] it is the language of *call* rather than substance that would

---

[81] It is of course possible at the level of consciousness to ignore the problem of death even to the point of accepting it either as a 'natural' fact or as a moral or religious obligation or 'blessing'. Yet, whether we are aware of it or not — usually we are not — death *conditions* our entire being and lies at the root of all that we do and think.

[82] See above, n. 76. The discussion of the distinction between humans and animals is still going on and is enriched every day with new findings. Theologians cannot, by appealing to fundamentalistic interpretations of the Bible or the Fathers, bypass the biological facts which are now well established on the basis of overwhelming evidence. From the point of view of the present essay, any natural (anatomical) differences between humans and animals, such as the size of the brain or the structure of the larynx, and the neural equipment to use syntax language, can be understood

express better the emergence of the human being from the 'hands' of the creator.

If we approach the divine act of the creation of the human being in this way, we do not have to contradict biological science in order to do theology, since we are interested in discovering not the *what* of humanity, its nature or substance, but its *how*, that is, its way or relating to God and other beings. By making the human being emerge as a particularity in creation through the divine call, we are defining it as a being distinguished from the rest of the animals not genetically, but by way of *relationship* to God and the rest of creation, that is, by its *freedom*.[83]

The human being emerges as other or particular *vis-à-vis* God and the other creatures only *by way of relationship*. It is by the 'mode of existence', the *how* of relating, that the human being can be either an animal or God. It was in this way that Adam turned his existence in the direction of animalhood and it is at the level of *tropos* that the human being can reach deification in and through the *hypostatic* union of God and man in Christ. The otherness of the human being hangs on the freedom to relate one way or another. Otherness and communion coincide.

But there are some further implications of this approach to the emergence of the human being as a particular being. If the appearance of the human being is a result of a call to otherness from outside, and if this event is *constitutive* ontologically of what it means to be human, there is no human being unless there is the Other to issue the call. This means that if there is no God there is no man, and there is no freedom for the human being to be ultimately other. Freedom without God would lose its ontological character; it would be reduced to freedom of the will.

---

as *consequences* of the event of the call, as *adjustments* or 'innovations' of the animal nature to the demands of freedom which resulted from the event of the call. This is supported by the amazing fact that there has been no change at all in the human brain since the appearance of *homo sapiens* about 150,000 years ago (see E. Mayr, *What Evolution Is*, p. 252). Once the human brain acquired the natural or anatomical equipment to exercise the distinctive characteristics of the human being (centred mainly on freedom) no evolution in this respect was necessary.

[83] A fundamentalistic use of patristic texts, which, in accordance with the then-prevailing philosophy, treat the *autexousion* of the human being as part of human *nature*, would lead us to the absurdity of looking for freedom in human genes! This would hardly be freedom, of course. In any case, it is important to bear in mind that, for the Greek Fathers, the *nature* of the human being always remains incomprehensible for our minds. E.g., Gregory Nys., *C. Eun.* 2 (PG 45, 245f.); 3.8 (PG 45, 825f.); Greg. Naz., *Theol. Or.* 2.22 (PG 36, 56f.).

This means, further, that by defining the human being through the freedom to respond to a call, we not only make human identity fundamentally an otherness in relation, but we also introduce *a-symmetry* into relationality. A call which comes from an Other needs an initiator, it does not spring automatically from the relationship. Otherness in this case is always a gift, it is grace. We cannot 'manufacture' it; it 'visits' us and calls us to be particular and unique.

Finally, if the human being is constituted as other by a *call* from an Other, requiring response and establishing a relationship, the identity of the human being is constantly formed through the response to this call of the Other. As long as there is freedom there is *history*: the 'yes' and 'no' to the call, which defines humanity and makes the human being an *historical* being. It is because the human being is defined by the freedom to relate its 'mode of being' to God and every other that history and culture exist as specific characteristics of humanity. According to the Greek Fathers, chiefly Irenaeus and Maximus, this history is endowed with a *telos*, a goal. The call has a specific content: the human being is called to bring creation into communion with God so that it may survive and participate in the life of the Holy Trinity. To this call, Adam in his freedom answered with a 'no'. It was Christ who fulfilled it, thus revealing and realizing in himself what it means to be truly human.

2. Otherness as the Tragedy of the Human Being

(a) Otherness and the Self

The rejection of God by Adam signified the rejection of otherness as constitutive of being. By claiming to be God, Adam rejected the Other as constitutive of his being and declared himself to be the ultimate explanation of his existence.[84] This gave rise to the *Self* as having ontological priority over the Other.[85] It also meant that otherness and communion could not ultimately coincide.

The priority of the self over the other has dominated Western philosophy almost from its beginning. When Parmenides declared 'being' to be identical with 'knowing', ontology and epistemology (gnoseology) became dependent on each other. This led ancient Greek philosophy to what Levinas called the idea of 'sameness', which he described as totalitarian ontology. It was thus inevitable for

---

[84] Cf. Maximus, *Thalas.* 62 (PG 90, 653A; 713A).

[85] Maximus, *Ep.* 2 (PG 91, 396D): the fall is connected with the appearance of φιλαυτία (self-love). Pleasure (ἡδονὴ) and passions all stem from this.

Levinas to reject ontology altogether[86] and seek the content of meta-physics elsewhere.

The ontological priority of the 'self' over the 'other' is dominant in modern Western thought, as Hegelianism, phenomenology and even existentialism show.[87] Hegel's otherness is essentially a circle of sameness in which the knowing subject dominates being and obtains stability through the law of dialectic in history. His idea of the Other, as expounded in his *Phenomenology of the Mind* and *Encyclopedia*, involves a movement of negation and assimilation, the negation of alterity being necessary in the first place in order to arrive at self-consciousness.[88]

For Husserl, the Other is in reality an instrument of self-discovery, the I's *alter ego*. Even while he admits that the Other constitutes me, he understands this in the sense that he constitutes me only as he is constituted by me as constituting me: the I is primary; the Other exists because I exist and for me.[89] The Other is, for Husserl, an intentional object of the self. Intersubjectivity, on which he insists, is thus of no significance for overcoming the transcendental solipsism of pure egology.[90]

Heidegger seems to attempt a departure from the foundational role of subjectivity and intentionality. By proposing the concept of 'being-with' (*Mitsein*) as an essential structure of existence, he moves

---

[86] It must be noted that Levinas rejected ontology precisely because it is identified in philosophy with comprehension. As J. Derrida (*Writing and Difference*, 1987, p. 83) summarizes his concern, he seeks to liberate philosophy 'from the Greek domination of the Same and the One (other names for the light of Being and of phenomenon) as if from oppression itself — an oppression certainly comparable to none other in the world, an ontological or transcendental oppression, but also the origin or alibi of all oppression in the world'. Yet the assumption that ontology must necessarily be tied up with comprehension and 'knowledge' is by no means an inevitable one. My aim in these essays is to question such an assumption.

[87] The beginnings are to be found in the Cartesian *cogito* as a philosophical development of Augustinian religious and philosophical introspectiveness.

[88] In a paper with the title, 'Earliest System-Programme of German Idealism', discovered in a bundle of Hegel's papers in his own handwriting, Hegel makes it clear that in metaphysics 'the first Idea is, of course, the presentation of *myself* as an absolute free entity (*Wesen*)' (H.S. Harris, *Hegel's Development: Towards the Sunlight. 1770–1801*, 1972, pp. 510-12).

[89] E. Husserl, *Formale und transzendentale Logik*, 1974, pp. 239f. and 244f. Cf. his *Cartesian Meditations*, trans. D. Cairns, 1964, p. 126: 'After these clarifications it is no longer an enigma how I can constitute in myself another Ego or, more radically, how I can constitute in my monad another monad, and can experience what is constituted in me as nevertheless other than me'.

[90] Cf. M. Theunissen, *The Other*, p. 162.

ontology in the direction of the Other: the comprehension of the being of *Dasein* includes the comprehension of the Other. Yet, in making the world the necessary medium of the encounter with the Other, he deprives the Other of a *constitutive* role in ontology. The Other is conditioned by the intermediary of the world; he forms *part* of the 'panoramic' nature of existence. This 'panoramic' view of existence leads Levinas to observe that Heidegger places the particular being within the horizon of Being, forcing us to identify it always with reference to the universal, and in this way ultimately to reduce the Other to the Same.[91]

Sartre seems to deny the intramundane character of the Other, proposed by Heidegger, and to emphasize that the Other, as the 'extra-mundane being', is not to be found in the world; he does not need the world for his existence, although he is directed towards it. The Other is present to me without mediation, suddenly, as 'immediate presence'. 'Being with' is not, for Sartre, an essential structure of one's being. The Other stands on his own feet as 'the concrete presence of this or that concrete being'. The Other is in this sense 'a factical necessity'.

This presence of the Other enables me to distinguish in me what I am for myself from what I am for the Other. What I discover in the Other's look is that I am an object for him, a sheer *nature*. Therefore, '[i]f there is an Other, whatever he may be, whoever he may be, whatever his relations with me may be...then I have an outside, I have a *nature*; the existence of the Other is my original fall [*ma chute originelle*]'. The same applies to the Other when I look at him: he is subjected to a degradation of his being; his freedom becomes '*liberté en soi*', or objectified freedom. The fundamental question in the end is to know whether it is possible to escape from this 'hell' of alienation ('*l'enfer, c'est les autres*' — *Huis clos*, 1943), and to establish with the Other a different kind of relationship, a quest which leads to constant struggles and conflicts in the human conscience.[92]

These examples from modern western philosophy in its preoccupation with the Other show that the self continues to dominate western philosophy as logically prior to the Other. To a decisive degree,

---

[91] On Heidegger's views, see his *Being and Time*, 1962, esp. pp. 149ff. On Levinas' criticism of Heidegger, see *Totalité et Infini*, 1971, pp. 63, 15, 16ff., 270ff. Levinas regards Heidegger's ontology as enslaved to comprehension and subjectivity (*Totalité et Infini*, p. 15).

[92] On the extra-mundane character of the Other and his unmediated presence, see Sartre, *L'être et le néant*, 1943, pp. 303ff. On the Other as 'original fall' and a threat to one's freedom, see *L'être et le néant*, p. 321.

the matter is cultural, in that it would appear to be absurd to think otherwise. This is so because this sort of thinking is congenial to our fallen existence, in which the Self is the ultimate point of reference (= the God) of the human being.

A decisive role in the formation of this culture must be attributed historically to the emergence of *consciousness* as a dominant factor in western anthropology. The contribution of St Augustine to this development can hardly be exaggerated.[93] There is a difference between this and the classical Greek association of ontology with gnoseology, although the two are not totally unrelated. The ancient Greeks did not operate in anthropology with the notion of *subject*, that is, of the Self as thinking its own thoughts and as being conscious of itself and preoccupied with its own 'intentions'. Their ontology had nothing to do with the modern existentialist conception of being as emerging in the horizon of the subject or of time as experienced by the subject (for example, as concern, anxiety, etc.). This introspectiveness is characteristic of the Augustinian tradition, which has never really been abandoned by the western mind and which has affected even modern Orthodox 'spirituality', as if self-consciousness and self-examination were the way to salvation. In fact, this introspectiveness is essentially nothing other than a confirmation of our fallen existence, of the domination of selfhood.

The emergence of consciousness and subjectivity as fundamental anthropological categories has led to a confusion between ontology and psychology in our ordinary way of thinking. The ultimate concern of modern man is how to 'experience' reality, something that applies also to religion. A characteristic manifestation of this attitude is that even matters as ontological as death are approached mainly as psychological problems (e.g., the main concern with such matters is suffering).[94] The human being is ultimately a Self, a centre of consciousness, that is all that matters.[95] It is also within this domination

---

[93] As far as we know, Augustine was the first among the early Christian writers to write *Confessions*, in which man's relationship to God passes through his consciousness or even self-consciousness.

[94] It is noteworthy that *Thanatology*, a recognized branch of medicine in our time, deals not with the nature of death itself but with the psychological and social aspects of death and dying. The definition of health and sickness is also based today on the idea of *suffering*. Cf. C.M. Culver and B. Gest, *Philosophy in Medicine: Conceptual and Ethical Issues in Medicine and Psychiatry*, 1982, *passim* and p. 71f.: 'A malady is a condition of the person that involves suffering or the increased risk of suffering an evil'.

[95] This is especially the case with psychoanalysis, which is based fully on intro-

of psychology that we must place man's thirst for power, be it mate-rial or spiritual power, a thirst that Nietzsche made a central theme of his philosophy of will.

A departure from the consciousness-centred philosophy of western thought is observable in two modern western philosophers of Jewish descent, and it is with them that the 'Other' is brought to the centre of philosophy as a primary concept, and not as one deriving from the Self. We must pay some special attention to their thought, and relate it to an understanding of otherness in the light of patristic thought.

The first representative of this trend is Martin Buber. In contrast with Husserl, Heidegger and Sartre, who essentially derive the Other from the 'I', Buber makes the Other co-constitutive with the I in the structure of being, and regards the two as of equal primordiality: 'The I exists only through the relationship with the Thou'.[96] Instead of focusing on perception and consciousness, he operates with answer and response (not excluding silence), that is, with language. All this sounds biblical and patristic. However, Buber's understanding of the Other lacks a-symmetry to the extent that relationship, that is, the 'between' the I and the Thou, becomes a category of primary onto-logical significance even with regard to the Thou: the I does not exist because of the Thou, but because of 'the relationship with the Thou'. What Buber calls the 'Between', that is, the point on which I and Thou meet, seems to be the ultimate ontological category for him.[97] Furthermore, the contrast between I-Thou and I-It relations with which Buber operates implies intentionality in the form of the *atti-tude* taken by the I *vis-à-vis* the Other, that is, an attitude either of the I-Thou or of the I-It kind. This implicitly makes the Other depend on the intention of the I, who can turn it either into an I-Thou or into an I-It relationship.[98] In the final analysis, does this not imply recog-nition of the primacy of the I over the Other?

---

spectiveness and self-consciousness. See S. Freud, *Wege der psychonalytischen Thera-pie*, 1918, Gesammelte Werke XII, pp. 184-86; XVII, pp. 159-61.

[96] See M. Buber, 'What is Man?', in *Between Man and Man* (English trans. by R.G. Smith), 1954, p. 205.

[97] M. Buber, 'What is Man?', p. 204: the dialogical situation 'is not to be grasped on the basis of the ontic of personal existence, or of that of two personal existences, but of that which has its being between them and transcends both'. Thus Buber can write that ' "Between" is not an auxiliary construction, but the real place and bearer of what happens between men' ('What is Man?', p. 203). M. Theunissen (*The Other*, p. 383) thinks that this 'Between' corresponds to the idea of God in the thought of Buber.

[98] See M. Buber, *I and Thou* (Eng. translation by R.G. Smith), 1958, p. 3: 'To man the world is twofold *in accordance with his twofold attitude*' (my emphasis). It is thus possible, for example, to treat a tree either as a Thou or as an It, according to the

With Levinas we come closer to the patristic understanding of otherness than with any of the philosophers mentioned above. For Levinas, the Other is not constituted by the Self (Husserl, etc.), nor by relationality as such (Buber), but rather is absolute alterity, which cannot be derived, engendered or constituted on the basis of anything other than itself. Consciousness is not only a manifestation of the priority of the I; it is always at the same time consciousness of something, that is, a process of turning the Other into an object. Levinas insists on the departure from the '*Il y a*',[99] that is, being in general, which is the equivalent of 'substance' and which enslaves the Other. It is of crucial importance that the 'same' should not integrate into itself as a totality every Other. The Other must have priority over consciousness, because it is the Other that provokes the identity of the I: 'The identity of the *same* in the *ego* (*je*) comes to it despite itself from the outside, as an election or an inspiration, in the form of the uniqueness of someone assigned'.[100]

All this reminds us of some of the key ideas of this essay: the constitutive character of the Other in ontology, the equally constitutive role of the call or election, the secondary significance of consciousness, the a-symmetry of ontological relations, and so on. Yet, Levinas leaves us with the problem of how to reconcile otherness with communion, in order to make sense of the Trinity, Christology and ecclesiology while regarding otherness as primary and constitutive. If 'being in general' is to be regarded as a 'nightmare', because it enslaves us in sameness, whereas otherness provides the 'exit' from it, where does this exit lead us? How is the fallen human being liberated from the 'general' so as to exist as 'other'?

Levinas rejects the idea of communion, because he finds in it a threat to otherness by the same and the general, a subjection of otherness to unity. However, this leaves us with the interference of nothingness in the relationship between others. Levinas himself insists on *separation* and *distance* as alternative ideas to that of relationship.[101] He is forced in this way to build his philosophy on *time* and to regard

attitude I choose to take towards it (*I and Thou*, p. 7f.). Equally, I can turn a man into an It, i.e., I can experience him as an object (*I and Thou*, p. 7f.).

[99] E. Levinas, *Existence and Existents*, 1978, p. 93f.

[100] E. Levinas, *Otherwise Than Being*, 1991, p. 52.

[101] E. Levinas, *Totalité*, p. 229: 'Le rapport avec Autrui n'annulle pas la séparation'. Also p. 271: 'L'extériorité de l'être ne signifie pas, en effet, que la multiplicité soit sans rapport. Seulement le rapport qui relie cette multiplicité ne comble pas l'abîme de la séparation, il la confirme'.

death as preferable to any impossibility of dying.[102] Without rupture and separation there is no otherness for him.

Levinas seeks to avoid using comprehension as a means of establishing otherness by insisting that the Other does not affect us in terms of a concept or theme, that is, of a universal, but in and through the concrete situation of speaking or calling or listening to the Other, by the mere 'face' of the Other, which calls us to engage actively in a direct, non-comprehensive relation with the Other. 'Expression', 'invocation', 'prayer', and finally 'ethics' can be regarded as the meeting point with the Other, instead of comprehension and substantive unity (or, for that matter, 'communion').

Levinas' attempt to liberate western philosophy from the primacy of consciousness, from the reduction of the particular to the general, from grasping, comprehending, controlling and using being by the human mind is most remarkable indeed. It brings us closer than any other philosophy to the Greek patristic view of otherness as irreducible to the universal, and of consciousness as belonging to the universal rather than to the particular, at least with regard to the Holy Trinity.[103]

But how, in Levinas' thought, is the liberation of beings from comprehension to be realized?

Levinas tries to escape from the totalitarianism of Being with the help of a metaphysic of transcendence expressed with the term 'Infini': in the face of the Other the 'I' experiences or realizes or undergoes a transcendence towards the infinite through an adventure into the unknown (*'aller sans savoir ou'*).[104] Being is thus replaced with *Desire*, which is distinguished from *Need* (*Besoin*) in that, as infinite, it knows of no satisfaction.[105] In this adventure of Desire and Goodness (*Bonté*), the I (*moi*) is not isolated 'as an I which would tend

[102] E. Levinas, *Le temps et l'Autre*, 1979, p. 29. Cf. his *Totalité*, p. 260: 'La constitution de l'intervalle qui libère l'être de la limitation du destin appelle la mort. Le néant de l'intervalle — un temps mort — est la production de l'infini'.

[103] According to the Greek Fathers, all things falling in the category of consciousness (e.g., knowledge, will, etc.) are common to all three Persons of the Trinity; they belong to the realm of the 'universal' (καθόλου) rather than the 'particular' (ἴδιον).

[104] E. Levinas, *Totalité*, p. 282. This is an allusion to Abraham contrasted with Ulysses — a very familiar contrast in Levinas' philosophy.

[105] Desire, in its metaphysical dimension, is nourished by its own hunger (*Totalité*, p. 4). Cf. R. Calin and F.D. Sebbah, 'Levinas', in *Le vocabulaire des philosophes. IV. Philosophie contemporaine (XXe siècle)*, 2002, p. 814. The affinity with Lacan is noticeable. See D. Evans, *An Introductory Dictionary of Lacanian Psychonalysis*, 1996, pp. 35f. and 121f.

afterwards towards a beyond', but is produced as an I by the same movement by which it is exteriorized, that is, by the encounter with the Other. Nevertheless, as Levinas admits, 'transcendence is a transcendence of an I (*moi*). Only an I can respond to the injunction of a face (*visage*)'.[106]

All this raises the question of the *eschatology of otherness* in Levinas' thought. Is the Other the ultimate destination of Desire? Levinas would seem to answer this in the negative: 'the Other is not a term: he does not stop the movement of Desire. The Other that Desire desires is again Desire'.[107] In sharp contrast with St Maximus, for whom the movement of Desire or *eros* finds its 'rest' in the Other, for Levinas the ultimate destination of Desire is not the Other but the Desire of the Other.[108]

These remarks may help us to understand the ambiguous phrase of Levinas: 'the Desire for (or of?) God' (*'le désir de Dieu'*). Since the Other we infinitely desire is not a particular being, in whom our Desire would ultimately rest, what we are left with in the end is nothing but our own Desire. Given that the Other we infinitely desire is one who attracts our Desire but does not himself desire us or any other, otherness finally evaporates in a Desire without the Other.[109] We are confronted with a fundamental difference from the Greek Fathers, such as Dionysius Areopagite and Maximus, for whom God, the Other *par excellence*, as *eros* both moves outside himself and attracts to himself as *the ultimate destination* of their desire those whose desire he provokes.[110]

---

[106] E. Levinas, *Totalité*, p. 282.

[107] E. Levinas, *Totalité*, p. 247.

[108] We are reminded at this point of D. de Rougemont's analysis of love in the tradition of the West (*L'amour et l'occident*, 1956), esp. p. 43: love 'n'est pas l'amour de l'autre tel qu'il est dans sa realité concrète'; it is love of loving rather than love of the Other; it springs from the Self rather than from the Other; 'un double narcissisme!'

[109] Cf. the pertinent remarks of J. Manoussakis, 'Spelling Desire with Two Ls: Levinas and Lacan', *Journal for the Psychonalysis of Culture and Society* 7 (2002), p. 22.

[110] Dion. Areop., *De div. nom.* 4.14 (PG 3, 712AB); Maximus, *Amb.* 23 (PG 91, 1260C). It must be noted that Levinas' concept of *eros* is fundamentally different from that of the Greek Fathers. For Levinas, *eros* is an 'instant', not an ultimate state in existence (*Totalité*, p. 283). In the case of *eros*, the infinite does not coincide with the erotic but with 'fecundity', with 'paternity', and is concretized in the family (*Totalité*, p. 283). *Eros* oscillates 'between the beyond of desire and the below of need'. As need (*besoin*), it is connected with a subject identical with itself. It is through fecundity that 'le sujet n'est pas seulement tout ce qu'il fera... Il sera autre que lui-même tout

For the Fathers, therefore, God, as the Other *par excellence*, is the 'object' of endless desire — a desire that knows no satiety — but at the same time the ultimate destination of Desire, its rest (στάσις). An interminable motion is inconceivable.[111] Desire cannot move beyond the Other, the desired one; the Other *is* the 'term' of Desire. At the same time, the Other, who is the term of Desire, is also the *cause* of desire, as he moves himself towards us, even to the point of uniting with us (Incarnation). This precludes any understanding of Desire as a movement of the Self: the Other initiates or 'causes' our Desire for him in and through his Desire for us. There is an event of *communion* of Desire at the very heart of otherness.[112]

We may conclude this section on otherness and the self in western philosophical thought by briefly considering the place of the 'Other' in the so-called 'postmodernity'. Is the Other of postmodernism compatible with an ontology of communion?

The first thing one must acknowledge with appreciation is the proclamation of the death of the Self by leading thinkers of postmodernism.[113] Certainly, a theology inspired by the Greek Fathers,

---

en restant lui-même... Cette altération et identification par la fécondité...constitue la paternité' (*Totalité*, p. 249f.). It is in this way that the I transcends itself though a *rupture* that brings about the other (the son), who is both other and identical with the father. The otherness acquired in fecundity ultimately takes the form of social 'fraternity' (*Totalité*, p. 256f.) which will be applied to the other human beings as goodness (*bonté*). Thus the original father-son relationship of otherness evaporates into social 'goodness' and the enjoyment of endless Desire. Time and death which intervene in the production of otherness through fecundity and paternity ultimately separate the son from the father — a separation which not only does not seem to bother Levinas, but on the contrary is regarded as the necessary 'intervalle' for the production of the infinite and of otherness. Cf. above, n. 102.

[111] Maximus, *Amb.* 7 (PG 91, 1072B); *Amb.* 15 (PG 91, 1220A).

[112] J. Lacan, who seems recently to have attracted the interest and appreciation of certain Orthodox theologians, also differs fundamentally from the way the Greek Fathers understand desire and otherness. For Lacan, desire is not a relation to an object but a relation to a lack; it is a lack of being which causes desire to arise (*The Seminar*, II, 1988, p. 223; cf. *Seminar XI, The Four Fundamental Concepts of Psycho-Analysis*, trans. A. Sheridan, 1977, p. 214: 'The desire of the Other is apprehended by the subject in that which does not work, in the lacks of the discourse of the Other'). The Other (with a capital 'O'), as distinct from the 'little other', designates radical alterity and is inscribed in the order of the symbolic. But he must first of all be considered as a *locus*, the 'locus' in which speech is constituted, and only secondarily as another subject that occupies this position (*Seminar* III, 1993, p. 274; *Le Séminaire*, VIII, 1991, p. 202). We are thus entirely outside the patristic conception of otherness and Desire.

[113] For example, M. Foucault, *The Order of Things: An Archaeology of the Human Sciences*, 1974, p. 385f.; *The History of Sexuality*, vol. II, 1992, p. 25f., and vol. III, 1990,

such as this essay wishes to expound, would welcome the questioning of self-identity, unity of consciousness and subjectivity, in spite of the fact that a great deal of modern Orthodox theology and 'spirituality' still operates with similar categories, borrowed from western modernity. The Self must die — this is a biblical demand (Mt. 16.25; Lk. 14.26; Jn 12.25; Gal. 2.20; etc.) — and any attempt to question the idea of Self at a philosophical level should be applauded, together with the rejection of substantialist ontology that supports it.

Postmodernism begins with the criticism that modernity repressed the 'other' in favour of the stability of 'the presence of the present and the present of the presence'.[114] The 'other' constantly disrupts every present. There is no possibility of 'embodying' reality. Difference is what determines existence.[115] Unity and closure, involving a substantialist ontology, are the characteristic ideas of modernity to be avoided. There is always and in all reality an excess, or 'other', that makes it impossible to stabilize, conceive and master reality and truth.[116] It is with the signifier rather than the signified that we should be preoccupied.[117] Reality is a ceaseless movement from signifier to signifier, a multiplicity marked by difference and heterogeneity, bereft of origin and purpose.[118]

We cannot enter into a full discussion of postmodernism for obvious reasons, not least because its significance lies mostly in the method, the way of doing theology, rather than in the content of doctrine as such.[119] Our scope is limited to the twofold question: is the 'other' of postmodernity conceivable at all, (a) as *primary* and *ultimate* in existence, and (b) as in any sense *relational*, that is, as in a state of communion?

The answer to both aspects of this question seems to be a negative one. The following are among the main reasons why the 'other' of patristic thought and the 'other' of postmodernism do not coincide.

---

p. 37ff.; M.C. Taylor, *Erring: A Postmodern A/Theology*, 1984, p. 40f.; *Journeys to Self-hood: Hegel and Kierkegaard*, 1980; cf. C. Schrag, *The Self after Postmodernity*, 1997.

[114] M.C. Taylor, *Disfiguring: Art, Architecture, Religion*, 1992, p. 50.

[115] See J.-F. Lyotard, *The Different: Phrases in Dispute*, 1988; J. Derrida, *Writing and Difference*, 1978.

[116] Cf. M.C. Taylor (ed.), *Deconstruction in Context: Literature and Philosophy*, 1986, esp. p. 31.

[117] D. Harvey, *The Condition of Postmodernity*, 2000, p. 53. Cf. J. Lacan (e.g., *Écrits: A Selection*, 1997, p. 153f., and elsewhere).

[118] Cf. C. Schrag, *The Self after Postmodernity*, p. 8.

[119] See G. Hyman, *The Predicament of Postmodern Theology: Radical Orthodoxy or Nihilist Textualism*, 2001. For an attempt to relate the discussion to doctrine, see K.J. Vanhoozer (ed.), *Postmodern Theology*, 2003.

(i) As I have already explained, patristic thought is deeply concerned with the eternal affirmation and survival of the *particular*. Otherness is threatened whenever the particular is faced with transience, decay and death. Postmodernism, on the other hand, is on the whole deeply suspicious of any notion of identity: 'as identity approaches, difference withdraws. When identity becomes absolute, difference is consumed'.[120] The 'other' cannot be domesticated; the 'other' is precisely what prevents reality from being located and thus mastered and 'identified'. The function of the 'other' is precisely to liberate beings from becoming 'substances', subject to comprehension, conception and control. Otherness becomes in this way 'the most liberative and therefore most appealing aspect of postmodernist thought',[121] yet at the expense of the ontology of the particular: the 'other' liberates by passing over or through all particulars. It is a 'heterotopia' (Foucault), which amounts to a movement of death.

(ii) In patristic thought, the Other is both the 'cause' of particular beings and their ultimate destination, their 'rest' (στάσις). In postmodernist thought, there is constant destabilization, a movement that constantly departs and never comes to rest, precisely because of the 'other'. In the name of the 'other', we become 'passers by' and wanderers.[122] The Other of patristic thought is conceived in terms of 'ever-moving rest' (ἀεικίνητος στάσις): in moving from one particular to another we do not 'leave behind' or 'negate' any of them, but we *affirm* their particularity in and through their mutual relationship and communion. Movement and rest are not contradictory, because the otherness of the Other is not threatened but confirmed through relationship and communion: every 'other', in moving to and relating with another 'other', confirms the particularity of the 'other', thus granting it a specific identity, an ontological 'rest'. In this movement, the ultimate destination of otherness is the Other *par excellence*, who affirms the particularity of every 'other' and in whom, in this way, all particulars find their ontological affirmation (= rest) as 'other'. Otherness does not lead us to a 'desert' or the 'white light' of the mystics, as with Taylor and de Certeau, but to a concrete personal Other.

(iii) It seems, therefore, that the crucial difference between the patristic and the postmodernist conceptions of otherness lies in the

[120] M.C. Taylor, *Nots*, 1993, p. 152.
[121] D. Harvey, *The Condition of Postmodernity*, p. 47.
[122] See M. de Certeau, *The Mystic Fable*, 1992, p. 299. Cf. the discussion of de Certeau's ideas in G. Hyman, *The Predicament of Postmodern Theology*, *passim*, and pp. 125-40.

way of 'filling the gap' between particulars, as these are engaged in
the movement of constant departure from one to another in the name
of the 'other'. Both postmodernity and patristic thought understand
reality and existence as a constant movement of new beginnings,[123] but
whereas for postmodernism alterity involves negation, rupture and
'leaving behind', for patristic thought the 'new' relates to the 'old' in a
positive way. This is illustrated by the way in which patristic thought in
the second century answered the question of whether the provisions
of the Old Testament (Passover, circumcision, sacrifices, etc.) that were
abolished by the Christian Church were 'good' or 'bad', that is, whether
by abolishing the 'old' the 'new' had negated it in the name of the
'other'.[124] By employing a teleological or eschatological ontology, Irenaeus and Melito of Sardis proposed that since every 'old' receives its
raison d'être from its significance for the 'new' that follows it, its replacement by the 'new' affirms rather than negates it.[125] Between the 'old'
and the 'new', just as between one particular and another, there is no
gap of nothingness, no rupture or separation, but mutual affirmation.
Once again, otherness coincides with communion.

Postmodernism would suspect such a coincidence of otherness
with communion, as leading to some form of totalizing reduction
bordering on violence. It is suspicions and fears of this kind that led
Levinas and others unambiguously to reject any relational otherness.
Patristic thought avoids such dangers of totalizing ontology by proposing a relational otherness which is always generated or caused
by the Other and which aims at and 'rests' in the Other. There is no
'self' or 'same' conceivable here. The otherness of the Other does
not dissolve in sameness through communion, because relations do
not take place at the level of the *logos of being* (= substance), but at the
level of the *mode of being* (= personhood). As we have shown,[126] while

---

[123] See Gregory of Nyssa, *Hom. Cant.* 8 (PG 44, 941C): the soul moves from beginnings to beginnings by means of beginnings which have no end.

[124] Second-century Christian theology was faced with the dilemma either to affirm
certain Old Testament institutions as 'good' and hence to make them binding, or
to say that they were never good and thereby explain why the Church had rejected
them. Thus Pseudo-Barnabas would regard such institutions as sinful and Justin
would attribute them to the hardness of the Jewish heart. See the discussion of the
problem in J. Daniélou, *Message évangelique et culture hellénistique*, 1961, p. 183ff.

[125] This was the position taken by Melito of Sardis and Irenaeus, who developed in
this way a theology of history. See J. Daniélou, *Message évangelique et culture hellénistique*, p. 185, and 'Figure et évenement chez Meliton de Sardes', *Neotestamentica et
Patristica* (Freundesgabe Oscar Cullman), 1962, pp. 282-92.

[126] See above, I, 2.

substance can lead either to an unbridgeable 'gulf', or to sameness and totality, the 'mode of being' is always and by definition 'other' in communion. Perhaps the loss or absence from western thought of this Maximian distinction between 'logos' and 'mode' of being, on which I insist so much in this study, accounts for the oscillation of western philosophy between 'totalizing' substantialism and 'liberating' fragmentation of being. If otherness is conceived in terms of personhood, it does not involve distance, rupture and secession or 'deconstruction'. By being 'other' and at the same time relational, the person differentiates by affirming rather than rejecting the 'other'. In personhood there is no 'self', for in it every 'self' exists only in being affirmed as 'other' by an 'other', not by *contrasting* itself with some 'other'.[127]

All this calls for a reconsideration of the concept of *love*. Love is not a feeling or disposition of the 'self' towards an 'other'. Rather, it is a *gift* coming from the 'other'[128] as an affirmation of one's uniqueness in an indispensable relation through which one's particularity is secured ontologically. Love is the assertion that one exists as 'other', that is, particular and unique, *in relation to* some 'other' who affirms him or her as 'other'. In love, relation generates otherness; it does not threaten it.

'Perfect love casts out fear' (1 Jn 4.18). The fear of the Other can only be overcome by love, that is, by acceptance and affirmation by the Other and of the Other as indispensable for our own otherness.

(b) Otherness and Nature

The rejection of God by Adam led not only to the rise of the *Self* as ontologically primordial in existence, but also to the subjection of *hypostasis* to *nature*, of the particular to the general. One of the most tragic implications of the Fall is experienced in the conflict that exists between the human being and its own nature.

---

[127] This is the philosophical significance of the doctrine of the Trinity as it was taught particularly by the Cappadocian Fathers: God's being consists in the mystery of the three Persons each of whom is radically 'other' in affirming each other's otherness through communion. See my *Being as Communion*, *passim*, esp. ch. 1. The same principle also underlies the doctrine of the Incarnation: God *in his otherness* — this is significant — i.e., *as one of the three Persons*, not as God (substance), enters into communion with creation *without prejudice to the otherness of either side*. It is precisely the difficulty of accepting the coincidence of otherness and communion that lies behind postmodernism's refusal to accommodate the Trinity and the Incarnation in its thought.

[128] 1 Jn 4.19: 'we love because he [God] first loved us'.

It is a fundamental philosophical assumption, in the thought of the Greek Fathers at least, that hypostasis or person signifies the *particular* (the ἴδιον), while nature or *ousia* expresses the common or general.[129] We humans are persons only if we can be distinguished as particular (ἴδια) from the nature we share commonly with other human beings. Personhood and nature are two aspects of existence which correspond to the two basic ontological principles of particularity and totality, the 'many' and the 'one'. This is a key idea in patristic thought.

The relationship between the particular and the general, person and nature, is experienced as a conflict in human existence. Whereas in God these two co-exist harmoniously, the human being can only aspire to a coincidence of the two. The reason is to be found in the fact that in the case of the human being nature precedes the person, whereas in God the two coincide fully. The divine persons exist not as a result of given natural laws, but because the Father freely brings them into being simultaneously as 'one' and 'many', as three persons and one substance. Human beings, on the contrary, are born as particular entities only as a result of pre-existing natural laws, common to all humans, the 'general' being in this case ontologically prior to the particular.[130]

The conflict between the particular and the general, person and nature, is experienced by the human being at the level not simply of psychology but of ontology. Psychologically, we may manage to avoid this conflict, albeit with great difficulty, but we can do nothing about it at the ontological level; the conflict remains deep and unredeemable.

There are two areas in which the ontological level of human existence manifests itself in a decisive and uncontrollable way: the way a human being is established as particular through biological birth, and the way it ceases to be particular through death. Both of these 'facts' are ontological and not merely psychological, since they are constitutive of a particular human being and totally uncontrollable by our minds or feelings, or even irrelevant to them. Both of them involve a conflict between the particular and the general, the 'hypostatic' and the 'natural'.

---

[129] E.g., Basil, *Ep.* 236.6 (PG 32, 884A); 38,1;5 (PG 32, 325f.); Amphilochius, *Frg.* 15 (PG 39, 112C-D); Maximus, *Ep.* 15 (PG 91, 545A); John Dam., *C. Jacob.* 52 (PG 94, 1461), *et al.*

[130] See my *Being as Communion*, pp. 50ff.

We should stress at this point the difference between the 'ontological' and the 'psychological' levels of existence, because ever since St Augustine the western mind has, on the whole, tended to treat the conflict between nature and person as a psychological experience of the 'self' and its consciousness, and for this reason any mention of such a conflict may easily be misconceived as 'existentialist personalism'. What I wish to refer to in speaking of the conflict between person/particular and nature/general takes place at the level not of consciousness but of being *quâ* being; it is not an experience of the thinking subject but a 'cosmic' reality affecting everything that may be said to be. By extending the notion of 'hypostasis' to every particular being, and not just to humans,[131] the Greek Fathers removed the conflict between the particular and the general from the level of consciousness and psychology, and made it an ontological matter: everything that exists, whether consciously or unconsciously, or even non-consciously, undergoes and 'suffers' this conflict. Human beings, and for that matter many animals possessing a degree of consciousness, 'suffer' this conflict psychologically and, if they are mentally developed or philosophically inclined, as is the case with the human being, they may reflect on it. But it is one thing to reflect on this conflict or possess 'knowledge' of it or experience it psychologically, and quite another to have your being established through it and determined by it. Unless we understand the world as a product of our consciousness, psychology and ontology must remain clearly distinct, and ontology must be given priority and ultimacy in our theological considerations.

The conflict between the particular and the general manifests itself in the form of a clash between 'hypostasis' and nature in the very event constitutive of every human being, that is, in the way each human being is born. Biological birth involves the deception that the otherness that emerges from it is ultimate ontological otherness: human nature brings forth particular beings whose particularity springs from the death of other particularities and is constructed in such a way as to produce other particularities at the expense of its own particularity. This is exactly what *sexual reproduction* is about.

The biological mechanism of human reproduction consists in a law of nature preceding the emergence of the particular being and uncontrollable by it,[132] according to which every particular being

---

[131] See, e.g., Maximus, *Ep.* 15 (PG 91, 549C).
[132] St Maximus underlines this in *Quest. ad Thal.* 21 (PG 90, 312f.): After the Fall,

coming into existence is 'tuned' to bring about other particularities which would secure the survival of the species, that is, of the general. This mechanism is tied up with a process of death,[133] that is, of the disappearance of the particular in the common, of the hypostasis in nature.[134]

This must be taken seriously by theology, as it coincides fully with the views of the Church Fathers.[135] The veneration and almost religious exaltation of human reproduction among Christian theologians and even official Churches, who produce 'theologies of marriage', and idealize 'natural law', can only be explained by the loss

man was condemned to a birth consisting in passion and sin, 'which sin has as a law the birth according to nature'. Therefore, 'no-one is sinless, as he is subjected in his nature to the law of birth introduced on account of sin (the Fall)'. Note the connection between nature, sin and sexual reproduction.

[133] To the connection between nature, sin and sexual reproduction, Maximus adds death as another link in the chain. Thus in *Quaest. ad Thal.* 61 (PG 90, 633 and 636), he writes: 'death occupied the entire nature owing to the transgression (of Adam)... All those who received their being from Adam according to the law of birth by pleasure (= sexually) necessarily and without their will (ἀναγκαίως καὶ μὴ βουλόμενοι) had their birth tied up with death to which nature was condemned'. Cf. *Quaest. ad Thal.* 65 (PG 90, 740B); *Amb.* 10 (PG 91, 1157A), etc.

[134] It is amazing that Maximus' ideas are confirmed today by biological science which links natural death and sexual reproduction. See, e.g., W.R. Clark, *Sex and the Origins of Death*, 1996, *passim*, and p. xi: 'Obligatory death as a result of *senescence* — natural ageing — may not have come into existence for more than a billion years after life first appeared. This form of *programmed death* seems to have arisen at about the same time that cells began experimenting with sex in connection with reproduction. It may have been the ultimate loss of innocence'. For the connection between death and sexual reproduction in biological science, see also: A. Klarsfeld and F. Revah, *Biologie de la mort*, 2000; J.D. Vincent, *La vie est une fable*, 1998. Cf. R. Dawkins, *The Selfish Gene*, 1989, pp. 40-42. Also, J. Lacan, *The Four Fundamental Concepts of Psycho-Analysis*, 1977: 'the link between sex and death, sex and the death of the individual, is fundamental' (p. 150); 'Is it surprising that its [sexuality's] final term should be death, when the presence of sex in the living being is bound up with death?' (p. 177).

[135] In addition to Maximus, see also Athanasius, *Exp. Psalm* 50.7 (PG 27, 240C); Gregory of Nyssa, *De hom. opif.* 16-18 (PG 44, 177ff.); John Chrysostom, *De virg.* 14 (PG 48, 543ff.). It would be a mistake to jump from this to the conclusion that marriage and sexual reproduction are 'evil'. Such a Manichaean position would amount to moralizing an ontological truth. In taking the above position, the Fathers made an ontological, not a moral, statement. All of them would explain that, *in the present circumstances*, i.e., in our fallen existence, sexual reproduction is 'good', both as a means of 'controlling' pleasure through childbirth (Chrysostom) and as the way of multiplying human nature. But in not condemning sexual reproduction as evil and even calling it 'good' (Chrysostom, *De virg.*, PG 48, 550), these Fathers did not free it of its *ontological* repercussions owing to its association with death.

of ontological concern in theology and by a consequent blindness to
the reality of death. Without the conflict between true otherness and
nature, life risks being ultimately a property only of the species and
not of the hypostasis or person. In the final analysis, sexuality serves
nature at the expense of the person, something that the person as
the particular *par excellence* refuses to accept. This is why the birth of
a particular human being, being as it is the product of a mechanism
of death, cannot but lead into a conflict between person and nature
at the ontological level.

Now, this death which takes place at the level of the human cell,
that is, at the most elementary and ontologically constitutive point
of our biological existence, is not caused by external circumstances
and does not provoke any defensive reaction, as would be the case in
any formal illness or accident. It is a death 'wanted' and 'desired' by
nature itself, a death that we might call 'healthy' or 'natural'.[136] Can
death be 'healthy' or 'desired'? This is the tragic paradox that lies at
the very heart of existence as it comes to us through our nature. But it
is a paradox that becomes tragic only if particularity or personhood
is raised to the level of ontological ultimacy, in other words only if
the particular human being that nature brings forth is regarded and
treated as absolutely unique and indispensable, that is, as a person
in the Trinitarian sense. Not only is nature incapable of producing such a truly and ultimately particular human being, in fact it
does everything through its very mechanism of reproduction to pre-
vent this from happening. Otherness may appear to be inherent in
nature, but it is ultimately swallowed up by death: it is not ontologically absolute.

This death of the particular, which takes place at the most elementary and constitutive level of man's biological existence,[137] is marked
by a manifestation of utter individualism: it is essentially nothing
other than the breakdown of communion. As Professor W. R. Clark
describes the process of the death of a cell (in the 'programmed'
form of death), 'the first hint that something unusual is underway
involves the cell's plasma membrane'. 'As a sign that a given cell has
somehow been singled out for a fate different from its neighbours',
the cell physically detaches itself from them. One by one it breaks the
points of contact between its own plasma membrane and the mem-

[136] W.R. Clark, *Sex and the Origins of Death*, p. 32.
[137] W.R. Clark, *Sex and the Origins of Death*, p. 61: the death of a cell and the death
of an organism are interrelated.

branes of surrounding cells, until it stands alone. And then the cell begins a slow dance of death'.[138] Communion and otherness interact ontologically at the very basis of biological existence. It is only when they coincide that true being emerges.

Now, the death of the particular cell or organism is a death that affects exclusively *the body*. In biological terms, the 'programmed death' involved in sexual reproduction consists in the split and segregation of the DNA between that part which is transmitted through the conjugation of cells (the genetic part or the germ cells) and the other one used for the nourishment, movement, and so on, of the body, as well as the protection and function of the germ cells themselves (the so-called 'somatic part' — an interesting association with *soma*, the 'body'). This means that the death we are talking about in our concern for the survival of the particular human being is *corporeal*; it is in *the body* that the conflict between person and nature takes place. It is the destruction and decomposition of the *somatic* part of ourselves that we lament when a beloved person dies; the genetic part of us is transmitted to the next generation to make sure that the unity and continuity of nature, from the original bacteria to ourselves, is secured. Why bother, then, about the loss of the body, since life still goes on? There is only one answer to that: not because at some point in evolution our brains have been turned into 'minds' that tend to 'think' about death,[139] but rather because particularity is built into ontology in such a way as to make it not just absurd to the mind but existentially unacceptable that any body with which we relate, establishing through this relationship our own particular being, should die and disappear. The death of a body may be nature's way of surviving, but the survival of the particular being is just as important in existence. We do not strive to prolong the life of a particular being because we 'think' or 'feel' in a certain way, but because consciously or unconsciously (significantly, this is irrelevant) our very being seems to depend on its existence. We *are* bodies; we do

---

[138] W.R. Clark, *Sex and the Origins of Death*, p. 35. As the formation of the nervous system in the womb shows, 'from the moment a neuron is spun out of the central nervous system toward potential target cells, it is destined to die. Only if it finds a connection with another cell will it be rescued from an otherwise certain death; it will receive chemical substances (called *growth factors*) from the target cell that in effect switch off the death program' (p. 38). Only communion can switch off the death programme!

[139] This is what a biologist such as W.R. Clark (*Sex and the Origins of Death*, p. 175f.) would propose as an answer to the crucial question of why the human being refuses to accept 'programmed', i.e., natural, death.

not *have* bodies (simply in order to host and transmit genetic material for future generations). And we acquire our ontological identities through the relationship of our own bodies with the bodies of others, that is, through that part of our being which nature throws away as 'unwanted' after the survival of the species is secured.

This leads us to a consideration of the importance of the human *body* for the ontology of otherness. The body, precisely that body which nature uses for its purposes and throws away after these purposes are satisfied, not the part of the body that is transmitted through sexual reproduction, *is* 'me' or 'you' as particular beings. From the point of view of nature, this body is not ontologically ultimate; it is a means to an end. The difference between naturalism and Platonism is, in this respect, not so radical: for both of them the body is not ontologically ultimate and does not have to survive eternally; its death does not matter ontologically; it is even desirable.[140]

The real conflict between *hypostasis* and nature arises only when the body, the dying part of it, is regarded as absolutely essential for a particular being to be itself and not someone or something else, and therefore to be at all. If a particular being ceases to be at all when it ceases to be particular, then particularity is ontologically ultimate for it. And if the body is absolutely essential for a human being to be particular, then the death of the body is a threat to this being's particularity and therefore to its very being. The conflict between otherness and nature becomes inevitable. In this case, we need *the resurrection of the body* if the conflict is to be resolved.

That the body is absolutely essential for the particularity and therefore otherness, that is, the ontological identity, of a human being was a fundamental belief in the earliest Christian tradition. From the Apologists, above all Irenaeus, to Methodius of Olympus in the fourth century, Christian anthropology could not conceive human identity without the body.[141] Indeed, in the words of the late Father

---

[140] One may argue that in the case of naturalism the matter which is transmitted and survives through procreation is itself 'part of the body', and therefore that natural procreation leads to the survival of the body. This, however, would be true only with regard to that part of the body (the germ cells) which does not guarantee or express particularity and otherness in a hypostatic sense. The aspect of the body that makes a certain being particular and therefore truly other is the 'somatic' part. This, however, from nature's point of view is ultimately irrelevant, if not 'dangerous' and unwanted, and must die. In Platonism, likewise, the particular body must ultimately die, but for a different reason, namely in order to liberate the soul imprisoned in it.

[141] E.g., Justin, *Dial.* 80 (PG 6, 664f); *De Resur.* 8 (PG 6, 1538B); Athenagoras, *De*

Florovsky, 'a body without a soul is a corpse, but a soul without a body is a ghost'[142] — not a human being. Under the influence of Origenism, this was obscured and weakened in the centuries that followed, but the Church could never abandon the faith, expressed in the Creeds, in the resurrection of the 'flesh' or the 'body', and not simply of the 'dead'.[143] After all, this was regarded as the most important implication of the Resurrection of Christ from the very beginning (1 Corinthians 15).

It is because the body is ontologically constitutive for the human being and so essential for its identity and particularity that the conflict between hypostasis and nature is observable above all in the body. For the human being, the key to the resolution of the conflict cannot be found outside the body itself: there is no escape from the body, for example by recourse to the immortality of the soul, for such an escape would amount to the loss of the human being itself. The body is constituted by the Creator in such a way as to be the *locus* both of the conflict and of its resolution. For the body is paradoxically the vehicle of otherness and communion at the same time. With the body we affirm and realize our particularity, and with the body we establish communion with other particular beings. If the body makes us particular beings not by bringing us into communion with other particular beings but by separating us from them, there is a conflict between otherness and communion experienced through the body. But such a conflict is not part of the body by definition; it is only a result of the fact that the body has been turned into a carrier of death. If the sting of death is removed from it, it ceases to perpetuate the conflict between particularity and nature and becomes the point where communion and otherness meet. This means that the conflict between *hypostasis* and nature cannot be resolved until death is conquered for all and for ever. Those who wish to remove or undermine this conflict already in our actual historical experience, and try to accommodate nature happily in personal existence, must turn a blind eye to the seriousness of death and consequently to the crucial importance of the Resurrection both as an historical event in the person of Christ and as the eschatological destiny for all humanity.

Resur. 15 (PG 6, 1004f.); Irenaeus, *Adv. Haer.* V.6.1 (PG 7, 1137f): 'Anima autem et spiritus pars hominis esse possunt, homo autem nequaquam'; Methodius, *De Resur.* (PG 18, 230B-C). Cf. Maximus, *Amb.* 7 (PG 91, 1101A-C).

[142] G. Florovsky, 'The Resurrection of Life', *Bulletin of Harvard University Divinity School*, XLIX, 71 (1952), pp. 5-26.

[143] See J.N.D. Kelly, *Early Christian Creeds*, 1952, pp. 46, 86, 89, 91, 103, esp. 163f.

3. *Otherness and the 'New Being'*

(a) Otherness and the *Logos* of Nature

I have insisted in the previous section on the fact that in human existence the conflict between otherness and communion, that is, the particular (the *hypostasis*/person) and the general (*ousia*/substance or nature), is not only ontological but also in itself *unredeemable*: nature not only precedes particular beings and dictates its laws to them, but also finally swallows them up through death. From the point of view of nature, the particular being has no hope for survival and ever-being (ἀεὶ εἶναι). Human nature is 'condemned' to follow this course, which has become part of its very definition.[144]

This 'negative' view of nature appears to many people, including theologians, to be an unacceptable exaggeration. Most people find it difficult, almost unbearable, to accept that the beauty of the nature in which we live, or the birth of a child and all of the joys and pleasures accompanying it and the child's growth, or the pleasure of sexuality itself, should be jeopardized by such a negative view of nature. They prefer to take a more positive view of nature, and the Church on the whole does everything in its power to cultivate this as a means of relieving the pain experienced when suffering and death show their ugly faces in existence. By substituting psychology for ontology, the Church has more or less forgotten the negative aspects of nature, often to the point of either idealizing suffering[145] or of treating it as a problem which can be faced, or rather covered up, by 'spirituality' and 'pastoral care'.

Probably for the same reasons that apply to people in general, theologians transfer to the theological level a similar undermin-

[144] See Maximus, *Quaest. Thalas.* 47 (PG 90, 424B); 64 (PG 90, 696Df.); 21 (PG 90, 312Bf.).

[145] There is a tendency, observable particularly in Russian Orthodox thought, towards a 'metaphysics of suffering'. This is exemplified in Dostoevsky, in whose thought true personhood seems to be fulfilled in the 'catholic sufferer'. See the interesting article of C. Paul Schroeder, 'Suffering Towards Personhood: John Zizioulas and Fyodor Dostoevsky in Conversation on Freedom and the Human Person', *St Vladimir's Theological Quarterly* 45 (2001), pp. 243-64. As is rightly observed by this author, my own position is different. Although 'experience teaches us that in the human realm of "capacity in incapacity" suffering and love are inextricably intertwined' ('Suffering Towards Personhood', p. 263), in my view, *in embracing suffering, love aims at transcending and overcoming — even eliminating — it.* Suffering, like death, remains an 'enemy' of love; the Resurrection rules out a 'metaphysics of suffering'. It is for this reason that I find it difficult to endorse the introduction of any form of 'kenoticism' into the immanent Trinity, as is done, e.g., by S. Boulgakov (see his *The Lamb of God*, 1933), or in J. Moltmann's *The Crucified God* (1974).

ing or dismissal of the conflict between person and nature, and either 'shake it off' as 'modern existentialism' or claim that there is a positive view of nature in patristic thought. That there is such a positive view of nature in the western theological tradition is evident from the fact that, at least since Augustine and throughout the middle ages, nature or substance has been regarded as the highest form of being with reference both to God and to creation. Even when the idea of the person became important and was contrasted or opposed to that of substance in western thought, otherness and personhood did not in reality acquire an ontological character, but remained attached to the psychological experience of the thinking subject.[146] In Greek patristic thought, however, things are different, as the following explanations will show.

With regard to the being of God, I have already made my position clear concerning the Greek Fathers, and I shall return to this in further parts of the present book: nature or substance coincides fully with personhood in God's existence, no conflict between the two being conceivable; in God, otherness and communion are mutually conditioned. With regard to the human being, it is mainly St Maximus the Confessor who can help us, since he refers extensively to human nature and it is in this regard that some explanations appear to be necessary.

Maximus speaks of being 'according to nature' (κατὰ φύσιν) as the highest form of existence, and of deviation from nature (παρὰ φύσιν) as synonymous with the Fall. But what exactly does he have in mind in saying this? At this point, writers on Maximus leave the matter without further explanation, allowing us to think that the 'natural' rather than the 'personal' way of existence is for this Church father the authentic form of being.

Maximus' use of 'nature' in the above positive sense must always be taken together with his expression λόγος φύσεως. We leave this untranslated for the moment because it requires more than two words to give it its proper meaning. 'Logos of nature' is for Maximus an expression that points not to nature as it is but to nature according to its aim (σκοπὸς) or end (τέλος), that is, to nature as it exists in the *hypostasis* of the divine *Logos*.[147] To exist 'according to nature'

---

[146] The view that 'existence precedes essence', promoted by modern existentialism, was always understood in terms of subjectivity; cf. J.-P. Sartre, *Existentialism* (English trans. by B. Frechtman, 1947), pp. 15-18: 'Man is nothing else but what he makes of himself. Such is the first principle of existentialism'.

[147] See esp. *Amb.* 7 (PG 91, 1080B-C; also 1084B).

(κατὰ φύσιν) means to exist 'according to the *logos* of nature' (κατὰ τὸν λόγον τῆς φύσεως), and this in turn means to exist in the way that God *intended* nature to be incorporated in the *hypostasis* of the *Logos*.[148] In speaking, therefore, of being 'according to nature', Maximus means this: the authentic and true way of being is that which conforms to the hypostasization of human nature in the hypostasis of Christ,[149] which will be realized when nature is purified from the passion of death,[150] that is, when communion and otherness will coincide onto-logically in the eschata. The 'logos of nature' for Maximus denotes not nature as such but nature *personalized*. Not emphasizing this may lead to two fundamental misunderstandings of Maximus' theology: (a) that the Fall and sin, including death, are simply the result of a deviation from a previous natural state of existence; and (b) that the authentic form of existence amounts to conformity to nature as such (nature being an ultimate ontological notion). The 'logos of nature' points to nature as it is hypostasized in a person; it is the particular-ization of nature. In other words, to exist 'according to the logos of nature' means to hypostasize your nature in true and authentic per-sonhood, to make the general (nature) exist in a state of otherness and particularity for ever. The 'logos of nature' is not to 'naturalize' the person but to 'personalize' nature by turning it from general to particular, by introducing otherness into its very 'being'.

This conclusion shows how very different a theological interpreta-tion of Maximus can be from a philological one. The latter draws its conclusions from the study of words. The former places the words in the broader theological mind of the author. In our particular case, the result of a theological interpretation is to affirm once more the ontological significance of otherness and personhood for patristic thought: true being is only that which exists for ever as 'other', as

---

[148] See the well-known text in *Quaest. Thalas.* 60 (PG 90, 620f.). Cf. *Myst.* 1 (PG 91, 668A-B); *Amb.* 7 (PG 91, 1081C): 'the one *Logos* is the many *logoi*, and the many *logoi* are one (εἷς — not ἕν — i.e., a person): with regard to the creative and sus-taining procession of the One, the One is many; while with regard to the providen-tial return of the many to the One...who will gather everything, the many are One (εἷς)'.

[149] *Amb.* 7 (PG 91, 1097B): 'For the mystery hidden before the ages and genera-tions is now manifest through the true and perfect incarnation of the Son of God who united to himself *according to the hypostasis* (καθ᾽ ὑπόστασιν) our nature...'

[150] 'Ever-being' (ἀεὶ εἶναι), i.e., the overcoming of death, is the grace given to us through our third — and final — birth in the resurrection of the dead, while our biological birth gives us simply our 'being' and Baptism grants us our 'well-being'. *Amb.* 42 (PG 91, 1325B).

particular, as personal. In the fallen state of existence, the conflict between the general and the particular results in the survival of the former at the expense of the latter. In the redeemed, eschatological existence, the general survives as *particulars*, nature is affirmed and survives through personhood.

In response to this conclusion, we may be asked: is nature not made up of particulars anyway? Do not the Fathers themselves, as we have already noted,[151] apply the term 'hypostasis' to everything that exists, whether 'personal' or 'impersonal'? Why make the survival of the particular depend on personhood?

To such questions, the strictly theological and 'dogmatic' answer would be: simply because, as we have just noted, the will or intention (βουλή) of God in creating the world was to 'recapitulate' it in his beloved Son or *Logos*, that is, in a person, and this applies to the redemption of the world as a whole. The *logoi* of creation on which the 'logos of nature' depends can only truly exist in the hypostasis of the *Logos*. From the Christian point of view, there is no other way for creation to exist authentically except 'in Christ', which from the patristic standpoint means to exist in the *hypostasis* of the Logos. There is no escape from personhood in Christian cosmology.

This 'dogmatic' answer finds its justification in a fundamental truth: all natural particularities are subject to corruption and death. 'Difference' or otherness in creation results in 'division', and this gives rise to the ontological question: how true is the being of a particular being if at some point it ceases to exist as a particular? How can a 'mouse' be truly a 'person' if personhood means particularity (*idion*) and if this animal's particularity is destined to disappear? Personhood or *hypostasis* aims at the survival, the ever-being (ἀεὶ εἶναι), of its particularity; only a particular being that is liberated from its death can be an ontologically true particularity, that is, a true person or hypostasis.[152]

Human beings were created 'in the image and likeness of God', which from the point of view of our subject here means that their par-

---

[151] See above, n. 131.

[152] In the eschatological perspective of Maximus' Christology, all particular beings in nature possess a *hypostasis* in a truly ontological sense only thanks to the final survival of creation in the *hypostasis* of the Son. Whatever is finally swallowed up by death is not 'true' ontologically. True being — and true particularity or *hypostasis* — like everything in Maximus' ontology, belongs only to 'the future state' (cf. *Scholia eccl. hier.* 3.2; PG 4, 137D), and derives its 'hypostasis' from it. Thus, it is thanks to a 'hypostasis' *in the sense of free personhood* that 'impersonal' entities acquire their hypostatic character. Being particular, and thus being in the true sense, whether 'personal' or 'impersonal', is a gift of personal freedom, not a 'natural' datum.

ticularities or *hypostases* should be ontologically true, like the persons of the holy Trinity, that is, not subject to disappearance and death. In addition to that, this means that as images of God human beings are called to offer the rest of creation the possibility of overcoming mortality, that is, showing them to be truly hypostatic by hypostasizing their 'hypostases' in a personal relationship with the immortal God so that they may obtain true hypostatic existence. This means that, if the particular beings that make up the world are called 'hypostases' or *idia*, they are so called in view of their survival in the human *hypostasis*, which again is called by this name because it is an image of the truly hypostatic God, in view of the final incorporation of humanity in the *hypostasis* of the Logos. If *hypostasis* means *idion*, that is, particularity — and this is what it means to the Greek Fathers — it follows that the only true particularity from the ontological point of view is to be found ultimately in divine personhood, and, as far as creation is concerned, in the *hypostasis* of the incarnate Son, in which it is called to be hypostasized in the end. It is such a particularity or *hypostasis* that the human being is called to be as an image of God, that is, a particularity that would be ontologically true by overcoming mortality, and at the same time capable of hypostasizing the rest of creation so that creation, too, may be saved through incorporation in the human being. This 'chain' of hypostatic existence, which connects with the Trinity every 'hypostasis' in creation through the *hypostasis* of the human being in its conformity (συμμορφία: Cyril Alex.) to the hypostatic existence of the incarnate Son of the Trinity (see above, n. 51), guarantees and expresses the survival of the world as a complexity of particular beings, as communion and otherness at the same time.

This eschatological ontology, which derives the meaning of philosophical terms such as 'nature' and 'hypostasis' not from the past or the present but from the *future*, that is from the 'new being', the *telos* or final purpose of creation, is the only way to do justice to the thought of Church Fathers like Maximus who locates the truth of things only in the future.[153] In this kind of ontology the terms we use to express reality acquire their meaning from the kind of existence *for which* reality, past or present, was created.[154] Only what will sur-

---

[153] Maximus, *Scholia eccl. hier.* 3.2; PG 4, 137D. The question of the authenticity of the *Scholia* does not affect the truth of this statement in the least, since the eschatological ontology permeates the whole of Maximus' thought.

[154] This means that 'reality' and 'truth' should be distinguished in ontology. The former denotes being *as it actually is*, including its cancellation by mortality, while the latter signifies *true* being, that is being *not nullified by non-being*.

vive in the end is true; the rest is either 'shadow' that 'announces' the future, or *'eikon'* that 'prefigures' and 'foretastes' it,[155] evil being neither of these and thus non-being.[156]

(b) *Otherness and Uniqueness*

Only if the ultimate goal of a particular being is the Other, and only if this Other is a person that can hypostasize the particular and elevate it to the status of ontological ultimacy, can this particular being survive as particular, and not be swallowed up by the general. This means that if the existence of a certain being has as its ultimate goal either its self or its nature or anything general, such as ideas or ideals or moral principles, its particularity cannot survive and be shown to be ontologically true; it will be a false particularity destined to be absorbed by the general and die. The crucial question, therefore, is whether *in all truth* the ultimate goal in our existence is — to put it in terms borrowed from patristic theology — the 'other' not as ἄλλο but as ἄλλος, that is, not as nature but as person or hypostasis.[157]

If this principle were to be translated into morality, into a code of behaviour, it would mean that any ethics based on natural law or the idea of justice and the 'rights of the individual' would become unacceptable. Given the fact, which we have already noted and analysed here, that in human existence there is a fundamental conflict between the self and the other, as well as between nature and the particular (between the 'other' as ἄλλο and the 'other' as ἄλλος), any translation of the above principle of otherness into morality would bring this conflict to the surface. If, for example, we were to translate into ethics the Sermon on the Mount, or in fact the Gospel in its entirety, which demands that we turn the left cheek to someone who strikes us on the right one, that we sell all our possessions and give them to the poor, and so on, this absolute priority of the Other would amount to the death of the Self and its 'punishment' by the laws of nature. There is no ethic of otherness, therefore, that would not lead to the Cross. But can the Cross be morally prescribed? Can

---

[155] Maximus, see above, n. 153.

[156] Maximus, *Quaest. Thalas.* 1 (PG 90, 253A-C). It is noteworthy that, at least for St Maximus, the reason why evil is non-being is that it is a deviation from, or deprivation of, the movement towards the 'end' (τέλος) for which the world was created. The eschatological ontology to which I have just referred is clearly implied: only that which survives in the end possesses true being.

[157] Gregory Naz., *Ep.* 101.4 (PG 37, 180A-B); Maximus, *Ep.* 15 (PG 91, 552B): ἄλλο = otherness of nature; ἄλλος = otherness of person.

martyrdom and asceticism be part of ethics? Can we have such an ethic of otherness?

But the application of otherness to morality also involves a logical difficulty. If we turn into a moral principle the idea that the Other can truly exist as Other only if it is ultimately regarded as person or *hypostasis* and not as self or nature, it will mean that *every being* should be treated as absolutely Other in the above sense. But if every particular being is absolutely Other, no being would be absolutely Other; it may be Other with regard to the self or to nature and everything general, but it will not be absolutely Other with regard to the other Others. Otherness is a notion that, in its absolute sense, that is, in its truth, excludes generalizations of all kinds. Ethics, on the other hand, operates with general principles, and thus is forced to subject to a general category of beings (those qualified as Other with regard to self or nature) an entity — a concrete Other — which by definition claims absolute particularity with respect to every other entity. Translated into existential, empirical terms, this leads to the conclusion: you cannot regard and treat all 'others' as absolutely and truly Other; in order for someone to be absolutely Other that someone must be *unique*. In the final analysis, otherness, by definition, implies *uniqueness*.

Before we turn to the question of how this otherness as uniqueness can be realized in existence in the light of Christian theology in particular, let us briefly consider one of its subtle implications: the distinction between otherness as uniqueness and otherness as *difference*.

Otherness and difference are often taken to mean the same thing in our minds. However, if we understand otherness as uniqueness, we must clearly distinguish it from the notion of *difference*. Difference does not involve uniqueness; it is not absolute or radical ontological otherness, since it does not require us to regard any 'other' as absolutely Other in relation to other Others. Difference can be symmetrical; it can be expressed in terms of *variety* or *diversity*, in which no Other necessarily exceeds or excels the others in the sense of ontological otherness. It is only when otherness is understood as uniqueness that we can speak of absolute metaphysical exteriority, in which case, however, the relation between 'others' would inevitably be a-symmetrical.

Difference is a natural or moral category; uniqueness belongs to the level of personhood. Two or more beings are different in terms of their natural or moral qualities, which, however, are not unique in the final analysis; they form part of a universal or *genus* (black or white, male or female, moral or immoral, etc.). A person, on the other hand, as *imago Dei*, is 'other' regardless of his or her natural or moral qualities, which may well be common to this person and to many 'others'; it is not natural or moral qualities that make the 'difference', in this case, but *a particular and unique relationship* (σχέσις) *in which a certain 'other' is singled out as uniquely Other.*

The highest example we can use to illustrate this distinction between difference and uniqueness is offered by the theology of the Holy Trinity. All qualities that we normally use in our culture to indicate difference are in fact common to all three divine Persons; they belong to divine nature (omniscience, holiness, might, goodness, energy, etc.). The only otherness we can speak of in the case of the Trinity is *personal otherness.*[158] It is an otherness that involves *uniqueness* and radical alterity stemming not from natural or moral qualities, or from a combination of such qualities, but from *unique relations.*[159] When unique relations generate or involve otherness, this otherness is not difference but uniqueness.

(c) *Otherness and* Eros

The possibility of experiencing otherness as uniqueness appears to be offered in the case of *eros. Eros* is a movement, an *ekstasis*, from one being to another.[160] Such an *ekstasis*, however, can be found in

---

[158] προσωπικὴ διαφορά: Maximus, *Ep.* 15 (PG 91, 553D). Cf. Basil, *Adv. Eun.* 1.19 (PG 29, 556B).

[159] Note how St Basil uses the example of three human beings to illustrate the difference between nature and *hypostasis*: the characteristics (ἰδιώματα) he mentions as distinguishing Peter or Paul from *anthropos* in general are borrowed not from *natural* qualities but exclusively from *personal relations and qualities*: in speaking of Peter we have in mind the son of Jonah, who comes from Bethesda, the brother of Andrew, etc.; and in speaking of Paul the 'concurrence of qualities (συνδρομὴ ἰδιωμάτων)' that we have in mind is that he is from Tarsus, a Hebrew, a Pharisee, the disciple of Gamaliel, etc.; *C. Eun.* 2, 4 (PG 29, 577Cf.). Gregory of Nyssa (*De com. not.*; PG 45, 184) uses natural qualities (baldness, height) to illustrate hypostatic difference, in addition to qualities stemming from personal relations (paternity, sonship, etc.). By being hypostasized in a particular person (Peter, Paul, etc.), these qualities turn nature into a specific (ἰδικόν) ἄτομον, a term which *from this particular point of view only*, i.e., specificity, is identical with πρόσωπον (*De com. not.*; PG 45, 179D). On the question of the equation of ἄτομον with πρόσωπον in patristic theology, see below, Appendix to Chapter 4.

[160] For a thorough exposition of the ecstatic character or *eros*, though one different from my own approach in many ways, see Ch. Yannaras, *The Person and Eros*, 1976 (in Greek).

nature itself, as the ancient Greeks and modern romanticism have so vividly described. But such a view of *eros* does not stem from the Other and is not ultimately destined to the Other; it is an *ekstasis* of the self and an expression and fulfilment of nature's inherent energies. It is natural rather than personal.

For *eros* to be a true expression of otherness in a personal sense, it must be not simply *ekstatic* but also and above all *hypostatic*: it must be caused by the free movement of a particular being and have as its ultimate destination another particular being. This cannot be the case either in the sexual or in the 'platonic' form of *eros*. In the case of sexual *eros*, the erotic movement stems from the self and is dictated by the laws of nature. It is neither caused by the Other nor is it directed ultimately towards the Other.[161] Equally, in the case of *eros* as presented by Plato, love is attracted irresistibly by the good and the beautiful; the concrete particular is used as a means to an end, and finally sacrificed for the sake of the idea.[162]

Thus, in the case both of the sexual and of the platonic *eros*, the other is shown to be an epiphenomenon and not a constitutive onto-

---

[161] This is obvious at the biological level. From the point of view of psychology, Freud's observations seem to confirm this, too, as they rule out any fundamental role of the Other in human sexuality: 'The sexual instinct is in the first instance independent of its object; nor is its origin likely to be due to its object's attractions' (S. Freud, 'Three Essays on the Theory of Sexuality', *The Complete Psychological Works of Sigmund Freud*, English trans. by J. Strachey *et al.*, vol. VII, 1953, p. 148). This means that the Other is not the *cause* in the case of sexual *eros*. And it is not the *aim* or ultimate destination, either: 'In childhood, therefore, the sexual instinct is not unified and is at first without an object' ('Three Essays on the Theory of Sexuality', p. 233). In infantile sexuality, 'the instinct is not directed towards other people, but obtains satisfaction from the subject's own body' ('Three Essays on the Theory of Sexuality', p. 181). Lacan seems to connect human sexuality with language and the symbolic, and thus with the Other who stands between the two sexual partners as a third party (J. Lacan, *Le Séminaire. Livre XX. Encore, 1972–73*, 1975, p. 64). But we must bear in mind his understanding of the Other as the *locus* of the symbolic rather than a concrete human being (see above, n. 112). As he himself explains, the sexual drive is directed not towards a 'whole person' but towards part-objects; there is no such thing as a sexual relationship between two subjects: the woman does not exist for man as a real subject, but only as a fantasy object (*Le Séminaire. Livre XX. Encore, 1972–73*, p. 58). Thus, according to Lacan, too, the particular 'other', as a concrete subject, is neither the cause nor the aim of sexual *eros*. He categorically rules out love as part of sexual *eros* by regarding it as no more than an illusion, designed to make up for the inevitable absence of harmonious relations between the two sexes (see his *The Seminar. Book II*, English trans. by S. Tomaselli, 1988, p. 263).

[162] See below, Chapter 7. Interestingly enough, Lacan applies his observations about the absence of love in sexual *eros* (see above, n. 161) also to platonic love as presented in the *Symposium*.

logical factor. Although the erotic movement appears to be related to one particular being, this being is not unique in an absolute sense; rather, it is 'used' as a means to an end, be it the satisfaction of a natural drive and purpose, or, in the case of Platonism, the participation in an idea.

Things are totally different in the patristic understanding of *eros*. Following and developing the teaching of Dionysius, St Maximus describes *eros* as a movement of *ekstasis* in which the vehemence of the motion is constantly intensified and does not stop until the loving one 'has become entire in the whole of the beloved one and is embraced by the whole, willingly (ἑκουσίως) accepting in freedom (κατά προαίρεσιν) the saving circumscription'.[163] *Eros* is described here as a free movement that begins from a free being and ends in communion (embrace, circumscription) with another free being, which is its final destination. The description of this ultimate state of *eros* as 'embrace' or 'circumscription' (περίληψις, περιγραφὴ) rules out any absorption of the particular in the general; it is the union of a whole with a whole in which both of the two beings retain their ontological integrity. It is also significant that both the cause and the ultimate purpose of the erotic movement in this case is nothing else (e.g., nature, ideal, or even the relationship of love itself) than *the concrete Other*, in whom the erotic movement stops and rests. In this conception of *eros*, there is no servitude to nature, no desire that goes beyond the Other,[164] no 'love of loving', but only love of the concrete Other.[165]

Now, the claim to otherness as absolute uniqueness which is built into the concept of *eros* can very easily be understood as a claim to *exclusiveness*: if the beloved one is absolutely unique and the only truly and absolutely Other, is there still a place for other particular

---

[163] *Amb.* 7 (PG 91, 1073C-D).

[164] This shows that there is no similarity whatsoever between Maximus' and Lacan's concepts of Desire. For the latter, the Other as the Object of desire is no longer desired once it is attained, Desire being always a desire not for what is attained but for what is lacking. Similar observations apply to Levinas' concept of desire (see above).

[165] Contrast this with the medieval concept of *eros* in the vivid analysis of D. de Rougemont, *L'amour et l'occident*, 1956: 'Tristan et Iseut ne s'aiment pas, ils l'ont dit et tout le confirme. *Ce qu'ils aiment c'est l'amour, c'est le fait même d'aimer...* [L]'amour qui les "demeine" n'est pas l'amour de l'autre tel qu'il est dans sa réalité concrète. Ils s'entr'aiment, mais chacun n'aime l'autre qu'à *partir de soi, non de l'autre*' (pp. 27, 37-38; emphases in the original). This very important book by de Rougement exists in English translation with the title, *Passion and Society*, trans. by Montgomery Belgion, 2nd edn, 1956.

beings to be Other in a true sense? Exclusiveness presupposes individualism and can make sense in the case of *eros* only if the erotic relationship is dictated by nature and is conceived and experienced psychologically rather than ontologically, as is in fact the case in our common experience. In order to exclude someone or something you need an 'ontology' of separation, that is, of isolating a particular being from the relations that constitute it, and defining it as Aristotle's τόδε τι, an entity in itself. When *eros* is understood merely as a psychological experience, you need to create conditions of distance and separateness in order to ascertain the uniqueness of the beloved one.[166] But in the case of an ontology of communion, the way to make someone or something unique is to see this particular being in relation to everything that exists. You establish its uniqueness not by *separating* this being from other beings, but by *including* them in its very identity. In a relational ontology there is no Other without Others, for every being obtains its identity through its relations and not through separation. Therefore, since the unique being, the object of *eros*, receives its identity from its relationship with other beings, in loving this being uniquely one also loves whatever relates to it and constitutes its identity.

But in that case what is the difference between the way one loves a unique being and the way one loves the beings with whom this being is ontologically related? What is the specific meaning of *uniqueness*?

There are several things that constitute the uniqueness which distinguishes *eros* from other forms of love. The most important difference has to do with *cause*: there is only one reason that causes our love for the other beings, and that is the one being we love uniquely. It is in and through and thanks to this unique being that we love the other beings that relate to it. The highest example of this is to be found in God's love for his creation. God the Father loves uniquely only one Person, that is his Son.[167] The adjective, μονογενής,

---

[166] Cf. again D. de Rougemont, *L'amour et l'occident*, p. 29: '*on peut dire qu'ils* [the two lovers] *ne perdent pas une occasion de se séparer. Quand il n'y a pas d'obstacle, ils en inventent*' (emphasis in the original). One is tempted to see a similarity between this description and the 'metaphysics of suffering' referred to above (see n. 145).

[167] The Holy Spirit is also loved eternally by the Father but he is not μονογενής. In a sense, the Spirit's relation with the Father — in the case of God, love is not psychological but ontological, i.e., not a feeling but generating *hypostasis* — passes through the Son; it is caused by the Father alone, yet hierarchically *after* the generation of the Son, in order that 'the mediating position of the Son in the divine life may guard his right to be the only begotten (μονογενής)', Gregory Nys., *Quod non sint* (PG 45, 133). Cf. below, Chapter 5.

with which the Father refers to his Son (Jn 1.14-18; 3.16), does not
mean simply the 'only begotten' but also the 'uniquely loved one' (ὁ
ἀγαπητός; Mt. 3.17; 12.18; 2 Pet. 1.17; etc.). It is in and through and
because of him that the Father loves all the beings that exist, for he
made them 'in him' and 'for him' (Col. 1.16-18). It is also by being
incorporated into this uniquely beloved Son that all created beings
can be both other than God and in communion with him. As the
Gospel of St John puts it in a striking way, it is because one loves the
only beloved Son that one is loved by the Father (Jn 16.27; cf. 14.21).
Uniqueness is not exclusiveness but inclusiveness; it is the *cause* of
inclusiveness.

Thus, the uniquely loved being is a *hypostasis* which hypostasizes
other beings, the Other that affirms Others, giving them an identity, a *hypostasis* of their own. In the Christological vision of existence, there can be no hypostases without their hypostasization in
the one and unique *hypostasis* of the Son, who is the unique *hypostasis* of the Father (Heb. 1.3). Love as *eros* hypostasizes beings, that is,
makes them exist as particular, by incorporating them into a unique
(a uniquely loved) *hypostasis*. Not only does uniqueness not exclude
other particular beings, it establishes their otherness in and through
communion.[168]

---

[168] V. Lossky (*In the Image and Likeness of God*, 1974, p. 188f.) describes the unity of
the Church in terms of the scheme of 'nature vs. person' and attaches to Christ the
unity of human *nature* and to the Spirit the multiplicity of *persons*. Thus he strongly
rejects the view that a hypostasis can contain other hypostases. In support of his
position he interprets Mt. 18.20 as excluding the sense of 'I contain them in me' or
'they (those gathered together in his name) are in me' — the 'in my name' meaning
'unity of nature' (p. 189). Such an interpretation, however, overlooks the fact that
in other sources (John and Paul) we encounter such expressions very frequently. As
I have argued elsewhere (see my *Being as Communion*, pp. 124-25), the application
of the scheme 'nature vs. person', as corresponding to that of 'Christ vs. Spirit', in
ecclesiology is extremely problematic. The 'many' are united not in the *nature* of the
'one' but in his *person* — both in ecclesiology and in Christology the unity is *hypostatic*. The 'polyhypostasity' of the Church corresponds to Christ 'polyhypostasized'.
This, Lossky believes, involves a contradiction: 'as for a person or hypostasis containing other persons as parts of a whole, such a notion would be contradictory' (*In the
Image and Likeness of God*, p. 188). For him, if there is unity in the Church this must
be attributed to nature and not to persons. His scheme is: Christ = nature = unity,
while Spirit = person = diversity in the Church. Such a scheme is problematic: the
Spirit not only diversifies, he also unites (1 Cor. 12.13; Eph. 4.4), and Christ unites
not via *nature* but 'hypostatically', i.e., via *personhood*. The position I present in this
essay is precisely the opposite to that of Lossky: it is not via nature but via personhood
that two or more Others can unite. This is so because, with the help of an insight borrowed from Maximus, *natures can unite only because they possess a hypostasis*; the princi-

This vision of existence may help us understand the well-known expression ἐν Χριστῷ, 'in Christ', which we encounter particularly in the writings of St Paul. There is no need to interpret this expression in mystical terms or to contrast it with the expression σὺν Χριστῷ, 'with Christ', as a more genuinely Pauline expression. Paul repeatedly refers to Christ as his own life and being and to the life of Christians as being hidden in Christ and, through him, in God (Gal. 2.19-20; Phil. 1.21, 23; Col. 3.1-4; etc.). For him, Christ is the unique Other, the one in and through whom all other beings are loved, not in a psychological but an ontological sense, since it is in him that everything exists (Col. 1.16) and acquires its particular identity. It is in Christ, through his resurrection, that the death which nature brings about through reproduction is eliminated, and that the particular beings in relation to which we exist survive as particular beings and acquire their true being as otherness in communion.

Life in Christ, therefore, means placing all our relations, in and through which we obtain our personal identity, in the *hypostasis* of Christ. Christ is the only one that can guarantee the ontological truth, the eternal survival, of every being we regard as unique and indispensable, for he is the only one in whom death, which threatens the particular with extinction, is overcome. It is for this reason that Christ can claim absolute uniqueness for himself to the point of demanding from us that we cease, for his sake, to regard any other being (father, mother, wife, children, etc.; Mt. 10.37; Lk. 14.26) as unique and indispensable. It is not that he wants to exclude in this way anyone we love uniquely, but rather that he is the only one who can hypostasize them and give them eternal being. Without him, their uniqueness would not be ontologically true, and our *eros* for them would tragically stumble on their death, the ultimate enemy of all uniqueness (1 Cor. 15.26).

(d) *Otherness and Ecclesial Existence*

The Church is the community in which otherness is experienced as communion in and through uniqueness. By being the body of

ple of unity is not nature but person. It is this that allows for communion to be unity *while* being diversity, and vice-versa, i.e., otherness and communion at the same time. In this case, persons are not contained 'as parts of a whole' — that would certainly be contradictory — rather, they are hypostasized in another hypostasis *as wholes in communion*. The point at issue is crucial: if unity is attached to nature and not to hypostasis, a totalitarian ontology, so much and so rightly feared by post-modernity, becomes inevitable. If unity takes place at the hypostatic level, as I am trying to show in this essay, the fear of such a totalitarian ontology is dispelled.

Christ, the Church exists as the hypostasization of all particular beings in the unique *hypostasis* of Christ, which guarantees the ontological truth, the eternal survival, the ἀεί εἶναι, of these beings thanks to his resurrection. This hypostasization takes place *in the Holy Spirit*, which means in freedom (2 Cor. 3.17) and communion (*koinonia*; 2 Cor. 13.13) and as a foretaste of the eschatological state of existence (Acts 2.18). The Spirit offers the particularizing force which guarantees that hypostasization in Christ will not end up in an absorption of the many into the one, in the loss of otherness. This applies to each member of the Church as well as to each Church community and its structure.[169] The Church in every respect is communion in otherness and otherness in communion.

In order to grasp this mystery of the Church as otherness in communion, we must recall what we have already noted concerning *eros*. Uniqueness is not exclusiveness, and hypostasization does not imply the disappearance of *hypostaseis* in a unique *hypostasis*. Christ, and ultimately the Father, is the equivalent, in our experience, of the unique person to whom *eros* is addressed (cf. Maximus, above) and with regard to whom no other being counts ultimately except in so far as it is part of the relations that constitute the identity of the uniquely loved person. In our common human experience of *eros*, the unique being to whom our love is addressed draws his or her identity from a limited range of relations; hence the real possibility that uniqueness may involve exclusiveness. It is not so with Christ, in whose *hypostasis* everyone and everything (τὰ πάντα; Eph. 1.10, 23; Col. 1.16f.) is incorporated. In loving Christ uniquely, that is, as the uniquely and absolutely Other, we love all those with whom he has freely chosen to relate; in and through the Church, we love everyone and everything that exists.[170]

Now, this may sound like an abolition of all uniqueness, and, effectively, in fact, like an abolition of *eros* itself for any other being except Christ. So, does uniqueness allow for a plurality of 'unique' objects

---

[169] This is developed in my *Being as Communion, passim*, and esp. in Chapters 3 and 6.

[170] The late Archimandrite Sophrony (Sakharov) developed the idea that, in Christ, the human being too, through love and union with him, acquires a hypostatic existence which encompasses the whole of creation and even the whole of God, and is expressed and realized especially in prayer for all creation. See especially his *We Shall See Him as He Is* (English trans. from Russian by Rosemary Edmonds), 1988 and 2004, pp. 190f. Cf. K. Ware, 'We must pray for ALL: Salvation according to St Silouan', *Sobornost* 19 (1997), pp. 34-55.

of love? Can *eros* be addressed to human beings as well as Christ, or is it only 'love' that we can apply to our fellow humans and not *eros*, which must be reserved for Christ, the truly unique one?

These questions are not academic; they are deeply connected with the actual life of the Christian, and, in particular, with what is (inadequately) called 'spirituality' and the 'spiritual life'.

Eros has been more or less anathematized in Christian tradition as if it were totally incompatible with the 'spiritual life'. This has happened for different reasons. One of them has to do with its common association, if not identification, with sexuality. This is especially observable in puritan Christian traditions, which cultivate an attitude of fear and repulsion for anything sexual or bodily. They do so not for ontological reasons, such as the association of sexuality with biological death, but for reasons of *morality* based on an opposition between 'flesh' and 'spirit' which amounts to a depreciation of the human body and perhaps even of matter in general.

It is not difficult to show how mistaken this negative attitude to *eros* is. If this notion was necessarily associated with sexuality, the Greek Fathers, for example Dionysius the Areopagite and Maximus, would not make such repeated use of it, applying it to God himself. As to the morality that depreciates the body, it would suffice to remind ourselves of the Incarnation and the Resurrection; there is no greater proof of the sanctity and ontological significance of the body in the Christian faith.

This anti-erotic morality is usually combined with a tolerant attitude to *eros* on the strict condition that it serves the natural function of reproduction. In this case, it is not only difficult to accept the patristic use of *eros* to describe God's love, but we are confronted with a morality which ignores or overlooks the fact that nature, particularly through sexual reproduction, paradoxically serves not only life but also death. The claim of the beloved one to absolute and eternal being, which is built into the very idea of *eros*, is thus shown to be a deception, and *eros* can no longer be conceived as death's most fierce enemy, as all genuinely erotic literature and art has portrayed it since time immemorial.

This is the moralistic attitude to *eros*. But there is also a trend in Christian 'spirituality' which does not object to the use of *eros* in the 'spiritual life' (especially since ascetic fathers, such as St Maximus, make extensive use of it), provided that it is applied only to our relationship with Christ and God, and not to our relationship with our fellow human beings. The ground for this attitude is not moralistic

but theological: it is exclusively God and Christ that can claim uniqueness in our love; we cannot have more than one unique person in our
existence.

We are now at the heart of the problem: if uniqueness is a fundamental aspect of the erotic relationship, all such relationships must
cease to involve uniqueness if they are not to contradict Christ's
uniqueness in our love, that is, they must cease to be erotic. We can
love all those whom Christ loves, but not in an erotic manner, that
is, not regarding them as unique in an absolute sense. Such seems to
be the attitude of the martyr and the ascetic, for whom the absolute
Other is Christ and God, for whose sake not only love of self but also
love of all Others is sacrificed.

Since the Church projects her martyrs and ascetics as models of
Christian life — she is in fact founded on martyrdom and asceticism
— it would be hard to question this position. Yet the erotic is a fundamental dimension of our existence — not of our nature, for we have
seen the problems entailed in that, but of our personhood, which is
inconceivable without its ecstatic and hypostatic dimensions. Personhood aims at uniqueness, and since we are persons, not only in relation to God but also in relation to our fellow human beings, *eros* is
not, in principle, a 'passion' that takes us away from God, but rather,
on the contrary, a mode of being that makes us capable of relating
to him. If the erotic capacity of the human being is killed and not
allowed to express itself in all aspects of our existence, if we cease to
be erotic beings seeking in all our relations the otherness of communion that admits no death (that is the ontological meaning of
uniqueness), then we would be so mutilated that our relationship
with God, too, would be deprived of its erotic nature.

How then are we to harmonize the uniqueness of a human person
to whom our *eros* is addressed with the uniqueness of Christ and
God, who are ultimately the unique beings *par excellence*? In order to
answer this question, the following remarks must be borne in mind.

(i) There is no way to God which does not pass through the human
being, as there is no way for God's love to reach each of us except
through the love of human beings. You cannot love God whom you
have not seen, and not your fellow human being whom you see (1 Jn
4.20).

(ii) If your *eros* is genuine love for the Other, and not a self-love in
disguise, or a love of loving,[171] or a natural necessity and attraction,

---

[171] As described by D. de Rougemont. See above, nn. 165, 166.

the ever-being of the beloved one cannot but be your ultimate concern. The person you love as unique cannot maintain his ontological uniqueness, cannot be truly unique, if death overcomes him in the end. He can be truly unique only in him who has conquered death. Therefore, the uniqueness of a human person and the uniqueness of Christ are not in competition. In an ontology of otherness, the one leads to the other inevitably.

(iii) Martyrdom and asceticism do not involve a rejection of all other beings for the sake of Christ, for that would amount to an individualization of Christ, who is the relational being *par excellence*.[172] They should rather be understood as a rejection of self-love and as an entrusting[173] of those we love in and through a particular person to him who so loves us as to offer himself to be the unique person who guarantees through his death and resurrection their ontological uniqueness by their eternal survival. Thus the concern for the ever-being of the beloved one, the claim to absolute ontological otherness, which is built into *eros*, is not a deception but a faith in the existence, the 'hypostasis', of things hoped for (Heb. 11.1).

Far from being anti-erotic, therefore, the Church, in her very way of being, is the truly erotic mode of existence. She is the place where God's love as the love of a particular and ontologically unique being (the love of the Father for his only-begotten, i.e., uniquely loved, Son) is freely offered to his creation in the person of Christ, so that every particular human being may freely obtain ontological otherness (i.e., true uniqueness not subject to annihilation by death) in him. This is the 'essence' of the Church — everything else is meant to be the means for its realization.

We can therefore describe the Church, fundamentally, as a *eucharistic way of being*,[174] for it is in the Eucharist that this love of God the Father is offered to humanity as the unique *hypostasis* in which all human beings can freely obtain otherness and uniqueness. In the Eucharist, otherness is not a psychological 'experience' of particularity; but rather, the event of the Eucharist is the ontological affirmation of otherness and particularity through the assurance and foretaste of immortality.[175]

---

[172] More about this in my *Being as Communion*, esp. chs 2 and 3.

[173] Cf. the words of the Orthodox liturgy: 'let us commit (or entrust, = παραθώμεθα) one another to Christ our God'.

[174] Cf. Nicholas Cabasilas, *De div. alt.* 37-38 (PG 150, 452-453): the *only* way to 'regard' the Church is to identify her with the Eucharist.

[175] It is for this reason that the Eucharist was quite early described as the 'medicine

It is, therefore, not accidental that the *sine qua non* condition for the Eucharist is Baptism. In its ontological significance, Baptism is a new birth, not from below or from 'blood or from the will of the flesh, nor from the will of man' (Jn 1.13), that is, from nature, but 'from above' (Jn 3.3), that is, from the Spirit (Jn 3.5-6). We are clearly faced here with what I described earlier as a conflict between nature and person. Unless we acknowledge this conflict and cease to draw otherness and particularity from natural reproduction ('from blood or the will of the flesh or the will of man'), we cannot understand the necessity of birth 'from above' or 'from the Spirit', that is, the necessity of Baptism.[176] Given the fact that otherness is ontologically constituted by the birth of a particular being and terminated by death, the only way for a particular being ontologically to be truly Other is to be born again, this time not from nature but from the Spirit, and to overcome death through the 'medicine of immortality'.[177] What Baptism initiates, therefore, the Eucharist fulfils. Otherness as the emergence of a new particular being through Baptism is granted eternal being through communion in the Eucharist. Thus the Church is communion and otherness at the same time.

All this may serve as an explanation of the reason why the ancient Church insisted that all aspects of human life which involve ontological relations should pass through the Eucharist, in order to be saved from the mortality inherent in human nature. Penance, ordination and matrimony, which medieval scholasticism turned into autonomous 'sacraments', were performed in the context of the Eucharist in the ancient Church. Penance originally mainly covered sins against one's fellow man, particularly against members of the eucharistic community itself,[178] thus indicating that the restoration of communion between human beings and participation in eucharistic communion are intrinsically inter-related. Its liturgical connection with the Eucharist was only natural: the eternal survival of the Other, which is

of immortality, an antidote against death' (Ignatius, *Eph.* 20.2; PG 5, 756A) and as '*antidotum vitae*' (Irenaeus, *Adv. Haer.* III.19.1; PG 7, 938Df.).

[176] Note how Maximus contrasts Baptism with biological birth in *Amb.* 42 (PG 91, 1348A-1349A): Baptism is a birth which 'abolishes' or 'rejects' (ἀθέτησις) the 'unfree' (ἀπροαίρετον) biological birth, and leads to 'ever-being' (ἀεὶ εἶναι) and 'immortality' (ἀθανασίαν).

[177] See above, n. 175.

[178] Mt. 5.23-24. Confession of sins was related to reconciliation in connection with the Eucharist; cf. the *Didache* 14.1; the *Epistle of Barnabas* 19.12 (PG 2, 780A-B); the Syriac *Didascalia* 11 (ed. Connolly, pp. 109-115); Tertullian, *Apol.* 39; and other early sources.

guaranteed by the Eucharist as the 'medicine of immortality', neces-
sitates our reconciliation with him or her through Penance. The existential context of Penance is reconciliation with the Other, not for
psychological or moral reasons (so that we may experience the joy of
peaceful co-existence) but for the reason that, thanks to Christ's resurrection, celebrated in the Eucharist, the Other will survive in the
Kingdom as a unique and indispensable partner in the relationship
that brings about our own identity.

Similar observations apply to ordination and matrimony. Their
performance by the early Church in the context of the Eucharist
indicated that the relationships established through these 'sacraments' are placed by the Church in the Kingdom, so that they may
acquire ultimate ontological significance. For this reason, both ordination and matrimony are actions of the Church involving ontological relations of eschatological, that is, ultimate, uniqueness.[179]

(e) *Otherness and the Ascetic Ethos*

In section (b), above, I discussed the difficulties entailed in any
ethics of otherness. This is not to be understood as excluding the
application of otherness to ordinary human life, nor as limiting such
an application to specific aspects of it, such as *eros* or ecclesial existence in its sacramental manifestations. On the contrary, communion and otherness are supposed to permeate and pervade our lives
in their entirety. They are to become an *attitude*, an *ethos*, rather than
an *ethic* and a set of principles.

Ethics operates on the basis of the polarity of good and evil. There
may be a diversity of views as to what ethical principles belong to the
category of good or of evil at a certain time in a particular culture or
moral system, but there can be no ethics without a categorization of
what *ought* and what *ought not* to be done.[180] As soon as human reason

---

[179] The service of matrimony in the Orthodox Church includes the crowning of
the two married persons, whose crowns are removed from their heads by the cel-
ebrant at the end of the service with the prayer to the Lord: 'retrieve' or 'recover'
them 'in your kingdom'. Both in ordination and in matrimony — the two services
resemble each other in their rite — the persons involved are placed in the Kingdom
through relations that only sin can break. The eucharistic acts of the Church are
not to be seen as 'means of grace' enabling us to continue our mortal existence by
making it more bearable psychologically, or morally permissible, etc. They are *ontologically* significant, as they place us in relations of an eschatological nature.

[180] Ethics is '[t]he philosophical study of voluntary human action, with the
purpose of determining what types of activity are good, right, and to be done (or
bad, wrong, and not to be done)... What the ethicist aims at, then, is a reflective,

is unable to categorize in this way by identifying an act or a person as either good or evil, just or wrong, the notion of ethics automatically collapses.

Now, I have argued here that the Other is not identifiable ontologically in moral terms, for he or she would cease to be truly Other if placed in a class or category applicable to more than one entity. By being a person, the Other is by definition unique and therefore unclassifiable. Only in this way can one remain truly and absolutely, that is, ontologically, Other.

This seems to suggest that otherness implies a demoralization or an a-moralization of human life, a naive attitude of turning a blind eye to the reality of evil in our fallen existence. How can we avoid a-moralism in treating the Other as a morally unclassifiable being? How can we free the Other from moral categorization, thus protecting his or her personal uniqueness, while recognizing the reality of evil in our existence?

I cannot find a better answer to this question than the one provided by the ascetic Fathers of the Church, particularly those known as the desert Fathers. No one has taken evil as seriously as they have, being engaged in a constant fight with the 'demons' and with everything demonic in existence. Yet in a remarkable way they insisted that the Other should be kept free from moral judgement and categorization. This they achieved not by disregarding evil but by *transferring it from the Other to the Self.*

'The beginning of salvation for everyone is to condemn himself'. This axiom, attributed to Nilus of Ancyra,[181] is the very foundation of asceticism for the desert Fathers.[182] The death of 'self' is the *sine qua non* condition for salvation. But this condemnation of the Self does not imply a negative attitude; it is tied up with one's positive attitude to the Other, with the liberation of the Other from his or her evil qualities, so as to be fully affirmed and accepted. Evil is not ignored or overlooked, but is passed from the Other to the Self.[183] The Other

---

well-considered, and reasonable set of conclusions concerning the kinds of voluntary activities that may be judged GOOD or suitable (or EVIL and unsuitable)...'
V.J. Bourke, 'Ethics', *New Catholic Encyclopedia*, 2nd edn, 2003, vol. 5, p. 388f. Cf. *The Cambridge Dictionary of Philosophy*, 1955, p. 244: 'the general study of goodness and the general study of right action constitute the main business of ethics'.

[181] Nilus, *Cap. paraen.* (PG 79, 1249), attributed to Evagrius by J. Quasten, *Patrology* III, 1960, p. 504.

[182] Thus Anthony, Arsenius, Ammoes, Poimen, Theophilus, John Colovos, etc. See *Apophthegmata Patrum* (PG 65, 72-410).

[183] The stories of such empathy with the Other's sin which are retailed in the lives of

has priority and supremacy over the Self; he must not be judged; he must be stripped of his moral qualities; he must be simply *himself* and loved for who he is.

A remarkable presentation of this ethos is also to be found in the *alloquia* of Zosimas, a desert Father of the sixth century. Not only is the evil act of the Other against someone forgiven and eliminated by him, but the Other is regarded as a benefactor for having helped him to blame himself for this evil act.[184]

All this may appear to be totally irrational or, at best, an exercise in the virtue of humility with no ontological foundation or truth for its justification. And yet, if it is carefully analysed, this attitude is found to be based on a firm theological and ontological foundation. The theological justification is Christological: Christ himself made his own the sins of others on the Cross,[185] thus paving the way to self-condemnation so that the others might be justified. 'Christ became a curse for us' (Gal. 3.13). 'For our sake he [God] made him to be sin who knew no sin, so that in him we might become the righteousness of God' (2 Cor. 5.21).

Behind the ethos of self-condemnation for the sake of the Other lies the Christology of *kenosis*. The application of this theme to the ascetic life was well developed by the late Father Sophrony (Sakharov). The famous saying of his spiritual master, St Silouan the Athonite, 'keep thy mind in hell and despair not', inspired Father Sophrony to develop the theology of ascetic *kenosis* by extending Christ's 'descent into hell' to the point of reducing oneself to nothing so that space may be made for the reception of the Other. *Kenosis* and its manifestation as self-condemnation are to be seen in their *positive* significance, as they develop 'the hypostatic *modus agens* — the entire giving over of the I to the other, and the *modus patiendi* — the receiving of the other

---

the desert Fathers are indeed striking and moving. One of the brothers does penance for the other's sins, as if he had committed them himself. Another one prays that the devil, who possessed a brother, might pass into himself so that the other might be liberated (which is, in fact, allowed by God to happen). The personal cost in such cases is very high but it is paid gladly in a Christ-like manner. As Barsanuphius indicates in his correspondence (see *Baarsanuphe et Jean de Gaza: Correspondance*, translated from the Greek by L. Regnault and Ph. Lemaire, 1971; letters 72-73), the 'perfect ones' are able to carry all of their brother's burden, while the weaker ones can only carry half of it. For more instances and a very good presentation of this subject, see D. Burton-Christie, *The Word in the Desert*, 1993, p. 282f.

[184] Zosimas, *Alloquia* (PG 78, 1680-1701); complete text by Augoustinos Iordanitis, in *Nea Sion*, vols. 12 (1912) and 13 (1913).

[185] Zosimas, *Alloquia* (PG 78, 1688D).

in his or her fulness'.[186] Therefore, self-condemnation has no meaning whatsoever outside an understanding of the Other as having primacy over the Self. Ascetic life aims not at the 'spiritual development'
of the subject but at the giving up of the Self to the Other, at the erotic
ecstasis of the I, that is, at *love*.

This theological justification of ascetic self-emptying for the sake
of the Other is deeply rooted in patristic thought, particularly in that
of St Maximus the Confessor. Maximus locates the roots of evil in
self-love (*philautia*).[187] All vices and passions spring from this source.
In vain would one fight evil in its concrete manifestations, the passions or vices, without uprooting self-love; the elimination of one
vice would amount to its transformation into another one.[188]

This leads Maximus to the conclusion that the ultimate purpose
of all ascetic effort is the attainment of love. The fullest effect of deification is in love, particularly love of enemies, even to the point of
dying for them.[189] Prayer and 'mystical theology' consist in 'depriving' oneself not only of all things but also of one's self.[190] Ecstasis
aims at nothing but love.[191]

All this is grounded by Maximus in the Incarnation, which for him
is the mystery of love.[192] Both the negative aspect of ascetic life, that
is the uprooting of self-love, and its positive goal, which consists in
the attainment of virtues and *theosis*, involve the priority of the Other
over the Self. The virtues to be attained through ascesis are *Christ's*
virtues, not our own,[193] and *theosis* is always *granted*, never achieved
by the individual.[194] This connects the ascetic life essentially with the
eucharistic ethos: we offer to God only what we receive from him;[195]

[186] N. Sakharov, *I Love Therefore I Am: The Theological Legacy of Archimandrite Sophrony*, 2002, p. 107.

[187] See I. Hausherr, *Philautie: De la tendresse pour soi à la charité selon saint Maxime le
Confesseur*, 1952.

[188] See the analysis of Maximus' ideas by Photius, *Bibl.* 192 (PG 103, 637f.).

[189] Maximus, *Quest. Thal.* 64 (PG 90, 725C); *Ep.* 2 (PG 91, 405A).

[190] Maximus, *Quest. Thal.* 25 (PG 90, 332C). Cf. P. Sherwood, *St Maximus the Confessor: The Ascetic Life. The Four Centuries on Charity*, 1955, p. 88ff.

[191] P. Sherwood, *St Maximus the Confessor*, p. 96. 'Than love there is nothing higher
to be sought...love knows no limits; or rather its limits are those of God' (p. 97).

[192] See especially his *Ep.* 2 (PG 91, 393C).

[193] Maximus, *Amb.* 7 (PG 91, 1081CD): Christ is the essence of virtues.

[194] *Theosis* is always κατὰ χάριν, i.e., by divine grace, according to Maximus — and
the entire patristic tradition. See the excellent work of N. Russell, *The Doctrine of
Deification in the Greek Patristic Tradition*, 2004, *passim* and pp. 262ff.

[195] 'Thine own of thine own, we offer unto thee in all and for all' (Prayer of the
eucharistic Anaphora of the ancient Liturgies of Chrysostom and Basil).

all that we have, indeed all that we *are*, is grace coming from the Other. The ascetic life culminates in the Eucharist. There is no *theosis* outside the Eucharist, for it is only there that communion and otherness coincide and reach their fullness.

The ascetic life, therefore, is not concerned with the inner psychological experiences of the individual. Its ground is ontological: one is truly oneself in so far as one is hypostasized in the Other while emptying oneself so that the Other may be hypostasized in oneself.[196] This hypostasization constitutes the essence of communion: 'it is no longer I who live, but Christ who lives in me' (Gal. 2.20). As St Maximus observes, commenting on this Pauline verse, this does not involve a destruction of freedom, but 'gnomic yielding (ἐκχώρησιν γνωμικὴν)',[197] in the context of an erotic ecstasis in which one lives the life of the beloved one,[198] freely and fully embraced by him.[199] No particular being can survive death, that is, truly *be*, except in and through this kind of communion with the Other.

But what about truth? Is it not a violation of truth, and therefore of ontology, to transfer the evil of the other to one's innocent self? The answer to this question is that, although ethics operates with a classification of human beings as either good or evil, the ascetic ethos presented above proceeds with the assumption that *all* human beings participate in the fall and are sinful. A man may not actually have committed adultery, but yet by simply 'looking at a woman with desire he has already committed adultery with her in his heart' (Mt. 5.28). It is precisely on this basis that Jesus declared the accusers of the adulterous woman incompetent to pass judgement on her: 'let him who is without sin among you be the first to throw a stone at her' (Jn 8.7).[200]

---

[196] Cf. above, n. 170.

[197] Maximus, *Amb.* 7 (PG91, 1076B).

[198] Dionysius Areop., *De div. nom.* 4.13 (PG 3, 712A).

[199] Maximus, *Amb.* 7 (PG91, 1073D).

[200] It is worthwhile reading Maximus, *Lib. ascet.* 32f. (PG 90, 937f.): 'Tell me, who of us have no part in the aforementioned evils?... Are we not all gluttonous? Are we not all lovers of pleasure? Are we not all mad for, and lovers of, material things? Are we not all savages? Are we not all nurturers of wrath? Are we not all bearers of malice? Are we not all traitors to every virtue? Are we not all revilers? Are we not all fond of scoffing?... Do we not all hate our brothers?... Are we not full of evil?' (Eng. trans. by P. Sherwood, *St Maximus: The Ascetic Life*, p. 122). In the same tradition, Dostoevsky presents the heroes of his novels always as a mixture of good and evil, recognizing good and evil qualities in all of them, and indeed being unable to draw a clear line of separation between good and evil characters. Contrast this with Jane

By transferring evil from the Other to the Self, therefore, one is not violating truth. It is only when the Other is identified by his or her qualities that his or her being appears to be affected ontologically by these qualities. When someone commits adultery or murder, and so on, we tend to say that he or she *is* adulterous or a murderer, and so on. But the use of the verb *to be*, enslaves the Other to his or her qualities forever.[201] This makes forgiveness a merely psychological matter — a sheer forgetting, not a removing of sin — which is not what Christian forgiveness means.[202]

It follows from this that the Christian ethos of otherness cannot be based on ethical principles such as justice and the pursuit of happiness. Unless we apply to Christology the Anselmian theory of satisfaction of divine justice, we cannot explain by reference to justice the otherwise scandalous sacrifice of the innocent Christ in place of us sinners. But in fact the idea of justice is absent from Christ's teaching in a way that is provocative to all ethics since Aristotle: he likens God to the householder who paid the labourers in his vineyard the same amount whether they had worked one hour or twelve hours (Mt. 20.1-16); this is the same God who 'sends rain on the just and on the unjust' (Mt. 5.45), and loves the sinner equally or more than the righteous (Mt. 9.13; Lk. 18.9-14 etc.).

In conclusion, the Christian ethos of otherness does not allow for the acceptance or the rejection of the Other on the basis of his or her qualities, natural or moral. Everyone's otherness and uniqueness is to be respected on the simple basis of each person's ontological particularity and integrity. Not only the rejection, therefore, but even the mere *tolerance* of the Other on the basis of such qualities would be incompatible with the Christian ethos.[203]

Austen, who clearly distinguishes between good and evil characters in her novels. She is rightly described by A. MacIntyre (*After Virtue*, 1981, p. 226) as an important moralist, 'in a crucial way the last representative of the classical tradition' of virtues, before the substance of morality becomes 'increasingly elusive'.

[201] It is, of course, common to apply the verb 'to be' to someone or something in a transient sense. But 'you cannot jump twice into the same river', and the use of the verb 'to be' in its truly ontological meaning implies and requires permanence and stability.

[202] God in Christ forgives our sins by *removing* them; Acts 3.19 (cf. Rom. 4.7-8, 11, 27; Heb. 10.4; etc.). Even when it is said that God no longer 'remembers' our sins (Heb. 8.12), the meaning is not psychological but ontological, since whatever God does not 'remember' ceases to exist. On the ontological significance of forgiveness, see Maximus, *Exp. orat. dom.* (PG 90, 901).

[203] There is a big difference between tolerance and acceptance. The Other is not

Obviously, this kind of ethos would be inapplicable in a justly, that is, morally, organized society. It would be inconceivable to regulate social life on such a basis, for there would be no room for *law and order* if this attitude to the Other were to become a principle of ethics. Societies are organized on the assumption that evil can be controlled only if it is somehow identified with the evil-doer, for it is not evil as such but the person who commits the evil act that can be the subject of law. Given that justice is a fundamental principle of ethics and law, any transference of moral responsibility for an evil act from the person who committed it to someone else would be totally unethical.

It would follow from this that no morality can be totally free from the fear of the Other. The very fact that the Other is identified by his or her qualities involves the fear that the Other *may* be an agent of evil and a threat to the Self. In the final analysis, therefore, morality is a necessary device for dispelling the fear of the Other.

In view of the inapplicability in social life of the ethos of otherness as it was described above on the basis of Christology and patristic teaching, one wonders whether it is at all meaningful for the Church to preach and teach such an ethos. For example, what is the point in preaching the Sermon on the Mount, including instructions such as the one to turn the left cheek to someone who strikes you on the right (Mt. 5.39), and so on, when they are inapplicable to social life? Should the Church continue to teach such a practically and even morally irrelevant ethos?

There is no doubt that the Church cannot abandon or betray or distort the Gospel, and present to society an ethos different from the one emerging from Christ's life. If this is inapplicable to social life, that simply means that the Church can never coincide with society; she lives *in* the world but she is not *of* the world (Jn 15.16). The ethos she preaches cannot take the form of a rationally or practically sustainable ethic. The optimism of a 'social gospel' which might transform history into the Kingdom of God simply cannot be sustained theologically. Society will never become the Church, and history will have to wait for the *eschaton* to redeem it from its antinomies.

Meanwhile the Church, as the sign and image of the eschatological community, continues to portray in history the genuine ethos of otherness, not only in her preaching and teaching, but also and above all in her *sacramental life* and in her *saints*. As a sacramental and eucharistic community, the Church is the place where the 'old man' of servitude to

---

to be simply tolerated (ἀνέχεσθαι), but to be cared for more than oneself: Maximus, *Quaest. Thal.* 64 (PG 90, 725C).

nature and selfhood dies in Baptism, and where the fear of the Other is replaced in the Eucharist and in the ascetic ethos by the acceptance of the Other *qua* Other: this is the meaning of *catholicity*.[204] And in the persons of her saints (martyrs, ascetics and innumerable anonymous Christian faithful) who in one way or another, though always imperfectly, sacrifice themselves for the sake of the Other, she manifests in history the holiness of the only truly holy one, Jesus Christ.

But the ethos of otherness will always remain a *sign* and an *eikon* of the Kingdom, devoid of permanent ontological roots in history and social life. So long as death prevails in fallen existence, the two enemies of otherness, namely the self and nature, will continue to claim ontological priority over personhood. The trinitarian model of existence in which otherness and communion coincide can become an ontological reality for creation only when the 'last enemy' (1 Cor. 15.26) which separates and disintegrates beings, thereby generating individualism, self-love and fear of the Other,[205] is finally conquered in the Kingdom. Until this happens, the ethos of otherness will remain a 'foretaste' of *theosis*, of the 'mode of being' which pertains only to God by nature, and which is promised as a permanent state to creation in the *eschata*.

(f) *Otherness and the Eucharistic Ethos*

Being is a *gift*, not a self-subsistent and self-explicable reality. As a gift, being presupposes the Other — there is no gift without a giver. This is the heart of *personal* ontology, as distinct from, and in a certain sense opposed to, *substantialist* ontology. In personal ontology otherness is *constitutive* of being. That is why in this kind of ontology *causation* is of primary and paramount importance. In a substantialist ontology causation occurs *within* being: beings derive from other beings but there is always, under or before them, a *substratum*, which remains eternal and uncaused, such as, for example, 'matter' or 'form' in the case of Aristotelian ontology.[206] Christian ontology, by introducing the idea of *creatio ex nihilo*, has made personal causation constitutive of being, and, by employing the notion of personal

---

[204] The ethos of the Church's catholicity lies precisely in the transcendence of all natural, moral and social divisions in the Eucharist. See my *Being as Communion*, p. 151f.

[205] It is regrettable that theology and the Church do not seem to realize that the real problem of the human being is *mortality*, not sin as such. As long as there is mortality, sin will remain uncontrollable, and ethics will disguise evil by transferring it from one vice to another.

[206] Thus, for example, Aristotle, *Phys.* 1.7–8.190a; *Metaph.* 7.7–9.1032a–1034b. Cf. below, Chapter 7.

causation even with reference to God's being,[207] it has brought otherness into ontology in an ultimate sense.

Therefore, the gift *par excellence* that comes from the Other is not a quality, an 'accident' of being, but *being itself*. In a personal ontology this means that the Other causes someone or something to be 'other' or particular, in the absolute sense of particularity, that is, as a being which cannot be confused with other beings, added or combined with them so as to be absorbed in a sum or totality of beings, or be swallowed up by another being or by Being itself. This is exactly what *love* is in its ontological notion, exemplified and manifested, as we have already seen, in the true meaning of *eros*.

Love as *eros* is not about feelings and emotions, or goodness. It is about a new birth, a 'call' giving someone a unique identity, totally incomparable to any other identity, a 'mode of being' distinguished and identifiable, after the model of the Holy Trinity, not by any natural or moral qualities, but by the sheer relation it has with the being who causes its identity to emerge. The beloved one is unique because he or she is the beloved *of* someone, *his* or *her* beloved one. This is the only identity that makes him or her unique; it is a relational identity (cf. Mt. 3.17 and parallels; Jn 1.18: 'beloved' and 'unique' combined with the possessive 'my'). Beings exist as particular, therefore, only as gifts of the Other, who grants them an identity by establishing a unique relation with them.

In this kind of ontology, in which the Other and not the Self is the cause of being, we not only leave behind the Cartesian ontology of 'I think, therefore I am', but we also go beyond 'I love, therefore I am', since the latter still presupposes the Self as somehow causing being (by love). The proper way of expressing the ontological character of love in an ontology of otherness would rather be: '*I am loved*, therefore I am'.[208] Being is a gift of the Other, and it is this very gift that constitutes love; if love does not grant or 'cause' a unique identity, it is not true love; it is self-love, a sort of narcissism in disguise.

---

[207] See below, Chapter 3.

[208] The question that may be asked, in response to such a thesis, of whether those who do not happen to be loved by anyone can still be said to exist, since they cannot say 'I am loved', can have only one answer: such persons *exist, because they are loved by God*. If there is no God at all, or if there is a God who is not love, there is no true existence for them. God as love both in himself (= Trinity) and towards creation (= Christ) is, in any case, the presupposition of the existence not only of those who are not loved by any human being but even of those who are fortunate enough to be so loved, since no human love can offer existence *for ever*, i.e., true being. God thus emerges as a logical 'necessity' from the axiom 'I am loved, therefore I am'.

Now, the Eucharist was originally conceived and practised precisely as an expression of thanksgiving (εὐχαριστια) *for the gift of being*. In the *Didache* (ch. 10), the Eucharist is described primarily as an act of thanksgiving to God the Father 'for your holy name', which is a way of referring to God's very identity,[209] his personal existence, revealed and made known to us through Jesus.[210] The most important gift to us, therefore, is the fact of God's existence, his 'name', that is, his existence as a person made known to us as the Father of his Son. This thanksgiving is extended to *the gift of creation*, that is, to our own existence: 'You, Lord *pantocrator*, have created everything (τὰ πάντα)'.

This ontological significance of the Eucharist survived well into the fourth century CE, as is evident from such sources as the *Mystagogical Catecheses* of Cyril of Jerusalem and the Liturgies under the name of Basil and John Chrysostom. In Cyril's account of the eucharistic canon there is commemoration 'of the sky, the earth, the sea, the sun...and *of all creation*, both rational and non-rational, visible and invisible'.[211] In St Basil's Liturgy, the *Anaphora* solemnly begins with the address to the Father as 'the One who Is' (ὁ ὤν), while in the Liturgy under the name of John Chrysostom the *Anaphora* includes giving thanks for the Father 'who exists (ὁ ὤν) always and without change' for 'having brought us from non-being into being' (ἐκ τοῦ μὴ ὄντος εἰς τὸ εἶναι).[212]

If by ethos we mean an *attitude*, an *orientation*, and *a way of relating* with whatever exists, the Eucharist involves and reveals above all the grateful acknowledgement of the Other's existence and of our own existence as a gift of the Other. The essence of the eucharistic ethos, therefore, is the affirmation of the Other and of every Other as a gift to be appreciated and to evoke gratitude. The Other of the eucharistic ethos is the extreme opposite of Sartre's 'hell' and 'original fall'. He does not threaten our ontological freedom, that is, our particu-

---

[209] The old saying, *nomen Dei est Deus ipse*, is substantiated by 'all the expressions in the Old and the New Testaments'; E. Lohmeyer, *'Our Father': An Introduction to the Lord's Prayer*, 1965, p. 74f. The *Didache* betrays and confirms its archaic character by this eucharistic text. For a helpful recent summary of the discussion concerning the eucharistic character of this text, see P.F. Bradshaw, *Eucharistic Origins*, 2004, pp. 24-42.

[210] *Didache* 10.5.

[211] Cyril Jerus., *Myst. catech.* 5.6 (PG 33, 1113A-B).

[212] Similar references to thanksgiving for the existence of creation are found in other early liturgical documents, such as the Strasbourg Papyrus (fourth–fifth century). See W.D. Ray, 'The Strasbourg Papyrus', in P.F. Bradshaw (ed.), *Essays on Early Eucharistic Prayers*, 1997, pp. 39-56.

larity. By remaining Other while constituting us as Others, the Other confirms our otherness, our ontological freedom to be Other.

If we understand the Eucharist in such ontological terms, the implications for our ethos will include the following:

(i) The only thing that *ultimately* matters in our ethos is the *existence* of the Other. The natural or moral qualities of the Other, whether positive or negative, 'good' or 'bad', do not affect our attitude to him or her. This opens the door to unlimited *forgiveness* — 'seventy times seven', that is, infinitely.[213] For forgiveness is about preventing *qualities* from affecting being as such. Forgiving 'debts' or 'trespasses' and any 'wrong' done to us implies that we are ultimately concerned with the Other's being and not with his or her qualities. Whereas an ethic of qualities puts limits and conditions on our attitude to the Other, a eucharistic ethos accepts and gratefully affirms the Other unconditionally. All that matters in such an ethos is that the Other *exists*.

It is not without reason, therefore, that patristic thought interpreted the biblical association of the Eucharist with 'the remission of sins' (Mt. 26.28) as meaning an 'antidote to death' and a 'medicine of immortality' (Ignatius, Irenaeus, etc.). In forgiving we do not perform a negative act; we declare our ultimate concern for the Other's being. It is *death* that we fight in forgiving sins.

(ii) In offering thanks for the existence of the Other in the Eucharist, we affirm the overcoming of death. This makes the Eucharist the feast of the Resurrection. But death is overcome in Christ only through death. This makes the Eucharist a *sacrifice*: the gift of being is offered to the Giver purified from the passion of self-love which has made it possible for death to conquer our being. A eucharistic ethos is sacrificial in that it gives priority to the Other over the Self.

The priority of the Other over against the Self reaches its climax on the Cross where, according to Christ's prayer in Gethsemane, it is the will of the Other that prevails: 'not as I will but as thou wilt' (Mt. 26.39). This attitude permeates the Christian's ethos throughout his or her life: 'let no one seek his own good but the other's' (1 Cor. 10.24; cf. Phil. 2.4). And this can go as far as to subject one's conscience to the conscience of the Other. 'For why should my freedom be determined by the conscience of the other?' (1 Cor. 10.29). The Other must always have priority, even if this means going against one's own conscience.

(iii) In the Eucharist the Other is inconceivable as an autonomous or independent 'individual'. The Eucharist is *communion*, and this

---

[213] Mt. 18.22. Cf. Floyd V. Filson, *The Gospel according to St Matthew*, 1960, p. 203.

means that otherness is experienced as *relational*. The eucharistic ethos, therefore, precludes any exclusiveness in otherness. The only exclusion that is permissible — even imperative — is of exclusiveness itself. All eucharistic discipline involving exclusion from eucharistic communion was originally connected with this anti-exclusivist ethos and not with a casuistic ethic or morality as such.[214]

As we have explained in a previous section of this essay, otherness, even in its absolute form of uniqueness, involves inclusiveness. Since otherness emerges from or through communion — there is no identity which is not relational — the Other is identifiable as particular not in *contrast with* but in *relation to* all Others with whom this particular Other is ontologically related. As there is no Other who is not ontologically a relational being, the eucharistic ethos involves an attitude of acceptance and confirmation of the Other, *including all the relations that make up his or her identity*.

(iv) This attitude of inclusiveness goes so far as to reach not only God, the primary constitutor of our ontological identities, but also *the entire creation* in relation to which these identities are established. Given the fact that there is not a single particular being whose otherness and identity does not depend directly or indirectly on its relation to the entire cosmos,[215] the eucharistic ethos automatically acquires an *ecological* significance. This ecological significance follows not from moral but from ontological reasons: all beings are ontologically inter-related, and any 'exclusion' of one being ontologically affects the rest.[216] A eucharistic way of being involves respect and care for

---

[214] Exclusion from the Eucharist was originally based on Mt. 5.23-24. Thus the *Didache* 14.2: 'whosoever is in conflict (ἀμφιβολία) with his fellowman (τοῦ ἑταίρου αὐτοῦ) should not participate in your assembly until the two are reconciled'. Even in the third-century eucharistic discipline, which was characterized by strictness, the offences that led to exclusion from the Eucharist (murder, adultery and apostasy) had to do, implicitly or explicitly, with the rejection of the Other. It was only later that moral conditions for eucharistic communion ceased to be necessarily related to love.

[215] In the prevailing view of modern physical science, the universe is a relational entity which is characterized by the mutual penetrability of the most elementary particles and by a constant interaction between them, the nature of each of them deriving from its relation with the rest. Thus, e.g., already M. Faraday, 'A Speculation Touching Electric Conduction and the Nature of Matter', in R. Laming (ed.), *On the Primary Forces of Electricity*, 1938, p. 7f., and more recently, Ilya Prigogine and Isabelle Stengers, *Order out of Chaos: Man's New Dialogue with Nature*, 1985, p. 95. Also, J. Polkinghorne, *Science and the Trinity*. Cf. C. Gunton, *The Promise of Trinitarian Theology*, 1991, p. 144f.

[216] The being of each one of us emerges from an endless chain of 'others', both personal and 'natural', in most cases without our being conscious of that. We would not be here but for this chain and complexity of known and unknown 'others'. The gift of being is not given to us directly and individually, but always and only through

the whole creation. The Eucharist is a 'cosmic liturgy'[217] in which the human being acts as the 'priest of creation'[218] offering to God with gratitude the gift of created existence as the body of him who freely assumed this existence in his own *hypostasis* in order to 'save' it, that is, to assure and confirm the survival of creation.

(v) In giving thanks for creation we do not simply utter words of gratitude to the Creator. We take creation *in our hands* and offer it to the Creator and to our fellow human beings as our own personal gift, as our own creation. Thus the eucharistic way of being involves an act of dedication or 'setting apart', a sacralization of creation.[219] This is not because of some sacred quality inherent in created nature but because of the sacrality of communion, of the relation between giver and recipient. In other words, it is personal relation that makes creation sacred, not something inherent in the nature of creation itself.

Such an attitude to creation not only protects us from falling into paganism (an understanding of creation as sacred in its own nature) but also protects creation itself from being conceived in immanent biological or 'natural' terms, as something possessing its own powers and qualities to be unlocked, transformed and used. The eucharistic ethos is incompatible with any treatment of nature as an object to be decontextualized, analysed and reduced to its primary qualities,[220] even to sheer energy,[221] ultimately beyond human control.[222] The

others. The fear and rejection of evolutionism in its fundamental claim is incompatible with the eucharistic ethos. As eucharistic beings we cannot but be thankful 'for all (things and persons) that we know and do not know of' (*Anaphora* of the Liturgy of St John Chrysostom), since we would not have come to being and would not exist without or apart from them.

[217] To use the pertinent description of St Maximus' theology by Hans Urs von Balthasar.

[218] Cf. my 'Preserving God's Creation', *King's Theological Review* 12 (1989), pp. 1-5, 41-45, and 13 (1990), pp. 1-5.

[219] 'Setting apart' and dedicating something or someone to some Other constitutes the essence of holiness and sacrality.

[220] Cf. A. Feenberg, *Questioning Technology*, 1999, p. 201f.

[221] According to M. Heidegger (*The Question Concerning Technology and Other Essays*, Eng. trans. by W. Lovitt, 1977), technology involves the 'challenging (*Herausfordern*) which puts to nature the unreasonable demand that it supply energy that can be extracted and stored as such. But does this not hold true for the old windmill as well? No! Its sails do, indeed, turn in the wind; they are left entirely to the wind's blowing. But the windmill does not unlock energy from the air currents in order to store it' (p. 14).

[222] See Heidegger (*The Question Concerning Technology*, p. 18ff.). From a sociological perspective, J. Ellul, too, in his *The Technological Society*, Eng. trans. by J.V. Wilkinson, 1964, comes to a similar conclusion. In his later work under the provocative title, *The*

eucharistic ethos involves an attitude of respect for the diversity of creation as it is realized and manifested in the specific *body*[223] of each created being, a body made to offer itself for communion, instead of being; in Heidegger's terminology, a *Bestand*, a 'standing-reserve' to be incorporated into a technological and economic system.[224] In a eucharistic approach to creation, the body of a particular entity, that which makes it 'other' in relation to the rest of the world, is treated as possessing its own desires and communion goals, and not as a source of energy to be extracted, reserved and distributed for any purpose and use that the human being chooses and decides.

But are we not thereby 'personalizing' nature? Are we not attaching to impersonal entities communion goals and purposes as if they were persons? Is it not the human being that gives purpose and goals to non-humans? Well, the latter is exactly what the human being has been doing ever since the emergence of modern science and technology: it is the human being that decides what the goal of each creature and of creation itself is. But we are now learning where this attitude is leading us.[225]

There is a paradox underlying the problem of the relation between human beings and nature — a paradox vividly illustrated by the technological approach to nature, and immediately related to the theology of personhood that we are advocating here. I have been arguing that we should be reluctant to approach being, both created and uncreated, from the angle of energy. Instead, I have been sug-

---

Technological Bluff (Eng. trans. by G.W. Bromilly, 1990), he writes: 'Are we then shut up, blocked and chained by the inevitability of the technical system which is making us march like obedient automatons thanks to its bluff? Yes, we are radically determined. We are caught up continuously in the system if we think even the least little bit that we can master the machinery...' (p. 411). 'Our back is to the wall' (p. 411).

[223] The danger of making even the human body redundant is apparent in modern technology, particularly as it takes the form of computer and internet information. Many, if not as yet all, of the things we do, which previously required the involvement of our bodies (meeting people, going to the shops, etc.) are now gradually being replaced by electronic communication from our homes.

[224] M. Heidegger, *The Question Concerning Technology*, p. 17f.

[225] The present ecological crisis is a direct result of this assumption that human beings can treat nature as a 'thing' and impose their will on it as its 'masters and possessors'. (Descartes already boasted that science would achieve exactly that: to make us 'maîtres et possesseurs de la nature', *Discours de la méthode. Introduction et notes de Etienne Gilson*, 1999, p. 127.) Lynn White, Jr, in his well-known 'The Historical Roots of our Ecological Crisis', *Science* 155 (1967), pp. 1203-1207, was among the first to draw attention to the responsibility this attitude bears for our ecological problems.

gesting that, following St Maximus, we must approach it from the angle of *hypostasis* or the 'mode of being', that is, the way it relates to other beings. Modern science and technology, in their cooperation, have been fascinated by the *energy* of entities: non-humans are analysed so as to produce useful results for human 'happiness'. However, this attitude to nature leads paradoxically to the depersonalization of human beings themselves. Because human beings, like the rest of creation, exist in the form of bodies, that is, potential sources of energy and a complex of natural qualities, science and technology cannot resist the temptation to treat the human body in the same way as the rest of creation, that is, by way of analysis into its most elementary constituents. Biotechnology, genetic engineering, and so on, promise a better human nature. But the danger of depersonalization of the human being lurks underneath this promise. Bioethics is desperately trying to save the human person from destruction, but it is doubtful whether it can manage to halt the force of the stream.

(vi) Now, the alternative to a depersonalization of nature is not necessarily the personalization of it. All creatures possess a *hypostasis*, a mode of being.[226] Yet not all creatures are gifted with the freedom to relate this *hypostasis* to the divine 'mode of being' which is not subject to death, and thus to allow or enable their *hypostasis* to exist for ever as particular, truly personal and hypostatic. By contrast, the human being, as the *imago Dei*, is gifted with this freedom. Unlike the animals or other creatures, therefore, the human being can properly be called a *person*, *as it is endowed with the freedom to reflect divine personhood in creation*. And it is *divine* personhood alone that can be the model of true personhood.[227]

This awesome privilege of the human being was not given by God for the sake of humanity alone. The human being is called to bring the rest of creation into communion with God so that the *hypostasis* of every creature might be saved from mortality and thus be shown to be a true *hypostasis*, that is, truly existing as particular and 'other', and not swallowed up by the general. *Hypostasis* as an ontological term carries with it a demand for the true and eternal existence of the particular — a demand that is obvious in the drive towards sur-

---

[226] See above, n. 36.
[227] Thus we do not have to borrow our concept of the person from existentialist philosophies, as some critics too readily suppose that I do in my studies (see the Appendix to Chapter 4, below). The Holy Trinity and the *imago Dei*, two thoroughly patristic ideas which no existentialist or any other modern philosophy would use, are the only proper basis for theological personalism.

vival, especially of all living creatures. In the patristic, and especially the Maximian, vision of creation, this drive can be fulfilled only in and through the human being. It is this that Christ, as the true human being, has fulfilled, and it is this that is realized and manifested in the Eucharist, when human hands, imaging those of Christ, lift up (*Anaphora*) creation to God, offering it thankfully to him with the exclamation, 'Thine own of thine own'.

The priestly function of the human being does not stop with the celebration of the Eucharist. It is exercised in human life every time that human beings take creation in their hands in order to liberate it from mortality and lift it up to truly hypostatic existence. Every form of genuine creativity, especially art, is a witness to this manifestation of human personhood.

In the long history of art, various philosophical ideas have determined its relationship to ontology, to the truth of being. In the patristic period and in Byzantium in particular, such ideas include, on the one hand, the idea that nature and matter are representable artistically only in and through their connection or relation with *personhood*, and, on the other hand, the idea that the object of art is to combine form and matter in order to bring forth the *eschatological* truth of creation, that is, the state of existence which is liberated from death.

Hence it is not by accident that it is almost impossible to find in Byzantine art any interest in the representation of nature *per se*, for example, landscape as such, except as part of the environment of persons. Similarly, the theological argument in support of the icons in Byzantium was based entirely on the idea of *hypostasis* as distinct from that of *ousia* or nature: matter is respected because it has been assumed by the *hypostasis* of the Son in the Incarnation,[228] and it is the *hypostasis* depicted in the icon, not the substance, that is venerated.[229] At the same time, the form of the persons represented, as well as their natural environment, point to the way things will be in the eschata and not to the way they are in the present state of mortality. Even the Crucifixion and burial of Christ are represented in such a way as to indicate that pain and suffering are qualified by faith that the persons involved are not under the dominion of decay and death but exist in the glory of eternal life.[230]

---

[228] So John of Damascus, *Imag.* 1.8, 16 (PG 94, 1237f., 1245f.).

[229] Theodore Studite, *Antirr.* 3.1 (PG 99, 405); cf. 3.3 (PG 99, 425).

[230] It is well-known, for example, that in Byzantine iconography there is no sen-

All this draws its inspiration from the eucharistic liturgy. The liturgical action of the human being, in which creation is 'changed' into the body of the *Risen* Christ, is the model of human art. Just as in the Eucharist, in the hands of human beings, the material creation is liberated from mortality by becoming the 'body of Christ' and by being drawn into the personal relationship of Christ with his Father in the Holy Spirit, in a similar manner art liberates nature and matter from death by granting them 'eternal life' through the personal seal of the creator. In this way, art is an *ontological* matter. It is not a means of expressing aesthetic beauty or of provoking pleasure or feelings of some kind, or of imitating nature, informed or not by some ideal standard. Nor is it even a means of giving expression to the artist's moods, feelings and responses. Art, here, is the bringing about of *a new identity*, as happens in the case of *eros*. In the words of Paul Valéry, with reference to music, it is 'the beginning of a world',[231] a new creation, albeit not *ex nihilo*, with all the tragic implications that this carries with it.[232] The eucharistic ethos leads to art as a truly *creative* manifestation of personhood, as the emergence of otherness in an ontological and personal sense. The culture produced by such an ethos is, therefore, foreign to the technological domination of the Self over matter, and has very little to do with the satisfaction of the psychological demands of the individual. It is not a product of the Self to be enjoyed by the Self, or by the various 'selves', but the bringing forth of a new identity which draws impersonal nature into personal relation with the creator in an attempt to liberate nature from its mortality.

(viii) Finally, the eucharistic ethos generates *faith*. Classical Greek thought seems to have initiated a *cognitive* approach to faith in God,[233]

---

timentality in the way Mary stands by the Cross or in the way the crucified Christ is depicted in his suffering. Similarly, the Byzantine hymnography of Good Friday strongly conditions suffering and mourning by constant references to the Resurrection. It was only at a later time and under Western influence that black vestments were introduced for the celebrating clergy in Good Friday services. In the original Byzantine worship the crucified was presented as the 'Lord of glory' (cf. 1 Cor. 2.8), and the Cross was venerated (as it still is in Orthodox worship) always in connection with the Resurrection: 'we worship your Cross, O Master, and glorify your Resurrection'.

[231] Paul Valéry, *Oeuvres* I, 1957, p. 1327.

[232] Cf. below, Chapter 6.

[233] Plato could not understand how one could be an atheist, if one looked at the movement of the stars and at the orderly conduct of the cosmos (*Laws* X, 903). Equally, Aristotle arrived at the First Mover by reasoning from physical movement and causality.

but it was mainly through scholasticism and Cartesian philosophy
that faith became a matter of *rational conviction*.[234] Modern atheism
seems to have presupposed this approach to faith, at least at the
time of the Enlightenment. By dismantling all ontological connection between God and the world, Protestantism marked a departure
from the intellectual path to faith and its replacement by a psychological or 'existentialist' approach: faith is to be understood in terms
of *trust*[235] rather than in terms of rational conviction and persuasion,
or as response and obedience to the Word of God.[236] In none of these
cases does the eucharistic ethos seem to play a decisive role as a way
to faith.

In the eucharistic ethos faith is closely linked with the idea of *personal causality*. Whatever exists or happens is *given* to us *by a person*.
'Every house is built by someone (= a person), and he who has built
everything is God' (Heb. 3.4). Faith does not spring from a rational
conviction or from a psychological experience, but from the ethos of
attributing everything to a personal cause. Whatever we are or have
is attributed to an *Other* — not to Self or to nature. And since everything, including our being, is a *gift*, we cannot but assume a giver
behind everything. This is the eucharistic path to faith. To this way of
thinking, atheism appears to be a form of ingratitude, a lack of the
eucharistic ethos.

In the eucharistic ethos you presuppose the Other as prior to
the Self and to anything that exists or happens. This makes you a
thankful being by ethos or attitude. Faith is thus an attitude of gratitude to every Other and of doxology to the Other *par excellence*,
the author of all otherness. This kind of faith offers no security of
rational conviction. The only certainty it offers lies in the *love* of
the Other. The only proof of God's existence is his love — demonstrated by our very being, in otherness and communion. We are
loved, therefore he exists.

---

[234] The 'ontological argument' for the existence of God, the *analogia entis*, etc., are
all based on the exercise of the human cognitive faculty. The Cartesian argument
for God's existence from the idea of infinity also makes faith a matter of logical
conviction.

[235] Thus the classical formulation of Luther in his *Large Catechism*: 'it is the trust
and faith of the heart alone that makes both God and an idol'.

[236] Thus Karl Barth, e.g., *Church Dogmatics*, I.1, 1975, p. 200f.; I.2, p. 270f., etc.

CHAPTER 2

ON BEING A PERSON:
Towards an Ontology of Personhood

Ontology is a word to which various meanings have been given, while for some people it indicates almost nothing at all. In this chapter, we take it to mean the area of philosophy (and theology) in which the question of *being* is raised more or less in the sense in which it was posed for the first time by ancient Greek philosophy,[1] applied here to the specific problem of personal identity. What does it mean that someone *is* rather than *has* a person? It is all too often assumed that people 'have' personhood rather than 'being' persons, precisely because ontology is not operative enough in our thinking. Personhood in this case becomes a quality added, as it were, to being: you first (logically speaking) *are* and then *act* or *behave* as a person. This assumption rules out *a priori* an ontology of personhood and is not taken into account here. Instead, we operate with the view that the assertion of personal identity, the reduction of the question, 'Who am I?', to the simple form of the 'I am who I am', that is, the claim of absolute metaphysical identity independent of qualities borrowed

[1] This was more or less the sense in which the term *ontology* was employed for the first time in the seventeenth century by authors such as R. Goclenius (*Lexicon Philosophicum*, 1613) and, more explicitly, J. Glauberg (*Metaphysica de Ente*, 1656), who defines it as the part of philosophy which speculates on being *qua* being. The same definition is recovered and employed without change by Ch. Wolff (*Philosophia prima sive ontologia*, 1729, esp. §§1 and 2), who is responsible for the establishment of this term in philosophy. Kant, in his *Critique of Pure Reason* (esp. ch. III) tried to give the term a different meaning, which however has not prevailed. Heidegger and the modern existentialist philosophers have also employed it with a different meaning in their attempt to take a critical view of classical philosophy, whereas authors such as E. Levinas in our time prefer not to attach to it the traditional metaphysical importance.

from other 'beings', is an assertion implied in the very question of personal identity. Personhood, in other words, has the claim of absolute being, that is, a metaphysical claim, built into it.

In the lines that follow we shall first pose the question that can be called 'personal' in the strictest sense, and try to elicit its ontological ingredients. We shall see how problematic a true ontology of personhood is, unless certain drastic revisions of philosophical thinking are introduced. These revisions will be considered as the presuppositions of an ontology of personhood. Against this background, suggestions will then be offered for an attempt to work out an ontology of personhood with reference to the Christian doctrine of God.

I. THE PERSONAL QUESTION AS AN ONTOLOGICAL QUESTION

1.

Who am I? Who are you? Who is he/she? This question analysed in its basic components contains the following fundamental and indeed *constitutive* ingredients:

(a) The ingredient *Who*. 'Who' is a call for *definition* or 'description' of some kind. It is a call of and for *consciousness*, a desire for *articulation*, for knowledge in the most fundamental sense. Wanting to know *who* you are is a human question which seems at first sight to require a developed degree of consciousness, a capacity for reflection, and yet it is a primordial cry, stemming from the fact that man is faced with a *given* world, and thus forced into self-assertion always via comparison with other beings *already* existing.

(b) The ingredient 'am' or *to be*. This is a cry for security, for ground to be based on, for fixity. It is uttered in the face of two basic facts: the fact that we have not always been there, and the fact that things disappear, are not always there. To assert 'being there' is to assert that you are overcoming not being there. It is a triumphalistic cry, or if you wish a doxological/eucharistic one, in the deepest sense of acknowledging being as a sort of victory over non-being. It is at the same time a cry of hidden fear in the face of non-being or the threat of death. The assertion of being is the recognition of the limitations or limits of being. It is a *kataphasis* implying an *apophasis*, the possibility or rather the actuality of a *beyond*, a movement of *transcendence*. Whether this 'beyond' leads to still other forms of being, or to pure and simple non-being, this is a matter of choosing between, on the one hand, various forms of idealism, and, on the other, extreme forms of existentialism. In either case, the expression 'I *am*' cannot be understood apart from some kind of transcendence, from what might be called 'metaphysics'.

(c) The ingredient 'I' or 'You' or 'He/She'. This is a cry for *particularity*, for *otherness*. Other beings, besides the one spoken of under the question, 'Who am I?', *are*. The second of our ingredients (the assertion of being) can be applied, therefore, to *many* beings, and so can the first one (the *who* ingredient), since it implies qualities borrowed from other beings. What this third ingredient implies is a sort of *uniqueness*, a claim of being in a unique and unrepeatable way. Many things 'are', but no one else is *me* (or you, etc.). This assertion is absolute: not simply because nothing else is 'me', but also because nothing else can *ever* be me.[2] Metaphysics in this case applies to 'me' as much as it does to 'am'. Hidden behind this is the cry for immortality, the desire not simply of the εἶναι but of the ἀεὶ εἶναι, being for ever. The fact that being continues after the 'I' disappears or falls into non-being cannot be a consolation here. If we answer the question, 'Who am I?', by simply saying 'I am a mortal being', we have removed the absoluteness from the ingredient 'I' and thus reduced it to something replaceable. This can be done, but immediately the problem of personal ontology will arise.

2.

Personal ontology is an assertion of the metaphysics of particularity. It is the endeavour to raise the particular to the primacy and ultimacy which transcends the changing world of coming and going particularities; to attach fixity to the 'many' as if they were the 'one', that is, absolute, unique and irreplaceable.

Ontology in the metaphysical sense of the transcendence of beings by being, that is, in the sense of going beyond what passes away into what always and truly *is*, was the primary preoccupation of ancient Greek thought. The flux in which things exist caused the Greek mind wonder and disturbance. You can never jump twice into the same river: how, then, can you say that this *particular* river *is*? 'Everything is in a

---

[2] This rules out any ontologies implying transformations of particular beings, leading to the emergence of *new* particular beings, as for example in the case of Platonic *metempsychosis*, or even the Aristotelian perpetuation of species through the emergence of particular beings. In both cases, particularity ceases to be absolute in a metaphysical sense, since it is implied that a particular being is replaceable by another one. Contrasted with these particularities, the personal 'I' or 'me' (or 'he/she') involves the claim that *never* can there be an 'I' other than this particular one to replace it in any way.

flux', and yet things are true, and can be said to *be*. If this is not so then we are driven either to sophistry or to madness. Particularity does not extinguish being. The latter goes on for ever, while particular beings disappear. True being, therefore, in the absolute, metaphysical sense, cannot be attached to the particular except in so far as the latter is part of a *totality*. Ancient Greek thought in *all* its forms (Parmenidean, Heracletan, Platonic and Aristotelian), in spite of its variations on other aspects, agreed on one thing: particularity is not ontologically absolute; the many are always ontologically derivative, not causative.[3]

This ontology of the classical Greeks made a personal ontology impossible, as the third of the above mentioned ingredients had to be somehow sacrificed. The truth of any particular thing was removed from its particularity and placed on the level of a universal form in which the particular participated: the thing itself passes away but its form *shared by more than one particular thing* survives. The survival of man was also subjected to the same principle. The Platonic soul of a human being, far from safeguarding the survival of the particular eternally, could be reincarnated in other beings, even in animals.[4] And Aristotle's concern with the particular did not lead to the survival of the concrete being for ever, except in the form of its species. The αὐτὸ passes away; what survives is the οἷον αὐτό.[5]

Thus, Aristotelian ontology operated with the first two of our three ingredients, but not with the third one. The 'who' question was answered with the help of categories taken from something general, not from the particular thing itself (the 'I'). The οἷον αὐτό — not the αὐτό — is the answer to the question of the 'who'. But the οἷον αὐτό comprises qualities shared by other beings besides the αὐτό (the 'I') — hence, the αὐτό cannot be ontologically ultimate. Participation in being is a condition for the particular's being as much for

---

[3] Plato's words in the *Laws* (X, 903 c-d) are revealing: 'But thou failest to perceive that all partial generation is for the sake of the whole in order that for the life of the whole blissful existence may be secured. For it (the whole) is not brought into being for thy sake, but thou (the particular) art for its sake'. Neoplatonism, by attaching ontological priority and ultimacy to the 'one' and by regarding the 'many' as a sort of deterioration or 'fall' of being, as a tendency towards 'non-being', confirms the fact that classical Greek thought was basically and consistently monistic in its ontology, as is rightly remarked by C.J. de Vogel, *Philosophia* I, *Studies in Greek Philosophy*, 1970, pp. 397-416.

[4] See Plato, *Timaeus* 41d-42e, in combination with *Phaedo* 249B, *Repub.* 618A, etc.

[5] See Aristotle's *De Anima* 2, 4.415A, 28-67. Cf. E. Rohde, *Psyche*, 1925, p. 511, and H.A. Wolfson, 'Immortality and Resurrection in the Philosophy of the Church Fathers', in K. Stendahl (ed.), *Immortality and Resurrection*, 1965, pp. 54-96.

Aristotle as it is for his master Plato. No ancient Greek managed to escape from this. The consequences on the existential level were inevitable. Classical tragedy enslaved its heroes — human *and* divine — in the destiny of natural or moral order and rationality. Man exists for the world, not the world for man.

The inability of Greek thought to create a personal ontology is not due to a weakness or incapacity of Greek philosophy as *philosophy*. None in the history of philosophy has so far managed to work out a consistent ontology of personhood in the sense of incorporating the third of our ingredients into the other two. The reason for this is both logical and existential. Logically, the particular is conceivable and can be spoken of only with the help of categories applicable to more than one thing. Such a category is οὐσία itself, which accounts at the same time for the being of the particular and of what transcends it, hence Aristotle's oscillating between first and second substance, brought out so well by D.M. Mackinnon.[6] Existentially, on the other hand, death conditions the particular being so radically that only by joining being with death in a Heideggerian 'panoramic' view of existence[7] can we give to the 'how' of things a primary ontological role, thus securing for the particular a place in ontology. But this panoramic view of being presupposes still a *horizon* in which the particulars emerge, as is exactly the case in Heidegger's philosophy, and this 'horizon' is a unifying principle conditioning the 'many' and hence prior to them. Otherness cannot acquire ontological primacy as long as one begins with the world as it is, as did the ancient Greeks and as all philosophy does, if it wishes to be pure philosophy. The observation of the world cannot lead to an ontology of the person, because the person as an ontological category cannot be extrapolated from experience.[8]

II. PRESUPPOSITIONS FOR AN ONTOLOGY OF PERSONHOOD

1.

In order to give to the particular an ontological ultimacy or priority it is necessary to *presuppose* that being is *caused* and cannot be posited as an axiomatic and self-explicable principle. This causation

---

[6] D.M. Mackinnon, 'Substance in Christology — a Cross-bench View', in S.W. Sykes and J.P. Clayton (eds.), *Christ, Faith and History: Cambridge Studies in Christology*, 1972, pp. 279-300.

[7] See the critique of Heidegger by E. Levinas, *Totalité et Infinie: Essai sur l'Exteriorité*, 1974[1], p. 15.

[8] For more on this, see below, Chapter 6.

must be absolute and primary in ontology, not secondary. Ancient Greek philosophy knew of causation, but it always posited it *within* the framework of being. Everything is caused by something else but the world as a whole is not caused *radically*, that is, in the absolute ontological sense, by anything else. Plato's creator is an artist and an organizer of pre-existing being, and Aristotle's *nous* is the First Mover causing the world to move always *from within* and on the basis of an eternal ὕλη (matter). The world is eternal; it is not ontologically caused. And so the particular is never the ontologically primary cause of being. This leads to necessity in ontology.[9] Being is not a gift but a datum to be reckoned with by the particular beings.

Biblical thought posited a different view of being. It is rightly said that Hebrew thought has no ontology to offer. For the Bible, being is caused in a radical way by *someone* — a particular being. There is no attempt in the Bible to describe this 'someone' in terms of being, for this would lead to associating him with the world and thus depriving him of the capacity of cause in the absolute sense. At some point in the Bible, he is described as ὁ ὤν rather to indicate in an apophatic manner that he is not to be described in any ontological way. Nevertheless, in terms of our initial question in this chapter, the 'I am that I am' of the Bible offers an illustration of an assertion in which the particular (the third ingredient) coincides fully with the other two, the 'who' and the 'am'. We thus have a step towards an ontology of personhood.

This principle of personal causation of being means that particularity is to be understood as causative and not derivative in ontology. To illustrate this, we may turn to patristic thought which tried to apply this principle, stemming from the Bible, to ontology. Two examples can be significant for this purpose.

First, the question of human being. What is it that causes particular human beings to *be*? Greek philosophy at the time of the Fathers was offering the choice between a Platonic 'substance standing above' (οὐσία ὑπερκειμένη) and an Aristotelian 'substance standing underneath' (οὐσία ὑποκειμένη). In other words, particular human beings *are* in so far as they participate either in the ideal 'human being' or in the 'nature' of humanity, its species. The particular is caused by the general.

To these two choices patristic thought added a third one which it borrowed from the Bible. What causes the particular human beings

---

[9] For an attachment of the idea of being to that of necessity, see E. Gilson, *L'esprit de la philosophie médiévale*, 1932, pp. 45-66.

to *be* is *Adam*,[10] that is, *a particular being*. This way of thinking would create immense difficulties to Greek philosophy — or perhaps philosophy as a whole? At this point, biblical thought introduced a paradox quite unknown to Greek or, for that matter, to our Western way of thinking, too. This paradox is known, ever since the British biblical scholar, H. Wheeler Robinson, coined the phrase, as *corporate personality*.[11] According to it, Semitic thought could move naturally from the 'one' to the 'many' and *vice versa*, by including in a particular being a unity of many, and by referring to a group of beings as one particular being. The examples from the Old Testament (as well as from the New) are numerous. It is noteworthy that they all refer to *human* beings — not to things or animals. In this sense ontology operates with the view that the fixed point of reference, the ground of being that offers security and truth, is a particular person and not a general idea or nature.

The second example is to be found in the patristic doctrine of God. Here we must specify the term 'patristic' to include mainly the Cappadocian Fathers. For before them the question of God's being, that is, divine ontology, was not raised as an issue *in itself* (not in relation to the world, as was the case even still with St Athanasius, while after them with Augustine things took an altogether different direction in ontology). What is it that causes divine being to *be* and to be *particular persons*? The analogy of Adam which was applied to the human being, and not the οὐσία (ὑπερκειμένη or ὑποκειμένη), was applied also to this question.

The discussion of this matter is to be found in a very explicit form in the correspondence between St Basil and Apollinaris.[12] Basil asks Apollinaris to explain to him how one could avoid assuming 'a substance lying above' (οὐσία ὑπερκειμένη) — a reference to Platonism — or 'a substance lying underneath' (οὐσία ὑποκειμένη) — a probable

---

[10] See below, n. 12.

[11] H. Wheeler Robinson, *The Hebrew Conception of Corporate Personality*, 1936, pp. 49ff. Cf. A.R. Johnson, *The One and the Many in the Israelite Conception of God*, 1942; J. de Fraine, *Adam et son lignage: Etudes sur la 'personnalité corporative' dans la Bible*, 1959.

[12] See Basil, *Epist.* 361 and 362. These letters form part of the corpus of the Basilian epistles. That there is no reason to doubt the authenticity of these letters is shown by G.L. Prestige, *St Basil the Great and Apollinaris of Laodicea*, 1956, and others (e.g., R. Weyenborg, 'De authenticitate et sensu quarundam epistolorum S.Basilio...', *Antonianum* 33 [1958], pp. 197-240, 371-414, and 34 [1959], pp. 245-98). In any case, the ideas expressed in these letters coincide fully with St Basil's theology found in the rest of his writings.

allusion to Aristotelianism — in dealing with God, and particularly with the relationship between the persons of the holy Trinity. The question arose because, as St Basil states, some people accused those who accepted the *homoousios* of introducing 'substance' as a principle in divine existence, either as ὑπερκείμενον or as ὑποκείμενον. This would correspond to the Platonic or the Aristotelian way of understanding the emergence of human beings. Apollinaris' reply seems to be fully acceptable to Basil and consists in the following significant thesis: there is no need to suppose either a 'substance above' or a 'substance underneath' the particular human beings, since human beings derive their being *not from a 'common substance'* (κοινὴ ὕλη) but from *the person of Adam*; he is the ἀρχή and ὑπόθεσις (in other words, the 'cause') of us, and not human substance. Equally, he argues, in the case of God such a supposition of a substance either above or below is unnecessary, because it is *God the Father* (θεὸς ὁ πατήρ) and not divine *ousia* that is likewise the ἀρχή and ὑπόθεσις of divine being.

God's being, the holy Trinity, is caused not by divine substance but by *the Father*, that is, a particular being. The one God is the Father. Substance is something common to all three persons of the Trinity, but it is not ontologically primary until Augustine makes it so. The Cappadocians work out an ontology of divine being by employing the biblical rather than the Greek view of being.[13]

2.

Now this can only make ontological sense if certain conditions apply. If Adam as a particular being and not as a human nature is the primary cause of human being, he must be in a *constant relationship* with all the rest of human beings, not via human nature — for this would make nature acquire again the decisive priority — but *directly*, that is, as a particular being carrying in himself the *totality* of human nature, and not part of it.[14]

---

[13] Those who fail to appreciate the importance of the idea of 'cause' (αἴτιον), introduced by the Cappadocian Fathers into Trinitarian theology, apparently overlook these important implications of the matter. Unless the ontological ἀρχή in God is placed clearly and unequivocally *in a person* — and who else but the Father could be such a person in the Trinity? — substance becomes the obvious candidate for such an ontological ἀρχή. This would leave the *homoousios* open to the accusations that prompted the above mentioned correspondence of St Basil and, of course, would render an ontology of personhood problematic, if not altogether impossible.

[14] Cf. the concept of *perichoresis* with which the Cappadocians (cf. Basil, *Ep.* 38.8; Gregory Naz., *Or.* 31.14) tried to express the unity of the Trinity: each person carries the full, undivided nature and co-inheres in the other persons, thus showing

The Fathers noted that this cannot be the case with Adam, because of creaturehood and death.[15] Humanity, therefore, *per se* cannot be a candidate for personal ontology. But it is instructive to see in what way divinity is such a candidate.

In God it is possible for the particular to be ontologically ultimate because *relationship is permanent and unbreakable*. Because the Father, the Son and the Spirit are always together,[16] the particular beings are bearers of the totality of nature and thus no contradiction between the 'one' and the 'many' can arise. What Adam *should* represent, God *does* represent.

This means that if we wish to build the particular into ontology we need to introduce *relationship* into substance itself, to make being relational.[17] In trying to identify a particular thing we have to make it part of a relationship and not isolate it as an *individual*, as the τόδε τι of Aristotle. This is a condition for an ontology of personhood. The result of such an ontology will be as follows:

The particular is raised to the level of ontological primacy; it emerges as *being itself* without depending for its identity on qualities borrowed from nature and thus applicable also to other beings, but solely on a relationship in which it constitutes an indispensable ontological ingredient, since it is inconceivable for the rest of beings to *be* outside a relationship with it. This results in a reality of communion in which each particular is affirmed as *unique* and irreplaceable by the others — a uniqueness which is *ontological*, since the whole being in question depends on it, due to the unbreakable character of the

---

substance to be commonly shared among the persons not by way of each person holding *part* of it (note how the English word 'partaking' can be misleading as implying partition of nature), but by each *coinciding fully into one and the same nature*, carried *in its totality by each person*. It is a question of *unity of identity* of substance (ταυτότης φύσεως; Didymus, *De Trin.* 1.16), not of participation in a substance conceivable in itself as a kind of 'reservoir' of divine being. The tendency of Basil to speak at times of ὁμοία φύσις — which has led to his classification with the homoiousians — is to be seen in the light of his concern that the *homoousion* not be taken to imply partition of divine nature. This is evident also from the above mentioned *Epist.* 361.

[15] See Gregory Nys, *Ex com. not.* (PG 45, 180). Cf. below, Appendix to Chapter 4. Cf. also Basil, *Epist.* 38.4 and Gregory Naz., *Theol. Or.* 3.5.

[16] Wherever one person of the Trinity is, the others are there, too. This is a basic patristic teaching related also to the idea of the unity of God's *opera ad extra*. (See Athanasius, *Ad Serap.* I.20; Basil, *De Spir. Sancto* 19.49; Cyril of Alex., *In Joan.* 10.)

[17] This kind of ontology was worked out, perhaps for the first time, by St Athanasius in his wrestling with the problems created by Arianism. More about this in my *Being as Communion*, 1985, p. 84f.

relationship. If we define *love* in ontological terms (i.e., as relationship creating absolute and unique identities), we must speak here of an ontology of love as replacing the ontology of οὐσία, that is, we must attribute to love the role attributed to substance in classical ontology.

The overall consequence of this is that as long as ontology depends solely or ultimately on substance or nature it cannot accommodate the particular in an ultimate or primary way. This does not cause any problems with regard to the being of God (except in so far as theologians force into God's being the priority of substance in order to make it more intelligible to the human being who, as a creature, is faced with the givenness of being, i.e., with the primacy of οὐσία or nature). God, by being uncreated, is not faced with given being: he, *as a particular being* (the Father), brings about his own being (the Trinity).[18] He is thus free in an ontological sense, and therefore the particular is primary in ontology in this case. But what about the human being?

3.

The human being, by asking the question, 'Who am I?', expects to raise the particular to the level of ontological primacy. This is built into this question of his being, as we have already seen. In so doing, man wishes to be God, for the conditions that we have set out for this ontology of personhood exist only in God. Is that the *imago Dei* in man? I believe it is. But the realization of this drive of man towards personal ontology cannot be provided by created being. Here *Chris-*

---

[18] The question of whether God's being is constituted *freely* or not was already raised in the fourth century. By distinguishing will from substance and attaching the generation of the Son to God's substance and not to his will, Athanasius provoked the accusation of the Arians that he was implying that the generation of the Son was not free but necessary. Athanasius (cf. *Contra Ar.* 3.66f.) replied by denying emphatically that the Father generated the Son 'unwillingly' (ἀθελήτως). Cyril of Alexandria offered a solution by stressing that, in God's being, will and substance are 'con-current' (σύνδρομος), but it was mainly the Cappadocians, and in particular Gregory of Nazianzus, who dealt successfully with this problem. In his *Orat. theol.* III.5-7, Gregory distinguishes between 'will' (θέλησις) and 'the willing one' (ὁ θέλων). The significance of his position for our purpose here is twofold. On the one hand, it implies that the question of freedom is a matter of *personhood*: God's being ultimately depends on a willing *person* — the Father; and, on the other hand, it indicates, as indeed Gregory explicitly states, that *even the Father's own being* is a result of the 'willing one' — the Father himself. Thus, by making a person — the Father — the ultimate point of ontological reference, the αἴτιον, the Cappadocian Fathers made it possible to introduce freedom into the notion of being, perhaps for the first time in the history of philosophy.

tology emerges as the only way of fulfilling the human drive to personhood. And this on the following conditions:

(a) That Christology is one *from above*, not from below. If 'above' stands for the uncreated — God — it is important to hold the view that man acquires personal identity and ontological particularity only by basing his being on the Father-Son relationship in which nature is not primary to the particular being (owing to the fact that being is not 'given' — this is what 'uncreated' means). Chalcedon, therefore, made an important *ontological* statement in speaking of the hypostasis of the Son as the only personal identity of Christ.

(b) If this point concerning the priority of the particular in ontology is taken as a *sine qua non* condition, it emerges that in Christology the crucial thing for our subject is not the *communicatio idiomatum* but the hypostatic union. What enables man in Christ to arrive at a personal identity in ontological terms is that in Christ the natures *are* only because they are particularized in one person. In Christ the general exists only in and through the particular; the particular is thus raised to ontological primacy. The 'Who' of Christ is the Son. In him the two natures give their qualities to the identity without making the identity depend, in the primary ontological sense, on these qualities, that is, in the sense in which our identities ultimately depend — and thus are unable to make the particular 'I' ontologically decisive. The natural qualities are not extrinsic to the identity — the question, 'Who am I?', does not aim at excluding natural qualities from the identity of 'I' — but by being 'enhypostasized' these qualities become dependent on the hypostasis for their being; the hypostasis is not dependent on them. Thus, the cause of being is the particular, not the general.

(c) For man to acquire this ontology of personhood it is necessary to take an attitude of freedom *vis-à-vis* his own nature. If biological birth gives us a hypostasis dependent ontologically on nature, this indicates that a 'new birth' is needed in order to experience an ontology of personhood. This 'new birth', which is the essence of Baptism, is nothing but the acquisition of an identity not dependent on the qualities of nature but freely raising nature to a hypostatic existence identical with that which emerges from the Father-Son relationship. If Baptism gives 'sonship', the ontological significance of this is that Man's identity is now rooted not in the relations provided by nature, but in the uncreated Father-Son relationship.

(d) Finally, this identity can never be fully realized in history as long as nature still dictates its laws to man, particularly in the form of death. When death ceases to be 'natural', humanity will experience the true ontology of the person. Meanwhile, man is called to fulfil the image of God in him as much as possible, striving to free himself from the necessity of nature, experiencing 'sacramentally' the 'new being' as a member of the community of those 'born again' (in the above sense), and maintaining an eschatological vision and expectation of the transformation of the world. The ontology of personhood with all the conditions we have just outlined cannot be extrapolated from history or nature. If it exists and is not wishful thinking on man's part, it is the only 'analogy' or proof we have that God exists. If it does not exist, then our faith in God is untrue; ontology in this situation is not applicable to personhood; we are left with a drive towards personal identity that will never be fulfilled. Even so, it is worth keeping it at all costs. For without it man ceases to be human.

III. CONCLUSIONS FOR AN ONTOLOGY OF PERSONHOOD

Who am I? This is a basically human question which no animal can raise. It is thus the question *par excellence* that makes us human and shows personhood to be an exclusive quality of the human being in the animal world. Even when it is not raised consciously (as it is raised in our Western culture), it conditions and colours everyone's attitudes and activities whenever we, unlike the animals, are not satisfied with our given being and wish to affirm freely identities of our own, thus creating our own world (e.g., in art, in unconditional love, in forgiveness, etc.).

In posing this question, however, the human being usually receives an answer pointing to *what* he is, not to *who* he is. This 'what' can take the form of a substantialist or idealist philosophy in which personal particularity is 'identified' — and thus lost — with ideas or ideals ultimately determining the human being. It can also take the naturalistic or biological form in which procreation of human species is more or less taken as identical with the emergence of persons. Connected with this is the problem of sex, highlighted today by the feminist movement. It is increasingly pointed out that women in our world feel a sort of loss of identity. To the question, 'who am I?', posed by a woman, the implicit answer in our culture is essentially determined by sex: you are a woman. But this is an answer of 'what', not of 'who'.[19] How can we arrive at the pure 'who' answer to this question?

[19] See above, Chapter 1. Similar remarks apply to the identification of the 'who'

Our discussion here has pointed to the following observations:

(a) The 'who' question can never be totally divorced from the 'what' question in our created existence. This causes the difficulty in any attempt to create a true ontology of personhood. Nevertheless, it always has to be kept *distinct* from the 'what' question, if the human being is to remain truly human. Personhood is not about qualities or capacities of any kind: biological, social or moral. Personhood is about hypostasis, that is, the claim to *uniqueness* in the absolute sense of the term, and this cannot be guaranteed by reference to sex or function or role, or even cultivated consciousness of the 'self' and its psychological experiences, since all of these can be *classified*, thus representing qualities shared by more than one being and not pointing to absolute uniqueness. Such qualities, important as they are for personal identity, become ontologically personal only through the hypostasis to which they belong: only by being *my* qualities are they personal, but the ingredient 'me' is a claim to absolute uniqueness which is not granted by these classifiable qualities constituting my 'what', but by something else.

(b) Absolute uniqueness is indicated only through an affirmation arising freely from a relationship which constitutes by its unbrokenness the ontological ground of being for each person. In such a situation what matters ontologically is not 'what' one is but the very fact that he or she *is* and is *not someone else*. The tendency of the Greek Fathers to avoid giving any positive content to the *hypostases* of the Trinity, by insisting that the Father is simply not the Son or the Spirit, and the Son means simply not the Father and so on, points to the true ontology of *hypostasis*: that someone simply *is* and *is himself* or *herself* and not someone else, and this is sufficient to identify him or her as a being in the true sense. This point acquires tremendous existential significance when placed in the context of ordinary human life. In relationships of genuine love, which are the proper context for the 'experience' of an ontology of personhood, one does not — and should not — identify the other with the help of their qualities (physical, social, moral, etc.), thus rejecting or accepting the other on that basis as a unique and irreplaceable partner in a relationship that matters ontologically (on which one's own personal identity depends). The more one loves

of man with, for example, 'a member of the working class', or 'a businessman', or any profession or social status. Even the identification with the 'ego' or the 'self', or the 'thinking agent' — categories used widely in modern depth psychology — can be reduced to the question of 'what' rather than that of 'who', as we have described it here.

ontologically and truly personally, the less one identifies someone as unique and irreplaceable for one's existence on the basis of such classifiable qualities. (In this case, one rather loves *in spite* of the existence or absence of such qualities, just as God loves the sinner and recognizes him as a unique person.) Here it is perhaps appropriate to introduce into our terminology the category of *ethical apophaticism*, so badly needed in our culture, with which to indicate that, exactly as the Greek fathers spoke of the divine persons, we cannot give a *positive qualitative content* to a hypostasis or person, for this would result in the loss of his or her absolute uniqueness and turn a person into a classifiable entity. Just as the Father, the Son and the Spirit are not identifiable except simply through being who they are, in the same way a true ontology of personhood requires that the uniqueness of a person escape and transcend any qualitative *kataphasis*. This does not place personhood in the realm of a 'misty' mystery any more than the absence of a positive content in our reference to the persons of the Trinity does. Both in the case of God and in that of human beings the identity of a person is recognized and posited clearly and unequivocally, but this is so only in and through a *relationship*, and not through an objective ontology in which this identity would be *isolated*, pointed at and described in itself. Personal identity is totally lost if isolated, for its ontological condition is relationship.

This hypostatic fulness as otherness can emerge only through a relationship so constitutive ontologically that relating is not consequent upon being but is being itself. The *hypo-static* and the *ek-static* have to coincide.

Chapter 3

THE FATHER AS CAUSE:
Personhood Generating Otherness

I. THE PATRISTIC BACKGROUND

1. *The Early Creeds*

If we take as our starting point the study of the old creeds, we note that all creeds begin with a clause containing reference to the Fatherhood of God. The origin is clearly baptismal, going back to Mt. 28.19. This is significant in itself: the idea of God as Father did not arise as a speculative reflection about God, but emerged from ecclesial experience. Only in and through incorporation into the ecclesial community can there be recognition of God as Father. This is what the baptismal origin of the idea of divine Fatherhood implies.

The idea of God as Father appears to be connected in the early creeds with *cosmology*: 'I believe in God the Father almighty', says the old Roman creed of the second century. But at this point a most interesting exegetical problem arises: is the word 'Father' to be attached to 'almighty' or to 'God'? In other words, is the clause to be read as, 'I believe in God who is Father almighty', or as 'I believe in God the Father, who is almighty'? This question bears great theological significance. Most exegetes of the past (e.g., Kattenbusch)[1] had decided that the word 'Father' belongs syntactically to 'almighty'. But as J.N.D. Kelly[2] rightly argues, there is no authority whatsoever for such an honorific periphrasis for God either in the Old Testament (Septuagint) or in the New. In the Old Testament, the most frequent collocation is 'Lord almighty' (Κύριος παντοκράτωρ) or 'God almighty' (ὁ Θεός

---

[1] F. Kattenbusch, *Das apostolische Symbol*, 1894, II, p. 517f.
[2] J.N.D. Kelly, *Early Christian Creeds*, 1950, p. 132f.

παντοκράτωρ). In the New Testament, 'almighty' appears very rarely, and when it does, as in 2 Cor. 6.18 and Rev. 1.8, and so on, it always follows the Septuagint usage, that is, 'Lord almighty'. Similar observations apply also to the second-century Fathers, such as Justin, the *Martyrium Polycarpi*, and Irenaeus: the term 'almighty' (παντοκράτωρ) is used either alone or combined with God (ὁ παντοκράτωρ Θεός), and never in connection with the word 'Father'.[3] On the other hand, the expression 'God the Father' is very frequent in the New Testament. Paul repeatedly uses such phrases as 'Grace and peace from God the Father' (Gal. 1.3), 'to the glory of God the Father' (Phil. 2.11), or 'in God the Father' (1 Thess. 1.1). Other New Testament authors, such as Jas 1.27, 1 Pet. 1.2, 2 Jn 3 and Jude 1, reflect the same usage.[4] What is the theological significance of this?

Being primarily an historian, Kelly sees the significance of this usage as a reflection of the baptismal formula: since Mt. 28 speaks of baptism in the name of the Father, the title 'almighty' must have been a later addition as a result of the influence of the language of the Septuagint on Christian theology, and, I would add, also as a reaction to Gnosticism which denied the direct involvement of the Father in creation. To a systematic theologian, however, the significance of this exegetical detail goes much deeper. It points in the direction of a clear-cut distinction between the God of the Economy (the Creator) and God in his own being. This was already observed by ancient authors, such as Cyril of Jerusalem[5] and Rufinus;[6] only by a misuse of language (καταχρηστικῶς), says Cyril, can the word 'Father' be understood as referring to God's relation to mankind; it properly belongs to God in virtue of his relation to the Son. This is obvious, too, from the language of the second article of the creed. The fourth-century Fathers, particularly St Athanasius, make full use of this distinction in their theology.[7]

If we follow this to its philosophical consequences, we are led to a sharp distinction between the *ontological* and the *moral* content of divine Fatherhood. It is interesting that it was mainly Western authors, such as Tertullian, Cyprian and, above all, Augustine, who stressed the moral content of God's Fatherhood. Thus Augustine comments on the creed: 'Observe how quickly the words are spoken, and how

---

[3] J.N.D. Kelly, *Early Christian Creeds*, p. 133.
[4] Cf. J.N.D. Kelly, *Early Christian Creeds*, p. 133.
[5] Cyril of Jerusalem, *Catech.* 7.4f. (PG 33, 608f.).
[6] Rufinus, *Com. in Symb. ap.* 4 (PL 21, 341).
[7] Athanasius, *C. Ar.* 2.32; 24-26; 3.66 (PG 26, 213f.; 196f.; 461f.); etc.

full of significance they are. He is God, and he is Father: God in power, *Father in goodness*. How blessed we are who find that our Lord God is our Father!'[8] In the Eastern Fathers, the ontological aspects of Fatherhood were predominant. In fact, there was a widespread suspicion that in any stress on the moral qualities of divine Fatherhood a latent Sabellianism could be observed. Divine Fatherhood is not to be confused with some sort of divine energy. Moral qualities in God were always understood by the Greek Fathers as properties common to all three persons;[9] they cannot in any circumstance indicate a particular person, such as the Father. The consequences of this point can go very far and reach fundamental differences between, for example, Augustine and the Cappadocians, with the former's description of the Trinity in psychological terms and the latter's insistence that the only categories we can apply to the persons of the Trinity are ontological and not moral.

Having said this, we must not lose sight of the fact that all of the old creeds relate divine Fatherhood also to creative power. Not that God is Father in being creator; the notion of Fatherhood, as I stressed earlier, is not attached to the word 'almighty' in the creeds, but to the word 'God'. This means that the Fatherhood of God does not arise with his creative activity.[10] Nevertheless, it is not unrelated to it. What does the word 'almighty' imply, excluding of course any dependence of the ontological identification of God on his creative act?

At this point, we seem to encounter once again a subtle difference between the Latin and Greek patristic language. The Latin equivalent of the English word 'almighty' would be *omnipotens*. This as well as the corresponding English terminology points to an understanding of God the Father in terms of *power*. The language of *potestas* remains characteristic of Western theology throughout the Middle

---

[8] Augustine, *Serm.* 213 (PL 38, 1060).

[9] G.L. Prestige, *God in Patristic Thought*, 1959, p. 263f.

[10] There was long discussion in the second century about whether the terms 'God' and 'Father' coincide fully. Tertullian, for example, took the view that God 'has not always been Father... He became Father by the Son' (*Adv. Herm.* 3) and 'there was a time when the Son did not exist with him' (*Adv. Herm.* 3). Novatian openly refuted this and wrote that the Son 'who was in the Father came forth from the Father; and he who was in the Father, because he was of the Father, was subsequently with the Father, because he came forth from the Father' (*De Trin.* 31). Therefore, according to Novatian, since time cannot be applied to God, God was always Father (*De Trin.* 31). The oscillations and unclarities concerning this matter in the second century came to an end with St Irenaeus who clearly and emphatically connected the Son with the Father as 'always co-existing', *semper coexistens* (*Adv. Haer.* II.30.9; II.25.3; IV.20.3; III.11.8).

Ages, and even later. It is a way of indicating God's *freedom*, conceived in a typically Western fashion as the power to *act* (*action* has
always been equal to, if not identical with, *being* in Western thought,
to the point of speaking of God as *actus purus* in medieval and later
theology).[11]

In contrast, the Greek equivalent of 'almighty' used in the early
creeds is παντοκράτωρ; not παντοδύναμος which would translate literally *omnipotens* (or almighty). In a certain sense, of course, παντοκράτωρ
means 'almighty', but with the emphasis placed not so much on the
power to act as on the capacity *to embrace and contain*, that is, *to establish a relationship* of communion and love. Thus St Irenaeus writes:
'Either there must be one God who *contains all things* and has made
every created being according to his will, or else there must be many
indetermined creators or gods...and the name of παντοκράτωρ [Latin
translation: *omnipotens*!] will come to naught'.[12] Similarly, Theophilus
of Antioch quite explicitly translates παντοκράτωρ as 'all-embracing'.
God is called almighty 'because he rules and *compasses* all things'.
'For the heights of the heavens and the depths of the abysses and
the limits of the world are in his hand'.[13] Here the freedom of God
is conceived not so much in terms of *potestas* and *actus* as in terms of
communio. We come very close here to an affinity between the idea
of divine Fatherhood as an ontological category to which I referred
above (i.e., God is called Father because he has a Son) and the understanding of God as Father in the sense of creator and παντοκράτωρ.
Indeed, with such an explanation of 'almighty' and 'maker of heaven
and earth and of all things visible and invisible', it is easy to understand the association of the Father's creative work with that of the
Son (God created the world in and through the Word — and, according to Irenaeus at least, also the Spirit). In this way, creation becomes
mainly an act not of divine power (omnipotence) but of divine communion, that is, of an involvement of created existence in the Father-
Son (and Spirit) relationship. The syntactical problem to which I
referred at the beginning, namely that of whether the word 'Father'

---

[11] See E. Gilson, *L'Esprit de la Philosophie Médiévale*, 1944, pp. 89, 94: 'être, c'est agir
et agir, c'est l'être'. The equation of God's being with God's activity is also reflected
in R.W. Jenson's interpretation of the Cappadocians (cf. Carl E. Braaten and Robert
W. Jenson [eds.], *Christian Dogmatics*, I, 1984, p. 139f.). The fact, however, that the
Cappadocians speak of divine *ousia* in terms of its *energeia* does not mean that they
identify *energeia* with either *ousia* or *hypostasis* in God. On the contrary, they insist
very much on the distinction between these terms.
[12] Irenaeus, *Adv. Haer.* 2.1.5 (PG 7, 712).
[13] Theophilus, *Ad Antol.* 1.4 (PG 6, 1029).

in the first clause of the creed is to be attached to the word 'God' or to that of 'almighty' loses its acuteness if by 'almighty' we mean παντοκράτωρ in the sense in which I explained it above. God is Father primarily because he has a Son, but also because he is creator and παντοκράτωρ, as he holds everything in his Son, embracing them with the same loving relationship that holds the persons of the Trinity together. It is no wonder, therefore, that the icon of παντοκράτωρ in Byzantine art depicts the Son and not the Father.

Now, one of the highly significant differences between early Western and Eastern creeds is that, with a striking consistency, the former limit themselves to the expression, *credo in deum patrem omnipotentem*, whereas the latter, with a similar consistence, add the word 'one' before that of 'God': πιστεύομεν εἰς ἕνα Θεὸν πατέρα παντοκράτορα.[14] The historical explanation of this difference is difficult to establish. Some scholars think that the Eastern creeds tend to be more theological than those of the West. But it would be fairer to say that both of them are theological throughout, albeit with a different theological motivation and concern underlying each of them — the Western creeds being interested more in God's action than in his being. But even this comparison may be misleading.

Although the historical explanation of this difference may be difficult to produce, the consequences of this divergence cannot be left unnoticed. By adding the word 'one' before 'God the Father', the Eastern creeds highlighted the problem of divine unity. If God = Father, as is the case already with the Roman creed,[15] and if now, in the case of the Eastern creeds, God is 'one', it follows that only the Father can properly be called 'God'. The phrase 'one God the Father' seems to attach divine unity to the divine Fatherhood. The Arians would then appear to be right in excluding the Son and the Spirit from the idea of the one God.

In order to solve this problem, theology could only choose between two options. One would be to dissociate logically the word 'God' from that of 'Father' and to attach 'one' to God without logical association with the word 'Father'. This would answer the Arian challenge, but the cost to be paid for it would be a radical departure from the biblical association of God with the Father, an association which, as we have noted, was faithfully preserved in the early creeds. This option, however, seems to have been preferred by Western theology, at least since Augustine. With the help of a substance language, employed

[14] See J.N.D. Kelly, *Early Christian Creeds*, pp. 181ff.
[15] See above.

by Nicaea for quite a different purpose,[16] Augustine proceeded to a disjunction between God and Father, making of divine substance a notion (*divinitas*) logically prior to that of the Father, and assigning to it the role of expressing divine unity. The 'one God' became thus identical with the 'one substance', and the problem posed by Arianism appeared to be solved. The absence of the word 'one' in connection with 'God the Father' in the early Western creeds must have facilitated this development.

However, things were different in the East. Devotion to the biblical identification of God with the Father was so strong in the East that theologians as influential as Origen would tend to speak of the Logos as a sort of 'second God',[17] in some sense inferior to the Father who alone can properly speaking be called God. Arianism could therefore not but be an Eastern heresy, something to which devotion to the biblical equation of God with the Father in the East could lead almost naturally. The East, therefore, did not adopt the easy way of dissociating the 'one God' from 'God the Father', and preferred to face the Arian challenge in a way that was faithful to the biblical equation of God with the Father. The difficult task of doing this was performed mainly by the Cappadocians.

2. *The Cappadocians*

Although the Cappadocian Fathers do speak of the one substance of God with reference to his unity, they never do what Augustine did, namely elevate the one divine substance above or before the person of the Father. Substance may indicate divine oneness, but the ground of unity remains the Father. St Gregory Nazianzen puts the matter clearly: 'The three have one nature...the *ground of unity being the Father*, out of whom and towards whom the subsequent persons are reckoned'.[18] The Father, therefore, remains the one God of the Bible by being the ground of unity of the three persons.[19]

That the identification of God with the Father, which we find in the Bible and in the early creeds, survives in the Cappadocians, is

---

[16] Nicaea's intention in introducing substance language was primarily to secure the difference between created and uncreated nature, and to place the Logos at the level of the latter. It is only by extension and implication that this language was utilised later to describe God's being as such. Cf. below, Chapter 5.

[17] Origen, *De Princ.* II.1-2, 12-18: only the Father is *Ho theos*, the Son is *theos* (adjectival). Cf. H. Crouzel, *Origen* (Eng. trans. by A.S. Worrall), 1989, p. 181.

[18] Gregory Naz., *Or.* 42.15.

[19] See more below, section II.

illustrated by their understanding of divine *monarchia* as indicating the one *arche* in divine existence, not simply in the sense of 'rule' and 'power' (*monarchia* did have such a meaning, too)[20] which would be common to all three persons and, therefore, relevant to the one divine substance, but also, if not mainly, in the sense of *personal onto-logical origination*, in which case it would be referred to the Father: the one ontological *arche* in the Trinity is the Father, who is in this sense the One God.[21] This was the way the Cappadocians sought to remain faithful to the biblical and early creeds' equation of God with the Father.

Now, if the Father is the one personal *arche* in God, his relation to the other two persons could not but be described in *causative* terms. The idea of *arche* implies a movement, and as Gregory Nazianzen put it, the Trinity is a *movement* from the one to the three ('The monad moved to triad', he writes),[22] which suggests that the One, that is, the Father, *caused* the other two persons to be distinct hypostases. This causation, the Cappadocians insist, takes place (a) before and outside time,[23] hence there is no subordination of the Arian type involved; and (b) on the hypostatic or personal level, and not on that of *ousia*,[24] which implies *freedom* and *love*: there is no coercion or necessity involved in this kind of causation, as would have been the case had the generation of the Son and the procession of the Spirit taken place at the level of substance. As is indicated by a passage from St Gregory Nazianzen, the Cappadocians insisted on the Father, rather than the divine *ousia*, being the *arche* of personal divine being precisely because they wanted to avoid necessity in ontological causation, a necessity which Gregory recognized and rejected in the Platonic image of God as a crater overflowing with love.[25] By making

---

[20] This seems to have been the earliest meaning: unity of rule. See Justin, *Dial.* 1; Tatian, *Or. ad Grec.* 14; Theophilus Antioch., *Ad Antol.* 2.35; Athenagoras, *Suppl.* 24; etc.

[21] In Gregory Nazianzen, we encounter both senses of *monarchia* (unity of rule, or what we may call the 'moral' sense, and unity of personal derivation, which can be described as the ontological sense): in the 'moral' sense, the *monarchia* is shared equally by the three persons, whereas in the ontological sense of personal derivation the *monas* is identified with the Father. See his *Theol. Orat.* 3.2. For an analysis of this key passage, see below, section II.

[22] Gregory Naz., *Theol. Orat.* 3.2.

[23] Gregory Naz., *Or.* 42.15.

[24] Basil, *C. Eun.* 1.14-15; Gregory Naz., *Theol. Or.* 3.15-16.

[25] Gregory Naz., *Theol. Or.* 3.2f.: we regard the Father as the *monas* from which the other two came because we want to avoid what 'some Greek philosophizing (i.e.,

the Father the origin of the Trinity, the Cappadocians introduced freedom into ontology, since the Father as a person, and not as substance, can only exist freely and in relation with the other persons.

The removal of the ontological *arche* from the level of substance to that of personhood found its way into the creed in a striking manner, thanks to the theology of the Cappadocians. The creed of Nicaea spoke of the generation of the Son 'from the substance of the Father'. This was altered by the Council of Constantinople (381 CE) which produced the Nicene-Constantinopolitan Creed by striking off the word 'substance' and making it read that the Son was born simply 'from the Father'. It is well known that Cappadocian theology influenced this council decisively (Gregory Nazianzen even presided over it for some time), and such an alteration — a bold act given the authority Nicaea enjoyed — could make sense only in the light of the Cappadocians' insistence on the emergence of the Trinity from a personal rather than an ousianic source. With this bold alteration, the Council of Constantinople made it clear that the introduction of the *homoousios* by Nicaea should not obscure the original biblical faith expressed in the phrase of the oldest Eastern creeds: 'I believe in one God the Father'.[26]

The proper understanding of this Patro-centric view of divine unity by the Cappadocians requires certain clarifications so as to avoid misunderstanding and bring out the existential consequences of this position. We have already noted that Fatherhood, being a personal notion, implies freedom. In the *Scholia* attributed to St Maximus the Confessor this is formulated beautifully in the statement that the Father 'outside time and lovingly' (ἀχρόνως καὶ ἀγαπητικῶς) moved to the generation of the Son and the spiration of the Spirit.[27] The accusation of the Arians against the Nicaeans, that by introducing the *homoousios* into the creed they made the generation of the Son necessary for the Father, was simply rejected by St Athanasius without any demonstration of why logically the Arian argument was wrong. Athanasius insisted that the Father generated the Son 'willingly' and 'freely',[28] but having made in his theology a clear-cut distinction between the creation of the world from God's will and the generation of the Son

---

Plato, *Tim.* 41D)' dared to say 'concerning the first and second cause' by likening God to an 'overflowing (with love) crater', in order 'not to introduce a necessary (ἀκούσιον) generation'.

[26] For a further discussion, see below, section II.

[27] Maximus Conf., *Schol.* 2.3 (PG 4, 221A).

[28] Athanasius, *C. Ar.* 3.66.

not from God's will but from God's substance, he had to say more in explanation of his statement that the Father generated the Son 'willingly'. His substantialist language, useful and even necessary as it was to indicate that the Son was not a creature, entailed logical difficulties. It was clear that only the employment of personal language could offer a satisfactory response to the Arian challenge, and this was precisely what the Cappadocians did.

St Gregory Nazianzen contributed the solution by making a distinction between 'will' (θέλημα) and the 'willing one' (ὁ θέλων):[29] the 'will' is common to all three persons of the Trinity; the Son shares this one divine will common to all three persons, which, as St Cyril of Alexandria put it, is 'concurrent with the divine ousia'.[30] Yet, there is no will without the willing one, as there is no ousia without hypostasis. The 'willing one' is a person, and as such is primarily none else but the Father. The one divine will shared equally by all three persons and lying behind the creation of the world, in accordance with Athanasius and Nicaea, does not emerge automatically and spontaneously as it were out of itself, but is initiated by a person, namely the Father, as 'the willing one'. It is a Cappadocian axiom, expressed particularly by St Basil, that everything in God begins with the 'good pleasure' (εὐδοκία) of the Father,[31] and this should not be limited to the Economy; it relates also to the way the immanent Trinity exists. Although, therefore, the Son, as Athanasius insisted, is not born out of the will of God, as is the case with creation, he nevertheless is not generated unwillingly, and this because he is born 'of the Father' who, as a person and not substance, is the 'willing one'. This is how crucial the employment of the notion of Personhood in Trinitarian theology is.

If, therefore, we recognize the one ontological *arche* in the Trinity in the Father, we are forced to say not simply that the Father causes the Son and the Spirit to exist as particular beings and to be who they are, that is, unique identities, but also that he is, in this way, as the 'willing one', the initiator of divine freedom. Freedom in this sense is ontological, not moral, that is, it springs from the very way the hypostases are constituted, with the person of the Father being the initiator at once both of personal being and of freedom, that is, of ontological otherness in the Trinity, if freedom is to be understood

---

[29] Gregory Naz., *Theol. Or.* 3.6-7.
[30] Cyril of Alexandria, *De Trin.*, Dial. II (PG 75, 780B).
[31] Basil, *De Sp.* 16.38.

ontologically, that is, as the freedom to be oneself, uniquely particular, and not as a freedom of 'choice', which would in any case be inappropriate for the Trinity.

In a sense, all this remains a puzzle to our common logic, because we tend to associate freedom with individuality: how can one be constituted freely if someone else with *his* freedom constitutes him? Has the Father 'asked' the Son and the Spirit for their free consent before he brought them into being? Such a question presupposes individualism, for how can you 'ask' someone's consent for his being if he does not already exist? Ontological individualism is precisely the establishment of an entity prior to its relationships. Its opposite is the establishment of the entity through the very relations that constitute its existence. This is what we mean when we speak of the relational character of 'divine substance',[32] or of Father, Son and Spirit as relational entities. The Father as a relational entity is inconceivable without the Son and the Spirit.[33] His freedom in bringing them forth into being does not impose itself upon them, since they are not already there, and their own freedom does not require that their consent be asked, since they are not established as entities before their relationship with the Father. This is the difference between moral and ontological freedom: the one presupposes individuality, the other causes individuality, or rather personhood.

The Fatherhood of God, therefore, has nothing in common with human fatherhood; no analogy between the two is possible. Human fatherhood presupposes a division in human nature, that is, individuality before relationality, since the entity of the human father is already established prior to that of his son. It would therefore appear impossible in such a context to speak of the idea of divine Fatherhood as 'oppressive' or 'paternalistic' or 'sexist', and so on.[34] All fears that by maintaining the biblical language of God the Father we encourage

---

[32] See my *Being as Communion*, 1985, p. 84f.

[33] Gregory of Nyssa, *C. Eun.* 4.8, expresses this in a prolific way: 'For what mutual relation is so closely and concordantly engrafted and fitted together as that meaning of relation to the Father expressed by the word "Son"? And a proof of this is that even if both of these names be not spoken, that which is omitted is connoted by the one that is uttered, so closely is the one implied in the other and concordant with it; and *both of them are so discerned in the one that one cannot be conceived without the other*'. Note the simultaneity of unity and discernment or otherness.

[34] W. Pannenberg, *Systematic Theology*, I, 1988, p. 261, arguing from a different angle, rightly stresses that the Father language in the Bible transcends all sexual differentiation. Cf. also his, *The Apostles' Creed in the Light of Today's Questions*, 1972, p. 31.

sexism in religion and society are dissolved in such a relational ontology. The Fatherhood of God is incompatible with individualism and, therefore, with notions of oppression, and so on. If we keep it and refer to it in theology, it is on the one hand because this is how God calls and indicates himself in revealing himself to us, and on the other hand because this is the only way for us to express, indeed to experience, our saviour Jesus Christ and our sanctifier, the Holy Spirit, as God. It must be stressed that the first article of the creed, which speaks of the Fatherhood of God, makes no sense without the second article, which speaks of the Son, and the third one, which refers to the Spirit. We are not allowed by our creed either to work out a metaphysic of fatherhood, such as the one suggested by Levinas,[35] for example, or to make an anthropomorphic projection of sexual differentiations and individualism into divine being. The creed, by its very structure, suggests that divine Fatherhood is relational and totally inconceivable in human terms, which are conditioned by individualism.

II. In Defence of the Cappadocians

The teaching of the Cappadocian Fathers that the Father is the 'cause' of the Son and of the Spirit in the immanent Trinity, an idea which I underlined and promoted in previous publications,[36] seems to have met with objections[37] that need to be discussed, for they reveal important problems with crucial implications both of an historical and of a broader existential significance.

Why is it so difficult for certain theologians to accept this Cappadocian teaching? What difficulties does such a teaching present, and how can they be answered?

Before I deal with these questions, it is relevant to repeat a point I have made elsewhere:[38] I believe that the theology of the Cappadocian

---

[35] E. Levinas, *Totalité et infini*, 1971, ch. 6.

[36] See, for example, my *Being as Communion*, pp. 17, 44, etc. Cf. Chapters 2, 4 and 5 of this book.

[37] See, for example, A.J. Torrance, *Persons in Communion: Trinitarian Description and Human Participation*, 1996. Professor T.F. Torrance also strongly objects to this teaching of the Cappadocians. See his, *The Christian Doctrine of God: One Being, Three Persons*, 1996, and, *The Trinitarian Faith: The Evangelical Theology of the Ancient Catholic Church*, 1988; also, W. Pannenberg, *Systematic Theology*, I, p. 322f. On the other hand, appreciation of the Cappadocian teaching on the Father as cause is strongly expressed by E.P. Meijering, 'The Doctrine of the Will and of the Trinity in the Orations of Gregory of Nazianzus', *Netherlands Theologisch Tijdschrift* 27 (1973), pp. 224-34.

[38] See below, Chapter 5.

Fathers, representing a third way between the Alexandrians and the Antiochenes, has not been fully appropriated by the West for historical reasons that need not be discussed at this point.[39] This may explain why theology in the West, with the help of St Augustine's decisive influence, has developed a substantialist rather than a personalist approach to Trinitarian theology, with many consequences; for example, classical divergences such as the issue of the *Filioque*, and the tendency to prefer the theology of St Athanasius from among the Greek Fathers and juxtapose it to that of the Cappadocians. It is only in our days that the first attempts to appreciate and integrate the Cappadocians into systematic theology have been made,[40] although an immense amount of study has been devoted to these fathers in the West by historians and patristic scholars. This may have something to do with the difficulty in accepting Cappadocian teaching that we are concerned with here.

In the lines that follow, I propose to deal with the major issues emerging from the Cappadocian teaching that the Father is the cause of the Trinity under the following headings:

- Causality and communion
- Causality and the ultimate reality in God
- Causality and ordering
- Finally, I shall try to draw some conclusions regarding the anthropological and broader existential implications of this particular teaching of the Cappadocians, as well as the significance of this teaching for inter-religious dialogue in relation to the question of monotheism.

However, before discussing these points, I ought to say a few words about language concerning *being* with reference to God. This seems to be necessary in view of certain assumptions made by the critics of Cappadocian theology concerning the issue under discussion.

1. *Being and Personhood*

There seems to be a widespread assumption that the term 'being' denotes the *ousia* or substance or essence of God, and that it is to be

---

[39] These may have to do with the fact that the Council of Constantinople in 381 was exclusively an Eastern council, with no participation from the Western Church, although it was later formally recognized by it as an ecumenical council. It must also relate to the fact that Augustine's theology dominated the West soon after the Cappadocians.

[40] Notably at King's College, London, under the inspiration and work of the late Professor Colin Gunton.

distinguished from the persons of the holy Trinity.[41] Being and personhood are juxtaposed as two parallel or different ideas, as if the notion of person did not connote being.

Such a use of language directly contradicts the ontology of the Cappadocian Fathers and accounts to a great extent for the difficulties in understanding and appreciating their Trinitarian theology, including their idea of causality in God. For the Cappadocians, 'being' is a notion we apply to God simultaneously in two senses. It denotes (a) the τί ἐστιν (*what* he is) of God's being, and this the Cappadocians call the *ousia* or substance or nature of God; and (b) it refers to the ὅπως ἐστιν (*how* he is), which they identify with his personhood.[42] In both cases, the verb is *to be* (ἐστιν or εἶναι), that is, *being*. Given the fact that, according to these Fathers, there is no *ousia* in the nude, that is, without hypostasis, to refer to God's substance without referring simultaneously to his personhood, or to reserve the notion of being only to the substance, would amount to making a false ontological statement. Any juxtaposition, therefore, of 'one being' to 'three persons' would not express faithfully the ontology of the Cappadocians. The three persons of the Trinity denote God's being just as much as the term 'substance'. In speaking of the divine persons we speak of God's very being.

This point relates directly to the criticism of the idea of the Father as cause. It is claimed that, in supporting this idea, we fail 'to take proper cognisance of the ontological significance of the union integral to the divine communion'.[43] But why? Is the notion of the Father not ontological enough to indicate divine unity ontologically? The criticism seems to take for granted the juxtaposition of being to personhood and thus the assumption that a person, in this case the Father, is not enough to safeguard 'the ontological significance of the union integral to the divine communion'.

There is no doubt that the reservation of being to *ousia* plays an important role in the difficulty of accepting the Father as an ultimate ontological category in God. The ultimate reality in God's being is,

[41] A.J. Torrance, *Persons in Communion*, p. 289 and *passim*, repeatedly assumes that personhood is something different from being. T.F. Torrance subtitles one of his books: 'One Being, Three Persons' (see above, n. 37). Equally, recent official translations of the Nicene Creed into English render the word 'homoousios' not as 'consubstantial', as was previously done, but with the expression, 'of one (or the same) being with the Father'.

[42] Thus, Basil, *C. Eun.* I.14-15; Gregory Naz., *Theol. Or.* 3.16; etc.

[43] A.J. Torrance, *Persons in Communion*, p. 289.

therefore, sought, in the final analysis, in *ousia*, be it in the static form of 'essence' or in the dynamic form of a communion constituting activity, that is, of a relational substance. In both cases, it is the *ousia* that is the ontological *arche* in God.[44] I shall discuss this matter later and the difficulties it presents. For the moment, let us make it clear that personhood is as ultimate and primordial ontologically as anything can be. In this case, there is no reason why we should go beyond the person in order to be ontological in our reference to the unity of the divine being. Quite the opposite: there are compelling reasons why we should not do that, as we shall see below.

2. *Causality and Communion*

Are we really being consistent with ourselves in saying that the Trinity derives from the Father as cause (it is caused by him) and at the same time making the Trinity, or communion, ontologically primordial? This seems to be one of the difficulties with the idea of the Father as cause.[45]

I have insisted throughout my writings that person is a *relational* term. This means that when we utter the word 'Father' we indicate automatically a relationship, that is, a specific identity which emerges from a relationship or connotes a relationship (*schesis*).[46] It is, therefore, impossible to make the Father ontologically ultimate without, at the same time, making communion primordial. When we utter the word 'Father' we imply his communion with the other two persons automatically.[47] There is no inconsistency in making communion primordial and at the same time making the Father ontologically ultimate. In that case, how did the difficulty arise?

The difficulty arises only when, in uttering the word 'person' or in making it ontologically primordial, we have in the back of our minds an assumption that we have uttered something incompatible with communion, or somehow dissociated from it. Thus, if a particular person (in this case, the Father) is regarded as ontologically ultimate, the apprehension arises that the other persons in communion — or communion itself — will no longer be safeguarded ontologically. I

---

[44] A.J. Torrance (p. 294) quotes T.F. Torrance identifying the one *ousia* with one *arche* in God.

[45] See A.J. Torrance, *Persons in Communion*, p. 292.

[46] Gregory Naz., *Theol. Or.* 3.16: 'The Father is a name neither of *ousia* nor of *energeia* but of *schesis* and of the *how* the Father relates (ἔχει) to the Son or the Son to the Father'.

[47] See Gregory of Nyssa, quoted above, n. 33.

cannot but attribute this apprehension to a latent individualism, to a deficient integration of communion into the notion of the person.

Now, the objection to what has just been said may be twofold: (a) it is not making the person of the Father as such a primordial concept ontologically; it is rather making him a 'cause' that creates the difficulty. In other words, one might be ready to speak of the Father as ontologically primordial, provided that one does the same thing about the Son and the Spirit, which would appear to do justice to the relational character, that is, the ontological interdependence, of the three persons, to which I have just pointed. Why single out the person of the Father and not make the Son and the Spirit equally causative of divine being? And (b) following this to its conceptual consequences, why not make communion as such, that is, the *perichoresis* and ontological interdependence of the three persons, the ultimate reality in God's being, and thus a 'cause'?

Before addressing these questions, let us consider the notion of cause and its application to divine being by the Fathers.

The idea of causality is as old as Greek philosophy, and it has decisively influenced our minds. It is based on the revolutionary distinction made by the ancient Greeks, as early as the Pre-Socratics, between 'being' and 'becoming' — a distinction absent in ancient mythological religions and cultures before or outside the Greek world — including primarily the conception of being as φύσις and the relationship of φύσις and λόγος. It is this distinction, which is not to be found outside the Greek language, that made it possible to distinguish cause and effect. Ever since then, our minds have been conditioned by the question of how and why something is caused, that is, has come into being. It would seem, therefore, to be a requirement for the inculturation of the Christian Gospel by the Greek Fathers — and why not by ourselves who continue to think as participants in the same culture? — to utilize the idea of causality, that is, to raise the question of how and why someone or something exists in our ontological references.

Now, this distinction between being and becoming and the consequent idea of causality was from the beginning tied up with *time*. In fact, it was again the ancient Greek mind that moved language from the mythic unity of being towards seeking a sufficient reason (αἴτιον or αἰτία) for all that is. Aristotle is known for the discussion of causality as an explanation of why things are the way they are, by reference to 'how' they come into being. However, Aristotle's discussion of causality in the fourfold description of cause presented difficulties to patristic theology, and it is extremely important to note how the Cappadocians employed this notion in theology. The following constitute some of the innovations of the Cappadocians with regard to the employment of this notion.

(a) The concept of cause was removed by the Cappadocians from its necessary association with time. There is no necessary involvement of time in causation.[48] By applying causation to the Trinity, the Cappadocians freed it from time and thus from cosmological implications. We do not have to read cosmological connotations into it.

(b) Timeless causality was also to be found outside patristic thought (e.g., in Neoplatonism), but the Cappadocians coupled their view of timeless causation with a rejection of *substantialistic* causation. This is extremely important, and it is overlooked by the critics of Cappadocian theology. Causal language is permissible, according to the Cappadocians, *only at the level of personhood, not of substance*;[49] it refers to the *how*, not to the *what* of God. Causality is used by these fathers as a strictly personalist notion presupposing a clear distinction between person and *ousia*. Thus we are driven away from the Greek idea of causality, which from its inception was tied up with the dynamic movement of *ousia* as *physis*. It is noteworthy that, although the Cappadocians used the term *physis* with regard to God, they refused to attach causality to it; they spoke of causation strictly with reference to persons, natural causality being applicable to the being of creation, not to that of God.

The result of this was to free causality with regard to God not only from the cosmological connotations suspected by critics of this idea,[50] but also from necessity, which would have made it a sort of Platonic emanationism.

Having clarified the sense in which the Cappadocians employed causality, we can now look at the reasons why they did so. Apart from the motif of inculturation, to which I referred above and which was by no means insignificant, as the doctrine of the Trinity had to be rooted into a culture shaped by the notion of causality, the way the

---

[48] E.g., Gregory Naz., *Or.* 42.15: 'The name of the unoriginate is Father; of that who has had a beginning (*arche*), Son; and of that who is together with the beginning (*to meta tes arches*), Holy Spirit. And *the union (henosis) of them is the Father*, from whom and to whom are referred those who follow...*with neither time nor will nor power instigating*'. Cf. *Or.* 31.10 and 5.14: 'those who exist (*onta*) from the first cause *without time (achronos)*'.

[49] Basil, *C. Eun.* 1.14-15; Gregory Naz., *Theol. Or.* 3.2; 15.

[50] E.g., A.J. Torrance, *Persons in Communion*, p. 291.

notion of causality was employed by the Cappadocians suggests the following reasons why it was applied at all.

In the first place, there was an important historical reason. As is evident from the argument of Gregory Nazianzen in his third *Theological Oration*,[51] the Eunomians based their argument on the following syllogism: The Father is greater than the Son (Jn 14.28) in as much as the Son owes his existence to him. But the giving of existence to the Son belongs to the Father by nature (here lies the crux of the matter); therefore, the Father is greater than the Son by nature.

In order to refute this syllogism while maintaining the validity of the scriptural reference, and to defend in this way the Nicaean *homoousios*, the Cappadocians ingeniously introduced the following subtle distinctions:

We must distinguish between the level of nature or *ousia* and that of person or *hypostasis* in divine being. Both denote being, but the former refers to the *what* and the latter to the *how* of being. Giving existence or being (εἶναι) to the Son by the Father is a matter not of nature, of the *what* God is, but of *how* God is.[52] This implies that the idea of causation is used in order to describe the *how* of divine being and avoid making the emergence of the Trinity a matter of transmission of *ousia*.[53] What the Father 'causes' is a transmission

---

[51] *Or.* 29.15.

[52] It is this that makes it important to avoid saying that the Son came 'from the *ousia* of the Father', as Nicaea first put it, not having faced as yet the Eunomian challenge, and to say instead that he came 'from the Father', thus making it impossible for the Eunomians to argue, as they did, by identifying nature and person in the Father. The change in the creed introduced by the Second Ecumenical Council was therefore of the utmost significance at that time and, for this reason, it must have been consciously made. Equally, it is important to avoid saying that the Father gives his *ousia* to the Son and the Spirit, as if he were by himself its original possessor, or as if the *ousia* existed somehow prior to the persons and was imparted to them by the Father, the original possessor. The *ousia* always denoted something *common* to the three persons and it was never an-hypostatic; its hypostasization was and is simultaneous with the personal differentiation, i.e., the coming forth of the Son and the Spirit from the Father. This point is totally missed if we say, with G.W.P. McFarlane (*Christ and the Spirit*, 1996, p. 64), that, by accepting my position, we 'identify the Father with the unity *of divine essence*'.

[53] In this respect, I do not fully subscribe to the conclusions drawn from John of Damascus by Vl. Lossky, *Mystical Theology*, 1957, p. 59f., implying that the divine *ousia* is identified with the Father primarily and transmitted to the Son: the Father 'confers *His one nature* upon the Son and upon the Holy Spirit' (p. 60, my emphasis).

St John of Damascus (*De fide orth.* I.8) teaches that the Son comes 'from the substance' of the Father, yet he never connects that, as Lossky seems to do, with the idea

not of *ousia* but of personal otherness (i.e., of the *how* of being). The principle of causality *distinguishes* the persons, it involves the emergence of *otherness* in divine being. The Father as 'cause' is God, or *the* God in an ultimate sense, *not because he holds the divine essence and transmits it* — this would indeed endanger the fulness of the divine being of the other persons and would also turn him into an individual conceivable prior to the other persons — *but because he is the ultimate ontological principle of divine personhood.* If this is truly understood, apprehension that the causal language of the Cappadocians endangers the fulness of the deity of the Son and the Spirit may disappear. For, in fact, the equality of the three persons in terms of substance is not denied by the Father's being the cause of personhood; it is rather ensured by it, since by being cause *only as a person and for the sake of personhood* the Father guards against locating substance primarily in himself.

Now, all this transcends the historical context in which it appeared and implies that causation in God does not destroy ontological equality. It produces otherness of 'wholes of the whole'. It brings about otherness in communion and communion in otherness. By not being a matter of transmission of substance, causality involves freedom in personal being and makes God the Trinity not a necessary but a free being, exactly as Gregory Nazianzen states in explaining why causality is a matter not of nature but of personhood: 'so that we may never introduce an unfree (ἀκούσιον) generation'.[54]

---

that the Father is the cause. Whenever he refers to 'cause', he calls the Father the ἀρχή and αἰτία of the *how* things are (PG 94, 821D). Nowhere does John of Damascus say, with Lossky, that *in being cause* the Father 'imparts *his ousia*'. It is one thing to say that the Son comes from the *ousia* of the Father, and quite another to say that in being the cause the Father imparts *his ousia*. The correct way of stating the matter would be to say that although the Son is *homoousios* with the Father, since he comes from the same *ousia*, common to the Father and to himself, the Father *causes* in generating him not a transmission of *ousia* but the emergence of a person, called the Son. This means that the person of the Father does not cause *sameness* (*ousia* connotes something common, i.e., sameness, within the Trinity) but *otherness*, i.e., personhood. It is this subtle distinction that is implied in the Cappadocian theology of causality as referring not to the level of substance but to that of personhood. Note how the author of Basil's *Letter* 38.4 carefully avoids the expression 'from the *ousia* of the Father' in referring to 'cause': 'But concerning the Father as cause (of the Spirit's) being (*einai*), from whom he proceeds this is a manner of knowing (or indicating) *the hypostatic particularity*... Everything indicating the particularity of the persons is incompatible (*asymbata*) and incommunicable in (the context of) the community of substance'.

[54] Gregory Nazianzen, *Theol. Or.* 3.2.

The idea of cause was introduced, therefore, in order to indicate that in God there is not only substance, relational and dynamic, but also otherness, which is also dynamic. It is, in fact, in and through this otherness, and in no other way, that substance in God is dynamic and relational. Causation is precisely part of God's dynamic being; it involves movement, not however a movement of substantial necessity, but a movement initiated freely by a person. Gregory Nazianzen describes the mystery of the Trinity precisely as movement initiated by a person, the Father: 'For this reason, the one (μονὰς) moved from the beginning to a dyad and stopped at the triad. And this for us is the Father and the Son and the Holy Spirit'.[55]

The movement, therefore, of divine personal being is not a spontaneous movement of the three persons, a dynamism of their *ousia* or of their mutual communion. It is clearly a movement with *personal initiative*. It is not that the Three, as it were, moved simultaneously as 'persons in communion'; it is the *one,* the Father, that 'moved' (μονὰς κινηθεῖσα) to threeness (cf. below). There is no movement in God which is not initiated by a person. When Gregory says the above words, he paraphrases causality: the Trinity is a 'movement' initiated by a person.

This brings us to the question of divine *monarchia*. What meaning did it have for the Fathers and for the Cappadocians, in particular? Did it relate to the Father or to all three persons? Let us try to answer this question with particular reference to the evidence of Gregory Nazianzen, who seems to be trusted more by the critics of the Cappadocians.

Monarchia means *one arche*. The idea was first employed to indicate that there is only *one rule* in God, amounting to one will, one power, and so on.[56] Soon, however, the concept had to be employed ontologically, as it applied not only to the Economy but to God in his eternal life. In such a case, it was inevitable for the question to arise as to its precise meaning for the being of God. The Cappadocian Fathers witness to this development by specifying what *arche* means with reference to God.

Basil clearly understands *arche* in the ontological sense of the beginning of being. As such, *arche* is attached exclusively to the Father. He writes: the names Father and Son 'spoken of in themselves indicate nothing but the relation (*schesis*) between the two'. 'For Father is the

[55] Gregory Nazianzen, *Theol. Or.* 3.2.
[56] Thus in Justin, *Dial.* 1; Tatian, *Or. ad Gr.* 14; etc.; see above, n. 20.

one who has given the beginning of being (*arche tou einai*) to the others... Son is the one who has had the beginning of his being (*arche tou einai*) by birth from the other'.[57]

Gregory Nazianzen seems to use the term *monarchia* in the early sense of one rule, will and power. As such, he refers it to all three persons of the Trinity. Yet he is not unaware of the ontological meaning which he expresses with the term *monas*. This he refers not to all three persons but to the Father. Let us consider carefully the following passage which is crucial for our subject.

> There are three opinions (δόξαι) about God, anarchy, polyarchy and monarchy. The first two were played by the children of the Greeks, and let them continue to be so. For anarchy is something without order; and the rule of many is factions, and thus anarchical and thus disorderly. For both these things lead to the same thing, namely disorder; and thus to dissolution, for disorder is the first step to dissolution. But *monarchia* is that which we hold in honour. It is, however, a *monarchia* that is not limited to one person, for it is possible for unity if at variance with itself to come into a condition of plurality; but one which is constituted by equality of nature, and agreement of opinion, and identity of motion, and a convergence (or concurrence) of its elements to one[58] ...so that though numerically distinct there is no division of *ousia*.[59]

So far, *monarchia* seems to refer to all Persons and not to any one of the Trinity. Yet we should note that Gregory uses *monarchia* in the sense of one will and concord of mind, that is, in the old moral or functional sense of the term, to which we referred earlier: monarchy is contrasted with anarchy and polyarchy, and the accent falls on order as opposed to disorder, and on common will, and so on. The

---

[57] Basil, *C. Eun.* 2.22. Note again the language employed by Basil: the Father gives the Son not *ousia* but *einai*, 'being'; there is a difference between these two terms: person *is* being, but does not denote *ousia*; *ousia* and *being* are not identical. See the implications of this above.

[58] This is the rather inadequate rendition given of this sentence in *A Select Library of Nicene and Post-Nicene Fathers*, vol. VII, p. 301. A translation and commentary more adequate and more interesting for our subject is given by J. Mason, *The Five Orations of Gregory of Nazianzus*, 1899, p. 75: 'This complete harmony of mind and will in the Godhead is itself based upon the concurrence of the other Blessed Persons with that One of their number from Whom they are derived, viz. the Father'. In this case, the monarchy is ultimately referred to the Father. Exegetically, the meaning depends on how we render the word 'one' (ἕν) and the 'from it' (τῶν ἐξ αὐτοῦ): do these refer to the One from whom the others derive, i.e., the Father, or to the elements that make up the unity of nature, motion, etc.? The sentence that immediately follows would support the first option. My argument, however, is unaffected in either case, as can immediately be seen.

[59] Gregory Naz., *Theol. Or.* 3.2.

ontological sense of *monarchia* comes with the text that immediately follows the one just quoted:

> For this reason, the One (μονάς) having moved from the beginning (from all eternity) to a Dyad, stopped (or rested) in Triad. And this is for us the Father and the Son and the Holy Spirit. The one as the Begetter and the Emitter (γεννήτωρ και προβολεύς), without passion of course and without reference to time, and not in a corporeal manner, of whom the others are one of them the begotten and the other the emission.

In this passage, the subject is transferred to the ontological level; it is now a question not of a moral unity in which disorder and anarchy are excluded but of how the three Persons relate to one another in terms of ontological origination. The crucial point here is the word *monas*: to what does it refer? Does it refer to something common to the three Persons out of which the Trinity emerged? Or to the person of the Father?

If the *monas* referred to something other than the Father, that is to *ousia* or something common to the three persons, we would have to exegete the text in the following way: 'The one *ousia* (*monas*) moved to a Dyad and finally stopped at the Triad'. This would mean that from the one *ousia* came first the two persons together (a dyad) to which a third one was added finally to make the Trinity. Unless we are talking about the *Filioque* such an interpretation would look absurd. If we wish to have the Trinity simultaneously emerging from the *ousia*, which is what I suppose those who refer the *monas* to *ousia* would prefer, the text would forbid that, for it would have to read as follows: 'The one *ousia* (*monas*) moved (not to a dyad first but simultaneously) to a triad'.

The text clearly refers the One (μονὰς) to the Father, for it explains itself immediately by saying: 'the one (moved) as the Begetter (γεννήτωρ) and Emitter (προβολεύς), of whom the others are the one begotten and the other the emission (τῶν δέ, τό μέν γέννημα, τό δέ πρόβλημα)'. Furthermore, in continuing his thought, Gregory explains all this by saying that the reason why he would insist on what he just said is that he wants to exclude any understanding of the Trinity as a derivation from an a-personal something, like an overflowing bowl (an explicit reference to Plato), lest the emergence of the Son and the Spirit be conceived of as 'involuntary', his intention being to 'speak of the unbegotten and the begotten and that which proceeds from the Father'.

In conclusion, when Gregory uses *monarchia* in the moral sense of unity of mind, will, and so on, he refers it to the three persons taken together (how could it be otherwise?). But when he refers to how the Trinity emerged ontologically, he identifies the *monas* with the Father.[60]

It follows from all this that the Cappadocians wanted to attribute the Trinity, that is the personal otherness in God, to a person and not to *ousia* or a 'tri-unity' of some kind, and it is this that lies behind their teaching on the Father as 'cause' of the other two persons. In so doing, they made the Father the ultimate reality of God's personal existence, in other words they made personhood ontologically ultimate. Is that theologically legitimate? How can it be supported, not just historically but also theologically?

3. *Causality and the Ultimate Reality in God*

Why do I object to the view that the ultimate ontological category in God is 'a structure of communion existing by itself'? I am asked to offer more 'sufficiently compelling arguments as to why it should be of "incalculable importance" that we do *not* conceive of the intra-divine communion of the Triunity as the ground of all that is?'[61] These questions imply that what is called 'intra-divine communion' would be an authentic way of referring to the ultimate reality in God, the ground of his existence. Such a view appears to be different from that of making substance the ultimate reality, yet the difference is actually very little and the difficulties it presents are exactly the same.

I should like to respond to the above question by making the following points:

(a) If we allow for anything beyond the Father as ultimate reality, we must bear in mind that biblical monotheism is at stake. Karl Rahner has pertinently reminded us that, in the Bible, God is the Father.[62]

(b) If we make 'Trinity', 'Tripersonality',[63] and so on, the ultimate ontological ground in God, we do away with any idea of *ontological*

---

[60] Other passages from Gregory would support this, e.g., *Or.* 42.15: 'The three have one nature...the Godhead. The principle of unity (ἕνωσις) is the Father, from whom the other two come and to whom they are referred back (ἐξ οὗ καὶ πρὸς ὃν ἀνάγεται)'. Thus, A. Meredith, *The Cappadocians*, 1995, p. 106f., rightly concludes that: 'On balance...Gregory prefers the idea of a monarchy where the Father is the source of order and being'.

[61] A.J. Torrance, *Persons in Communion*, p. 293.

[62] K. Rahner, *The Trinity*, 1986, p. 17f. and *passim*.

[63] D. Staniloae, *The Experience of God*, 1994, p. 129, prefers to use the expression 'Tripersonality': 'God can be said to be the Tripersonal superessence or the super-essential Tripersonality'. Father Staniloae understands the divine — and human — person as subject and centre of consciousness (*The Experience of God*, p. 256: Being

derivation in divine being. In this case, the three persons *co-emerge* and co-exist simultaneously and automatically — not of course in terms of time but logically. Divine being acquires what Levinas, with reference to Heidegger, critically calls the character of a 'panoramic' ontology,[64] in which the particular Other is not the ultimate reality. In this case, otherness — the persons of the Trinity — is not derived from a particular Other but is itself the ultimate explanation of itself.[65]

We are thus unable to ascribe ultimate ontological significance to the credal — and biblical — expression 'from the Father' (ἐκ τοῦ Πατρὸς),[66] for this expression cannot be understood in any other way than in terms of ontological derivation. A co-emergence of the three persons, which is implied in 'Triunity' and so on, cannot be made into the ultimate ontological reality in God without depriving the ἐκ τοῦ Πατρὸς of its ultimate ontological significance.

(c) If the co-emergence and co-existence of the three persons is the ultimate reality in God, what is it that accounts for or constitutes the *unity* of the three, that is, for their being *one* God, besides their personal otherness? For in trinitarian theology it is not enough to make the Trinity ontologically ultimate, we must regard the *oneness* of God, that is, that which makes the three one, as equally ultimate.

If the three persons co-emerge and are not derived from anyone, from any Other, their unity must be sought in the very 'fact' of their co-emergence or co-existence, that is, in their *communion*: the three are one because they *relate* with each other. Of course, there is always the Augustinian view that the three are one because they are relations within the one divine substance.[67] But if, by making 'Triunity' the ultimate reality in God, we wish to avoid making divine

does not exist really except in a hypostasis, or — in the case of spiritual being — in the *conscious subject*...we speak of the divine hypostases *as subjects...a conscious relation between subjects*' etc.; my italics). This is very different from the Cappadocian and Greek patristic view of personhood, which in fact excludes an understanding of the person in terms of subjectivity, consciousness being something common and identical to all three of the divine persons. Cf. G. Prestige, *God in Patristic Thought*, 1959, p. xxxii: the three persons are not to be regarded as three 'consciousnesses' in Greek patristic thought. See also below, Chapter 4, esp. the Appendix.

[64] E. Levinas, *Totalité et infini*, 1971, pp. 270f.; cf. 16f.

[65] This resembles the understanding of otherness in post-modernism. See Chapter 1, V, 2 (a) above.

[66] Cf. J.N.D. Kelly, *Early Christian Creeds*, p. 181f.

[67] Cf. Augustine, *De Trin.* 5.3 and 7f.; *In Ioann. tract.* 39; *Ep.* 170; *De civ. Dei* 11.10; etc.

substance this kind of ultimate reality, the only alternative at our disposal is to say that what makes the three one, accounting for or expressing their unity, is their relationship or communion with each other.

Viewed, therefore, from the aspect of divine unity, that is, the one God, 'Triunity' implies that *relationality* is the ultimate ontological ground of God. We are thus not far from Buber's 'Between' as the ultimate ontological reality.[68] Having ruled out ontological derivation, and having replaced it with ontological co-emergence or 'co-inherence',[69] we have inevitably turned relationality into the ultimate reality: the one God is not the Father; it is the *unity* of Father, Son and Spirit in their co-inherence or inter-relatedness.[70]

(d) Is there anything wrong with that? Indeed there is, and a great deal wrong! If the one God is not a particular *hypostasis*, our prayer cannot be addressed to the one God but only to the Trinity or to the 'Triunity'. But monotheism belongs to the *lex orandi*. In praying to the Trinity, we must be praying at the same time to the one God. If the one God is not a particular *hypostasis*, the one God is left out of our prayer, since we can only pray to a particular *hypostasis* and not to a 'Triunity' of some kind. It is not accidental that all of the early eucharistic prayers were addressed *to the Father*.[71] The gradual intro-

---

[68] On Buber, see above, Chapter 1 (nn. 96-98). According to M. Theunissen, *The Other*, 1986, p. 383, Buber identifies the 'Between', i.e., relationality itself, with God.

[69] It is noteworthy that in proposing 'Triunity' as the ultimate reality in God, A.J. Torrance, *Persons in Communion*, p. 293f., seems to connect divine *monarchia* with *perichoresis* and Triunity: 'the Monarchia is identified with the Triunity of God' (p. 294). Quoting T.F. Torrance, *The Trinitarian Faith*, 1988, p. 338, he claims that the doctrine of co-inherence (*perichoresis*) amounts to a rejection of causal relations within the Trinity! Such a view would make the Cappadocian Fathers look logically inconsistent, as they teach both causality and coinherence in divine being. *Perichoresis*, however, was never used by the Fathers as an alternative to causation, since it was meant to indicate how the three persons *relate* to each other, not how they come into being. See next note.

[70] C.E. Gunton, *The Promise of Trinitarian Theology*, p. 196, in his rejection of the idea that the Father is the cause of the Trinitarian persons, makes 'all three persons...*together* the cause of the communion in which they exist in *relations of mutual and reciprocal constitution*' (my italics). It is evident that in rejecting the Father as the cause of the Trinity we are inevitably led to the position that it is the *relations* that *constitute* the Trinity. Relationality is thus made into the ultimate ontological (constitutive) reality.

[71] The historical and liturgical evidence is overwhelming. See, e.g., J.A. Jungmann, *Public Worship*, 1957, p. 50f.: 'the person who is meant (in the eucharistic address to God) is God the Father... Only in later times, under the influence of

duction of the Trinity into these prayers was never meant to obscure the truth that, in praying to the Trinity, we are ultimately praying to the one God, the Father.[72]

Now, speaking to (or of) the one God — the Father — and the Holy Trinity *at the same time* does not involve a contradiction, because the Father denotes a particular *hypostasis* which is 'other' while being *relational*, that is, inconceivable apart from his unity with the 'other' divine persons. The one God and the triune God are thus conceived simultaneously, thanks not to an impersonal relationality or 'Tri-unity' but to a *hypostasis* which is both particular and relational.[73] The Father's otherness and particularity does not subject or negate but, on the contrary, affirms the particularity and integrity of the other 'others', being as he is their free and loving originator from whom 'flows both the equality and the being of equals'.[74]

4. *Causality and Ordering*

Let us now consider another objection or apprehension caused by the Cappadocian teaching of the Father as 'cause' of the Holy Trinity. It is claimed that this teaching entails the danger of projecting into God subordinationist notions which 'smack of a cosmological theology'.[75] The following remarks can be made in response:

There *is*, in fact, an ordering or τάξις in the Trinity, since the Father *always* comes first, the Son second, and the Spirit third in all biblical and patristic references to the Holy Trinity. It is of the utmost significance that we cannot reverse or upset this order and place any of the other persons before the Father. Gregory Nazianzen

---

the Gallico-Frankish liturgy, were there employed any prayers addressed directly to Christ'. Cf. P.F. Bradshaw (ed.), *Essays on Early Eastern Eucharistic Prayers*, 1997, *passim*.

[72] This rejoins the biblical faith that ultimately all of Christ's and the Church's work, and all that exists, will be offered to 'God the Father'. Thus, 1 Cor. 15.24; Eph. 2.18; etc.

[73] Here lies the crucial contribution of the Cappadocian Fathers in particular, who spoke of the divine persons not simply as relations, as did Augustine, but also as concrete *hypostases*. As C.E. Gunton pertinently observes, for the Cappadocians the designation of the persons as *hypostases* meant that the persons 'are not relations, but concrete particulars in relation to one another' (*The Promise of Trinitarian Theology*, p. 39; cf. also p. 152, comparing the Cappadocians with Augustine). To a great extent, it seems that the difficulty in accepting the Father as the ultimate ontological reality in God has something to do with this difference between Augustine and the Cappadocians.

[74] Gregory Naz., *Or.* 40.43. Cf. below, sections 4 and 5.

[75] A.J. Torrance, *Persons in Communion*, p. 289.

is explicit in speaking of ordering (τάξις) in the immanent Trinity: '[t]he union (ἕνωσις) is the Father from whom and to whom the *ordering* (τάξις) of persons runs its course'.[76] To make this ordering refer only to the economic Trinity and to soteriology, as Vl. Lossky and others seem to do,[77] would be to force the patristic texts, such as the one just mentioned, which refer to the *immanent* Trinity, as the context clearly indicates, and to dissociate too much the economic Trinity from God's eternal being. For example, the Son's filial 'Yes' to the Father, which we encounter in Gethsemane and elsewhere, can only make sense ontologically if it points to the eternal filial relationship between the two persons. It is mainly this unbroken eternal filial relationship that accounts for the fact that Christ's humanity, or rather Christ in his humanity, never sinned, that is, contradicted the will of the Father, although he was tempted to do so in the desert and before going to the Cross. It may be going too far to project Jesus' obedience to an eternal obedience of the Son to the Father,[78] but I would certainly agree with C. Gunton[79] in seeing, behind Jesus' obedience to the Father, the eternal response of the Son to the Father's love. Every movement in God, *ad extra* as well as *ad intra*, begins with the Father and ends with him, as Gregory Nazianzen's words, quoted above, indicate. This inevitably establishes an ordering in both the economic and the immanent Trinity.[80]

---

[76] Gregory Naz., *Or.* 42.15; cf. Basil, *C. Eun.* 1.20; 3.1: the Son is second to the Father 'because he came from him (ὅτι ἀπ'ἐκείνου)', i.e., not in the economy but in the immanent Trinity. Gregory of Nyssa insists on this order, too, with regard to the third place, that the Spirit occupies in the immanent Trinity; see *Quod non sint* (PG 45, 133).

[77] See Vl. Lossky, *In the Image and Likeness of God*, 1974, p. 92f. Cf. T.F. Torrance, *Trinitarian Perspectives*, 1994, p. 32, referring also to Calvin as having the same opinion. C. Gunton, *The Promise of Trinitarian Theology*, p. 196f., seems to hold a similar view. It is noteworthy that this position is maintained alongside the affirmation that the Economy and God's eternal being should be held inseparably together!

[78] Gregory Naz. (*Or.* 30.6; PG 36, 109C) openly rejects transferring Jesus' economic obedience to the Father to the Logos of the immanent Trinity: 'As the [eternal] Logos, he was neither obedient nor disobedient... But having taken the form of a servant...he honours obedience and experiences it'.

[79] C. Gunton, *The Promise of Trinitarian Theology*, p. 196.

[80] It may be appropriate to insert at this point a comment concerning the tendency observed in Vl. Lossky and other Orthodox theologians to undermine, or even eliminate, the notion of filiation (υἱοθεσία) in referring to God's manifestation *ad extra* and its soteriological content. Soteriology is thus built almost exclusively on the basis of the idea of divine energies, and the accent falls on that which God offers to us for participation out of what is *common* to the three persons, i.e., their 'natural' qualities through the divine energies (e.g., divine glory, light, etc.). This

It is almost unnecessary to add that such an ordering in the immanent Trinity should not be understood in temporal, moral or functional terms. The phrase, 'the Father is greater than I' (Jn 14.28),
does not imply a hierarchy of value or importance, for such an implication would be anthropomorphic and would have no place outside
created existence. Neither does it endanger, as is feared by certain
theologians, the wholeness and equality of each person's deity. I have
already shown above how the attachment of causality exclusively to the
level of personhood by the Cappadocians not only does not endanger
but actually ensures the equality of the three persons in terms of deity.
It is only when divine nature is somehow confused with the person

---

is supposed to be grounded on the theology of Gregory Palamas, who, however,
always understands the divine energies as given to us in a hypostatic, i.e., personal,
form. It is therefore not enough to speak of the divine energies purely and simply.
In the Economy, God gives us not simply his energies, but mainly his Son and his
Spirit (Jn 3.16, 34; Rom. 5.5; 1 Thess. 4.8; 1 Jn 3.24; 4.9; etc.), with whom and in
whom we know the Father (Jn 14.7; 17.3) through filiation (Rom. 8.15; Gal. 4.6;
etc.). The employment of the energy language should not obscure the importance
of personal communion in God's relationship with us in the Economy. Cf. above,
Chapter 1, n. 51.

Thus, it would be unnecessary to ask with Dorothea Wendebourg the question,
'how could they (the divine hypostases) enter the world, since they belong to that
level in God which is defined as being unalterably [*sic*] beyond the sphere of soteriological contact with the energies, namely the Divine Essence?' ('From the Cappadocian Fathers to Gregory Palamas: The Defeat of Trinitarian Theology', *Studia
Patristica* 17.1 [1982], p. 196). A study of Maximus the Confessor shows that the
characteristic of divine personhood, as opposed to divine nature, is precisely the
change of *tropos* so that the hypostasis may perform a soteriological purpose. It is
simply wrong, at least for the Cappadocians, to say that, 'the trinitarian persons
have no soteriological functions...the hypostases do not enter the created world,
they simply *are*' ('From the Cappadocian Fathers to Gregory Palamas: The Defeat of
Trinitarian Theology', p. 196), and this would be the case also with Palamas, albeit
not so clearly, due to his preoccupation with the *essence* versus *energy* scheme. Only
by reading these authors with Neopalamite spectacles, which we have just rejected,
can one arrive at conclusions like those just quoted. Wendebourg assumes too
quickly (p. 197) that, because the Cappadocian Fathers distinguished between the
essence and the energies of God and declared the impossibility of passing beyond
them to the divine *ousia*, they automatically excluded the hypostases from direct
involvement in human history. Such an assumption seems to overlook the insistence of the Cappadocians not only on the distinction between essence and energy,
but also on that *between essence and hypostasis*. This allows them to keep the essence of
God beyond direct contact with the world while bringing the hypostases into such
a contact. It is at this point that I disagree with Lossky and the Neopalamites, who
tend to exhaust God's soteriological work with the divine energies and undermine
the involvement of the *divine persons* in salvation. Consequently, I disagree also with
anyone who would interpret the Cappadocians and Palamas in the same way and
draw conclusions from such an interpretation.

of the Father, and personal causation with a process of *imparting of divine nature* by the Father to the other two persons, that the equality of the Trinitarian persons as fully divine is put at risk. As Basil puts it: 'Why is it necessary, if the Spirit is third in rank (τάξει), for him to be also third in nature?... Just as the Son is second to the Father in rank because he derives from him...but not second in nature, *for the deity is one in each of them*, so also is the Spirit'.[81] Divine nature does not exist prior to the divine persons, as a sort of possession of the Father who grants it to the other persons — that would be the Eunomian position which the Cappadocians vigorously rejected. Divine nature exists only when and as the Trinity emerges, and it is for this reason that it is not 'possessed' by any person in advance. An *a priori* possession of divine nature by any person would imply the existence of this nature prior to personhood. In saying that 'God as person — as the hypostasis of the Father — makes the one divine substance to be that which it is: the one God',[82] we automatically exclude the priority of substance over personhood, and at the same time its privileged possession by the Father, which would introduce the risk of inequality of deity in the Trinity. The co-emergence of divine nature with the Trinitarian existence initiated by the Father implies that the Father, too, 'acquires', so to speak, deity only 'as' the Son and the Spirit are in existence (he is inconceivable as Father without them), that is, only 'when' divine nature is 'possessed' by all three. Thus, the Father is shown to be 'greater' than the Son (and the Spirit) *not in nature*, but in the way (the *how*) the nature exists, that is, in the hypostasization of nature. Trinitarian ordering (τάξις) and causation protect rather than threaten the equality and fulness of each person's deity.

5. *Consequences for Anthropology*

Human beings have been created 'in the image and likeness' of God (Gen. 1.26). They are called to become 'partakers of divine nature' (2 Pet. 1.4) by being adopted 'sons of God' (Gal. 4.6) in the only-begotten Son of the Father. What does the idea that the Father is the 'cause' of divine personhood, the cause of the Son and the Spirit, tell us about our way of being 'in the image and likeness' of God?

The first thing we must underline is that our own way of being persons cannot be transferred or projected into God. Existentialist philosophy can only help us to appreciate the limitations, the anti-

---

[81] Basil, *C. Eun.* 3.1.
[82] In my *Being as Communion*, p. 41.

nomies and the tragic experience of personhood, and this in itself
is important in order to make it clear to us that, as human beings,
we are not content with what we actually are as persons, and long
for true personhood.[83] But it is precisely because we realize the tragedy of our personal existence that we cannot transpose our concept
of person to the being of God. It is the reverse that we should do,
namely *allow God's way of being to reveal to us true personhood*. Patristic theology offers important illumination concerning divine personhood and allows us to place our own personhood in the light of our
faith in the Triune God.

All this — which I hope will be sufficient to protect me from the
accusation of being under the influence of existentialist personalism![84] — can and must be related also to the idea of divine causality.
The statement that 'the Father is the cause of personhood in God's
being' can throw light on our own personal existence. Causality in
this case, like personhood itself, would not be an idea borrowed from
our experience and transferred to God, in an existentialistic way, but
would receive its meaning from its application to the way God exists.
What would this mean for our existence as persons?

In the first place, it means that there is not and should not be personal existence which is self-existent, self-sufficient or self-explicable.
A person is always *a gift from someone*. It is demonic to attribute one's
own personal identity to oneself or to an a-personal something. The
notion of self-existence is a substantialist notion, not a personal one.
Persons have a 'cause', because they are the outcome of love and freedom, and they owe their being who they are, their distinctive other-

[83] See below, Chapter 6.
[84] A charge made by A. J. Torrance, *Persons in Communion*, p. 290. Cf. below, Appendix to Chapter 4. Such a charge betrays a failure to distinguish between, on the one
hand, using existentialist personalism to describe the impasse of human personhood as it is, left to itself, and, on the other hand, transferring this human personhood to God's being. I have used the former extensively in my writings, for without
that theology would remain irrelevant to the human condition. But I have persistently objected to and refused to do the latter. Only a superficial reading of my work
can overlook words such as the following: 'The presence-in-absence paradox, therefore, shows that personal presence *quâ presence* is something that *cannot be extrapolated from created existence*. It is a presence that seems to come to us from outside this
world — which makes the notion of person, if properly understood, perhaps the
only notion that can be applied to God without the danger of anthropomorphism...
Personhood thus proves to be *in* this world — through man — but not *of* this world'
(my 'Human Capacity and Human Incapacity: A Theological Exploration of Personhood', *Scottish Journal of Theology* 28 (1975), p. 419f.; Chapter 6 in the present
volume).

ness as persons, to another person. Ontologically, persons are givers and recipients of personal identity. Causality in Trinitarian existence reveals to us a personhood which is constituted by love.

Secondly, if we allow our notion of personal causality to be conditioned and determined by the kind of causality I have described here as being characteristic of God's being, we are bound to attribute our personal existence *to a person and not to a nature*, whether human or divine. Our personal origins lie in a person. It is instructive to note how Basil illustrates the thesis that the Father is the cause of the Trinity:

> We therefore find in thinking this way that our concept of [the Father's] ungeneratedness does not fall under the category of discovering the *what is* (τοῦ τί ἐστίν), but rather...the *how is* (τοῦ ὅπως ἐστίν)... Just as, in speaking of human beings, when we say that so and so has come into being (ἐγένετο) from so and so, we do not speak of the what (τό τί), but of the whence he came forth... And in order to make it clearer, the evangelist Luke, in describing the genealogy of our Lord and saviour Jesus Christ according to the flesh...began with Joseph; and having called him the offspring of Heli, and him of Matthat, and thus leading the description to Adam, he then arrived at the earliest ones and said that Seth came from Adam, and Adam from God, at which point he ended the ascent. [In so doing, Luke] *did not declare the natures of each one's birth*, but the immediate principles (or beginnings: ἀρχάς) from which each of them came into being... This is what we do when by the appelation of the unoriginate we are taught the *how of God* rather than his nature itself.[85]

The same point is made in one of Basil's letters to Apollinaris, where he agrees with him that the ἀρχή of human beings should not be sought in human nature, either ὑπερκειμένη (standing above), in the Platonic sense, or ὑποκειμένη (standing underneath), in the Aristotelian sense, but *in Adam*.[86] It is Adam, not human nature, that is the 'cause', the 'father', of each one of us. As offspring of human nature, we are not 'other' in an absolute sense; neither are we free. If we attribute either ἀρχή or 'cause' to a person, Adam, we acquire otherness in unity.

The fact that causation in God has nothing to do with divine substance or nature, but only with his personhood, shows that true personhood in humans as 'images of God' must be free from the necessity of nature if it is to achieve otherness. Freedom from nature and dependence on the person is a lesson learnt from divine causality.[87]

---

[85] Basil, *C. Eun.* 1.14-15; cf. Lk. 3.23-38.

[86] Basil, *Ep.* 361 and 362; see above, Chapter 2.

[87] For a further discussion, see above, Chapter 2. The implications of such a thesis are far-reaching and subject to discussion and even controversy. Ever since Augustine, we tend to confuse person with personality, i.e., with natural qualities, and for

Thirdly, what divine causality teaches us is that personal otherness is not symmetrical but *a-symmetrical*. There is always in this otherness a 'greater' one (Jn 14.28), not morally or functionally but ontologically. Otherness is, by definition, 'hierarchical', since it involves absolute specificity emerging not from qualities — as is the way with natural otherness — but from the gift of love as being and being other: we are not 'other' by ourselves but by someone else, who in this way is 'higher', that is, ontologically 'prior' to us, the giver of our otherness.

'Hierarchy' has acquired a pejorative sense in our modern minds. It is connected with oppression and suppression of freedom. It is normally treated as a moral problem, but its roots are ontological. Hierarchy is evil and ontologically problematic when the 'greater' one, the 'causing other', does not let the 'inferior' one, the 'receiving other', be *fully other*, fully 'himself' or 'herself', equal in nature and 'whole of the whole'. In the Holy Trinity, the Father is 'greater', precisely while generating others of full and equal ontological status ('wholes of the whole').[88] If this is to be applied to the human being

this reason the thesis 'freedom from nature' appears to be provocative. In God's being, nature and personhood are distinct, yet they coincide and therefore such a thesis would be absurd. Humans, however, particularly in their fallen state, being subject to the necessity of death and individualism inherent in their nature, are also subject to natural causation: death and individualism, among other things, are 'caused' by their nature in spite of what they aspire to as persons, i.e., immortality, freedom and love. The passage from human to divine personhood inevitably involves this problem. The Cross is precisely this passage which God himself went through in the Incarnation, i.e., owing to the fact that the Son freely assumed human nature. This passage of the Cross is as real as anything, and it is implicit in all my references to Christology. The fact that I insist that Christ finally overcame the tragic aspect of human personhood and the necessity of biological nature because of his Trinitarian personhood (i.e., because the Father raised him from the dead in the Spirit; Rom. 4.25; 8.11; Acts 3.15) and *not* because of God's 'receiving non-being into himself' (A. Lewis quoted with praise by A.J. Torrance, *Persons in Communion*, p. 304) does not turn my position into 'a docetic tendency' (Torrance, p. 304). The reality of the Cross does not depend on the infiltration of God's being by non-being (an idea totally foreign, if not blasphemous, to patristic thought). It is not denied or undermined by the fact that, on the Cross, being encountered non-being only in order to swamp it, as the Resurrection proved, unless of course — and this may in fact be the case — we take the view that what makes the Cross real is the involvement of non-being in it and not the presence and power of being, i.e., divine love. This raises a broader issue: does an historical event involving some form of evil (such as the Cross) need the acceptance (receiving) of evil (= non-being) by being (= God) in order to be real and not 'docetic'?

[88] Cf. Gregory Naz., *Or.* 40.43: Gregory, like the other Cappadocians, does not avoid the term 'cause', precisely because for him, too, 'the Father is greater, since from him flows both the *equality* and the being of *equals*... For the humiliation of

as 'image of God', it will mean that the a-symmetry of hierarchical *taxis* is not *per se* problematic; it only becomes so when the 'cause' brings forth 'inferior' others, both ontologically and morally. Thus, the idea of the Father as personal cause implies the following important consequences for personal existence:

(a) Hierarchical ordering is inherent in personhood, all personal relations being ontologically a-symmetrical, since persons are never self-existent or self-explicable, but in some sense 'caused' by some 'other', by a 'giver' who is ontologically 'prior' and, in this sense, 'greater' than the recipient.

(b) The 'cause' of a personal identity brings forth, 'causes', fully other, that is, ontologically free and fully equal, identities. A-symmetry is not, therefore, incompatible with equality.

(c) Most importantly, no personal otherness can be conceived without ultimate ontological reference to the ultimately Other, who is the source of all otherness. Every other, not being self-explicable and always being understood as the gift of some other, owes his otherness ultimately to the Other *par excellence*, who is the uncaused cause of otherness. In other words, all 'others' owe their being who they are as absolutely particular, that is, ontologically free, identities to the person who even in his own being generates otherness, that is, the Father. To him all that exists is referred back, as it was from his 'good pleasure', that is his free love, that it originally came forth. This makes the Father the ultimate giver of personhood, whose own personhood is not given or caused by someone else, the uncaused cause of all personhood.[89]

This is what emerges as the conclusion for our personal existence from an analysis of the Cappadocian theology of the Father as cause.

the one who comes from him is no glory to the one from whom (the other comes: τῷ ἐξ οὗ)... For the [term] greater refers not to the nature but *to the cause* (αἰτίαν)'. Such a reconciliation of monarchical and hierarchical notions with ideas of equality may serve to dispel fears that monotheistic monarchianism leads to dangerous religious-political ideologies, fears expressed, for example, in J. Moltmann, *The Trinity and the Kingdom of God*, 1981, esp. p. 131f. Similar concerns were expressed earlier by E. Peterson, *Der Monotheismus als politisches Problem*, 1935, who seems to have influenced Moltmann. For a critical discussion of the problem, see Ch. Schwöbel, 'Radical Monotheism and the Trinity', *Neue Zeitschrift für systematische Theologie und Religionsphilosophie* 43 (2001), pp. 54-74.

[89] The idea that the relation between giver and recipient of personhood is asymmetrical precludes the logical possibility that the ultimate giver (the Father) receives his personhood from those who receive it from him (e.g., the Son). Reciprocity in this case would make the relationship symmetrical, putting monotheism at risk. See below.

A rejection of this theology would automatically result in a different understanding of human existence. It would entail either a total rejection of hierarchical ordering, for fear that it would threaten otherness, paradoxically resulting in an egalitarianism in which otherness is finally reduced to functionalism and personal identity to personality-based utilitarianism; or a submission of the particular to a 'class' of social or natural stereotypes and 'universals' in which otherness would cease to be personal and become natural, that is, determined by natural qualities.[90]

6. *Consequences for Ecclesiology*

From the point of view of the implications drawn above from Cappadocian theology, ecclesiologies can be grouped as follows:

(a) There is a kind of ecclesiology in which all hierarchical notions are suspected as threatening communion as well as otherness.[91] The most typical and representative expression of this non-hierarchical (if not anti-hierarchical) ecclesiology is to be found in Congregationalist and Free Church Protestantism. In the rest of Protestantism, hierarchical structures are centred mainly on ministries of Word and Sacrament, which, however, are conceived in terms of function rather than ontology, having little to do with the establishment and experience of *personal relations of an ontological kind* between the minister and the rest of the Church. Such an ecclesiology naturally and understandably reacts against the Cappadocian teaching of the Father as 'cause', fearing that such a Trinitarian theology might have undesirable consequences for ecclesiology.

(b) There is an ecclesiology in which hierarchical structures are regarded as central and necessary, but they are so on the basis of a Trinitarian model in which otherness is secondary to unity and is understood as existing only in order to serve unity. A substantialist Trinitarian theology is, in this case, transferred into ecclesiology.[92]

---

[90] See more on this in Chapter 1, above.

[91] An illustration of this is offered by M. Volf, *After Our Likeness: The Church as the Image of the Trinity*, 1998, pp. 215-17 and *passim*. See also C. Gunton, *The Promise of Trinitarian Theology*, p. 197. A similar position in J. Moltmann, *The Trinity and the Kingdom of God*, 1981, p. 200f.

[92] A typical example is J. Ratzinger's ecclesiology in which the universal Church ontologically precedes the local Church, and the highest ministry exists in order to safeguard and express the one, universal Church. See K. Rahner and J. Ratzinger, *Episcopat und Primat*, 1962, p. 26; also J. Ratzinger, *Church, Ecumenism and Politics*, 1988. Persons are 'pure relations' and ecclesial structures are conceived by way of the one substance of God; cf. M. Volf, *After Our Likeness*, pp. 67ff.

This priority of the 'one' over the 'many', or of substance over personhood, turns hierarchy into a means not of producing and securing otherness, as is the case in the Cappadocian understanding of divine causality, but of enforcing unity. Juridical and legal notions become part of ecclesiology and, as C. Gunton observes, as a consequence, the Church, like any legal institution, 'employs constraint in order to maintain unity'.[93] No wonder, therefore, that the term 'hierarchy' provokes negative reactions and is rejected in ecclesiology.[94]

(c) There is an ecclesiology in which hierarchical structures are regarded as essential to the Church only because on the Trinitarian model, as I described and analysed it above, otherness is ontologically primordial and is asymmetrical in its character. There can be no unity except in the form of otherness, and this implies that there should be no hierarchy which serves unity without at the same time allowing for, or even generating, otherness. Everything in the Church is a *gift*, including her being. The sacraments are gifts, and so is the word and the truth of revelation. Gifts presuppose a giver and a receiver. Even in the most 'congregationalist' type of Church, there are those who give (e.g., by preaching the word or performing the sacrament) and those who receive (by listening to the word, being baptized, etc.). The fact that such ministers are not permanent simply means that between the 'giver' and the 'receiver' there is no permanent (ontological) relationship, but only a functional one. However, the relationship is there, and it is an asymmetrical one, even if only for as long as the function lasts.

Now, one may argue that calling this relationship hierarchical is an abuse of terminology, but terms mean what the source from which they derive dictates, and if our source is the revelation of God as Trinity, as the Fathers interpreted it for us, the essential aspect of divine hierarchy is precisely this relationship of 'giver' and 'receiver', provided that it generates otherness and respects particularity as 'whole of the whole'. The issue, therefore, is not whether there is hierarchy in the Church, but what kind of hierarchy it is that does justice to the Trinitarian model.

We have already repeatedly made the point that the Trinitarian model involves a *taxis*, a hierarchy, which brings forth 'others' of full

---

[93] C. Gunton, *The Promise of Trinitarian Theology*, p. 60.

[94] Thus, C. Gunton, *The Promise of Trinitarian Theology*, p. 70: 'much ecclesiology has been dominated by *monistic or hierarchical* conceptions' (my italics). The association of hierarchy with monism reveals the deeper reason for its rejection.

ontological integrity and, therefore, equality of nature, dignity, and so on. This suggests an ecclesiology in which the one Church is constituted as many local churches of full 'catholic' ecclesial integrity, with no one of them being subject to another as 'part' of another or of a whole, but each being 'whole of the whole'. I have developed this sufficiently in my book, *Being as Communion*, and need not repeat it here. Equally, I have shown in the same study that all ministry both within and without the local church is to be understood in such a way as to allow for every ministry, even the most modest one, to be indispensable and ontologically significant for the rest (1 Corinthians 12). We must now consider the question of why such a relational structure should involve a *taxis* similar to that of the Holy Trinity in a more than functional or provisional way. Why, in other words, a hierarchical structure, albeit under the conditions stated above, is part of an ecclesiology inspired by the Cappadocian interpretation of Trinitarian theology.

I shall leave aside the argument from tradition, to which a great deal of discussion has been devoted in the past. Hierarchical notions are not totally absent even in the New Testament,[95] and they are certainly abundant in the patristic period and after that. Already *1 Clement* argues that there should be in the Church a *taxis* and a ministry which should claim authority and demand obedience.[96] The same is true of Ignatius and of all the subsequent patristic tradition. To attribute hierarchical ecclesiology to Neoplatonic influences is to close our eyes to all this early, persistent and unbreakable tradition, at least up to the time of the Reformation. It is another matter that *taxis* and hierarchy were at some point in history contaminated with legalistic ideas and finally provoked the well-known reaction of the Reformation. The doctrine of the Trinity, as I expounded it above, points to a notion of hierarchy that is free from monistic and legalistic or pyramidal Church structures, and it is such a kind of hierarchy that systematic theology should consider and discuss.

If Church hierarchy is modelled on the personal relations of the Holy Trinity, it becomes part of the *esse*, and not simply of the *bene esse*, of the Church. Just as, in the Trinity, the very being of God is

---

[95] In the Pauline communities, there are 'leaders' (προϊστάμενοι; Rom. 12.8; 1 Thess. 5.12), who should enjoy 'double honour', and it is not accidental that the ministries are listed in 1 Cor. 12.17f. with an order of first, second, third, etc., the apostles occupying the place of the 'first'. Whether leadership is corporate or not is another matter; the fact remains that an order (τάξις: 1 Cor. 14.40) of some kind existed from the beginning. Paul is hierarchically minded, perhaps like all his contemporaries, as is evident from 1 Cor. 11.3; Eph. 5.23; Col. 1.18; 2.10, 19; etc.

[96] *1 Clem.* 42.1-4; 44.1-4; 57.1f.; etc.

a movement from the Father to the Son and to the Spirit, which is returned finally to the person of the Father, so in the Church, too, everything moves from a ministry reflecting and imaging the Father to the rest of the members, in order that it may finally be returned to 'the Father who is in heaven'.

This is precisely what happens in the Eucharist. The earliest patristic sources, such as *1 Clement*, Ignatius, Hippolytus, the Syriac *Didascalia*, as well as the ancient eucharistic liturgies, speak of the Eucharist as *Gifts* and as food coming *from the Father* (Jn 6.32) and given to the people by the minister who is 'in the place (or type) of God the Father' (Ignatius), and who by so doing becomes for the community its 'father'. If we follow the history of the term 'father' in the early Church, we note that its original use was related to the Eucharist and it was for this reason that it was applied, in the first instance, to the bishop, as the president of the eucharistic assembly, and then was eventually transferred to the presbyters when they themselves became presidents of eucharistic assemblies (and in this way 'priests'), with the appearance of parishes in the fourth century CE.[97] This eucharistic context precludes any legalistic or monistic views of 'fatherhood' in the Church, as well as any 'paternalistic' or 'sexist' ideas borrowed from society at large and transferred to ecclesiology. Ecclesial fatherhood reflects Trinitarian Fatherhood in that membership in the Church requires 'generation' or 'birth'[98] or 'regeneration',[99] which is given 'from above' in an act or event (Baptism) of *sonship*, that is, our acceptance by the Father as his sons by grace through our incorporation into his only-begotten Son whom he eternally generates. The Eucharist is the fulfilment and 'enjoyment' of this baptismal incorporation, and in this sense it is a movement from the Father through the Son in the Holy Spirit, reaching us in order to be returned by us in the same way to the Father. It is precisely this movement that lies behind the 'hierarchies' of the Areopagitic writings, which, by using Neoplatonic concepts, seek to present the Church's eucharistic experience as a reality significant for the

---

[97] See the discussion of the evidence in my book, *The Unity of the Church in the Holy Eucharist and the Bishop in the First Three Centuries*, 1965 (in Greek); English edition, *Eucharist, Bishop, Church* (Holy Cross Orthodox Press, Brookline, 2001). Cf. also my 'Episkopé and Episkopos in the Early Church', in *Episkopé and Episcopate in Ecumenical Perspective* (WCC, 1980; Faith and Order paper 102), pp. 30-42.

[98] The apostle, for example, is called 'father' because he 'gives birth' to the members of the community 'in Christ Jesus' (1 Cor. 4.15).

[99] 1 Pet. 1.3, 23; cf. Jn 3.3, 7.

whole universe or cosmos. In so doing, Dionysius never ceases to be eucharistic, for he firmly and explicitly bases all hierarchical notions on the *synaxis* of the community, that is, of *all* the people, without whom no 'hierarchy' is conceivable.

To sum up, we must free ourselves from legalistic and monistic ideas in ecclesiology, and understand the Church not simply as an occasional 'happening', where the Word of God is preached and listened to and the sacraments are performed, but as the reality of *sonship in the Spirit*, that is, as a constant movement of filial grace from the Father, giving his Son to us in the Spirit, and as a return of this by us, 'giving grace' to him by offering back to him his Son in his incarnate, sacrificial and risen state as the head of a body comprising all of us and all that exists (τά πάντα). The *taxis* of the immanent Trinity itself becomes, in this way, the ordering of the economic Trinity. The Church is nothing other than the work of the economic Trinity applied to us and through us and together with us to the whole cosmos, an image of the Trinity and a foretaste of the *eschata*, when the whole world will become a movement back to the one God, the Father (1 Cor. 15.24) from whom everything, even the persons of the Trinity in their eternal being, comes forth.

7. *Consequences for Monotheism*

The crucial question concerning monotheism is whether the one God is a person or something else, that is, a substance or a relational reality of some kind, for example, 'triunity', 'tripersonality' or even Trinity, as such. We have already noted that if the relationship between giver and recipient of personal otherness were symmetrical, allowing for the Father to be 'caused' as a person by the Son and the Spirit, monotheism would be at risk. I must explain this further.

Christianity emerged from a monotheistic religious milieu. The claims associated with Jesus because of his special relationship with God, calling him 'Abba',[100] his identification with the eschatological 'Son of Man',[101] his appellation 'Son of God', and, above all, his Resurrection and Ascension, which led to the application of Psalm 110 to his person, as the one 'sitting at the right hand' of the Father and receiving the adoration and worship due, for a Hebrew monotheist,

---

[100] On the significance of this aramaic term as an indication of familiarity and special relationship between Jesus and God, see J. Jeremias, *New Testament Theology*, 1971, pp. 62ff.

[101] Cf. J. Jeremias, *New Testament Theology*, p. 272f.

to none but the one God, exercised the first pressure on biblical monotheism. This pressure was strengthened further by the demand to
baptize those accepting the Christian faith 'in the name of the Father
and of the Son and of the Holy Spirit' (Mt. 28.19),[102] thus introducing Trinitarian ideas into Hebrew monotheism, and making it
imperative to maintain biblical monotheism in a Christian context.

When the Christian gospel was accepted by Greek intellectuals in
the second century CE, the problem acquired a philosophical character and involved the question of how to reconcile monotheism with
the Trinitarian faith without ending up in polytheism. This constituted the main problem of patristic theology in the first four or five
centuries.

The solutions proposed at that time could be classified in the following way:

(a) The *modalist solution*: God remains one in spite of the Trinity,
because the Trinity is in fact three different ways or roles in which
the one God appears or acts in history. Sabellianism represented the
extreme form of this view.

(b) The *Cappadocian solution*: this was marked by a vigorous and
even passionate reaction against Sabellianism, and therefore by a tendency to stress the ontological integrity of each person of the Trinity.
Such a position inevitably involved the risk of tritheism.[103] The Cappadocians avoided this risk by introducing the principle of *ontological
origination* and making the Father the 'cause' of Trinitarian existence.
By so doing, they placed monotheism at the level of personhood,
which, owing to its simultaneous association with unity (relationality)
and particularity (otherness), served as the most appropriate means
to eliminate any logical contradiction between monotheism and Trinitarianism. This way of treating the problem also had the advantage
of bringing Christian monotheism into harmony with the biblical
equation of God with the Father.

(c) The *Augustinian solution*: according to this, monotheism is safeguarded by the one *substance* of God, the *divinitas*, which logically
precedes the three persons. In this case, monotheism survives at the
expense of Trinitarianism. The Trinity is not the way in which the
one God *is*, that is, in the sense of a primary ontological category,
but rather indicates relations within the one God, that is, instances
of his one nature, realized and expressed mainly in psychological or

---

[102] Cf. A. Wainwright, *The Trinity in the New Testament*, 1962, p. 237ff.
[103] Cf. J.N.D. Kelly, *Early Christian Doctrines*, p. 267f.

moral terms, as the memory, knowledge and love of a certain *individ-ual* substance. This is followed faithfully by Aquinas, for whom, when we generalize or abstract from the Trinitarian persons, what remains for thought is the one divine nature which is in general to be called 'God', not the three persons or only one of them.[104] Such a solution makes it difficult logically to reconcile the one and the three in God, and must be counted responsible for the eclipse of Trinitarian theology in the West for such a long time. It may also account for the emergence of modern atheism, particularly of the existential type, which has rejected the substantialist approach to God and thus God as such.[105]

We have already discussed here the recent attempts in Western theology to remove from Trinitarian theology the individualism inherent in traditional views of God by proposing the idea of *relational substance* and in this way making the Trinity coincident with the one substance. This, however, would still leave the substance, albeit relational, to express and safeguard monotheism. In that case, monotheism would be located in all three persons simultaneously and the only oneness available for monotheism would be either the one substance or a 'Triunity' of some kind, that is, a relationality of a more or less Buberian type.

I have already dealt with this matter extensively above. The question arising at this point is in what sense is Christianity a monotheistic religion, faithful to the biblical belief in one God *in spite of its Trinitarian faith*? This question would appear to be crucial in the context of the inter-religious dialogue that is so relevant, even imperative, today.

It would not be difficult to agree that both Judaism and Islam would refuse to accept a Trinitarian God of the substantialist type, whether substance precedes the persons, as in the Augustinian form of Trinitarianism, or coincides with them, as in the modern version

---

[104] Cf. K. Rahner, *Theological Investigations*, vol. 4, 1966, pp. 77ff.

[105] A modern type of solution, based on the Hegelian idea of God as the absolute subject (one subject, three modes of being) which relates to itself by an eternal process of self-differentiation and self-identification is exemplified, according to J. Moltmann (*The Trinity and the Kingdom of God*, pp. 17f. and 139f.) in K. Barth and K. Rahner. I do not assign a special category to it, because from the point of view of monotheism which concerns us at this stage, it does not differ fundamentally from the substantialist solution. As J. Moltmann observes, 'here the problems for the doctrine of the Trinity resemble those discovered in the earlier Trinity of substance: the unity of the absolute subject is stressed to such a degree that the Trinitarian persons disintegrate into mere aspects of the one subject' (*The Trinity and the Kingdom of God*, p. 18).

of relational substance and 'Triunity'. For both of these religions, the one God is a personal agent, not a substance — individual or otherwise. The possibility of dialogue would seem to rule out *a priori* all versions of Trinitarian theology that do not identify the one God with the Father. Identifying the one God with the Father does not automatically solve the problem of the kind of monotheism that the three major faiths adhere to. This would only be the starting point. But it is easier and sounder to build a discussion of Trinitarian theology on this basis than to begin with a theology that contains no common ground at all. A Trinitarian theology which identifies the one God with the Father may be argued more convincingly in the context of a dialogue with monotheistic religions.

I do not intend to enter into a full discussion of how such a dialogue would proceed if this basis were to be accepted. This would require a special study, which would undoubtedly be of great importance to a dialogue of this kind. I can only indicate here by way of illustration some points of significance emerging from the Cappadocian notion of the Father as 'cause'.

Old Testament religion and Christianity share a faith in *one* God, who is so transcendent that the world is not necessary in order to speak of the being of God. Yet both faiths would agree that, although God does not exist *because of* the world, or *together* and *simultaneously with* it, he exists *for* the world: he is a God who goes outside himself to create the world and to care for it, albeit only through a chosen people with whom he establishes a covenant. This implies that God *loves* the world; he is a God that loves.

It would be easy to subscribe to such a statement. The next step would be to enquire whether God *is* love, that is, whether his love is as free and transcendent as to be true and real regardless of the existence of the world. Admittedly, this is a culturally conditioned question which a believer at the time of the Bible would not bother to raise. And yet, in a culture such as ours, which is dominated by the verb *to be* in every sentence we utter, such a question would be inevitable. The New Testament already includes statements of this kind when it says that 'God *is* love' (1 Jn 4.8). If someone was ready to make such an affirmation, he would have to face the question of whether God is love only in so far as he loves the world, that is, on condition that the world exists, in which case his love is not as free and transcendent as his being, or that his love is as transcendent as his being, which would imply that he is love in himself and not because of the existence of the world.

This is not, of course, a compelling argument for someone who may simply refuse to associate God's love with his being: one may argue that the statement 'God is love' applies only to his relationship with the world, and not to his being apart from the world's existence. It would, however, be a logically compelling argument for anyone who wishes to maintain as axiomatic that God is both radically transcendent, that is, he exists before and regardless of the world, and at the same time loving in his very being. The only way to escape from the logic of this argument would be to regard love as a category *added* to being, and not constitutive of it. This is how people normally think of love: you first *are* and then you may or may not love (you may still be who you are and not love). If this way of thinking were to be adopted, we would end up with the difficulty of relating love to the ontological constitution of the divine persons, that is, making the Trinity ontologically primary to God's identity. However, if love is not understood as an *attribute* of a substance that precedes the persons, or as an *act* of already existing persons, but as constitutive of personal identities, it is logically inescapable to maintain that, in loving, a radically transcendent God either constitutes his existence in love or he does not exist at all.[106]

All this can serve as an apology, or explanation, for the Christian doctrine of the Trinity, which would be based on a logical assumption acceptable also to all those who share the biblical faith, namely that God loves because he *is* love. In other words, what the Christian does, in believing in the Trinity, is to extend to God's eternal and transcendent being the love with which he loves the world.

Now, if this divine love constitutes divine being in a *personal* way, and not as the self-love of an individual, otherness would have to be an inevitable aspect of it, as indeed the divine Trinity implies. This would make monotheism problematic, and it would be difficult to reconcile it with the doctrine of the Trinity. The Cappadocian idea of *aition* appears to be relevant in this case. Love in God's personal existence is *a-symmetrical*; it is not self-explicable but derives from a source which grants it as a personal gift, freely offered and freely, that is, personally, received. This source or 'cause' is the Father or God of the Bible. By introducing asymmetry and causation in God's

---

[106] This kind of difficulty is also present in any attempt to build Trinitarian theology on God's economic acts, which are then extended to God's being. God's actions in the economy are manifestations of his love, but divine love is *more* than these actions; it is God's way of being. Act points to being but it is not being (see above, n. 11).

Trinitarian existence, the Cappadocians safeguarded biblical monotheism, while maintaining the Trinitarian faith. The one God is the
Father of Jesus Christ and the Spirator of the Holy Spirit; the Trinity
depends ontologically on the Father and is not in itself, that is, *qua* Trinity, the one God. If the Trinity is God, it is only because the Father
makes it Trinity by granting it *hypostases*.[107]

There are bound to be many questions and problems that an
adherent to the biblical faith would still raise with regard to such
a theology. Yet, compared with the other Trinitarian theologies we
have mentioned, this one seems to come closest to the biblical concept of God. It would, therefore, provide the best basis available in
Christian theology for a dialogue with other monotheistic faiths.

---

[107] Love may be common to all three persons of the Trinity, but it is by no means
uncaused; it is 'the love of the Father' (2 Cor. 13.13) that is expressed in the economy
as the χάρις of Jesus Christ and the κοινωνία of the Holy Spirit (2 Cor. 13.13). Cf. the
pertinent remarks of C. Gunton, *Act and Being*, 2002, p. 140.

Chapter 4

THE TRINITY AND PERSONHOOD:
Appreciating the Cappadocian Contribution

INTRODUCTION

Cappadocia, which lies in the heart of Asia Minor, became an important centre of Christian theology in the fourth century CE. Already at the time of St Paul there was a small Christian community in Cappadocia where Christianity spread so rapidly as to produce a number of martyrs and confessors in the second century, and to contribute seven bishops to the Council of Nicaea in 325 CE. But it was mainly in the second half of the fourth century that Cappadocia became famous for its theological thought. This was due to four leading figures whose theological and philosophical originality sealed the entire history of Christian thought: St Basil the Great, bishop of Caesarea in Cappadocia (c. 330–79); St Gregory of Nazianzus, known as the 'Theologian' (c. 330–89/90), at first briefly bishop of Sassima in Cappadocia and later on, also briefly, Archbishop of Constantinople; St Gregory, the younger brother of Basil, bishop of Nyssa (c. 335–94?), and, finally, their friend St Amphilochius (340/45-?), bishop of Iconium. The first three of these left behind them a considerable number of writings (dogmatic treatises, exegetical works, ascetic writings, orations, sermons and letters), which allow us to appreciate their thought, while St Amphilochius' work survives only in a limited number of homilies and letters, some of them only in fragments.

Although the theological contribution of these Cappadocian Fathers is universally recognized and acknowledged, its importance is by no means limited to theology. It involves a radical reorientation of classical Greek humanism, a conception of man and a view of existence, which ancient thought proved unable to produce in spite of its many

155

achievements in philosophy. The occasion for this was offered by the theological controversies of the time, but the implications of the Cappadocian Fathers' contribution reach beyond theology in the strict doctrinal sense and affect the entire culture of late antiquity to such an extent that the whole of Byzantine and European thought would remain incomprehensible without a knowledge of this contribution.

How does the doctrine of God appear, if placed in the light of Cappadocian theology? What problems concerning the doctrine of the Trinity and its philosophical integrity could be overcome with the help of this theology? What consequences does this theology have for our understanding of the human being and of existence as a whole? These kinds of questions are the essential concerns of this chapter. Needless to say, however, such vast and complex questions cannot be dealt with in an exhaustive way in such a limited space. Only some suggestions will be put forth and some central ideas underlined. The Cappadocian contribution still awaits its comprehensive and exhaustive treatment in theological — and philosophical — research, in spite of the considerable number of works devoted to its individual representatives.

In order to understand and appreciate correctly the contribution of the Cappadocians to the doctrine of the Trinity we must first set the historical context. What were the Cappadocians reacting against? Why did they take the view they took, and how did they try to respond to the challenges of their contemporaries? After trying to give an answer to these questions we may consider the lasting significance of these Fathers' theology for other times.

I. The Historical Context

If we try to single out the sensitivities — we might call them obsessions — of the Cappadocian Fathers *vis-à-vis* their contemporaries, we may locate them in the following areas:

1. *Sabellianism*

Sabellianism represented an interpretation of the doctrine of the Trinity which involved the view that the Father, the Son and the Spirit were not full persons in an ontological sense but *roles* assumed by the one God. Sabellius seems to have used the term person in the singular, implying that there is 'one person' in God.[1] This modal-

---

[1] Cf. G.L. Prestige, *God in Patristic Thought*, 1936, pp. 113f. and 160f.

istic interpretation made it impossible to understand how the Son, eternally or in the Incarnation, had a relation of reciprocal dialogue with the Father, praying to Him, and so on, as the Gospel stories require us to believe. It would also make it impossible for the Christian to establish a fully personal dialogue and relationship with *each* of the three persons of the Trinity. Furthermore, it would appear that God was somehow 'acting' in the Economy, pretending, as it were, to be what he appeared to be, and not revealing or giving to us his true self, his very being.

For these and other reasons the doctrine of the Trinity had to be interpreted in such a way as to exclude any Sabellian or crypto-Sabellian understanding, and the only way to achieve this would be by stressing the fulness and ontological integrity of each person of the Trinity. The Cappadocians were so deeply concerned with this that they went as far as rejecting the use of the term *prosopon* or person to describe the Trinity[2] — a term that had entered theological terminology since Tertullian in the West and found its way into the East probably through Hippolytus — particularly since this term was loaded with connotations of acting on the theatrical stage or playing a role in society, when used in the ancient Graeco-Roman world. In their attempt to protect the doctrine from such connotations, the Cappadocians were at times ready to speak of 'three beings' in referring to the Trinity. For the same reason they preferred to use images of the Trinity that would imply the ontological fulness of each person, such as 'three suns', 'three torches', and so on, thus introducing a fundamental change in the Nicaean terminology which was inclined towards the use of images indicating one source extended into three ('light of light' etc.). By doing this, the Cappadocians came to be known as being interested in the Trinity more than in the unity of God. (Cf. the well-known textbook thesis that the West began with the unity of God and then moved to the Trinity, while the East followed the opposite course.) This stress on the integrity and fulness of the persons was full of important philosophical implications, as we shall see below.

Out of this concern for the ontological integrity of each person in the Trinity came the historic revolution, as I should like to call it,[3] in the history of philosophy, namely the identification of the idea of person with that of *hypostasis*. It would lead us too far to discuss here the history of these terms. Suffice it to recall that only a gen-

---

[2] See Basil, *Ep.* 236.6.
[3] See my *Being as Communion*, 1985, p. 36f.

eration before the Cappadocians the term *hypostasis* was fully identified with that of *ousia* or substance[4] (indeed, the Latin term *substantia* would literally translate into Greek as *hypostasis*). St Athanasius makes it clear that *hypostasis* did not differ from *ousia*, both terms indicating 'being' or 'existence'. The Cappadocians changed this by dissociating *hypostasis* from *ousia* and attaching it to *prosopon*. This was done in order to make the expression 'three persons' free from Sabellian interpretations and thus acceptable to the Cappadocians. That this constitutes an historical revolution in philosophy we shall have an opportunity to point out later, when we discuss the philosophical significance of the Cappadocian contribution.

Now, the Cappadocians seem to have done well with pointing out and defending the fulness and integrity of each person, but what about the unity or oneness of God? Were they not in danger of introducing tritheism?

To avoid this danger, the Cappadocians suggested that *ousia* (substance) or *physis* (nature) in God should be taken in the sense of the general category which we apply to more than one person. With the help of Aristotelian philosophy they illustrated this by a reference to the one human nature or substance which is general and is applied to all human beings, and to the many concrete human beings (e.g., John, George, Basil) who are to be called *hypostases* (plural), not natures or substances.[5] In this way they removed all apparent illogicality from their position, since it *is* logically possible to speak of one substance and three *hypostases* (or persons), as the above example shows. But the theological difficulty was there, since in the above example of the one human nature and three (or more) human beings we have to do with *three men*, whereas in the Trinity we do not imply three Gods, but one.

In order to meet this theological difficulty, the Cappadocian Fathers posed the question of what accounts for the difficulty in reconciling the one and the three in human existence. This was of paramount significance anthropologically, as we shall see later. The reason why human beings cannot be one and many at the same time involves the following general observations, inspired by and drawn from Cappadocian thought.

(a) In human existence, nature precedes the person. When John or George or Basil are born, the one human nature precedes them; they, therefore, represent and embody only *part* of the human nature.

---

[4] See Athanasius, *Letter to the Bishops of Egypt and Libya* (PG 26, 1036B).
[5] E.g., Basil, *Ep.* 236.6; 38.5; etc.

Through human procreation humanity is *divided*, and no human person can be said to be the bearer of the totality of human nature. This is why the death of one person does not automatically bring about the death of the rest — or, conversely, the life of one such person the life of the rest.

(b) Because of this, each human person can be conceived as an *individual*, that is, as an entity independent ontologically from other human beings. The unity between human beings is not ontologically identical with their diversity or multiplicity. The one and the many do not coincide. It is this existential difficulty that leads to the logical difficulty of saying 'one' and 'many' with the same breath.

Now, if we contrast this with God's existence, we see immediately that this existential and hence logical difficulty is not applicable to God. Since God by definition has not had a beginning, and space and time do not enter his existence, the three persons of the Trinity do not share a pre-existing or logically prior to them divine nature, but coincide with it. Multiplicity in God does not involve a division of his nature and energy, as happens with man.[6]

It is impossible, therefore, to say that in God, as is the case with human beings, nature precedes the person. Equally and for the same reasons, it is impossible to say that in God any of the three persons exists or can exist in separation from the other persons. The three constitute such an unbreakable unity that individualism is absolutely inconceivable in their case. The three persons of the Trinity are thus one God, because they are so united in an unbreakable communion (*koinonia*) that none of them can be conceived apart from the rest. The mystery of the one God in three persons points to a way of being which precludes individualism and separation (or self-sufficiency and self-existence) as a criterion of multiplicity. The 'one' not only does not precede — logically or otherwise — the 'many', but, on the contrary, requires the 'many' from the very start in order to exist.

This, therefore, seems to be the great innovation in philosophical thought, brought about by the Cappadocian Trinitarian theology, which carries with it a decisively new way of conceiving human existence, as we shall see below.

2. *Eunomianism*

Eunomianism marked a problematic unknown to Athanasius and Nicaea, since it introduced a far more sophisticated philosophical

---

[6] E.g., Gregory of Nyssa, *Quod non sint tres dii* (PG 45, 125).

argument than original Arianism had done. Eunomius, who came himself from Cappadocia, was made by the Arians bishop of Cyzicus, and was the most radical and perhaps the most sophisticated of the extreme Arians known as Anomoeans. In order to prove by way of Aristotelian dialectic that the Son is totally *unlike* the Father, the Eunomians placed the substance of God in being unbegotten (*agennetos*) and concluded that since the Son is 'begotten' (Nicaea itself calls him so) he falls outside the being or substance of God.

The refutation of such an argument requires that we make a sharp distinction between substance and person in God. By being a person the Father was to be distinguished from divine substance, and thus it would be wrong to conclude that the Son is not God or *homoousios* with the Father. When God is called Father or 'unbegotten', he is called so not with reference to his substance, but to personhood. Indeed, about the substance of God nothing can be said at all: no property or quality is applicable, except that which is one, undivided and absolutely simple and uncompounded, descriptions pointing to total unknowability rather than knowledge of the divine substance. The properties (*idiomata*) of unbegottenness or fatherhood for the Father, begottenness or sonship of the Son and *ekporeusis* (spiration) of the Spirit are personal or hypostatic properties which are incommunicable — unbegottenness being precisely one of them — whereas substance is communicated among the three persons. A person is thus defined through properties which are absolutely *unique*, and in this respect differs fundamentally from nature or substance. The reaction against Eunomianism produced, therefore, on the one hand, a clear and fundamental distinction between person and nature, thus allowing the concept of person to emerge more clearly as a distinct category in ontology, and, on the other hand, underlined the idea that personhood can be known and identified through its absolute uniqueness and irreplaceability, something that has not ceased to be of existential relevance in philosophy.

Now, this incommunicability of hypostatic properties does not mean that persons in the Trinity are to be understood as autonomous individuals. We must beware of making this incommunicability the definition of person *par excellence*, as Richard of St Victor seems to do, for although the hypostatic properties are not communicated, the notion of the person is inconceivable outside a relationship. The Cappadocians called the persons by names indicating *schesis* (relationship):[7] none of the three persons can be conceived without reference to the other two, both logically and ontologically. The problem is how to reconcile incommunicability with relationship, but this again is a matter of freeing divine existence from the servitude of personhood to substance, a servitude which applies only to created existence. By being uncreated, the three persons are not faced with a given substance, but exist freely. Being is simultaneously relational and hypostatic. But this leads us to a consideration of the philosophical consequences of Cappadocian theology.

II. THE PHILOSOPHICAL IMPLICATIONS

Here again history must give us the starting point. It is normally assumed that the Greek Fathers were Platonic or Aristotelian in their thinking, and yet a careful study of them would reveal that they were as obsessed with Greek philosophy as they were with various heretical ideas of their time. The doctrine of the Trinity offered the occasion to the Cappadocians to express their distance both explicitly and implicitly from Platonism in particular and thus to introduce a new philosophy.

One of the references to Plato made by St Gregory of Nazianzus is worthy of particular mention. He refers at one point to the philosopher as having spoken of God as a crater which overflows with goodness and love, and rejects this image as implying a process of natural or substantial, and therefore necessary, generation of existence. Gregory would not like to see the generation of the Son or the spiration of the Spirit understood in such terms, that is by way of a substantial growth. (Here we may perhaps observe some departure from the Athanasian idea of the 'fertile substance of God'.) He would insist, together with the rest of the Cappadocians, that the *cause* or *aition* of divine existence is the Father, which means a person, for this would make the Trinity a matter of ontological freedom. In fact, in one of his theological orations, Gregory takes up the defence of Nicaea against the Arian accusation that the *homoousios* implies necessity in God's being and develops it further than Athanasius — who in fact said very little on this matter — by stressing the role of the *Father* as the cause of divine being. Generation (and spiration) are not necessary but free because although there is one will 'con-

---

[7] E.g., Gregory Naz., *Or.* 29 (PG 36, 96): 'The Father is a name neither of substance nor of energy but of *schesis*'.

current' (as St Cyril of Alexandria would say)[8] with the divine substance, there is the 'willing one' (*ho thelon*)[9] and that is the Father. By
making the Father the only cause of divine existence, the Cappadocians aimed at understanding freedom in ontology, something that
Greek philosophy had never done before.

It is in the light of this observation that we can appreciate two
more points emerging from the study of the sources. The first is a
'detail' that we observe in the Creed of Nicaea-Constantinople, a
detail dismissed normally by historians of doctrine (e.g., Kelly)[10] as
insignificant. I am referring to the fact that the Council of Constantinople of 381 CE, operating clearly under Cappadocian influence
— Gregory of Nazianzus, then Archbishop of Constantinople, was
presiding over it for a time — took the bold step of altering the
Creed of Nicaea at the point where it referred to the Son as being
'from the substance of the Father' (*ek tes ousias tou patros*) and making
it simply read 'from the Father' (*ek tou patros*). This change, at a time
when fights took place over words, could not be accidental. It is a
clear expression of the Cappadocian interest in stressing that it is the
person of the Father and not divine substance that is the source and
cause of the Trinity.

The other point relates to the content that the term *monarchia*
finally received in the Greek Fathers. The one *arche* in God came to
be understood ontologically, that is, in terms of origination of being,
and was attached to the person of the Father. The 'one God' is the
Father,[11] and not the one substance, as Augustine and medieval Scholasticism would say. This puts the person of the Father in the place of
the one God, and suggests a kind of monotheism which is not only
biblical but also more akin to Trinitarian theology. If, therefore, we
wish to follow the Cappadocians in their understanding of the Trinity
in relation to monotheism, we must adopt an ontology which is based
on personhood, that is, on a unity or otherness emerging from relationships, and not one of substance, that is, of the self-existent and
in the final analysis individualistic being. The philosophical scandal

[8] Cyril Alex., *De Trin.* 2.
[9] Thus Gregory Naz., *Or. theol.* 3.5-7.
[10] Cf. J.N.D. Kelly, *Early Christian Creeds*, 1950, p. 333.
[11] See, e.g., Gregory Naz., *Or.* 42, 15. Cf. G.L. Prestige, *God in Patristic Thought*,
p. 254: '...their [the three Persons'] ground of unity (*henosis*) is the Father, out of
whom and towards whom are reckoned the subsequent Persons, not as to confuse
them but so as to attach them. The doctrine of monarchy had begun by basing the
unity of God on the single Person of the Father...'

of the Trinity can be resolved or accepted only if substance gives way to personhood as the causing principle or *arche* in ontology.

I have called the Cappadocians revolutionary thinkers in the history of philosophy. We may see this by a brief survey of ancient Greek thought in relation to that of the Cappadocians.

Ancient Greek thought in all its variations, ever since the pre-Socratic philosophers and up to and including Neoplatonism, tended to give priority to the 'one' over the 'many'. At the time of the Greek Fathers, this had taken several forms, some of them more theological and some more philosophical. On the theological level, the predominant pagan Greek philosophy at the time of the Cappadocian Fathers, namely Neoplatonism, had identified the 'One' with God himself, considering the multiplicity of beings, the 'many', to be emanations basically of a degrading nature, so that the return to the 'One' through the recollection of the soul was thought to be the purpose and aim of all existence. Earlier on in the first century, Philo, whose significance as the link between classical Platonism and Neoplatonism was decisive, had argued that God is the only true 'One' because he is the only one who is truly 'alone'. The doctrine of the holy Trinity as developed by the Cappadocians ran counter to this priority and exaltation of the 'One' over the 'Many' in philosophy.

With regard to human existence, too, classical Greek philosophy at that time had given priority to nature over particular persons. The views current at the time of the Cappadocian Fathers were either of a Platonic or of an Aristotelian kind. The first spoke of human nature as an ideal humanity, a *genos hyperkeimenon*, whose image every human being is, whereas the latter preferred to give priority to a substratum of the human species, a *genos hypokeimenon*, from which the various human beings emerge.[12] In both cases, man in his diversity and plurality of persons was subject to the necessity — or priority — of his nature. Nature or substance always preceded the person in classical Greek thought.

The Cappadocian Fathers challenged this established view of philosophy through their Trinitarian theology. They claimed that the priority of nature over the person, or of the 'one' over the 'many', is due to the fact that human existence is a *created* existence, that is, it is an existence with a beginning, and should not be made into a metaphysical principle. True being in its genuine metaphysical state,

---

[12] See Basil, *Ep.* 361 and 362. For a discussion of these letters and their philosophical significance, see above, Chapter 2.

which concerns philosophy *par excellence*, is to be found in God, whose uncreated existence does not involve the priority of the 'One' or of nature over the 'Many' or the persons. The way in which God exists involves simultaneously the 'One' and the 'Many', and this means that the person has to be given ontological primacy in philosophy.

To give ontological primacy to the person would mean to undo the fundamental principles with which Greek philosophy had operated since its inception. The particular person never had an ontological role in classical Greek thought. What mattered ultimately was the unity or totality of being of which man was but a portion. Plato, in addressing the particular being, makes it clear that 'the whole was not brought into being for thy sake, but thou art brought for its sake'. With a striking consistency, classical Greek tragedy invited man — and even the gods — to succumb to the order and justice that held the universe together, so that *kosmos* (meaning both natural order and proper behaviour) may prevail. Underneath the variety of beings, the 'many', there is the one Reason (*Logos*) that gives them their significance in existence. No digression from this one Reason can be allowed for the 'many' or for the particular beings without a disruption of being, even the very being of these particular beings.

The Trinitarian theology of the Cappadocian Fathers involved a philosophy in which the particular was not secondary to being or nature; it was thus *free* in an absolute sense. In classical thought, freedom was cherished as a quality of the individual but not in an ontological sense. The person was free to express his views but was obliged to succumb finally to the common Reason, the *xunos logos* of Heraclitus. Furthermore, the possibility that the person might pose the question of his freedom from *his very existence* was entirely inconceivable in ancient philosophy. It was, in fact, first raised in modern times by Dostoevsky and other modern existentialist philosophers. Freedom in antiquity always had a restricted moral sense, and did not involve the question of the *being* of the world, which was a 'given' and an external reality for the Greeks. On the contrary, for the Fathers, the world's being was due to the freedom of a person, God. *Freedom* is the 'cause' of being for patristic thought.[13]

Cappadocian theology stressed this principle of freedom as a presupposition of being by extending it to cover the being of God himself. This was a great innovation of the Cappadocian Fathers, even with regard to their Christian predecessors. The Cappadocian

[13] For further discussion, see my *Being as Communion*, especially ch. 1.

Fathers, for the first time in history, introduced into the being of God the concept of cause (*aition*), in order to attach it significantly not to the 'one' (God's nature) — but to a *person*, the Father. By distinguishing carefully and persistently between the nature of God and God as the Father they thought that *what causes God to be is the person of the Father*, not the one divine substance. By so doing, they gave to the person ontological priority, and thus freed existence from the logical necessity of substance, of the 'self-existent'. This was a revolutionary step in philosophy, the anthropological consequences of which must not pass unnoticed.

III. THE ANTHROPOLOGICAL CONSEQUENCES

Man, for the Fathers, is the 'image of God'. He is not God by nature, since he is *created*, that is, he has had a beginning, and thus is subject to the limitations of space and time which involve individuation and ultimately death. Nevertheless, he is called to exist in the way God exists.

In order to understand this, we must consider the distinction made by the Cappadocian Fathers between nature and person or 'mode of existence' (*tropos hyparxeos*), as they called it. Nature or substance points to the simple fact that something exists, to the *what* (*ti*) of something. It can be predicated of more than one thing. Person or *hypostasis*, on the other hand, points to *how* (*hopos* or *pos*) and can only be predicated of one being, and this in an absolute sense. When we consider human nature (or substance: *ousia*), we refer it to all human beings; there is nothing unique about having a human nature. Furthermore, all the 'natural' characteristics of human nature such as dividedness — and hence individuation leading to decomposition and finally death — are all aspects of human 'substance' and determine the human being as far as its nature is concerned. It is the *how* of human nature, that is, personhood, that by acquiring the role of ontological cause, as is the case with God's being, determines whether nature's limitations will finally be overcome or not. The 'image of God' in man has precisely to do with this *how*, not with the *what* man is; it relates not to nature — man can never become God by nature — but to personhood. This means that man is free to affect the *how* of his existence either in the direction of the way (the *how*) God is, or in the direction of *what* his, that is, man's, nature is. Living according to nature (*kata physin*) would thus amount to individualism, mortality, and so on, since man is not immortal *kata physin*. Living, on the other hand, according to the image of God means living in the way God exists, that is, as an image of God's personhood, and this would amount to 'becoming God'. This is what the *theosis* of man means in the thinking of the Greek Fathers.

It follows from this that although man's nature is ontologically prior to his personhood, as we have already noted, man is called to an effort to free himself from the necessity of his nature and behave in all respects as if the person were free from the laws of nature. In practical terms, this is what the Fathers saw in the *ascetic* effort which they regarded as essential to all human existence, regardless of whether one was a monk or lived in the world. Without an attempt to free the person from the necessity of nature one cannot be the 'image of God', since in God, as we have noted above, the person, and not nature, causes him to be the way he is.

The essence, therefore, of the anthropology which results from the Trinitarian theology of the Cappadocian Fathers lies in the significance of personhood in human existence. The Cappadocian Fathers gave to the world the most precious concept it possesses: *the concept of the person, as an ontological concept in the ultimate sense*. Since this concept has become, at least in principle, not only part of our Christian heritage but also an ideal of our culture in general, it may be useful to remind ourselves of its exact content and significance as it emerges from a study of the theology of the Cappadocians.

(a) As it emerges from the way personhood is understood by the Cappadocian Fathers with reference to God, the person is not a secondary but a primary and absolute notion in existence. Nothing is more sacred than the person since it constitutes the 'way of being' of God himself. The person cannot be sacrificed or subjected to any ideal, to any moral or natural order, or to any expediency or objective, even of the most sacred kind. In order to *be truly* and *be yourself*, you must be a person, that is, you must be free from and higher than any necessity or objective — natural, moral, religious or ideological. What gives meaning and value to existence is the person as absolute freedom.

(b) The person cannot exist in isolation. God is not alone; he is *communion*. Love is not a feeling, a sentiment springing from nature like a flower from a tree. Love is a *relationship*; it is the free coming out of one's self, the breaking of one's will, a *free* submission to the will of another. It is the other and our relationship with him that gives us our identity, our otherness, making us 'who we are', that is, persons; for by being an inseparable part of a relationship that matters onto-

logically we emerge as *unique* and *irreplaceable* entities. This, therefore, is what accounts for our being, and our being ourselves and not
someone else: our personhood. It is in this that the 'reason', the *logos*
of our being lies: in the relationship of love that makes us unique and
irreplaceable *for another*. The *logos* that accounts for God's being is
the uniquely beloved Son, and it is through this loving relationship
that God, too, or rather God *par excellence*, emerges as unique and
irreplaceable by being eternally the Father of a unique (*monogenes*)
Son. This is the great message of the patristic idea of the person.
The *raison d'être*, the *logos tou einai* of each one's being, for which the
Greek mind was always searching, is not to be found in the *nature*
of this being, but in the *person*, that is, in the identity created freely
by love and not by the necessity of its self-existence. As a person
you exist as long as you love and are loved. When you are treated as
nature, as a thing, you die as a particular identity. And if your soul is
immortal, what is the use? You will exist, but without a personal identity; you will be eternally dying in the hell of anonymity, in the Hades
of immortal souls. For nature in itself cannot give you existence and
being as an absolutely unique and particular identity. Nature always
points to the general; it is the person that safeguards uniqueness
and absolute particularity. The immortality, therefore, of one's soul,
even if it implies existence, cannot imply personal identity in the
true sense. Now that we know, thanks to the patristic theology of personhood, how God exists, we know what it means truly to exist as a
particular being. As images of God we are persons, not natures: there
can never be an image of the *nature* of God, nor would it be a welcome thing for humanity to be absorbed in divine nature. Only when
in this life we exist as persons can we hope to live eternally in the
true, personal sense. This means that exactly as is the case with God,
so with us, too: Personal identity can emerge only from love as freedom and from freedom as love.

(c) The person is something *unique* and *unrepeatable*. Nature and
species are perpetuated and replaceable. Individuals taken as nature
or species are never absolutely unique. They can be similar; they can
be composed and decomposed; they can be combined with others
in order to produce results or even new species; they can be used to
serve purposes — sacred or not, this does not matter. On the contrary, persons can neither be reproduced nor perpetuated like species; they cannot be composed or decomposed, combined or used
for any objective whatsoever — even the most sacred one. Whosoever
treats a person in such ways automatically turns him into a thing, he

dissolves and brings into non-existence his *personal particularity*. If one does not see one's fellow human being as the image of God *in this sense*, that is, as a person, then one cannot see this being as a truly eternal identity. For death dissolves us all into one indistinguishable nature, turning us into 'substance', or things. What gives us an identity that does not die is not our nature but our personal relationship with God's undying personal identity. Only when nature is hypostatic or personal, as is the case with God, does it exist truly and eternally. For it is only then that it acquires uniqueness and becomes an unrepeatable and irreplaceable particularity in the 'mode of being' which we find in the Trinity.

CONCLUSION

If we are allowed or even incited in our culture to think or hope for true personhood in human existence, we owe it above all to the Christian thought that Cappadocia produced in the fourth century. The Cappadocian Church Fathers developed and bequeathed to us a concept of God, who exists as a communion of free love of unique, irreplaceable and unrepeatable identities, that is, true persons in the absolute ontological sense. It is of such a God that man is meant to be an 'image'. There is no higher and fuller anthropology than this anthropology of true and full personhood.

Modern man tends on the whole to think highly of an anthropology of personhood, but the common and widespread assumptions as to what a person is are by no means consonant with what we have seen emerging from a study of the Cappadocian Fathers. Most of us today, when we say 'person' mean an *individual*. This goes back to St Augustine, and especially to Boethius in the fifth century CE, who defined the person as an individual nature endowed with rationality and consciousness. Throughout the entire history of Western thought the equation of person with the thinking, self-conscious individual has led to a culture in which the thinking individual has become the highest concept in anthropology. This is not what emerges from the thought of the Cappadocian Fathers. It is rather the opposite of this that results from a study of their thought. For according to it, true personhood arises not from one's individualistic isolation from others but from love and relationship with others, from communion. Only love, free love, unqualified by natural necessities, can generate personhood. This is true of God whose being, as the Cappadocian Fathers saw it, is constituted and 'hypostasized' through a free event of love caused by a free and loving person, the Father, and not by the necessity of divine nature. This is true also of man who is called to exercise his freedom as love and his love as freedom, and thus show himself to be the 'image of God'.

In our times, several attempts are being made by Western philosophers to correct the Western equation of the 'person' with the 'individual'.[14] Christianity's encounter with other religions, such as Buddhism, is forcing people to reconsider this traditional individualistic view of personhood. Today, then, is perhaps the most appropriate time to go back to a deeper study and appreciation of the fruits of Christian thought produced in Cappadocia in the fourth century, the most important of which is undoubtedly the idea of the person, as the Cappadocian Fathers saw and developed it.

This, therefore, is the existential — in the broader sense — significance of the Cappadocian contribution to Trinitarian theology: it makes us see in God a kind of existence we all want to lead; it is therefore basically a soteriological theology. But I think the Cappadocians also have something to say to some of today's issues concerning the doctrine of God. I refer particularly to the issues raised by feminist theology, especially concerning the use of names for God. The Cappadocians, in accordance with the apophatic tradition of the East, would say that all language concerning the substance of God and its qualities or energies is bound to be inadequate. Yet a distinction must be made between nature and person also at the level of human discourse. The names Father, Son and Spirit are indicative of *personal* identity. And since these are the *only* names that indicate personal identity they cannot be changed. Names indicating energies are changeable (e.g., God is good, or powerful), because they are drawn from our experience, which cannot adequately describe God. But what about Father, Son and Spirit — are they drawn from experience? Is there any analogy possible between God's Fatherhood and human fatherhood? There may be something of an analogy in what concerns moral qualities attached to Fatherhood (Creator, loving and caring person, etc.). But these are not *personal* properties — they apply to all three persons of the Trinity, that is, to the common substance or energy. Father, Son and Spirit are names of personal identity, names by which God in Christ reveals himself and names himself for us. This is the big difference between Trinitarian language and even the

---

[14] Thus, J. Macmurray, *The Self as Agent* (London: Faber & Faber, 1957), and *Persons in Relation* (London: Faber & Faber, 1961).

appellation 'God', which, in the sense of *divinitas*, is not a name of God. Only as person is he nameable. But his name is known and revealed to us only in Christ, which means only in and through the Father-Son relationship. He is therefore only known as Father.

The distinction between nature and person is, therefore, crucial also with regard to the issue of what is called 'comprehensive language'. Equally, it is crucial whether we identify the one God with the Father or with the one substance. For if he is Father only secondarily and not in his ultimate personal identity, Fatherhood is not the name *of* God but a name *about* God. In this case, it can be changed so as to convey better the message we wish to convey about God's being.

The Cappadocians have taught us that the Trinity is not a matter for academic speculation, but for personal relationship. As such, it is truth revealed only by participation in the Father-Son relationship through the Spirit which allows us to cry '*Abba*, Father' (Rom. 8.15; Gal. 4.6). The Trinity is therefore revealed only in the Church, that is, the community through which we become children of the Father of Jesus Christ. Outside this, it remains a stumbling block and a scandal.

APPENDIX:
Person and Individual — a 'Misreading' of the Cappadocians?

In this chapter, as indeed throughout my writings on personhood, I have insisted that the concept of person, if derived from a study of Greek patristic thought, and especially from Cappadocian Trinitarian theology, should not be understood as an 'individual' in the sense of an identity conceivable in itself, an 'axis of consciousness' and a concurrence of natural or moral qualities, or a number that can be subject to addition or combination. This is so because, according to the Greek Fathers, none of the above characteristics can be applied to the divine persons. For the persons of the Trinity, according to the above Fathers, are not 'individuals', either in the psychological sense of a centre of consciousness, or in that of a combination and concurrence of natural or moral qualities, or in the sense of a number that can be added or combined.

This view has recently been attributed to a 'misreading' of the Cappadocians and to the influence of modern existentialist philosophers.[15] To answer this criticism would appear to any student of theology as defending the obvious.[16] For what sort of being would God be if he possessed such a kind of personhood, defined as three individuals, three 'axes of consciousness', on which natural or moral qualities concur, and who can be regarded as numbers subject to addition and combination? He would be an anthropomorphic monstrosity, unworthy of the name of God, and, in the eyes of the Fathers, a sheer blasphemy. Nevertheless, a discussion of this matter appears to be necessary, because it raises some fundamental theological issues. These issues are related, on the one hand, to ways of reading the Fathers, and on the other hand, to the question of whether human or divine personhood should be the basis of the concept of the person in Christian personalism. This is the reason that compels me to comment on the above mentioned criticism.

---

[15] L. Turcescu, ' "Person" versus "Individual", and Other Modern Misreadings of Gregory of Nyssa', *Modern Theology* 18 (2002), pp. 527-39.

[16] For an excellent reply to this criticism, see A. Papanikolaou, 'Is John Zizioulas an Existentialist in Disguise? A Response to Lucian Turcescu', *Modern Theology* 20 (2004), pp. 601-607.

If we read the Cappadocian Fathers carefully, and especially Gregory of Nyssa, who is almost exclusively used as the ground of criticism, we notice that they are very conscious of the limitations and deficiencies of the analogy between human and divine being which they use, solely in a logical and not in a theological sense, in their theology. In his *Ex communibus notionibus*, Gregory of Nyssa is anxious to state that, in using the example of Peter, Paul, Barnabas, and so on, as three particular human beings or *hypostases* in order to illustrate the three persons of the holy Trinity, we do so 'by misuse of language' (καταχρηστικῶς) and not 'accurately' (κυρίως). Therefore, he adds, we must avoid applying to the Trinity things 'which are not to be seen in the Holy Trinity'. Such things, which account for the deficiencies of the analogy, and are 'causes' (αἰτίαι) of the deficiencies for Gregory, are the following:[17]

(a) *Human mortality involving separation* between human beings ('for in the place of those who have previously died, others are constituted in their stead').

(b) *The possibility of addition or subtraction* of human beings ('for this reason of addition [προσθήκης] and subtraction [ἀφαιρέσεως]').

(c) *The transience and change* of human persons (τῇ τροπῇ καί ἀλλοιώσει τῶν προσώπων).

(d) *The derivation of human persons from different personal causes* ('Human persons do not all derive their being immediately from the same person').

These factors apply purely to *human* personhood, and the Cappadocians deliberately avoided applying them to the divine persons. Thus, in speaking of the divine persons we must exclude:

(a) *Addition or diminution* (προσθήκης καί μειώσεως);
(b) *Alteration or change* (τροπῆς τε καί ἀλλοιώσεως);
(c) *More than one ontological cause* (the Father); and finally,
(d) *Any other properties or qualities except those of ontological relations* (μόνον ὅτι ὁ πατήρ, πατήρ ἐστι καί οὐχ υἱός, and so on; only that the Father is Father and not Son, etc.).

This last point is even more clearly stated in Gregory's letter to Ablabius, where he writes that '*the only* distinction between the other and the other' of divine persons is that of 'cause and being caused', which indicates 'the difference according to the *how* (God is)',[18] namely divine personhood.

---

[17] PG 45, 177-180; Jaeger's edition, III.1, p. 23f.
[18] *Ad Ablabium, Quod non sint...* (PG 45, 133; Jaeger, p. 56).

The conclusion, therefore, is clear: *divine persons*, in contrast with human ones, *cannot be regarded as a concurrence of natural or moral qualities of any kind*; they are distinguished only by their relations of onto-logical origination.[19] It is thus clear that the analogy between human and divine persons breaks down when we speak of persons as a col-lection of properties. In speaking of persons as the concurrence of natural or moral qualities (baldness, tallness, etc.), Gregory describes a *human* hypostasis. *No natural or moral quality* would be used by any of the Fathers to describe a *divine* person, simply because such qual-ities are common to all three divine persons and cannot be *personal* qualities.[20] All natural and moral qualities, such as energy, goodness, will (or consciousness in the modern sense), and so on, are qualities commonly possessed by the divine persons and they have nothing to do with the concept of divine personhood.[21] Therefore, the concept of personhood, *if it is viewed in the image of divine personhood*, is, as I have insisted in my writings, *not* a 'collection of properties' of either a natural or a moral kind. It is only a 'mode of being' comprising rela-tions (σχέσις) of ontological constitutiveness.[22]

We can now consider the question of the enumeration of persons. There is no doubt that the Cappadocians apply numbering to indi-cate divine personhood. Yet again they do so reluctantly and with full consciousness of the deficiency of the use of such a language. In one of the letters under the name of St Basil, attributed now to Eva-grius, numbering is excluded categorically from divine being.[23] But human language has no other means to indicate otherness except by

---

[19] Cf. G. Prestige, *God in Patristic Thought*, 1959, p. 228.

[20] Prestige, *God in Patristic Thought*, p. 244: 'the differences that distinguish dif-ferent human beings are *manifold*, but the differences that distinguish the divine persons consist *simply in the "idiotetes" expressed in the names of Fatherhood, Sonship and Sanctification*' (my italics). This, Prestige stresses, 'needs to be remembered' — indeed, I would add, for it rules out any idea of a 'collection of properties' in divine personhood. It would, of course, be nonsense to describe the above hypostatic 'idio-tetes' as a concurrence of qualities, let alone qualities of a natural or moral kind, as there is no 'concurrence' and there are no qualities of any kind to 'concur'. It is surprising that my critic should appear to ignore this and define person as 'concur-rence of qualities'.

[21] Prestige, *God in Patristic Thought*, p. xxxii: the three persons are not to be regarded as three independent 'consciousnesses'.

[22] Gregory of Nazianzus and Amphilochius are explicit on this; see below, n. 33. As Ps.Cyril puts it, 'ἀγεννησία and γέννησις and ἐκπόρευσις: in those hypostatic partic-ularities alone do the three holy hypostases differ from one another' (*De s. Trin.* 9; PG 77, 1140D).

[23] Basil, *Ep.* 8.

numbering the particular beings. Persons, therefore, cannot but be numbered — I have never denied that. What I have denied is that persons can be numbered in such a way as to involve *addition* and *combination*.²⁴ And it is precisely this that the Cappadocians exclude in the use of the category of number. We have already noted that Gregory of Nyssa excludes the idea of addition or subtraction from the divine being, while allowing it in the case of human beings. Basil is equally explicit: we must apply the notion of number to the Trinity 'reverently' (εὐσεβῶς), and this means that *we cannot number the persons by addition*.²⁵ This is precisely what I have been saying throughout. Numbering persons in the sense of adding or combining them with each other would be absolutely inadmissible with regard to the divine persons, not only for the Cappadocians but for the entire Greek patristic tradition. As John of Damascus²⁶ summarizes this tradition: 'In their mutual relations (ἐν ἀλλήλαις) the hypostases exist not so that they might be confused, but as they carry each other or relate to each other (ἔχεσθαι)²⁷…not composed (or added together: συντιθεμένων)²⁸… For they are united in a way not of confusion but of mutual relation (ἔχεσθαι ἀλλήλων); and they have their *perichoresis* in each other without coalescing (συναλοιφήν) or admixture (σύμφυρσιν)'. As Athanasius had already underlined, any idea of addition applied to the divine persons would be extremely dangerous, for it would amount to Arianism.²⁹

We may now consider the other topic in dispute, namely the use of the term ἄτομον interchangeably with that of πρόσωπον and ὑπόστασις by the Cappadocians — in fact, notably, by Gregory of Nyssa alone.³⁰ Does this mean that my distinction between person and individual stands in contrast or in disagreement with the theology of the Cappadocians? Hardly! For one thing, the term ἄτομον, as used by the Greek Fathers, does not fully coincide with the term individual, by

²⁴ See my *Being as Communion*, p. 47: the person cannot be regarded as an 'arithmetical concept', precisely in the sense that it cannot be 'set alongside other beings' (= added), or be 'combined with other objects'.
²⁵ Basil, *De Sp. S.* 44-45: 'we do not number (the divine persons) by addition (or composition: κατὰ σύνθεσιν)'.
²⁶ John of Damascus, *De fid. orth.* 1.14 (PG 94, 829A).
²⁷ On ἔχεσθαι as meaning 'relating to', see Plato, *Laws* 661B. The verb is loaded with meaning in the text of John of Damascus.
²⁸ συντιθεμένων literally means what I called above (in n. 24) being 'set alongside other things' and added together.
²⁹ Athanasius, *C. Ar.* 1.17 (PG 26, 48A); 1.40 (PG 26, 96A).
³⁰ Gregory Nys., *Ex com. not.* (PG 45, 177).

which for the purposes of criticism it is inaccurately rendered, and from which I distinguish the idea of person. A careful reading of Gregory of Nyssa shows that his use of ἄτομον in relation to πρόσωπον covers only one aspect of personhood, namely the idea of concrete, specific (ἰδική) and indivisible existence of *ousia*: 'for it is the same thing to apply to *prosopon* the (notion) of specific *ousia* as it is to apply it to *atomon*' (ταὐτόν γάρ ἐστιν ἰδική οὐσία τῷ προσώπῳ ἐπί τῶν ἀτόμων λεγομένη).[31] If this aspect of indivisible concreteness which ἄτομον denotes in the case of human beings were to be transferred and applied to divine personhood in an unqualified way, as meaning person *tout court*, we would end up with three Gods. We are back again to the same problem: would we be faithful to Cappadocian theology if we were to transfer what the Cappadocian Fathers say about human persons to divine personhood?

It is a striking fact, which any reading of the Fathers should take into account, that the term ἄτομον never found its way into the official dogmatic vocabulary with regard to the holy Trinity.[32] Is this an accident? If πρόσωπον and ὑπόστασις were identical with ἄτομον in patristic thought, why do we never encounter the dogmatic formula 'one *ousia*, three *atoma*', but only 'one *ousia*, three *prosopa* or *hypostaseis*', with reference to God? Obviously because this equation of πρόσωπον with ἄτομον, made by Gregory of Nyssa, was not meant to be applied to divine personhood; Gregory himself limits its application to human beings.

While this is true of the term ἄτομον, it is not so with regard to other terms used by the Cappadocian Fathers to explain person and hypostasis when applied to God. Terms used repeatedly by them and by other Greek Fathers following them include τρόπος ὑπάρξεως and σχέσις. This should be emphasized. The Cappadocians, and especially Gregory of Nazianzus and Amphilochius, who cannot be accused of 'misreading' or contradicting Gregory of Nyssa, use these particular terms without any hesitation, but not ἄτομον, to define the divine persons: the names Father, Son and Holy Spirit indicate 'a mode of existence, *that is* (ἤτουν) of relation'.[33] The term ἄτομον is

---

[31] Gregory Nys., *Ex com. not.* (PG 45, 177).

[32] This resistance is noteworthy, as it renders meaningless the only two pieces of evidence to the contrary, found in Leontius of Byzantium (PG 86, 1305C) and Ps.Cyril (PG 77, 1149B).

[33] Amphilochius, *Fragm.* 15 (PG 39, 112). See also Gregory Naz., *Or.* 29 (PG 36, 96): 'The Father is a name neither of *ousia* nor of *energeia* but of *schesis*'. Gregory of Nyssa himself, in summing up his argument in *Ex com. not.* (PG 45, 185), avoids

avoided precisely because it does not carry with it the dimension of relation, which the term πρόσωπον does carry. This is the explanation implied by John of Damascus in his reference to the distinction between πρόσωπον and ὑπόστασις: 'they often distinguish πρόσωπον from ὑπόστασις by calling πρόσωπον *the relation of entities* (τινῶν) *with one another*'.[34] The only terms, therefore, that can be employed to indicate divine personhood are those of 'person' and 'hypostasis' because they convey the sense of *ontological relationship* or *relational ontology* which the word ἄτομον does not carry. Is this not enough to justify, if not necessitate, the definition of personhood as it appears *in the light of divine personhood*, as a *relational category*, which *differs from the notion of 'individual'*? Is this not the reason why we never encounter in the established theological tradition the expression, 'God, one *ousia*, three *atoma*', and therefore we cannot say that the persons of the Trinity are three 'individuals'?

This leads us to the real issue behind this discussion. Dispute about words contributes only to philology and history. Theology is about fundamental matters of faith. What appears to be the fundamental question behind this discussion — and this is the only reason why I enter into it — is the following: *are we as theologians to draw our concept of human personhood from the study of the human person or from God?* If we draw it from the observation of humanity, we shall inevitably arrive at an identification of personhood with individuality, collection of qualities, centre of consciousness, and all the rest, as my critic thinks the Cappadocians do. If, on the other hand, we derive personhood from the holy Trinity, the result will be different. For divine personhood, being defined *solely* and *exclusively* in terms of a *relational 'mode of being'*, admits of no individualism in the sense of an entity conceivable in itself, subject to addition and combination, a centre of consciousness and a concurrence of natural and moral properties. Such characteristics of personhood, when used by the Cappadocians, in the context of a *logical* not a *theological* analogy, refer strictly to human personhood and are not transferred by them to the divine persons. Any application of such characteristics to divine personhood would not simply be a gross misunderstanding of Cappadocian thought. Ironically enough, it would also amount to a real — not imaginative — submission of patristic thought to modern existen-

using ἄτομον in referring to the Trinity: 'Therefore, we speak of one God, the creator of all, though he is seen in three *prosopa*, that is *hypostaseis*, of Father, Son and Holy Spirit'.

[34] John of Damascus, *Haer.* 7 (PG 94, 749C).

tialist philosophy. For it is precisely modern existentialist personalism that refuses to do what I have been trying to do throughout my writings, namely to work out a concept of the person that would be a reflection of *divine*, not human, personhood.

In conclusion, there is no 'misreading' whatsoever of the Cappadocians in saying, as I do, that the person, viewed in the light of the Trinity, is *not* an 'individual', in the sense of an identity which is conceivable apart from its relations; or an 'axis of consciousness'; or a concurrence of qualities, natural or moral; or a number that can be subject to addition or combination. There is, on the contrary, a gross misunderstanding of patristic thought in transferring to the Trinity the analogies from human personhood, which the Cappadocian Fathers use in full awareness of the deficiencies of these analogies and by 'misuse of language', as they themselves admit. To take these deficiencies and use them as points of criticism, for not applying them to my idea of personhood, is more than bad criticism, it is a bad reading of the Fathers.

As to the influence of modern existentialist philosophy on my concept of the person, such criticism entirely misses the point on which patristic theology and modern existentialist philosophy fundamentally differ. For *not a single one* of these philosophers would draw his personalism from a source other than a study of the human being. This is exactly what I consistently refuse to do. And this is what I am accused of not doing, because of a 'misreading' of the Cappadocians!

Both the Cappadocians, read correctly, and I myself stress that, in spite of any 'deficient' analogies between human and divine persons, true personhood is *only* what we observe in the Trinity, not in humanity, and this *excludes* individualism, conscious subjectivity, concurrence of natural or moral qualities, addition, combination, and so on. If modern existentialist thought also happens to reject some of these elements in its personalism, *starting as it does from observation of the aspirations and tragic failures of human personhood*, this is not an indication of its *influence* on those who, like the Cappadocians and myself, draw their personalism from the Trinity. To be in dialogue with modern philosophy and discover points of convergence, as well as fundamental difference, can be construed as 'influence' only by a superficial observer.[35]

---

[35] Cf. above, Chapter 3, p. 141. For a further discussion of the subject, see A. Papanikolaou, 'Is John Zizioulas an Existentialist in Disguise?', p. 604f. I have dealt with this matter more extensively in my article, 'The Being of God and the Being of Anthropos', *Synaxi* 37 (1991), pp. 11-35 (in Greek).

Chapter 5

PNEUMATOLOGY AND THE IMPORTANCE OF THE PERSON:
A Commentary on the Second Ecumenical Council

INTRODUCTION

The subject of this chapter is a vast one, to which scholarship has already paid so much attention as to make any new effort dealing with it repetitious, if not entirely unnecessary. My object in this chapter is to offer neither a scholarly contribution to the history of dogma nor a lecture of the kind offered to students in universities. While care will be taken to use the findings of scholarship as much as possible on this subject, my main purpose will remain that of offering an *interpretation* of the theology of the Holy Spirit professed by the Council of Constantinople (381), bearing in mind particularly our present ecumenical situation, its problems and its aspirations. This chapter, therefore, is basically systematic in nature and will concentrate on the *issues* lying behind the historical developments.

But in order to arrive at the selection of the basic issues involved in the teaching of Constantinople on the Holy Spirit, it is necessary to dig deep into the historical background of the Council. Constantinople is extremely brief in stating its faith in the Holy Spirit. Although amplifying the Creed of Nicaea considerably on this matter, it does not, as is to be expected of all credal formulations, itself offer a theology in the proper sense. This makes it inevitable that we seek illumination from sources outside the Council itself in order to focus on the issues with which it was preoccupied. These sources for our present purpose will be approached with the following questions in mind:

(a) What *issues* had emerged as *crucial* between 325 and 381 CE, which are reflected as basic concerns for the Fathers of Constantinople? I have underlined the words 'issues' and 'crucial' in order to indicate that we are going to be selective in our treatment of the vast historical material. Many problems will have to be left out as irrelevant for our purpose, not however on the basis of an arbitrary judgement, but after careful examination of the question: *what really mattered* to the Council on our subject?

(b) What *conceptual tools* or *theological ideas* emerged between Nicaea and Constantinople, which the Fathers of 381 CE were able to use in formulating their pneumatology? The struggles that marked so vividly the life of the Church after Nicaea were not without their creative results. The post-Nicaean generation which produced such creative minds as the Cappadocian Fathers, contributed new ideas to theology as well as to *philosophy* without which we cannot properly understand the pneumatology of the Second Ecumenical Council. Few periods in history have been as creative as that between 325 and 381 CE. The pneumatology of Constantinople cannot be accurately interpreted without reference to these ideas.

Finally, our interpretation of the doctrine of Constantinople will have to be related to our ecumenical situation today. What can we learn from the Second Ecumenical Council for our own faith in the Holy Spirit? How many of the concerns of the Fathers of 381 CE remain relevant for us today? How much of their doctrine constitutes our common ground and how much do we still have to strive to understand and profess in common? Pneumatology has been a divisive factor for many centuries, especially between East and West. The polemical atmosphere that had prevailed for long periods had tended to exaggerate the differences on many points, while the irenic tendencies of later periods have not helped much to clarify what is essential and what is simply 'theologoumenon' in this doctrine. We now live at the crucial point in history when all sides in the pneumatological debate seem to be willing to listen to each other with the greatest of good will and desire for unity. The study of the pneumatology of the Council must be directed towards deepening our faithfulness to Tradition in such a way as to grasp not its words but its deeper meaning and its existential concerns. This chapter is written as part of such an attempt towards a *re-reception* of the Second Ecumenical Council in a way that would imply faithfulness to the past without an enslavement to its mere formulations and wordings.

I. From Nicaea to Constantinople: The Crucial Issues and the
New Theological Ideas

1. *The Establishment of the Dialectic between 'Created' and 'Uncreated'*

Arianism did not appear as a storm out of the blue. It was connected with an issue that became crucial once the Church tried to
relate the Gospel to the educated and philosophically inclined Greeks
of late Antiquity. This issue can be summed up in the question of
the relationship between God and the world. To what extent is this
relationship a dialectical one? For the ancient Greeks, the world and
God were related to each other with some kind of ontological affinity (*syggeneia*). This affinity was expressed either through the mind
(*Nous*), which is common between God — the '*Nous*' *par excellence* —
and man, or through the Reason (*Logos*), which came to be understood, especially by Stoicism, as the link, at once cosmic and divine,
that unites God and the world.[1] Attempts, like that of Justin, to identify Christ, the Logos of the Fourth Gospel, with this Logos of the
Greeks concealed a problem which remained unnoticed as long as the
issue of the relation between God and the world was not raised in the
form of a dialectical relationship.[2] For many generations after Justin
the Logos (Christ) could be thought of as a projection (προβολή) of
God *always* somehow connected with the existence of the world.[3] Origen's attempt to push the existence of the Logos back to the being
of God himself did not help very much to clarify the issue,[4] since

---

[1] In spite of the complexity that this subject presents, it can be established that
classical Greek thought never departed essentially from the early Pre-socratic tendency to unite *being* and *thinking* (εἶναι and νοεῖν) in such a way as to form a *unity*.
See, e.g., Parmenides, *Fragm.* 5d,7; cf. Plato, *Parmen.* 128b. This basic ontological monism (in spite of any elements of 'transcendence' that may be found in the
ἐπέκεινα τῆς οὐσίας idea of the Platonic Good, or in the Aristotelian Θεὸς-νοῦς), persists in Greek philosophy well into the time of Neoplatonism, for which the One,
the Nous and Being form an unbreakable unity. See, e.g., Plotinus, *Enn.* V.1.8. On
this survival of the original Greek monism, cf. C.J. de Vogel, *Philosophia I. Studies in
Greek Philosophy* (Philosophical Texts and Studies 19,1), 1970, pp. 397-416.

[2] That Justin did not help to clarify this problem is evident not only from his well-
known idea of the λόγος σπερματικὸς, but mainly from his belief that between God
and Man there is an affinity (συγγένεια) through the νοῦς which allows man to 'contemplate' (καθορᾶν) that being which is the cause of all intelligent beings (νοητῶν).
See *Dial.* 3-4 (PG 6, 481D-484B).

[3] See the problem as discussed by J. Daniélou, *Message évangélique et Culture hellénistique*, 1956, pp. 317ff.

[4] The ambiguity is especially evident in passages such as Origen, *In Jo.* II.2 (PG
14, 108-109): 'it must be said...that God (the Father) is God in Himself (αὐτοθεὸς)...

he admitted a kind of eternal creation, thus giving rise to the question whether the Logos was not in fact to be understood in terms of an eternity related to this eternal existence of the world.[5] This is why both the Arians, who wanted the Logos to be related to creation rather than to God's being, and their opponents could draw inspiration and arguments from Origen himself.

Thus Arianism highlighted the philosophical issue of the ontological relation between God and the world, by forcing the Church to become more conscious than ever before that there is no ontological *syggeneia* between God and the world, between created and uncreated, and that there is no way of compromising between these two. No being can be both created and uncreated; the Logos is either created or uncreated; to mix up creature and creator is to commit the most unacceptable theological as well as logical mistake.[6] Both the Arians and the Nicaeans seem to have reached a silent agreement on this methodological principle to such an extent that it was regarded as sufficient to prove that Christ was God if it was shown that he could not be a creature — and vice versa.

It is well known how Nicaea and Athanasius himself tried to express this dialectic between created and uncreated. The employment of the language of *substance* (*ousia, physis*) was intended precisely to express this. The world owes its existence to the *will* (βούλησις) of God, not to his substance. The Logos owes his existence to the *substance* of God; he is *homoousios* with him — hence not a creature.[7] Substance was the highest ontological category to indicate that something *is* and at the same time is *itself*, and not something else.[8] Its employment by Athanasius and Nicaea was not intended to create a speculative or metaphysical theology, as some historians seem to think, but to express

and that all that exists outside Him who is God in Himself, being divinized by participation, should not be properly called ὁ Θεὸς but Θεὸς. This name applies fully to the first born of all creation, as the first one to be with God (πρὸς τὸν Θεόν)... The others are 'θεοί' formed in the image of him as images (εἰκόνες) of the prototype. But again, among these many images the archetypal image is the Logos who is with (πρός) God...'

[5] Cf. the discussion of this matter in G. Florovsky, 'The Concept of Creation in St Athanasius', in *Studia Patristica* IV (ed. F.L. Cross), 1962, pp. 36-57.

[6] This is the argument used repeatedly by St Athanasius in his *Letters to Serapion* (e.g., I.20-22f.), as well as by St Basil in his work of the Holy Spirit.

[7] E.g., Athanasius, *C. Ar.* II.2; 20 (PG 26, 149f.; 188C-189B), etc.

[8] On the notion of 'Substance', see especially C. Stead, *Divine Substance*, 1977. Cf. the important discussion of this subject by D.M. Mackinnon, 'Substance in Christology: A Cross-bench View', in S.W. Sykes and J.P. Clayton (eds.), *Christ, Faith and History* (Cambridge Studies in Christology, 1972), pp. 279-300.

the *utter* dialectic between God and the world. The *homoousios* is to be understood not so much as a positive statement, telling us something about God's being, but rather as a negative one, indicating what the Logos is *not*, namely a creature. When substantialist language is taken out of the created-uncreated dialectic and is turned into a ground of divine metaphysics, it is taken away from its original context. This, as we shall see, relates directly to the doctrine of the Spirit.

2. *The Questioning of Substantialist Language and the Emergence of the Notion of Person*

The *homoousios*, by becoming part of the Nicaean decision, acquired sanctity for those who accepted Nicaea, while constituting the stumbling block of all attempts at unity and the cause of continuous divisions. This, we must emphasize, was not because this term was used as a way of describing God's being as such, that is, as a way of professing a divine metaphysic. Neither in Athanasius nor in any of the Fathers of that century is there any indication that *ousia* was used for any other purpose than to indicate simply that the Son is God (and not a creature) — not *how* he is so, or what this means for God's being as such (e.g., its unity, etc.). The use of substance for such purposes is a later phenomenon and does not apply to the period we are examining here.

This observation is important in order to understand the reluctance of theologians like St Basil to employ the *homoousios* for the Holy Spirit, a reluctance that becomes a notable and open refusal to do so by the Fathers of Constantinople.[9] Since this is immediately related to the pneumatology of the Second Ecumenical Council, we cannot avoid asking the question: *why* this reluctance on the part of Basil, and this notorious omission on the part of the Council? The question, as we shall see, is not merely of interest to the historians.

---

[9] It is extremely significant that the Fathers of Constantinople not only avoided the use of *homoousios* for the Holy Spirit, but also, while keeping it with regard to the Son — probably because of the authority it had acquired particularly through St Athanasius — they quite consciously omitted from the Creed the phrase of Nicaea, τοὐτέστιν ἐκ τῆς οὐσίας τοῦ πατρός, making it simply to read that the Son was ἐκ τοῦ πατρός γεννηθέντα πρό πάντων τῶν αἰώνων. The omission is certainly revealing: substantialist language in theology was being gradually replaced by that of the person, undoubtedly under the influence of the Cappadocians, and this for reasons which, as we shall see immediately, were far more than merely tactical. As to the reluctance of St Basil to use the *homoousios* for the Spirit, this was already noted and criticized by his contemporaries. See Gregory Naz., *Ep.* 58 (PG 37, 113C-116B) and *Or.* 43.69 (PG 36, 589BC).

Students of St Basil's pneumatology have tried to explain this attitude by pointing mainly to *tactical* reasons:[10] Basil did believe in the *homoousios* of the Spirit, but wanted to win over to Orthodoxy those who found this language difficult to use. This explanation is certainly valid and, as we shall see later, it can teach us very much, even today. But it is not sufficient to do justice either to Basil or to the Council of Constantinople. For it would be unworthy of the theological seriousness which marked the Fathers of that time to reduce this attitude to mere diplomacy. Thus, I should like to point to two facts which go beyond the mere tactical concern and which reveal deeper theological developments that took place between Nicaea and Constantinople.

In the first place, Basil's attitude is not simply one of saying: it is not necessary to use the *homoousios* for the Spirit. He says something more positive than this: *if one professes that the Spirit is not a creature, then one does not have to profess the 'homoousios' of the Spirit.*[11] This proves the point I made earlier, namely that the real — and perhaps the only — issue behind the use of the notion of substance in theology was to safeguard what we have called here the dialectic between created and uncreated.[12] Once you accept this, the question remains whether the Holy Spirit is to be placed on the level of creation or of the uncreated, and this would suffice. The term *homoousios*, sacred

[10] The theory that Basil's silence on the consubstantiality of the Spirit should be attributed to the distinction he makes between δόγμα and κήρυγμα, the latter being public whereas the former is not, was introduced by C.F.H. Johnston, *The Book of St Basil the Great...on the Holy Spirit*, 1892, pp. 127-28, and developed further by H. Dörries, *De Spiritu Sancto. Der Beitrag des Basilius zum Abschluss des trinitarischen Dogmas*, 1956, pp. 121-28 and 181-83. For the theory that this attitude of St Basil is to be attributed to reasons of 'pastoral economy', see B. Pruche, *Basile de Césarée: Sur le Saint-Esprit* (Sources chrétiennes, 17 bis), 1968, pp. 94-110.

[11] See Basil, *Ep.* 113 and 114 (PG 32, 525B-529B). One must accept the faith of Nicaea in order to be in communion; in addition to this, one thing more is necessary: to profess 'that the Spirit is not a creature'. See also, *Ep.* 140 (PG 32, 585C-589A).

[12] It is interesting, for example, how St Gregory of Nyssa paraphrases the *homoousion* in contrasting substance with person in the Trinity: The Holy Spirit is '*in his nature uncreated in unity with the Father and the Son* and, on the other hand, is distinguished from them by his own proper characteristics (γνωρίσμασι)... One with the Father *in that he is uncreated*, he is distinct from him in that he is not Father; one with the Son *because both are uncreated* and deriving their substance from God, etc.' (*C. Eunom.* I.22; PG 45, 355f.). Thus, for Gregory, divine substance indicates the unity of the three persons of the Trinity *not as such but in so far as it points to the dialectic between created and uncreated reality.* Speculation about divine substance *per se* is not only absent but impermissible in Greek patristic thought.

as it is because of its use by Nicaea, becomes unnecessary. Basil, and for that matter the Fathers of the Second Ecumenical Council, were brave enough not to use this sacred term for the sake of the peace and unity of the Church, and creative enough to single out and support the dogmatic *raison d'être* of the *homoousios*, that is the faith that the created and the uncreated cannot be mixed up and that the Spirit belongs to the realm of the uncreated.

Secondly, there is more to be said concerning St Basil's silence on the *homoousion* of the Spirit. If we read carefully his *De Spiritu Sancto* and his *Letters*, we get the impression that Basil prefers to speak of the unity of God's being in terms other than that of substance. One could even risk saying that Basil does not particularly like this terminology, and prefers to use *koinonia* wherever reference is made to the oneness of the divinity.[13] There is a profound reason for this.

Basil, as we know, was one of those Easterners who were anxious to stress and safeguard the distinct and ontologically integral existence of each of the persons of the holy Trinity. The fear of Sabellianism (which destroyed this ontological integrity) was for him as deeply-seated as for many of his contemporaries in the East.[14] The *homoousios* was of little help to dispel such fears, for it could itself be subject to Sabellian interpretations. Basil must have seen that the best way to speak of the unity of the Godhead was through the notion of *koinonia* rather than that of substance. His reluctance to use the *homoousios* for the Spirit cannot be entirely dissociated from all this.[15]

---

[13] See, for example, *De Sp. S.* 18 (PG 32, 194C): 'the unity (of God) is in the Κοινωνία τῆς Θεότητος'; cf. 153A, 156A. A careful study of Basil shows that for him the meaning of ὁμοούσιος can be rendered by expressions such as 'οἰκεία καί συμφυής καί ἀχώριστος κοινωνία' or 'Κοινωνία κατά φύσιν', etc., in other words, by the use of κοινωνία. See, *De Sp. S.* 63 (Sources chrétiennes, 17 bis, 1968, p. 474); *C. Eun.* II.12 (PG 29, 593C); etc. Cf. on this A. Jevtich, 'Between the "Nicaeans" and the "Easterners". The "Catholic" Confession of St Basil', *St Vladimir's Theological Quarterly* 24 (1980), p. 244. The term, κοινωνία, unlike that of οὐσία, lends itself to a wider use which would include the *community of glorification and honour*, which is so important to Basil, as well as the *distinctiveness of the hypostases*, which is, again, fundamental to his particular theological position. The latter is especially evident in *Ep.* 38, where the author constantly qualifies the terms οὐσία or φύσις with words such as τό κοινόν, ἡ κοινότης, ἡ κοινωνία.

[14] Basil complains for the same reason that the Westerners remained insensitive to the Sabellian danger implied in the theology of Marcellus of Ancyra (*Ep.* 69). The same problem was already evident in the third century in the 'controversy' between Dionysius of Rome and Dionysius of Alexandria. The traditional (since Origen) Alexandrian use of 'three hypostases' was always directed in the East against Sabellian tendencies, a fact that was not fully appreciated in the West.

[15] The Synodical Letter of Alexandria (362 CE) lies in the background of subse-

This leads us to the next important point which has to do with the emergence of new theological tools and concepts between 325 and 381 CE. Basil, and the Cappadocian Fathers in general, are known in history for their contribution to the notion of the *person*. This contribution, however, is not sufficiently appreciated and needs to be discussed here, as it affects the pneumatology of Constantinople in a decisive way. With regard to this subject, two points appear to me to be of fundamental significance:

(a) For the first time in the history of philosophy, particularly of Greek thought, we have an identification of an ontological category, such as *hypostasis*, with a notion, such as person. In classical antiquity, both Greek and Roman, these terms always remained clearly separate and distinct. *Hypostasis* was identical with substance or *ousia*[16] and indicated that something *is*, and that it is *itself*, while *prosopon* indicated, in a variety of nuances and forms, the way something relates to other beings.[17] By calling the person a 'mode of being' (*tropos hyparx-*

---

quent developments. This letter, amending as it were the anathematization by Nicaea of all those who profess that the Son is 'of another *hypostasis* or *ousia*' from that of the Father, allowed for the use of the expression 'three hypostases' on condition that this does not imply separation between these hypostases. This resulted in two things: (a) it made it orthodox to speak of 'three hypostases', and (b) it called for the need of a theology which would explain how the expression 'three hypostases' does not imply division but safeguards the unity of God's being. It was the merit of the Cappadocians to respond to this challenge of their time.

[16] This was the case even at the time of St Athanasius, who clearly identifies ὑπόστασις with οὐσία. See his *Ep. ad episc.* (PG 26, 1036B). Cf. the Synodical Letter of Antioch (325 CE), as edited by Ed. Schwartz and translated into English by J.N.D. Kelly, *Early Christian Creeds*, 1972³, p. 209f. On the basis of this identification between οὐσία and ὑπόστασις it was even possible to speak of three οὐσίαι in God. E.g., Basil the Great, *Homily* (23) *on St Mamas* 4 (PG 31, 597C).

[17] The history of the term πρόσωπον is long and complex. Originally, it must have had simply the anatomical meaning of the part of the face which is between or towards the eyes (πρός + ὤψ). Cf. Homer, *Iliad* Σ 24, H 212; Aristotle, *Hist. Anim.* 1.8.491b. It was then associated with the theatre where it signified the role played by the actors and the mask they wore. Cf. Aristotle, *Probl.* 31.7.958a; Lucian, *De Calumn.* 6, etc. Thus it lent itself to a purely relational connotation: the role played on the stage and that played in real life. The meaning of the concrete individual was given to πρόσωπον much later (according to S. Schlossmann, *Persona und πρόσωπον im Recht und im christlichen Dogma*, 1906, pp. 41-42: not until the fifth century CE). Equally, *persona* in Latin seems to have originated from theatrical life and passed into everyday life — more rapidly than the Greek equivalent — where it occasionally meant the concrete individual but more often the role (social, etc.) played in life and, later, technically in legal life. See on this the detailed study of M. Nedoncelle, 'Prosopon et Persona dans l'antiquité classique', *Revue des sciences religieuses* 22 (1948), pp. 277-99. In general, it is clear that these two terms were not

eos), the Cappadocians introduced a revolution into Greek ontology, since they said for the first time in history, (i) that a *prosopon* is not secondary to being, but its *hypostasis*; and (ii) that a *hypostasis*, that is, an ontological category, is relational in its very nature, it is *prosopon*.[18] The importance of this lies in the fact that person is now the *ultimate* ontological category we can apply to God. Substance is not something ontologically prior to person (no classical Greek would say this), but its real existence is to be found in the person.[19]

(b) On the basis of this, the Cappadocians went on to develop another philosophical and theological position, for which some theologians of our time accuse them of having deviated from earlier tradition.[20] Since the person in its identification with hypostasis is an ultimate — and not a secondary — ontological notion, it must be *a person* — and not a substance — that is the source of divine existence. Thus, the notion of 'source' is complemented by the Cappadocians with the notion of 'cause' (*aitia*), and the idea emerges that the cause of God's being is the Father. The introduction of 'cause' in addition to 'source' was meant to indicate that divine existence does not 'spring', so to speak, 'naturally' as from an impersonal substance,

understood in an ontological way (like that of 'hypostasis') until the time of the Cappadocians. See the following note.

[18] As a proof that at the time of Basil πρόσωπον was not ontological enough to protect doctrine from the danger of Sabellianism, and that ὑπόστασις was needed *precisely in order to add to the relational character of πρόσωπον an ontological content*, the following passage of Basil is strikingly clear and revealing: 'Those who say that οὐσία and ὑπόστασις are the same are compelled to confess only different πρόσωπα and, by avoiding the use of the words τρεῖς ὑποστάσεις, they do not succeed in escaping the Sabellian evil' (*Ep.* 236.6). This constitutes important evidence for the historian of dogma, showing (a) that with Basil *something radically new* happens with regard to terminology, since even as recently as St Athanasius no need was felt for such clarifications (see above, n. 16); and (b) that the novelty in this development consists in *the introduction of ontological content into the notion of person*. The profound philosophical and existential implications of this fact are normally unnoticed by historians of philosophy.

[19] For a fuller discussion of the philosophical and existential implications of this, see my *Being as Communion*, 1985, esp. pp. 36-41.

[20] See, for example, E.P. Meijering, *God Being History: Studies in Patristic Philosophy*, 1975, pp. 103-27. The view expressed there (cf. A. Harnack's thesis), that there is an affinity between the Neoplatonic and the Cappadocian notion of αἰτία, is another example of how difficult it has been in modern theology to appreciate the Cappadocian idea of the person. For there is nothing more incompatible than the impersonal One of Plotinus and the Father on whose *personal* character the Cappadocians insist, precisely by making him the free αἴτιον of other free entities (see below, nn. 21 and 22). It is for this reason that Gregory Naz. (*Or. theol.* III.2) *explicitly rejects* the Platonic notion of first and second αἰτία.

but is brought into existence, it is 'caused', by *someone*.[21] Whereas *pege* (source) could be understood substantially or naturalistically, *aitia* (cause) carried with it connotations of personal initiative[22] and — at least at that time — of *freedom*. Divine being owes its being to a *free person*, not to impersonal substance. And since hypostasis is now identical with person, freedom is combined with love (relationship) and the two together are identified with the *Father* — a relational notion in its very nature.[23]

3. *The Emergence of Doxological Theology and the Contrast between 'Theologia' and 'Oikonomia'*

Basil's treatise on the Holy Spirit reveals certain important new developments in theology which lie behind the Creed of Constantinople. They constitute indispensable tools in any attempt at interpreting this Creed and can be summarized as follows:

There is a fundamental distinction between what we can say about God *as he is in himself* (immanently or eternally), and what we can say about him *as he reveals himself to us* in his *Oikonomia*. The two ways are indicated by the use of two different doxologies. The doxology which prevailed during the early centuries, probably of an Alexandrian origin, was 'Glory be to the Father through (*dia*) the Son, in (*en*) the Holy Spirit'. This was replaced by Basil with another one which

---

[21] It is evident from many passages that behind the emphasis on αἰτία by the Cappadocians there lies the stress on the *freedom* of God's Trinitarian existence. For example, Gregory Naz., *Or. theol.* III.2: 'we would never have the audacity to speak of a love which emerges, as a Greek philosopher has dared to say, like an overflowing bowl. For we shall never admit a generation which is forced (necessary), a sort of natural overflow, which would by no means befit our notion of the Godhead'. The errors of Eunomianism could not be combatted without the introduction of the notion of αἰτία. Without this notion, there is no guarantee that the one οὐσία of God cannot be misconceived as a substance producing or generating something *by necessity*. Behind this lies the distinction between οὐσία and *hypostasis*, as well as the ontological ultimacy of the person. For if it is the οὐσία that is ontologically ultimate, then the Father alone is the οὐσία of God, as the Anomoeans would say. See Gregory Naz., *Or. theol.* 3.15-16.

[22] That the 'cause' (αἰτία) terminology is related to the concept of person in the Cappadocians, see, among other sources, Gregory of Nyssa, *Quod non sint* (PG 45, 133D): 'while we confess the invariable character of the divine substance, *we do not deny the difference with regard to the cause and that which is caused, by which we only mean that each person is distinguished from the other*...in speaking of the cause and that which is from the cause we do not indicate by these words the nature but the difference in the *mode of being*'.

[23] Cf. above, nn. 17 and 18.

he claimed was just as ancient as the first one, namely 'Glory be to the Father with (*meta*) the Son, with (*syn*) the Holy Spirit'.[24]

In introducing and trying to justify the second doxology, Basil offers a theology which includes the following points:

(a) If one looks at the Economy in order to arrive at *Theologia*, one begins with the Holy Spirit, then passes through the Son and finally reaches the Father. The movement is reversed when we speak of God's coming to us; the initiative starts with the Father, passes through the Son and reaches us in the Holy Spirit.[25] In the latter case, the Spirit can be said to come third in order, but Basil does not seem to insist on that. The main point when referring to the Economy seems to be that the Spirit is a *forerunner* of Christ. There is no phase or act of the Economy which is not announced and preceded by the Spirit.[26] So even in the Economy, for Basil at least, the Spirit does not seem to depend on the Son.

All this may well be an idea related to an old liturgical practice in the areas of Palestine and Syria (with which Cappadocia is closely related) according to which the giving of the Spirit in the form of Chrismation or Confirmation preceded Baptism in water.[27] There is, one may say, in these areas a reversal of the liturgical order existing elsewhere in this respect, and this may well have been accompanied by an analogous theology (perhaps Theodoret's strong repudiation of Cyril of Alexandria's views on the relation between Son and Spirit[28] has something to do with the fact that the former is an Antiochene?).[29] This means that the *dia/en* doxology can be interpreted in

---

[24] See *De Spir. S.* 1.3f.; 7.16; 25.58ff. etc. (Sources chrétiennes, 17 bis, pp. 256f., 298f., 456ff.).

[25] *De Spir. S.* 18.47 (Sources chrétiennes, 17 bis, p. 412f.): 'the way, therefore, of knowing God is from the one Spirit through the one Son to the one Father, and, reversely, the natural goodness and natural sanctification and the royal dignity comes from the Father and passes through the only-begotten (Son) on to the Spirit'.

[26] See *De Spir. S.* 16.39 (Sources chrétiennes, 17 bis, p. 386).

[27] This may well go back to New Testament times, as is hinted at by 1 Jn 5.7. See on this point T.W. Manson, 'Entry into Membership of the Early Church', *Journal of Theological Studies* 48 (1947), pp. 25-33.

[28] See Cyril Alex., *Apologeticus contra Theodoretum* (PG 76, 432CD).

[29] In saying this, I do not wish to subscribe to the view that Theodoret's pneumatology was exactly that of the Cappadocians (i.e., a concern with the hypostatic causation of the Spirit in God). See on this the convincing argument of A. de Halleux, 'Cyrille, Théodoret, et le «Filioque»', *Revue d'Histoire Ecclésiastique* 74 (1979), pp. 597-625. Quite apart from this particular controversy between Cyril of Alexandria and Theodoret, there is, I believe, a close link — still awaiting a detailed study —

a way indicating either the precedence of the Son or the precedence of the Spirit in our relation to God.

(b) If, on the other hand, one speaks of God in terms of liturgical and especially eucharistic experience, then, Basil argues, the proper doxology is that of *meta/syn-* and this makes the inter-trinitarian relations look entirely different. The three persons of the Trinity appear to be equal in honour and placed one next to the other without hierarchical distinction.

The existence of God is revealed to us in the Liturgy as an event of communion. Basil, in agreement with the Fathers of both East and West, stresses the unity of divine operations *ad extra*,[30] and cannot see how else one can speak of God in his own being: 'If one truly receives the Son, the Son will bring with him on either hand the presence of his Father and that of his own Holy Spirit; likewise he who receives the Father receives also in effect the Son and the Spirit... So ineffable and so far beyond our understanding are both the communion (*koinonia*) and the distinctiveness (*diakrisis*) of the divine hypostases'.[31] From whatever end you begin in speaking of the holy Trinity, you end up with the co-presence and co-existence of all three persons at once. This is the deeper meaning — and the merit — of the *meta/syn-* doxology and, for that matter, of a theology inspired by the Liturgy. As Gregory of Nazianzus put it later, the worship of one person in the Trinity implies the worship of the Three, for the Three are one in honour and Godhead.[32]

---

between, on the one hand, the tendency to give priority (first liturgically, and owing to this also theologically) to the work of the Holy Spirit in areas such as Syria and Palestine, and, on the other hand, the Antiochene tendencies in Christology, etc. Cappadocia, of course, is a 'third world' between Alexandria and Antioch. But its historical links with the latter in what concerns liturgical life cannot be overlooked in any attempt to answer a major historical question: *why* and *how* the Cappadocians made such a *distinct* contribution to theology and saw things which the Alexandrian theologians, including St Athanasius, did not immediately see? Perhaps a deeper investigation of the history of patristic thought would show the great merit of the Cappadocians to have been their success in bringing forth a transcendence of the Alexandria-Antioch dilemma that threatened the Church so seriously with division. This would prove these Fathers to be truly 'catholic' and 'ecumenical' teachers, a title accorded to them by tradition.

[30] See J. McIntyre, 'The Holy Spirit in Greek Patristic Thought', *Scottish Journal of Theology* 7 (1954), esp. p. 357f., where the entire question of the unity of divine operations *ad extra* (indivisible but not undifferentiated) receives a profound and balanced analysis. On the fact that both the Eastern and the Western Fathers agreed on this principle, see Y. Congar, 'Pneumatologie ou "Christomonisme" dans la tradition latine?', in *Ecclesia a Spiritu Sancto edocta*, Mélanges G. Philips, 1970, pp. 41-63.

[31] *Ep.* 38.4 (PG 32, 332Df.). The question of authorship is irrelevant.

[32] *Or. theol.* 5.12; 14 (PG 36, 148; 149).

This language, which is taken up by Constantinople, opens the way to an argument based on liturgical experience and worship and thus to a theology which does not rest merely upon historical or 'economical' experience. The only thing we can say about God in this case is that he is three persons and that these three persons are clearly distinct from each other in that they each exist in a different manner. Nothing more can be said about *the way they exist* on the basis of the way they appear in the Economy or on any other basis. This is why, Gregory of Nazianzus argues,[33] we cannot say what the difference is between generation and procession. The safest theology is that which draws not only from the Economy, but also, and perhaps mainly, from the vision of God as he appears in worship. The Cappadocian way of thinking is thus strongly present behind the Eastern preference for a meta-historical or eschatological approach to the mystery of God,[34] as contrasted with the Western concern with God's acts in history. Constantinople is, in this respect, theologically and not only historically speaking, an eastern Council, but its interpretation can and must be, as we shall see later, truly ecumenical.

II. Important Points of the Pneumatology of the Second Ecumenical Council

Viewed against the background of the theological developments that took place between 325 and 381 CE, the doctrine of Constantinople on the Holy Spirit involves the following main theses.

1. *The Holy Spirit Is God*

This assertion of the Council is given indirectly and in a way that leads us back to the observations we made in the previous section of this chapter.

First, there is no mention of the word *homoousios*. This seems to be a victory for Basilian theology (whether this was simply tactical or based on the theological presuppositions which marked Basil's avoidance of this term is not clear with regard to Constantinople). It is thus significant that the way in which the assertion of the divinity of the Spirit is made by the Council reminds us vividly of Basil's way of speaking of God.[35]

---

[33] *Or.* 31.8 (PG 36, 141).
[34] Noticed, a long time ago, by Y. Congar in his 'Conclusions', in B. Botte *et al.*, *Le Concile et les Conciles*, 1960, p. 287.
[35] My entire approach in this chapter is based on the conviction, amply, in my view,

It has been remarked by some scholars[36] that the Council deals with the doctrine of the Spirit by using strictly scriptural language. It describes him as *Lord* (*kyrion*), a reference to 2 Cor. 3.17, as *Life-giving* (*zoopoion*), which is taken from Jn 6.63, and as 'having spoken through the prophets' (2 Pet. 1.21). This scriptural language is, in its choice, significant theologically, for it seems to be based on soteriological and existential rather than on strictly speaking speculative or metaphysical terminology. The *homoousios* is, therefore, not replaced with another philosophical term, not even with that of *hypostasis* or person which had become current terminology with the Cappadocians, but with terms which are not significant for the sake of being scriptural but are chosen in such a way as to make the doctrine of the Spirit directly related to the life of human beings and of the Church.

The only non-scriptural language used to denote the divinity of the Spirit is the reference to him as 'worshipped and glorified together with the Father and the Son'. This is another Basilian victory, for it was he who argued for the divinity of the Spirit in terms of equal honour (*homotimia*) in worship. The fact that the Council resorts to this kind of terminology in order to assert the divinity of the Spirit is in itself very significant. It is as though the Council considered it sufficient merely to refer to the worship of the Spirit together with the Father and the Son in order to indicate that he is God. The argument from worship, viewed against the distinction between *Theologia* and *Oikonomia* which we discussed earlier, reveals that not only the dialectic between created and uncreated is maintained as a crucial issue (one cannot worship a created being), but also that the doxological theology based on the vision of God's being as it is offered primarily in worship, and as contrasted with the way of the Economy and history, is the way chosen by the Council to speak of the divine existence of the Spirit. As we have already remarked, it is significant that

demonstrated by the evidence discussed here, that behind the teaching of Constantinople on the Holy Spirit lies not simply the wish to indicate the uncreated nature of the Spirit, but also the concerns of Cappadocian theology (hypostatic distinction of persons in God, etc., see above) which, by 381 CE, had become the major theological development, undoubtedly known to the Fathers of the Council (after all, the two Gregories were present there). For a different view, see A. de Halleux, 'Pour un accord oecuménique sur la procession de l'Esprit Saint et l'addition du Filioque au Symbole', *Irénikon* 51 (1978), pp. 451-69; also in his contribution to L. Vischer (ed.), *Spirit of God, Spirit of Christ*, 1981, pp. 69-84.

[36] See J.N.D. Kelly, *Early Christian Creeds*, p. 341f., and A.M. Ritter, *Das Konzil von Konstantinopel und sein Symbol*, 1965, p. 295f.

of the two doxologies mentioned in St Basil's *De Spiritu Sancto* it is the *dia/syn-* doxology that seems to find its way into the Creed. This certainly does not mean that the other doxology is excluded. But the way the Creed speaks about the Spirit calls for an investigation into the manner in which these two doxologies, representing as we saw two different theological methods, can be synthesized.[37]

2. *The Holy Spirit Proceeds from the Father*

This is another scriptural quotation which again, however, should not be approached as having no theological significance in itself. If Basilian theology has affected the pneumatology of Constantinople as much as it appears to have done, the reference of the Creed to the procession of the Spirit from the Father should be placed in the light of this theology, the main components of which have already been mentioned here. What is the importance of the idea that the Spirit proceeds from the Father if placed against this background?

First, in asserting that the Spirit proceeds from the Father we must understand, in strictly Basilian terms, that the ultimate ontological ground of the Holy Spirit is a *person*, and not substance. We have already referred to the idea of 'cause' as a peculiar Cappadocian contribution to theology and to its significance. The whole point seems to be that whereas the notion of 'source' can be impersonal, that of *aition* is personal (there are clear references to this reasoning in the Cappadocians).[38] The concern of the Council in making this assertion is not simply to keep the traditional idea of the *Monarchia*, since that could be done by simply keeping the notion of 'source' to describe the one 'principle' or *archē*. It is rather to safeguard the faith that the *person 'causes' God to be*. The Spirit, therefore, is not simply a power issuing from divine substance; he is another personal identity standing *vis-à-vis* the Father. He is a product of love and freedom and not of substantial necessity. The Spirit, by proceeding *from the Father*, and not from divine substance as such, is a person in the true sense. And this seems to be the most important implication of the phrase: 'from the Father'.

---

[37] This relates to the two approaches in theology, the 'historical' and the 'eschatological', and the need for a synthesis of the two. See my *Being as Communion*, 1985, pp. 171-208.

[38] See above, nn. 21 and 22. This point is missed by P. Evdokimov, *L'Esprit Saint dans la tradition Orthodoxe*, 1969, p. 74f. His strong rejection of the notion of 'cause' is apparently due to the assumption that causality necessarily implies 'production', something the Cappadocians explicitly deny in introducing the idea of αἴτιον.

Following this observation, we can now raise the thorny question of whether the Spirit proceeds also from the Son. Constantinople is clear in this respect, and it is unquestionably obvious that the *Filioque* is an *addition* to the original Creed. But in what sense can it be said to contradict the theology of the Council on the Holy Spirit? Again we cannot answer this question without reference to the theological presuppositions which emerged between Nicaea and Constantinople.

That the Son has some kind of role in the procession of the Spirit can follow from a study of patristic sources without any difficulty. Not only do Alexandrian theologians, such as Cyril, seem to hold this view,[39] but also Cappadocians like Gregory of Nyssa[40] appear to be saying the same thing. The Son in some sense 'mediates' in the procession of the Spirit. The Fathers do not seem to say much as to *how* this mediation is to be understood. But, certainly, it is something that has to do with the eternal and ontological reality of the Spirit, and not simply with the Economy.

This being said, we must add that what we regarded as an important point in our interpretation of the 'from the Father' phrase has to remain intact and not be threatened by this 'mediation' of the Son. None of the Greek Fathers, certainly none of the Cappadocians, would understand the mediation of the Son in the procession of the Spirit as in any sense implying that the Son is another 'cause' in divine existence. The Father remains the *only cause*, and this for reasons which go deep into the philosophical and theological presuppositions with which the Cappadocians operate in theology. Thus, between the Alexandrian (Cyrillian) tendency to involve the Son in the ousianic procession of the Spirit — this is how a careful study of Cyril's pronouncements on this subject seems to me to read — and the Antiochene (Theodoretan) tendency to limit the role of the Son in the coming into being of the Spirit to the Economy, Gregory of Nyssa's position seems to strike a middle road which does more justice to the intention of the Fathers of Constantinople. In Gregory's words:

> we do not deny the difference between that which is by way of 'cause' and that which is 'caused', and by this alone can we conceive of one being distinguished from the other, namely by the belief that one is 'cause' and another 'from the

---

[39] See particularly Cyril Alex, *Thes.* (PG 75, 585A and 608AB); *De recta fide...* (PG 76, 1408B); *De adorat.* I (PG 68, 148A), etc. Cf. H.B. Swete, *On the History of the Doctrine of the Procession of the Holy Spirit*, 1876, pp. 148ff.; J. Meyendorff, 'La Procession du Saint-Esprit chez les pères orientaux', in *Russie et Chrétienté*, 1950, pp. 158-78.

[40] E.g., *C. Eunom.* (PG 45, 464) and especially *Quod non sint tres dii* (PG 45, 133). Cf. below.

cause'. In the case of those who are from the cause, we recognise a further difference; one is derived immediately from the first, and the other through that which comes immediately from the first. Thus the mediating position of the Son in the divine life guards his right to be the only begotten [Son], while the Spirit's natural [ousianic = *physikes*] relation to the Father is not excluded.[41]

Thus, Gregory's position seems to be similar to that of Cyril in that it clearly allows for a mediating position of the Son in the eternal spiration of the Spirit. But he differs from him in that, (a) he introduces the notion of 'cause' which he clearly reserves to the Father alone,[42] putting the Son and the Spirit on equal footing in this respect (both of them are *ek tou aitiou*),[43] and (b) unlike Cyril, he does not leave any doubt as to the fact that even the ousianic or 'natural' relation of the Spirit to God is one of the relationship *with the Father*.

If, therefore, we are allowed to interpret Constantinople in the light of Cappadocian theology, we must conclude that the phrase *ek tou Patros*, (a) does not exclude a mediating role of the Son in the procession of the Spirit, (b) does not allow for the Son to acquire the role of *aition* by being a mediator, and (c) does not allow any detachment of divine *ousia* from the Father (or from the other persons of the Trinity): when we refer to *ousia* we do not refer in any way to some-

---

[41] *Quod non sint...* (PG 45, 133).

[42] On this point we must make an important distinction between two expressions which appear to be similar at first sight. The expression, μόνος αἴτιος ὁ πατήρ (the Father is the only cause), goes back to the teaching of the Cappadocians and is formulated by St John of Damascus (*De Fide orth.* 1.12; PG 94, 849B). This is not to be fully identified with the expression, ἐκ μόνου τοῦ πατρὸς (from the Father alone), which established itself through Photius. The difference between the two formulae is that the first clearly specifies the reason why the Father is the only originator of the Spirit by referring to the notion of αἴτιον, whereas the second remains open to interpretations which can — and in fact did — reject the *Filioque* on grounds not necessarily related to the concept of αἴτιον (and of what it implies).

[43] In *C. Eunom.* 1 (PG 45, 464), there is an ambiguous reference to the Son as preceding the Spirit κατὰ τόν τῆς αἰτίας λόγον. Does this mean that the Son is αἴτιον of the Spirit *or* that the Spirit's order in the Trinity (third in line) is to be related to the process of causation (κατὰ τόν τῆς αἰτίας λόγον)? In the latter case, the meaning of the phrase would be: the Spirit comes after the Only-begotten with regard to the process of causation which is initiated by the hypostasis of the Father, the ultimate and in this sense the only αἴτιον of the Trinity. If we accept the first option, then we have a contradiction with what is said in *Quod non sint*...and, indeed, with the way Cappadocian theology was received and understood in the East. Clarification of Gregory's position on this matter comes with the distinction he makes in *Quod non sint*...between αἴτιον (= the Father) and the ἐκ τοῦ αἰτίου (= the Son). The ambiguity, therefore, of the passage from *C. Eunom.* receives its proper clarification in the light of that passage.

thing conceivable *besides* the persons, that is, we do not refer to an *impersonal ousia*.

This much can be concluded as an interpretation of the Council's teaching on the Holy Spirit. Anything more than this, namely any attempt to define the content of this mediation of the Son by making him some kind of secondary cause, or by distinguishing between personal — relational and hypostatic — and ousianic levels of operation, cannot be concluded from either Constantinople or the Cappadocians.[44]

This little, however, that can be concluded is by no means negligible. For its deeper meaning has to do with an absolute and indispensable existential truth, namely with the ontological ultimacy of the person. If God's being is not caused by a person, it is not a free being. And if this person is not the Father alone, it is impossible to maintain the divine unity or oneness without resorting to the ultimacy of substance in ontology, that is, without subjecting freedom to necessity and person to substance.[45]

[44] The views expressed by B. Bolotov on the nature of the procession of the Holy Spirit (see 'Thesen über das *Filioque* von einem russischer Theologen', *Revue Internationale de Théologie* 24 (1898); also in French in *Istina* 17 (1972), and utilized further by contemporary theologians — see the contributions of D. Staniloae, J. Moltmann and J.M. Garrigues in the volume, *Spirit of God, Spirit of Christ*, cf. above, n. 35), constitute a *considerable* step beyond the Cappadocian Fathers in that they indicate something positive about the *how* or the *content* of the intra-Trinitarian relations on which the Cappadocians *constantly* and *persistently* refused to speculate. It is not accidental that the Fathers never said or implied any positive thing about the content of the words 'Father' or 'Son' (e.g., that 'Father' implies the begetting of a Son, hence the Father is such 'only in so far as he begets a Son'). The same is true about the content of the word 'Spirit' (e.g., that he is 'love' etc.), or about the number 3 (a third person is necessary for a complete existence; see D. Staniloae, *Spirit of God, Spirit of Christ*, p. 185f., cf. P. Florensky, *La Colonne et le Fondement de la Vérité*, French trans., C. Andronikof, 1975). This attitude of the Fathers relates to their sensitivity towards the Arian arguments (danger of anthropomorphism, etc.) as well as to their respect for the mystery of God's being, which is to be taken simply as it is *given* in Revelation and *worshipped*, instead of being speculated upon. Thus it is interesting that Gregory of Nyssa, in arguing that the Spirit has to come third in order after the Son, does not argue from the viewpoint of the meaning of the word 'Son' (this would have been very dangerous in view of the Arian arguments), but he bases his arguments on the meaning of Μονογενὴς: the Spirit is third so that the Son would remain the only-begotten one.

[45] This is perhaps the case with medieval scholastic thought, if E. Gilson is right in his presentation of it in his *L'esprit de la philosophie médiévale*, 1932, esp. pp. 45-66. His argument is extremely powerful as he shows the legitimacy, even the necessity, of a Christian philosophy; but if this philosophy is to be based on the notion of Being linked with necessity, it can hardly be called 'Christian'. Being must be

III. From Constantinople to Today

Many centuries separate us from the Second Ecumenical Council and during this time the doctrine of the Holy Spirit has been one
of the thorniest problems in theology. As it does not fall within the
scope of the subject to which this study is specifically addressed, I
do not intend to discuss the arguments that have been produced for
and against one of the main issues that have divided East and West
in their understanding of this doctrine. What I have tried to do here
is to point out what I regard as *the main issues* that lie behind the doctrine of Constantinople on the Holy Spirit and, as I promised in
my introduction, to establish which of these issues were essential to
the Fathers of that time and which of them, in accordance with an
essential continuity of Tradition, continue to constitute fundamental
issues for us today. I can now sum up this effort by underlining the
following points:

1.

As regards the *Filioque* problem, much of the polemic that has prevailed since the time of Photius has tended to obscure the real issues,
and therefore has to be re-examined today.

From what I have said so far, the following clarifications appear to
be necessary:

(a) The real issue behind the *Filioque* concerns the question whether
the ultimate ontological category in theology is the person or substance. It seems to me that the choice here is limited. If the Son is
understood as a kind of second *cause* in divine existence — alongside or even below the Father — the dilemma is that either the substance or a person is the ultimate ontological category in God (that
which has the priority and which safeguards the unity of divine existence). If we go back to the biblical and Greek patristic identification
of God with the *Father* — to which theologians like K. Rahner point
today[46] — the ultimate ontological category cannot be other than the
person, the hypostasis of the Father *alone*, since two hypostases being
such an ultimate category would result in two gods. Profound and

---

inseparably linked with freedom, and this can be done only if the notion of *person*
becomes an *ultimate* ontological category. What the Cappadocian Fathers did in the
context of their Trinitarian theology is extremely important for the creation of a
Christian philosophy — a task still awaiting its realization.

[46] K. Rahner, *The Trinity*, 1970, p. 58f.

crucial existential reasons argue against making substance ultimate in ontology; I have only hinted at them in this chapter.

(b) The position of Western theology with regard to this issue, which in my view is the only essential one, cannot be properly appreciated without taking into account the following observations:

(i) As has been so clearly shown by Y. Congar,[47] the Western interpretation of the *Filioque*, based on the theology of St Augustine, does not necessarily reject or exclude the thesis that the Father is the *only cause* of divine existence in the holy Trinity. Augustine refers to the Father as the one from whom the Spirit proceeds *principaliter*.[48]

(ii) It must be noted — and this is crucial — that the West was satisfied with the notion of *archē* or *pēgē* (cf. Augustine's *principaliter*) in what concerns the 'how' of the Trinitarian being. The East, on the contrary, as is shown by the case of the Cappadocians, *was not*: it went further and introduced the notion of *aitia* or *aition*, and with it, as I have argued in this chapter, also the idea of the ontological ultimacy of the person in God. The reasons for this development in the East are, on the one hand, *idiosyncratic* (if we may call them so), relating to the strongly liturgical approach to the mystery of God which always marked the Eastern areas (Syria, Palestine, Cappadocia, etc.)[49] and,

[47] See esp. vol. III of his *I Believe in the Holy Spirit*, 1983, pp. 80-95.

[48] *De Trin.* XV.17.29 and 26.47; *Sermo* 71.26 (PL 38, 459); and other references to be found in Y. Congar, *I Believe in the Holy Spirit*, vol. III, p. 93 n. 25f. As Congar puts it: 'The Son...has this faculty of being the co-principle of the Spirit entirely from the Father. Augustine stresses this fact very forcibly, either by using his term *principaliter* or in formulae which could be taken to mean *a Patre solo*' (p. 86). This is not very far from the *ek tou aitiou* of the Cappadocians (see above). See also the interesting distinction between the formula *ex Patre Filioque* and *a Patre Filioque*, the latter not contradicting the *ex unico Patre* according to J.M. Garrigues (in *Spirit of God, Spirit of Christ*, p. 161). Father L. Bouyer, *Le Consolateur* (1980), p. 221, does not seem to attach so much significance to the *principaliter* of St. Augustine; he sees in it only 'vaguely' a return to the ancient patristic idea of the *monarchia*. Instead, he offers another basis for an East-West rapprochement by presenting the non-Augustinian roots of western pneumatology (*Le Consolateur*, pp. 231-44) and, especially, by pointing out a common spirituality in what he calls 'theological conflict and spiritual accord' (pp. 299-334) between the two traditions.

[49] We have alluded above to the liturgical peculiarities of Syria and Palestine (with which Cappadocia is linked) in what concerns the order of the sacrament of confirmation celebrated there before Baptism. This is closely related to the strongly pneumatological approach to the mystery of the Church which had deep roots in the eucharistic-liturgical ethos of those areas of the East (e.g., St Ignatius of Antioch, etc.). The West tended to be more *ethical* in its approach, as a result of being less liturgical and eucharistic. We are, of course, talking in terms of *emphasis*: the West never lacked entirely the liturgical dimension, nor the East the ethical. This needs further analysis which cannot be given here.

on the other hand, purely *historical* and circumstantial: the rise of Eunomianism, for example, to the refutation of which the Cappadocians had to devote so much of their energy, inevitably brought forth the necessity of a Trinitarian theology based on the ontological ultimacy of the person.[50]

Thus, the Cappadocians marked the beginning of a theological ethos and a philosophical expression of the mystery of God which the West practically never fully appreciated or shared. In classical — perhaps also in modern — Western theology, the person never played the role of an ultimate ontological category, due to the tendency to place the person of the Father, *under* the ontological priority of the 'one God', that is of divinity in general.[51] The same is even more true about the Medieval Scholastics. It is in the light of this absence of an ontology of the person in the West that we must place the entire history of East-West relations in theology,[52] an absence which has affected other areas of doctrine and not simply the doctrine of God.[53]

Now, such an absence of a philosophical tool in the West may well indicate a basic difference in the understanding of the mystery of God, but not necessarily so. Since even St Augustine's intention

---

[50] Eunomianism, in the final analysis, was nothing but a conception of divine nature in such terms as to make it impossible to distinguish between the οὐσία of the Father and the person of the Father. This point was seen by the Cappadocian Fathers who thought that Arianism could not finally be refuted until the distinction between the 'Father' and the οὐσία of God could be made, so that the generation of the Logos would not necessitate a movement of God outside his being, his οὐσία (see above, n. 21). It was in this context that the notion of person as an ontological category was born.

[51] See L. Chevalier, *St Augustin et la pensée greque. Les relations Trinitaires*, 1940, pp. 63, 168f., etc. Related to this is also the strong psychologization of the notion of person in Augustine, on which see L. Bouyer, *Le Consolateur*, pp. 218-21. This psychological understanding of person survives up to now in Western thought: e.g., C.C.J. Webb, *God and Personality*, 1918; J.E. Walgrave, *Person and Society*, 1965; P.F. Strawson, *Individuals*, 1964.

[52] Even at the time of St Gregory Palamas, the argument seems to have been centred on the question whether substance precedes person in God's being. See Gregory Palamas, *Triads* III.3,2: 'When God was conversing with Moses, He did not say I am the essence but I am the One Who Is. Thus it is not the One who Is who derives from the essence, but the essence which derives from Him'. Cf. P. Evdokimov, *L'Esprit Saint dans la tradition Orthodoxe*, p. 61. Also, J. Meyendorff, *The Byzantine Legacy in the Orthodox Church*, 1982, p. 192.

[53] This is particularly true in the realm of ecclesiology (the question of the priority of Christology with regard to pneumatology, etc.). Cf. my *Being as Communion*, esp. pp. 123ff.

in supporting the *Filioque* does not seem to have been the recognition of two *archai* in God, the absence of the concept of *aition* (and with it of the ultimacy of the person) from his theology does not necessarily involve a radical departure from the faith of Constantinople. It is unfortunate that in the course of Church history Cappadocian and Western thought were never given the opportunity really to meet except in the context of a polemic that sought after differences rather than better understanding. In this sense, it could be said that the history of the reception of Constantinople was interrupted and never came to full maturity. Modern theologians, both of the Eastern and of the Western tradition, must work towards a recapturing of the ancient patristic threads that may rejoin us with the first dynamics of this unfinished history of reception.[54] In any such attempt of contemporary theology the crucial question, according to the main argument of this paper, will be to what extent both East and West can appropriate the Cappadocian theology that lies behind the Second Ecumenical Council, including its most important and existentially decisive intention to give ontological priority to the person in God and in existence in general. Thus, the *Filioque* issue remains an open question which may only be decided on the premises of such a deeper theological re-reception of Constantinople.

(iii) In any attempt to appreciate correctly the weight of the *Filioque* issue in East-West relations, one must take into account certain differences in the meaning attached to the expression *ekporeuetai* (proceeds) of Jn 15.26. Latin writers, including St Augustine, do not seem to make the distinction we find in the Greek Fathers between that and the expression *exēlthon kai ēkō* of Jn 8.42, taking the verbs *ekporeuesthai* and *proienai* as synonyms.[55] This confusion in vocabulary was regarded already by St Maximus the Confessor as sufficient reason for dispelling all suspicions of heresy that the Byzantines had against the Romans concerning the *Filioque*. He claimed that he had secured from the Romans the explanation that the *Filioque* does not imply for them any other *aition*, except the Father, in divine existence — it is noteworthy that the entire issue seems to be judged by the Cappadocian idea of *aition* — and asked the Byzantines to respect the fact that the Romans 'cannot render their thought in a language and words which

---

[54] Such a hopeful beginning is to be found in works like Y. Congar's three volumes of *I Believe in the Holy Spirit*, and L. Bouyer's *Le consolateur*. J.M. Garrigues' studies display a creative step in this direction; cf. his book, *L'Esprit qui dit 'Père'!* (1981).

[55] For references, see J.M. Garrigues, 'Procession et Ekporèse du Saint-Esprit', *Istina* 17 (1972), pp. 345ff. and Y. Congar, *I Believe in the Holy Spirit*, III, p. 87f.

are foreign to their mother tongue, exactly as this is the case with us (Greeks)'.[56]

Having said this, we must immediately observe that this terminological problem was not entirely free from theological implications. Maximus himself, in the above mentioned letter, makes explicit reference to St Cyril of Alexandria and the support that the Romans drew from him in their defence of the *Filioque*. Cyril, as we have already noted,[57] speaks clearly of the Spirit as coming from the Father *and* the Son with regard to the substance (*ousiōdōs*). But Maximus notes in his letter, and no doubt had discussed this with the Romans, that Cyril uses the verb *proienai* — not *ekporeuesthai* — in all such cases. *Ekporeusis* is applicable only to *ek tou Patros*.[58]

Now the theological issue behind this is that for Cyril the term *proienai* is related *simultaneously* to both the eternal being of God and to his *opera ad extra*, that is, the Economy. Cyril seems to push the economic 'mission' of the Spirit back into the eternal being of God, into the divine *ousia*.[59] In so doing, he displays insensitivity towards an issue which, as we have seen, was so important to the Cappadocians, namely the distinction between *Theologia* and *Oikonomia*. Are we confronted here with another Cappadocian novelty — in addition to that of the notion of *aition* — in the history of theology? The historian must certainly take note of this. As far as this concerns our purpose here, it is noteworthy that the same problem marks the relations between Eastern and Western theology with regard to the *Filioque*. If Cappadocian theology is of decisive importance for the interpretation and reception of the Pneumatology of Constantinople, the

---

[56] Maximus, *Letter to Marinus* (PG 91, 136A-C).

[57] See above, n. 39. Cf. also A. de Halleux, 'Cyrille, Théodoret et le «Filioque»', *passim*.

[58] The fact that Cyril uses the preposition ἐκ for the relation of the Spirit to both the Father and the Son (L. Bouyer, *Le consolateur*, p. 276f.) need not be given special significance. It is only later on, with St John of Damascus (*De Fid. orth.* 8; PG 94, 832B), that precisions of this kind are made.

[59] A. de Halleux ('Cyrille...', p. 615) rightly notes that Cyril 'comprend dans un sens économique l'ekporèse elle-même, c.-à-d. qu'il n'interprète pas encore Jn 15.26 au sens exclusif de la procession intra-divine... Le sens de la transcendance divine n'a donc pas conduit l'archevêque d'Alexandrie à séparer autant que les Pères cappadociens la Trinité immanente de l'économie de la création et du salut' ['understands the *ekporeusis* itself in an economic sense, that is, he does not yet interpret Jn 15.26 in the exclusive sense of the intra-divine procession... A sense of divine transcendence did not, therefore, lead the Archbishop of Alexandria to separate as much as the Cappadocian Fathers the immanent Trinity from the economy of creation and salvation'].

extent to which East and West can come to a common understanding on this issue will affect the removal of misunderstandings that may still exist between the two traditions concerning the *Filioque*. I regard it, therefore, as imperative to add a few words on this subject.

2.

The question of the distinction between 'economic' and 'immanent' relations in the holy Trinity has justly received considerable attention in modern theology, especially in the West. The problem takes the form of the question: is the economic Trinity the same as the immanent Trinity? Such a question seems to call for a positive answer, and indeed this has been the answer of most Western theologians in our time, both Protestant (K. Barth, J. Moltmann, etc.) and Roman Catholic (notably K. Rahner). But is the matter so simple?

In dealing with K. Rahner's views on this question, Y. Congar discusses this problem in such a brilliant way that I regard it as sufficient to repeat here what he writes in criticism of Rahner's position.

Congar agrees fully with the axiom proposed by Rahner that 'the economic Trinity is the immanent Trinity', but finds it difficult to accept without further qualification the idea which Rahner adds to this axiom, namely that this thesis is also true 'reciprocally' (*umgekehrt*), that is, that the immanent Trinity is also the economic Trinity. Congar offers a detailed analysis of the reasons why he disagrees with Rahner on this point and concludes with the following words:

> The economic Trinity...reveals the immanent Trinity — but does it reveal it entirely? There is always a limit to this revelation, and the incarnation imposes its own conditions, which go back to its nature as a created work. If all the data of the incarnation were transposed into the eternity of the Logos, it would be necessary to say that the Son proceeds from the Father and the Holy Spirit — *a Patre Spirituque*. In addition, the *forma servi* belongs to what God is, but so does the *forma Dei*. At the same time, however, that latter form and the infinite and divine manner in which the perfections that we attribute to God are accomplished elude us to a very great extent. This should make us cautious in saying, as Rahner does, 'and vice versa'.[60]

As to the question, posed by Congar in the same context, of what would be St Gregory Palamas' reaction if he were to comment on K. Rahner's views, I agree fully with what Congar writes. I would only add by way of further clarification that the distinction between 'essence' and 'energy' in God — a classical topic in Orthodox theology since Palamas — significantly enough goes back to the Cappa-

[60] Y. Congar, *I Believe in the Holy Spirit*, III, p. 16.

docians, that is to those who developed and stressed more than any of the ancient Fathers the distinction between *Theologia* and *Oikonomia*. It is, therefore, essentially nothing other than a device created by the Greek Fathers to safeguard the absolute transcendence of God without alienating Him from the world:[61] the Economy must not be understood as implying a loss of God's transcendence, an abolition of *all* difference between the immanent and the economic Trinity; at the same time, God's transcendence must be understood as a *true* involvement of the very being of God in creation. 'Energy', by being *uncreated*, involves in history and creation the very being of God; yet, by being *distinct* from God's 'essence', it allows for God's immanent being to be 'incomprehensible' and truly *beyond* history and creation.

The 'essence-energy' dialectic can be a useful means of approaching the problem posed by K. Rahner and others today if it is seen against its Cappadocian background. For 'energy', that is God's love towards creation, stems from his very being and is not to be dissociated from it. But it is clearly addressed *ad extra*, and, unlike the personal existence of God (the Trinity), it does not point to 'immanent' relations (differentiations) in God.[62] With the help of the notion of 'energy', therefore, we can avoid the risk both of saying that the

---

[61] See, for example, Gregory Palamas, *Triads for the Defence of the Holy Hesychasts* III.2.24 (ed. J. Meyendorff, 1959, pp. 686-87). J. Meyendorff (*The Byzantine Legacy*, pp. 191 and 193) also regards 'the distinction in God between "essence" and "energy"...[as] nothing but a way of saying that the transcendent God remains transcendent even as He communicates Himself to humanity... *The only* concern of Palamas was to affirm simultaneously the transcendence of God and His immanence in the free gift of communion in the body of Christ' (my italics).

[62] See, for example, Gregory of Nyssa, *Quod non sint* (PG 45, 25C): '...πᾶσα ἐνέργεια ἡ θεόθεν ἐπὶ τὴν κτίσιν διήκουσα'. It is very important to bear in mind that the Greek Fathers, especially the Cappadocians, clearly *exclude* any differentiation in the ἐνέργεια of God within the immanent Trinity as if 'generation' and 'spiration' could be conceived as different forms of the one divine energy. Thus, Gregory Naz., *Or. theol.* III.16 (PG 36, 96), and Gregory of Nyssa, *Quod non sint* (PG 45, 133Α): 'The Father is God and the Son is God, but God is proclaimed to be one; for *neither with regard* to nature nor with regard to ἐνέργεια can we contemplate any difference (διαφοράν)'. This contrasts with the energy *ad extra*, because in the Economy each person of the Trinity has a *different* — though not separable — function or activity. If we identify the economic relations of the divine persons *fully* with the immanent personal differentiations in God, we risk ontologically defining the 'person' (in God) on the basis of his activity. Such a thing, as is rightly remarked by J. McIntyre ('The Holy Spirit in Greek Patristic Thought', p. 359), would imply that we regard a person as an accident of God, an idea strongly criticized by St Gregory of Nazianzus.

Economy does not involve the very being of God, and of necessarily implying that the very being of God, the immanent Trinity, is identified with the Economy in a way that would rule out all apophatic elements in theology.[63]

All this is related to pneumatology in a decisive way. As the case of Justin, Origen, and others, illustrates,[64] pneumatology is weakened whenever the approach to God is dominated primarily by epistemological concern. If we make *revelation* the decisive notion in theology (this was the case with Justin and Origen and it is today with K. Barth and K. Rahner — the latter works out his Trinitarian theology on the basis of the idea of 'self-communication'), Christology dominates pneumatology, since it is Christ who links God and the world ontologically, the Spirit pointing always *beyond* history.[65] A strong pneumatology, therefore, leads to a stronger sense of this 'beyond creation' aspect and this to the emergence of meta-historical and eschatological tendencies in theology. It is not accidental, therefore, that the Basilian *meta/syn-* doxology is historically linked with all the peculiarities of Eastern theology already mentioned, namely a strong apophaticism in theological epistemology and a eucharistic, liturgical ethos as opposed to a preoccupation with history and a kerygmatic ethos in theology,[66] which were more prominent in the West. Cappadocian theology proves once more to be crucial in any attempt at a fuller understanding and reception of the pneumatology of Constantinople.

3.

Finally, related to all this is the issue of what we have called here the 'created-uncreated' dialectic. We have argued in this chapter that

---

[63] This allows Gregory Palamas to use paradoxes and say that God 'being transcendent, incomprehensible and ineffable, consents to be partaken of...and indivisibly visible' (*Triads*, ed. J. Meyendorff, p. 128).

[64] Cf. G. Kretschmar, 'Le développement de la doctrine du Saint-Esprit du Nouveau Testament à Nicée', *Verbum Caro* 22 (1968), pp. 5-51.

[65] Cf. H.U. von Balthasar, 'Der Unbekannte jenseits des Wortes', in *Interpretation der Welt* (Festschrift R. Guardini), 1966, pp. 638-45.

[66] Cf. the distinction between 'kerygmatic' and 'doxological' theological methods, discussed by E. Schlink, *Der kommende Christus und die kirchlichen Traditionen*, 1961. It must be made clear that in liturgical (apophatic) theology we do not say *nothing* about God's being (we are not silent about it), but what we say about it *transcends* history and the Economy. Hence, to use Basilian terminology, the *meta/syn-* doxology points to the Trinity as it is eternally, whereas the *dia/en* doxology directs our attention to God's acts in history. *Both*, however, imply that something positive is said about God.

this was very much behind the concern of the Fathers of Constantinople (and indeed of all the Greek Fathers of the first four centuries), and the explicit evidence for this is to be found in the Synodical Letter of 382 CE, which interprets the decisions of Constantinople.[67] Why is this issue so important?

The answer to this question would lead us back to the problem of the distinction between the 'immanent' and the 'economic' Trinity, while revealing the *soteriological* significance of the pneumatology of Constantinople.[68] The insistence of the Fathers on the idea that the Spirit cannot be both created and uncreated is due to the assumption, so central to their thinking, that creation cannot survive if it is self-centred and autonomous, and that the only way for it to be 'saved' or 'deified' (*theōsis*) is through *communion* with the uncreated. This communion is the work of the Holy Spirit, who becomes in this way 'life-giving' (*zōopoion*) as the Creed of Constantinople[69] calls him. Life and communion coincide only in the realm of the uncreated, since in creation death overcomes communion. The Spirit gives true life, because he is uncreated and the communion he offers comes 'from above', from the *uncreated* God. If the created and the uncreated are so confused in pneumatology as to make of the Spirit a creature or abolish any distinction between the immanent and the economic existence of the Spirit, what is at stake is nothing less than the life of the world. The description of the Holy Spirit as 'life-giver' is another way of saying that he is God, only that this truth is now put in soteriological terms. In fact, on this description hangs the entire existential significance of the pneumatology of the Council. As both Athanasius and Basil argue throughout their writings on the Holy Spirit, faith in the divinity of the Spirit involves so much of our salvation and of the life of the world that man cannot afford to abandon or lose it.

CONCLUSION

These are the issues which, in my view, lie behind the teaching of the Second Ecumenical Council on the Holy Spirit and which con-

---

[67] '…so that the blasphemy of the Eunomians, the Arians and the Pneumatomachi will not prevail, namely that the *ousia* or the nature of the Godhead can be divided and a posterior or *created* or a nature of another *ousia* be added to the uncreated and homoousian Trinity' (original text in G. Alberigo *et al.* (eds.), *Conciliorum Oecumenicorum Decreta*, 1958, p. 28).

[68] B. Bobrinskoy (in L. Vischer [ed.], *Spirit of God, Spirit of Christ*, p. 146f.) rightly insists on this point.

[69] Cf. my *Being as Communion*, 1985, ch. 3, on 'Christ, the Spirit and the Church'.

tinue to be crucial for us today. And yet the Fathers of this Council teach us a great deal not only by what they have said but also by what they have avoided saying, often quite consciously, for the sake of the unity of the Church and a creative re-reception of the faith of Nicaea. The fact that they were bold enough to avoid the controversial *homoousios* in the case of the Holy Spirit and creative enough to amplify the Creed and find other ways of asserting the divinity of the Spirit and the faith of the Church is extremely instructive for us today, as we seek our unity through a re-reception of Tradition.

In concluding this chapter, therefore, with particular reference to current efforts to promote a better understanding and, ultimately, an agreement between East and West with regard to pneumatology, I think that any attempt to go further than the Cappadocian Fathers or to say more than the Fathers of 381 CE said about the Holy Spirit would only complicate the issue even more. The 'golden rule' must be St Maximus the Confessor's explanation concerning Western pneumatology: by professing the *Filioque* our Western brethren do not wish to introduce another *aition* in God's being except the Father, and a mediating role of the Son in the origination of the Spirit is not to be limited to the divine Economy, but relates also to the divine *ousia*. If East and West can repeat these two points of St Maximus *together* in our time, this would provide sufficient basis for a rapprochement between the two traditions. For while these points do not necessarily imply speculations about the *how* or the content of the intra-trinitarian relations — speculations which could be very dangerous indeed — they imply a great deal concerning the *existential* significance of pneumatology. And this is what, in the final analysis, matters.

Thus, any progress in the pneumatological *rapprochement* between East and West cannot avoid posing the *ecclesiological* question: do we all accept that the Spirit is *constitutive* of the Church, and that in so being he points to the ontological priority and ultimacy of the *person* in existence? Are we prepared to let this truth affect our ecclesial institutions, our ethics, our spirituality, and so on, in a decisive way? If East and West can say 'Amen' to this, the intention and the theology of the Second Ecumenical Council in speaking the way it did about the Holy Spirit will be fully respected. In such a case, no further formulae would be necessary; the Creed of the Second Ecumenical Council would suffice.

Chapter 6

HUMAN CAPACITY AND HUMAN INCAPACITY:
A Theological Exploration of Personhood

INTRODUCTION

INTRODUCTION

Theology, unlike other disciplines dealing with man, is faced with a fundamental methodological problem in its attempt to understand the human being. This problem is due to the Christian view of the Fall. Whatever we may wish to mean by the Fall, the fact remains that there is something which can be called 'sin', and which gives rise to the question: is man that which we know and experience as 'man'?[1] If we answer the question in the affirmative, then we are bound to imply that sin is not an anthropological problem and redemption from sin does not essentially alter our view of man; in fact, if we follow up the consequence of this position, we are bound to say that unfallen man or man restored by redemption is not properly speaking 'man' but something of a super-man. If, on the other hand, we do not approach man from the angle of his actual sinful situation, how can we approach him? Is there another angle from which to look at man except from that of what we *actually* see as man?

This difficulty becomes even clearer when we pose the question of human capacity and human incapacity. For this question stems from man's difficulty in *defining* himself. It is a question that only a human being can ask, precisely because it seems to be a unique characteristic of this sort of being to be unwilling to accept his actual limits and to tend to move beyond them. Thus, even if one looks at the actual human being of our experience, one is confronted with

---

[1] I use the word 'man' throughout this chapter in the sense of *anthropos* or human being, which includes both male and female.

the fact that most of man's actions, consciously or unconsciously, go beyond his actual state in a movement of transcendence of actual human limitations. This is to be seen not only in the impressive history of man's discoveries and conquests over nature, but also in the commonest everyday struggles of man to survive by surpassing all obstacles, whether of a natural or of a moral character. Thus, the empirical man does not represent the reality of the human being in its fulness even for a purely humanistic approach to man. Whether one speaks, in terms of natural sciences, about the evolution of man, or, in terms of social sciences, about the man of the evolving society, it remains true that the empirical man is essentially 'the raw material' for the conception or creation of the real man. Only by setting up the empirical man against a certain vision do we make him a real man. Marxism in our day speaks openly of its aspirations to go beyond the actual, to a better type of man.[2]

It is precisely this peculiarity of the human phenomenon that makes the question of human capacity and incapacity a complex one. At what point exactly can we draw the line of demarcation between capacity and incapacity? At what point does the actual man cease to be actual, or, to put it bluntly, at what point does man cease to be man and become something else — a sub-man or a super-man or God?

In the lines that follow, I shall deal with two possible approaches to the problem of human capacity and incapacity as they are reflected in the theological discussion of the relation between God and man. I should like to emphasize that these approaches represent two anthropological methods, decisively different for the study of human capacity and incapacity. The first of these is to be found in man's attempt to answer the question of human capacity and incapacity by an *introspective* movement and, in general, by looking primarily into man himself. The second method presupposes — and the reasons for this will be argued — that man's capacity and incapacity can be properly discussed only if man is approached as an indefinable being which can be grasped only by being put in the light of his ability to relate to extra-human realities. The whole argument will finally be placed in the light of some strictly theological doctrines, such as Christology and pneumatology.

---

[2] See on this point the pertinent remarks of Archbishop Anthony Bloom in his *God and Man*, 1971, p. 30f.

I. THE SUBSTANTIALIST APPROACH

1.

Ever since Christian theology encountered Greek thought, with its concern for *ousia* and with its monistic view of reality,[3] it was forced to stress the utter difference between God and the world, which it had inherited from the Bible, by juxtaposing the *ousia* or nature of God to that of creation and of man. This defence of the biblical view of God against Greek monism is to be seen behind the doctrine of *creatio ex nihilo* as well as the long Christological debate which ended up with the Chalcedonian formula of the *two natures* of Christ united *without confusion*. Those who see Greek metaphysics entering Christian faith through this formula, should note also that Greek metaphysics, which is basically monistic in its approach to reality, is there only in order to be denied in and through the affirmation of *two* natures, divine and human, co-existing without confusion.

This juxtaposition of divine to human nature seems to suggest that it is possible and even permissible to approach man from the viewpoint of his 'substance' and try to understand him by drawing the limits between divine and human nature. But in order to do so, it is, strangely enough, necessary to go back to Greek ontology, because in fact the main characteristic of Greek thought lies in its concern with the *ousia* of things, with being *quâ* being and with the unity between thought and being.[4] This employment of Greek

---

[3] Greek thought in all its variations (Platonic, Aristotelian, etc.) always operated with what we may call a *closed ontology*. As E.L. Mascall puts it, 'for both [Platonic and Aristotelian thought] every being had a nicely rounded-off nature which contained implicitly everything that the being could ever become... What Greek thought could not have tolerated...would have been the idea that a being could become more perfect in its kind by acquiring some characteristic which was not implicit in its nature before' (*The Openness of Being*, 1971, p. 246f.). The 'dualism' between the intelligible and the sensible, which characterizes the development of Platonic thought, is not to be taken as an ontological dualism. Between the ideas and the mind there is an ontological *syggeneia*. This preserves ultimately the unity of being in one whole, while everything which falls outside this unity is to be regarded as non-being. This applies even to Neoplatonism as shown by C.J. de Vogel, *Philosophia I. Studies in Greek Philosophy* (Philosophical Texts and Studies, 19), I, 1970, pp. 397-416. See also K. Kremer, *Die neuplatonische Seinsphilosophie und ihre Wirkung auf Thomas von Aquin*, 1966 (1971), p. 79f.

[4] Ever since Parmenides, the unity between *einai* and *noein* was the ultimate concern for classical Greek thought (*Fragm.* 5d 7; Plato, *Parmenides* 128b). For Aristotle, the *ousia* of beings was the ultimate object of all ontology. (See, e.g., D.M. Mackinnon, 'Aristotle's Conception of Substance', in R. Bambrough [ed.], *New Essays on Plato and Aristotle*, 1965, pp. 97-119.)

ontology has, indeed, occurred in the theology of the great medieval Scholastics who not only found Aristotelian philosophy helpful and used it extensively, but by using the Latin concept of *natura* which, as Heidegger has shown,[5] was an unfortunate translation destined to obscure the Greek notion of *physis*, they reinforced the Western approach to *natura* as an *objectified substance*. As a result of this, theology was able to speak of man as a substance possessing certain qualities of its own and, again in the sense of the typical Aristotelian idea of *entelecheia*, as a being with a certain *potency* inherent in its nature. Thus, man's tendency to go beyond himself was understood as the expression of this natural potency which makes him *capax infiniti* or *capax Dei*. In order to stress that the doctrine of the *creatio ex nihilo* was not endangered by such views, theology was led to develop the notion of *gratia creata* which would serve as a reminder of both the creaturely character of this potency and the difference between the nature of God and the nature of man.

This was enough to prepare the stage for the argument between 'natural' and 'revealed' theology. The acceptance of an inherent human capacity appears to threaten the notion of revelation as an unconditional manifestation of God. Furthermore, this idea of an inherent capacity raises the entire issue of grace in an acute way: if there is such a thing as an inherent capacity for God, then God's grace is conditioned and in a sense dependent on what is already there in creation. And a conditional grace is not grace at all, as the idea of grace relies entirely on that of an absolutely free and unconditional gift. The reaction, therefore, to the idea of the inherent capacity was one of the denial of this capacity — capacity and incapacity became a matter of either-or. Man in himself is utterly incapable of knowing God; only God can reveal himself to man. Karl Barth, at least in his early period, has become a symbol of this reaction.

This discussion represents another variant of the old problem concerning the creation of man in the image of God. It is noteworthy that, as in the case of Grace and Revelation, so in this case, too, the argument has been one of either-or: the *imago Dei* has either been 'lost' (total depravity) or 'preserved' after the Fall. As a result of this, man has been presented either by stressing his state of sin (e.g., R. Niebuhr) or by emphasizing his capacity for God (e.g., K. Rahner). Capacity and incapacity have, in fact, never ceased to represent two options of a dilemma in theological discussion.

[5] *An Introduction to Metaphysics*, 1959, p. 13f.

210 Communion and Otherness

2.

I do not intend to enter into the historical development of these problems except in so far as it is necessary to illustrate the main issue that lies behind it. Thus, it must be noted that although East and West were from the beginning anxious to stress the difference between the nature of God and the nature of man — hence their agreement at Chalcedon — there was, nevertheless, always a tendency in the West to view the two natures from the angle of their particular qualities, and to go to the mystery of salvation with a somewhat overdeveloped interest in *what happens to man as man*. This is to be noticed already in Tertullian and it becomes quite evident in the case of the Augustinian-Pelagian controversy which was essentially preoccupied with the question of how much *man* contributes to salvation: nothing or something? In an approach like this, the scheme '*natural* versus *supernatural*' was almost inevitable, and it is interesting historically that the Aristotelian Scholasticism of the Middle Ages did not abolish this, essentially Platonic, Augustinian scheme, in spite of the many differences between Augustine and Thomas. In the East, the same kind of approach appears in the Antiochene theological tradition with its accent on the autonomy of each of the two, human and divine, natures in Christ. It can be demonstrated — but this is not the place for that — that in all of these cases the real issue lies in the attempt to understand man by looking introspectively at him either as an autonomous ethical agent (Tertullian, Antiochenes) or as the *Ego* of a psychological complex (Augustine) or as a substance possessing certain potencies (Scholastics).

The consequences of this approach for understanding human capacity and incapacity are, historically, of paramount importance and should be noted here, although only briefly for the limited extent of this paper. With the help of a cross-fertilization between the Boethian and the Augustinian approaches to man, our Western philosophy and culture have formed a concept of man out of a combination of two basic components: *rational individuality*[6] on the one hand and *psychological experience and consciousness* on the other.[7] It was on the basis of this combination that Western thought arrived at the conception of the person as an *individual* and/or a *personality*, that is,

---

[6] On the basis of Boethius' definition of the person as *naturae rationabilis individua substantia* (*Contra Eutych. et Nest.* 3).

[7] Augustine's *Confessions* stand out as a decisive contribution to this psychological approach to person.

a unit endowed with intellectual, psychological and moral qualities centred on the axis of consciousness.[8] Man's distinctive characteristic became in this way identical with his ability to be conscious of himself and of others and thus to be an *autonomous self* who intends, thinks, decides, acts and produces results.

3.

Now, the great difficulty for theology in raising the question of human capacity and incapacity in the context of this approach lies not only in its consequences which are beginning to worry theologians and simple Christians all over the world,[9] but also in the fact that there is something about the human phenomenon that seems to resist strongly any definition of man from the point of view of his 'substance' or qualities. Attempts at making out of the Aristotelian adjective 'rational' a *substantial* qualification of man (e.g., by explaining the uniqueness of man in terms of his 'mind', 'consciousness', etc.) cannot be seriously regarded as having demonstrated that there is something radically, and not simply by way of degree, different between man and the rest of the animals, 'the difference in mind between man and the higher animals' being, as Darwin wrote in *The Descent of Man*,[10] 'certainly one of *degree*, not of kind'. The linguists, on the other hand, who are trying to prove that man's uniqueness

---

[8] Western thought on the whole has operated with this concept of the person for a long time. We can see this even in some remarkable studies of our time, as, for example, C.C.J. Webb, *God and Personality*, 1918; J.H. Walgrave, *Person and Society*, 1965, and more explicitly in his recent article, 'Godservaring door het geweten', in *Tijdschrift voor Theologie* 12 (1972), pp. 377-95. P.F. Strawson in his *Individuals*, 1964, simply assumes the definition of person in terms of consciousness. For examples of a different approach in our time, see n. 12, below.

[9] By becoming an *individuum* definable by its own substance and especially its intellectual capacities, man has managed to isolate himself from creation, to which he naturally belongs, and having developed an indifference to the sensitivity and life of creation has reached the point of polluting and destroying it to an alarming degree. The American historian Lynn White, in examining the historical roots of our ecological crisis ('The Historical Roots of our Ecological Crisis', *Science* 155 (1967), pp. 1203-207; *Machina ex Deo: Essays in the Dynamism of Western Culture*, 1968, pp. 75-94), is quite categorical in attributing this to the Western intellectual tradition with its rationalistic image of man. But theology must also share the blame. One has simply to look at the predominant forms of Christian worship and spirituality or at the prevailing theories of the atonement and the sacraments: in all cases the cosmic dimension of man is missing; man in his relation to God singles himself out from nature as the autonomous self, as if his capacities and incapacities had nothing to do with those of the entire cosmos.

[10] Vol. 1, 1898, p. 193.

lies in his language have not managed to satisfy their many critics. In addition to all this, the growing prospect of the production of intelligent beings by technological means (e.g., with the help of computer science), makes the approach to the uniqueness of man from the angle of his 'substance' more and more questionable.[11]

Is there, therefore, no such thing as *human nature*? Does the Chalcedonian formula by explicitly mentioning 'human nature' point to nothing concrete and real? Of course, the answer can only be that there *is* a human nature, but this is not enough to indicate what the proper approach to man is. For the question is not whether or not there is such a thing as 'human nature' but *whether it is possible to approach man via his 'nature' or 'ousia' itself.* The problem is as old as the patristic issue concerning the *ousia* of God but it can be applied equally well to all issues that relate to the question of the adequacy of Greek and especially Aristotelian ontology for theology. And our problem depends very much on this.

In the lines that follow, I shall try to argue for an approach other than the 'substantial' one to the human being and for the fact that the entire problem of human capacity and incapacity rises precisely from man's resistance to any such 'substantial' definition. More concretely, I shall seek to raise the question of human capacity and incapacity in the context of man's *personhood* and all that this notion involves.

II. PERSONHOOD AS *EKSTASIS* AND *HYPOSTASIS* OF BEING

1.

Man's personhood should not be understood in terms of 'personality', that is, of a complex of natural, psychological or moral qualities which are in some sense 'possessed' by or 'contained' in the human *individuum*. On the contrary, being a person is basically different from being an individual or 'personality' in that the person cannot be conceived in itself as a static entity, but only as it *relates to*.[12] Thus, personhood implies

---

[11] See the discussion in A.J.P. Kenny, H.C. Longuet-Higgins, J.R. Lucas and C.H. Waddington, *The Nature of Mind*, 1972.

[12] Even if we understand person in terms of consciousness, as P.F. Strawson, arguing from a logical point of view, has shown: 'One can ascribe states of consciousness to oneself only if one can ascribe them to others. One can ascribe them to others only if one can identify other subjects of experience. And one cannot identify others if one can identify them *only* as subjects of experience, possessors of states of consciousness' (*Individuals*, p. 100).

The understanding of the person as a *relational* category in our time has marked a sharp contrast with the Boethian individualistic tradition. Some representative exam-

the 'openness of being', and even more than that, the *ek-stasis* of being, that is, a movement towards communion[13] which leads to a transcendence of the boundaries of the 'self' and thus to *freedom*. At the same time, and in contrast to the partiality of the individual which is subject to addition and combination, the person in its ekstatic character reveals its being in a *catholic*, that is, integral and undivided, way, and thus in its being ekstatic it becomes *hypostatic*, that is, the bearer of its nature in its totality.[14] *Ekstasis* and *hypostasis* represent two basic aspects of personhood, and it is not to be regarded as a mere accident that both of these words have been historically applied to the notion of person. Thus the idea of person affirms at once both that personal being cannot be 'contained' or 'divided', and that the mode of its existence, its *hypostasis*, is absolutely unique and unrepeatable. Without these two conditions, being falls into an a-personal reality, defined and described like a mere 'substance', that is, it becomes an a-personal thing.

The combination of the notion of *ekstasis* with that of *hypostasis* in the idea of the person reveals that personhood is directly related to ontology — it is not a quality added, as it were, to beings, something that beings 'have' or 'have not', but it is *constitutive* of what can be ultimately called a 'being'.

The notion of *'hypostasis'* was for a long time identical with that of 'substance'. As such, it basically served the same purpose as the term

ples of this trend are to be found in M. Buber's *I and Thou*, J. Macmurray's *Persons in Relation* and *The Self as Agent*, W. Pannenberg's important article, 'Person', in *R.G.G.* (3rd edition), V, pp. 230-35, etc. David Jenkins' studies on Man move also along similar lines (e.g., *The Glory of Man*, 1967; *What is Man?*, 1970, and *Living with Questions*, 1969).

[13] The term *ek-stasis* in this sense is known today mainly through the philosophy of M. Heidegger. Yet, long before him, this term was used in the mystical writings of the Greek Fathers (Pseudo-Dionysius, Maximus, etc.) in basically the same sense. C. Yannaras (*The Ontological Content of the Theological Notion of Person*, 1970 — in Greek) makes a remarkable attempt to utilize Heidegger's philosophy for a re-interpretation of Eastern Orthodox theology today. In spite of fundamental reservations that one may have concerning the possibility of such a use of Heidegger, Yannaras' work remains extremely helpful.

[14] That in every human person we see not part but the totality of human nature is essential to the biblical anthropology of 'Adam' — both the first and the last one (Christ). Such an understanding of the person also helps us to make sense of the so-called 'corporate personality' idea which biblical scholars have regarded as a central biblical theme ever since the works of H. Wheeler Robinson (*The Hebrew Conception of Corporate Personality*, 1936), and A.R. Johnson (*The One and the Many in the Israelite Conception of God*, 1942). There is no need to say how important, indeed how indispensable, such a concept of person is for Trinitarian theology and especially for Christology (Christ is a 'catholic' man) to which reference will be made below.

'substance' served since Aristotle, namely to answer the ultimate ontological question: what is it that makes a particular being be itself and thus be at all? Suddenly, however, in the course of the fourth century CE and under the pressure of conditions that are worth studying, the term *hypostasis* ceased to denote 'substance' and became synonymous with that of 'person'. The implications of this shift in terminology cannot but be of paramount importance for ontology, for it can hardly be conceivable that those who made this shift dissociated *'hypostasis'* from ontology entirely. The Greek Fathers were, after all, Greeks, and the Greek mind could not avoid thinking ontologically.

If the notion of *hypostasis*, no longer in the sense of 'substance' but of 'person', points to that which makes a being be itself, then we are indeed confronted with a revolution with regard to Greek and especially Aristotelian ontology. For the identification of *hypostasis* not with *'ousia'* but with personhood means that the ontological question is not answered by pointing to the 'self-existent', to a being as it is determined by its own boundaries, but to a being which in its *ekstasis* breaks through these boundaries in a movement of communion. That for which an ultimate ontological claim can be made, that which *is*, is only that which can be *itself*, which can have a *hypostasis* of its own. But since *'hypostasis'* is identical with personhood and not with substance, it is not in its 'self-existence' but in *communion* that this being is *itself* and thus *is at all*. Thus, communion does not threaten personal particularity; it is constitutive of it.

Ontological identity, therefore, is to be found ultimately not in every 'substance' as such, but only in a being which is free from the boundaries of the 'self'. Because these boundaries render it subject to individualization, comprehension, combination, definition, description and use, such a being free from these boundaries is *free*, not in a moral but in an *ontological* sense, that is, in the way it is constituted and realized as a being. Ontological identity requires freedom in this fundamental ontological sense and as such it is ultimately applicable only to *personal* beings and not to a-personal things — this is what the shift of *hypostasis* from *ousia* to personhood implies. Ultimately, therefore, a particular being is 'itself' — and not another one — because of its *uniqueness* which is established in *communion* and which renders a particular being unrepeatable as it forms part of a relational existence in which it is indispensable and irreplaceable. That which, therefore, makes a particular personal being be itself — and thus be at all — is, in the final analysis, *communion, freedom* and *love*, and that should not surprise any Christian who believes that the world exists only because of God's free love and that even God himself *is* love.[15] For, if the notion of God carries with it the ultimate ontological claim, 'I am that I am', it is because only God can claim to be a personal being in the genuine sense I have just indicated: he is the only being that is in an ultimate sense 'itself', that is, *particular*, but whose particularity is established in full ontological freedom, that is, not by virtue of its boundaries (he is 'incomprehensible', 'indivisible', etc.), but by its *ekstasis* of communion (he is eternally Trinity and love), which makes it unique and indispensable. When we say, therefore, that God *is*, we do not refer to a being as being but to the *Father* — a term which denotes being in the sense of *hypostasis*, that is, of person.[16]

It would seem, therefore, that the identification of *hypostasis* with person — this historic cross-fertilization between Greek and biblical thought that took place in the fourth century — has ultimately served to show that the notion of person is to be found only in God and that human personhood is never satisfied with itself until it becomes in this respect an *imago Dei*. This is the greatness and the tragedy of man's personhood and nothing manifests this more clearly than a consideration of his capacity and incapacity, especially from an ontological point of view. We can see this by considering one of the most important capacities of human personhood, namely *creating*: man is capable of creating, of bringing things into being.

2.

When we employ the terms 'creation', 'creating' or 'creativity' in relation to personhood, we must not have in mind the idea of 'manufacturing' with which we usually associate man's ability to be a creator.

---

[15] This, of course, calls for an understanding of freedom and love not in moral but in ontological terms — an understanding which still has to be worked out and to find the place it deserves in philosophy and theology. Such an ontology of love is, for example, the only way to understand the view of the Greek Fathers (e.g., Athanasius in his *De Incarn.*) that a break in communion with God means the return of the world to non-being.

[16] I am aware of the fact that God's being, his ultimate ontological identity, is often, or rather normally, understood in terms of 'substance'. This is so because the shift of *hypostasis* from *ousia* to personhood during the Trinitarian discussions of the fourth century has not yet been fully understood and applied in Western theology. For those who made this shift at that time, however, the ontological identity of God and the unity of his being were not to be found in divine 'substance' but in the *hypostasis of the Father*. This has been a major difference between East and West, as is noted by Karl Rahner who argues in his *Trinity* for a return to the Greek patristic and biblical identification of God's being with the *Father* rather than the divine *ousia*.

Admirable as it may be, man's capacity to manufacture and produce useful objects even of the highest quality, such as the machines of our modern technological civilization, is not to be directly associated with human personhood. Perhaps on this point the contrast we have been making here between man as a person, on the one hand, and man as an individual thinking or acting agent, on the other hand, becomes more evident. The 'creation' of a machine requires man's individualization both in terms of his *seizing, controlling and domi-nating* reality, that is, turning beings into things, and also in terms of *combination* of human individuals in a collective effort, that is, of turning man himself into a thing, an instrument and a means to an end. Hence, it is only natural that the more collectivistic a society, that is, the more it sacrifices personhood, the better the products its achieves. But when we say that man is capable of creating *by being a person*, we imply something entirely different, and that has to do with a double possibility which this kind of creation opens up. On the one hand, 'things' or the world around acquire a 'presence' as an inte-gral and relevant part of the totality of existence, and, on the other hand, man himself becomes 'present' as a unique and unrepeatable *hypostasis* of being and not as an impersonal number in a combined structure. In other words, in this way of understanding creating, the movement is from thinghood to personhood and not the other way round. This is, for example, what happens in the case of a work of real art as contrasted to a machine. When we look at a painting or listen to music we have in front of us 'the beginning of a world',[17] a 'presence' in which 'things' and substances (cloth, oil, etc.) or qual-ities (shape, colour, etc.) or sounds become part of a personal pres-ence. And this is entirely the achievement of personhood, a distinctly unique capacity of man, which, unlike other technological achieve-ments, is not threatened by the emerging intelligent beings of com-puter science. The term 'creativity' is significantly applied to art *par excellence*, though we seldom appreciate the real implications of this for theology and anthropology.

Now, this possibility of 'presence', which is implied in human personhood, reveals at the same time the tragic incapacity which is intrinsic in this very capacity of personhood. This is to be seen in the paradoxical fact that the presence of being in and through the human person is ultimately revealed as an *absence*. The implications

---

[17] 'C'est le commencement d'un monde', to use the profound observation of Paul Valéry with regard to music (*Oeuvres* I, 1957, p. 1327).

of this are of decisive importance for what we are trying to say here. If we take again our example from the world of art, the fundamental thing that we must observe with regard to the 'presence' it creates, is that the artist himself is absent. This is not an entirely negative statement. The tragedy lies in the fact that it is at once positive and negative: the artist exists for us only because he is absent. Had we not had his work (which points to his absence), he would not exist for us or for the world around, even if we had heard of him or seen him; he *is* by *not being there* (an incidental actual presence of the artist next to us while we are looking at or listening to his work would add nothing to his real presence in and through his work, which remains a pointer to his absence).

This presence which is realized in absence will be ruled out as sheer fantasy or feeling by all empirically inclined thought. For indeed, this presence is not graspable empirically and it does not appear to be compelling rationally. At the same time, it is not to be understood or explained idealistically either, that is, as an imposition of the mind upon reality, for the word 'absence' which is *inseparably* attached to 'presence' is to be taken seriously: the 'present' person is *not* there. In what sense, then, is this presence a presence at all? Where does the ontological content of this presence lie?

The first indication that this presence is not a matter of psychology but of something far more fundamental and *primordial* is to be found in the fact that it does not rest upon conscious reflection but *precedes* it. When — to use an example offered by Sartre for a different purpose — I have an appointment in a café with a friend whose existence matters to me, and on my arrival there I discover that this person is not there, the absent person *precisely by not being there* occupies for me the entire space-time context of the café. It is only *after* I reflect consciously on the situation that I realize empirically who 'is' and who 'is not' there. But as I do that a significant distinction emerges between the presence of personal and the presence of a-personal beings.

After my conscious reflection on the situation, those who 'are' and those who 'are not' there are not *particular* beings in a personal sense: their identities are established not in communion and freedom but by their own boundaries (as a realist would say) or through those imposed by our own minds (as an idealist would prefer to say). Their presence is compelling for our minds and senses but not for our freedom; they can be turned into things, they can lose their uniqueness and finally be dispensed with. (Those who 'are' in the café 'are' — from the point of view of personhood — in the same sense that the chairs 'are' there.) The presence, therefore, of a-personal beings is ultimately demonstrable through mind or sense perception (which allows for them being described, conceived, and finally manipulated or even dispensed with), whereas the presence of persons is ultimately demonstrable through love and freedom.[18]

The implications of this distinction for ontology are extremely important and present philosophy and theology with a dilemma they can hardly afford to ignore. For there seem to be two possibilities open to ontology. One is to attribute being to being as such, that is, to the *nature* of things, in which case being (and its recognition) emerges as *compelling* ontologically: presence is ultimately attributed to the very being of a being, to its own nature, that is to say, to something one simply *has to* recognize. In this case, ontology operates on the assumption that the world is a *given datum*; it does not raise the radical question of the *beginning* of the world in the radical ontological sense of the possibility of the non-being of what is so obviously — that is, compellingly there. On the other hand, there is the presence of personal beings, which is not established on the basis of a *given* 'nature' of the being but of love and freedom: persons can neither be particular — and thus be at all — by way of a nature compelling them to 'be' so, nor be present, that is, recognized as being there, by compelling us to recognize them.[19] In this case, ontology cannot ulti-

---

[18] It was after struggling to express these thoughts that I came across the following words of W. Pannenberg, which, I find, express the same thing in a clearer way: 'Human beings are persons by the very fact that they are not wholly and completely existent for us in their reality, but are characterized by freedom and as a result remain concealed and beyond control in the totality of their existence. A person whose being we could survey and whose every moment we could anticipate would thereby cease to be a person for us, and where human beings are falsely taken to be existent beings and treated as such, then their personality is treated with contempt. This is unfortunately possible, because human beings are in fact also existent beings. Their being as persons takes shape in their present bodily reality, and yet it remains invisible to one whose vision — unlike the vision of love or even that of hatred — looks only at what is existent in man' (*Basic Questions in Theology*, vol. III, 1973, p. 112).

[19] Maximus the Confessor puts his finger on this crucial issue by raising the question: does God know his creatures according to their own nature? The answer he gives is most interesting: no! God does not know (or recognize) beings in accordance with their nature but 'as the concrete results of his will' (*'idia thelemata'*. See esp. *Amb.* 91; PG 91, 1085A-B). From the angle of personhood, which is God's way of being, to recognize beings in accordance with their nature would amount to a compulsory recognition. The implications of this for theological epistemology are far-reaching and their proper treatment would demand a special study outside the limited space of this chapter.

mately take for granted the being of any being; it cannot attribute the ultimacy of being to a necessity inherent in the nature of a being; it can only attribute it to freedom and love, which thus become ontological notions *par excellence*. Being in this case owes its being to personhood and ultimately becomes identical with it.

In so far, therefore, as the human person is an entity whose being or particularity is realized by way of a transcendence of its boundaries in an event of communion, its personhood reveals itself as *presence*. But in so far as the human person is a being whose particularity is established *also* by its boundaries (a body), personhood realizes this presence as *absence*. Since both of these have their focus on one and the same entity, they represent a paradox, the two components of which must be maintained *simultaneously*, if justice is to be done to the mystery of human personhood. For taking the first aspect alone would mean that only bodiless beings can be called persons — which would exclude man from being a person. And taking the second aspect alone would mean that only bodily beings are persons, which would imply that the transcendence of the boundaries of the body is not ontologically constitutive of personhood — hence *all* bodies are actually or potentially persons.[20]

The presence-in-absence paradox is, therefore, inevitable in a consideration of man as person, particularly from the point of view of his capacity to be a creator.[21] A consideration now of the reasons which

[20] The main difficulty created by Professor Strawson's view is that particularity — and for that matter ontology as a whole, since, as he rightly insists, there is no ontology without particularity — inevitably requires a 'body' and hence a space and time context (*Individuals*, p. 126). Needless to say that for theology such a view would inevitably lead to the dilemma: either God's particularity is also one determined by space and time (by a 'body'), or it is impossible to attribute particularity to God at all, in which case it is also impossible to attribute ontology to him; we are simply forced to say that he *is* not. The only way out of such a dilemma — which, if I am not mistaken, is *the* difficulty in which theology constantly finds itself — is to admit the possibility of a particularity which is not determined by space and time, i.e., by circumscribability or, in other words, by individuality. My argument in this chapter relates precisely to this crucial problem. My thesis consists in trying to show that not only is it possible to speak of such a particularity, but it is indeed *only* such a kind of particularity that expresses the particularity of a person; even when it is determined by a body (as in the case of man), the person is particular only when its presence is constituted in freedom from its boundaries, as a being which is particular because it is unique and indispensable in the context of communion.

[21] Karl Mannheim, in his *Essays on the Sociology of Knowledge* (ed. P. Kecskemeti, 1952, p. 50f.), points, I think, in the same direction as my presence-in-absence argument here, when he speaks in connection with art of an 'aesthetic space' which is determined neither by the space of the object ('this slab of marble') nor by the

account for the absence aspect in this capacity of man may help us to understand this paradox better.

<h1 style="text-align:center">3.</h1>

I have been speaking of man's capacity for creation as a movement from thinghood to personhood. This is precisely what we find in a genuine work of Art, as contrasted with technological 'creation' which is realized through the reverse movement. But at this point a hypothesis emerges. Suppose that there are no 'things' to begin with but only 'persons', what happens then to creativity as a movement from 'thinghood to personhood'?

This supposition is compelling for anyone who assumes that a personal being ontologically precedes the world, that is, of anyone with the biblical view of creation in mind. It is a supposition that no Greek philosopher would ever raise. For the Greeks, 'Being', or the 'world', precedes the *'person'* — hence, if we say that God creates, we cannot but imply that he creates out of some pre-existing matter. To deny this would imply a denial of the ultimacy of 'being *quâ* being' and give ontological priority to personhood. This is why for the Greeks the world constitutes a *given datum* of ontology: it *is* because it has always been and will always be. 'Creation' or 'creativity' does not have to do in this case with ontology in a primary sense but with the *fashioning* of pre-existing matter.

Now, it is all too easy to admit *on a doctrinal level* that for a Christian things are different because the world was created *ex nihilo*. But I venture to suggest that unless we admit *on a philosophical level* that personhood is not secondary to being, that the mode of existence of being is not secondary to its 'substance' but *itself primary* and constitutive of it, it is impossible to make sense of the doctrine of *creatio ex nihilo*. But this is precisely what Christian theologians would not normally do: even the doctrine of God is based normally on the assumption that God is personal because he *first* 'is' and *then* 'relates' — hence the classical treatment of the doctrine of the Trinity and the problems of intelligibility it has never ceased to present.

The priority of 'being' as 'substance' over against the person, which is a basic Greek idea, seems to have extended its roots well and deep into our minds. And yet without the assumption that personhood is identical with being and prior to thinghood not only the doctrine of creation out of nothing collapses, but what is more directly relevant

mere experience of the subject, but which nonetheless has its own 'objectivity' — or, as I would prefer to say, its own ontological content.

for our subject, it becomes impossible to explain why there is in all creation the paradoxical structure of presence-in-absence to which I have referred.

The fact that presence in and through personhood is revealed to man in the form of absence constitutes the sign *par excellence* of the *creaturely* limitation of humanity. The idea of *creatio ex nihilo* was employed by the Fathers in order to oppose the Greek view of a creation of the world out of pre-existing matter. At first sight, it may not seem quite clear why this idea is so significant for illustrating the difference between being an uncreated creator and being a creator as creature, but it becomes evident that this is so as soon as we look at it anthropologically rather than simply and primarily cosmologically and theologically. In this particular case, in which as I have argued the mystery of personhood is at stake, creating out of pre-existing matter implies the distance (*diastēma*) due to what we call space and time, that is, categories indicating a relational event by emphasizing simultaneously *unity* and *distance*, that is, absence and presence, or rather presence-in-absence. The characteristic of creatures, as contrasted with God, lies precisely in this distance which accounts for their multiplicity: creatures are not one, but, taken all together, many and diverse because they are divided up in separate places (Athanasius).[22] The limitation of creaturehood lies in this 'distance' which makes the creatures 'comprehensible' and 'containable' (*chōrēta*). Space and time, when viewed from the angle of the *nature* of creaturehood, are two terms which reveal a relationship of separateness (*chōrismos*) and hence of individualization; only when they are viewed from the angle of personhood do these terms reveal a relationship of unity (*katholou*) and hence of communion. Thus personhood, when applied strictly to creatures, results in a contradiction between the *katholou* and the *kata meros*. And since personhood affirms the integrity and catholicity of being (cf. *hypostasis*) and must of necessity overcome the distance of individualization (cf. *ekstasis*), being a person implies, existentially speaking, the frustration of the contradiction between presence and absence. This frustration would not have existed had there not been the spatio-temporal roots of creaturehood, that is, in the last analysis, *beginning*.[23] Thus, the fact that the artist is absent through his

---

[22] *Ad Serap.* I.26; III.4.

[23] The notion of beginning is tied up inseparably with that of distance, individualization, fragmentation, etc., and because of that finally with the possibility of absence, decomposition and death. Creaturehood, being based, by definition, on beginning, cannot purely and simply *be*; non-being constantly conditions its ontol-

personal presence in his work is due primarily to the fact that he has used pre-existing matter, because this means that his personal presence is embodied in something that is already part of the space-time structure which makes it containable (*chōreton*) and thus present only by being distant from other things. Had God done the same thing, that is, used pre-existing matter, he would be caught in the same predicament and his presence in his creation would be a presence in absence for him — something that would rule out entirely the possibility of a presence without absence.

4.

Similar observations apply to man as an *historical being*. Man's *capacity for history* is not determinable by any substantial qualities of his nature; his capacity for memory is not necessarily a unique characteristic of the human being. It is again personhood that makes man historical and this is to be seen in a way similar to that of the presence of being in terms of space through the creation of art. Just as in the case of art human personhood creates 'the beginning of a world' (a presence which is not *causally* determined by the given reality), in the same way history means that the already given in terms of events — the 'past' — does not produce an irresistible causality for man, a necessity such as the one we find in the survival of species or the transformation of various substances or the movement of the stars. The 'events' created by man through history bear the seal of the freedom that is inherent in personhood. Presence in terms of space or art and presence in terms of time or history are *two sides of the same coin*: they refer ultimately to being as freedom and communion and not as a compelling presence. It is this that explains why an ontological term *par excellence*, namely that of *Parousia* (presence), which has been used here as a key term in connection with creativity and art, has in Christianity become a technical term to denote an *event*: the coming of Christ.[24] This would have been inconceivable

ogy. In this respect, Heidegger's idea of 'being-unto-death' faithfully describes the ontology of the world. It is another matter, as we shall see in a moment, that such an ontology cannot stand on its own feet, but depends on the possibility of 'being-into-life', of a presence, that is, without absence.

[24] The fact that in the Bible the *Parousia* is so persistently — almost to the point of obsession — removed from historical causality (the Kingdom does not come through observation; the Lord will come as a thief in the night; etc.) shows that we must apply to history exactly the same observations as we applied to creativity: 'presence' is not ultimately determined by a compelling ontology which implies

had it not been for the fact that we cannot properly understand history in an un-ontological way (in terms of man's decisions, consciousness, actions, etc.), but only in close connection with the question of being as a whole. History is an ontological matter. The time of history is the same time as that in which natural events occur.[25] The 'future' or the 'eschaton' of history is, therefore, identical with the final incorruptibility of the world, as the Greek Fathers insisted with particular force from Ignatius of Antioch and Irenaeus.

But if this is the case, then the presence-in-absence paradox which I discussed with regard to art must be applied here, too. The future which is offered by history, like the presence offered by art, is subject to the antinomy of its negation, to the threat of nothingness. It is this antinomy that accounts for man's fear of the future and which finds its resolution only in *hope* as a distinctive characteristic of personhood related inseparably with love and freedom. This antinomy is due to creaturehood and makes man tragically conscious of a past which is present only in the form of absence and of a future threatened by nothingness. The consciousness of *transience* which accompanies man's historical existence is part of this picture. Thus, *becoming* implies for man *passion* (*pathos*), due to the fact that creaturehood, taken in itself, has its being rooted in beginning and thus under the constant threat of nothingness, as a presence-in-absence. Its becoming in time therefore reveals being in the form of *change* and *decay*, that is, threatened by death. The *ekstasis* of personhood implies a certain kind of 'movement', but for the creature this is realized in the form of *pathos*, whereas for God's personhood, whose being is not threatened by decay and death, *ekstasis* is *impassible* (*apathēs*; the doctrine of the impassibility of God acquires, in this way, a meaning

causality, but depends on freedom and love. It has been rightly observed (by W. Pannenberg) that the idea of history develops in connection with Israel's doctrine of creation. I should like to add that all *evolutionary* ideas of history — detectable even in modern 'theologies of hope' — remain impossible as long as such a doctrine of creation is maintained. The Greek mind could not entertain the possibility of a 'creatio ex nihilo' *for the very same reason* that it could not avoid looking for causality in historical events (a characteristic theme of Greek tragedy as well as of Greek historiography). It is, therefore, no wonder that interpretations of history in terms of a linear 'Heilsgeschichte', such as that developed by O. Cullmann, appear in the end as identical with the Greek idea of history, as is shown so convincingly by Professor John McIntyre's criticism of Cullmann (*The Christian Doctrine of History*, 1957, p. 42f.).

[25] To repeat an important point made by Professor D.M. Mackinnon in connection with Kant (*The Problem of Metaphysics*, 1974, p. 9).

which does not contradict the ekstatic and creative love of God, both within and without space and time). Man's *ekstasis* of personhood cannot be impassible in itself, but only in God; possibility is part of creaturehood, yet something that personhood tends to find unacceptable through *ekstasis*.

The presence-in-absence paradox, therefore, shows that personal presence *quâ presence* is something that *cannot be extrapolated from created existence*. It is a presence that seems to come to us from outside this world — which makes the notion of person, if properly understood, perhaps the only notion that can be applied to God without the danger of anthropomorphism.[26] Man — especially, though not exclusively, through art and history — creates a 'presence', thus showing that he is a person. The significance of art (obviously the reference here is made not to those so-called artists who simply copy things of nature in a more or less photographic fashion) lies in that it shows that man as a person is not content with the presence of beings as they are given to him in the world. In a God-like fashion, he wants to recognize beings not 'according to their own nature', that is according to their compelling givenness, but as 'results of his own free will' — as *idia thelēmata*, to recall Maximus the Confessor.[27] In this he succeeds, yet only, as we saw, in the form of the tragic paradox of presence-in-absence. This in itself is very significant. For it means that personhood prefers to create its presence as absence rather than be contained, comprehended, described and manipulated through the circumscribability and individualization which are inherent in all creaturehood. Personhood thus proves to be *in* this world — through man — but not *of* this world.

All this means that the ekstatic movement towards communion, which is part of personhood, remains for man an unfulfilled longing for a presence-without-absence of being as long as there is no way of overcoming the space-time limitations of creaturehood. This situation implies that there is no possibility of a creature developing into something of an 'uncreated' being, and there is nothing that shows this more dramatically than this 'capacity-in-incapacity' which

---

[26] The right notion of the person is of crucial importance for theology. The individualistic and psychological conceptions of personhood which have prevailed throughout the history of Western thought have led inevitably to a rejection of the understanding of God as person (e.g., Fichte, Feuerbach, Tillich, etc.). This is an additional reason why we should seek an understanding of personhood away from the ideas of individuality and consciousness.

[27] See above, n. 19.

is implied in human personhood. At the same time, this reveals that there is a future, an *eschaton* or a *telos*, a final goal in creation, which must resolve the problem created by personhood.

This is not a kind of wishful thinking but an ingredient of personhood as fundamental — indeed as constitutive — as that of presence for the notion of being. For if there is ultimately no personal presence without absence, then there is no personal presence at all. The very use of the word 'presence' becomes then arbitrary and in the end meaningless. Those, therefore, like the atheistic existentialists, who do not wish to admit any ontology of pure presence, which would force them to go beyond the actual human situation, will have to answer the question of the meaning of the word 'presence' in the presence-in-absence paradox. For it is of course true that in actual human existence the two categories, presence and absence, are inseparably linked when applied to personhood. But unless there is something like an 'outside-the-actual-human-existence' in which both of these words point to something 'real', then they make no sense in this context either — they represent inventions of the most arbitrary kind. For where have we got the category of presence from, when we apply it to personhood? Is it an extrapolation or an analogy from the experience of the presence of objects as they are observed and recognized through our senses or minds? But the presence of which we are talking in the case of personhood is the very opposite of this experience: in terms of this experience, presence in this case is, as we have seen, absence. It is, therefore, impossible to regard the experience of the actual world as the source of the category of presence in the paradox, presence-in-absence. And if that is the case, then there are only two alternatives before us. Either what we call presence is an arbitrary use of a category which in this case bears no ontological significance whatsoever and which will prove the empiricist right in calling this kind of presence sheer fantasy.[28] Or if we wish to disagree with the empiricist and attach an ontological significance to the presence of the presence-in-absence paradox, we shall have to admit that presence in this case points to an ontology which does not ultimately depend on the experience of this world. Those who accept this paradox as pointing authentically and ontologically to personal existence are not as far as they may think from an implicit assumption of God.

---

[28] He will have to tell us, of course, where fantasies come from, but that is another, though very relevant, question.

5.

This shows that man has a capacity (in incapacity) for *faith*. Thanks to his ekstatic personhood man confronts nothingness not as a sort of acceptable 'nirvana', but as a *painful absence* which makes him long for presence. The fact that this absence remains unacceptable to man[29] is due to his personhood which drives him towards communion, and this is what makes faith a possibility for him: *he is confident in presence in spite of absence*. Thus, a man who escapes from the open confrontation with the threat of non-existence with the help of various securities (ideals, ethics, etc.) is closer to faithlessness than the one who — to remember the Dostoyevskian scene of Christ's confrontation with the Grand Inquisitor — has no objectified security to rely upon. For a person who has become indifferent to the problem of existence has made a decisive step towards thinghood, and things are incapable of faith.

6.

All this 'longing for communion' may sound as if it were a matter of psychology rather than ontology. Although what has already been said about the ontological content of the notion of 'presence' ought to be enough to warn the reader against such a misunderstanding, the ontological point will become clearer when we apply the presence-absence scheme to an area in which human incapacity reveals itself in the most tragic manner, namely *death*. Death appears to be the most tragic event of human life only if man is viewed from the angle of his personhood. To a biologist, death may be a form of life, and to an idealist a meaningful sacrifice of the individual for a higher cause, but to Christian theology it remains the worst enemy of man, the most unacceptable of all things. This cry against death, which is so deeply rooted in us, precedes our cognitive activity and even our consciousness in that it constitutes our primary and ultimate fear, expressed or hidden, the condition of all that we do. It is for this reason that the fear of death is a matter not just of psychology but of ontology; it is the threatening of being with non-being, the possibility that personhood may be turned into thinghood. The absence that death brings is the absence that threatens presence, as we tried to describe it here. Creativity and art are thus the person's defence

[29] This unacceptability of absence must be underlined. Faith as an ingredient of personhood does not address itself ultimately to some kind of *Deus absconditus* or to a 'being-into-death', but to presence and life. See below, n. 31.

against death and at the same time his taste of death, as this creativity leads to a presence-in-absence.

Now, death has always been associated with matter and body. In a substantialistic approach to man this fact has led to the idea that there is something like a soul or spirit which possesses *in its nature* a capacity for immortality. The difficulties that this view implies hardly need to be mentioned, and it would suffice to underline that this idea of a natural immortality of the soul is not only unbiblical, but it can hardly explain man's fear of death, as we described it a little while ago. Only if we associate being with its 'mode of being', that is, person as the bearer of being, can we make any ontological sense out of this unacceptability of death. It is at this point that the association of death with the body becomes evident.

The body of man is not a *part* of his being in the sense of a bipartite or tripartite division of man to which, in various forms, a substantialistic approach to the human phenomenon has led theology (in sharp contrast to the position of modern medicine and psychology). The body is an *inseparable aspect of the human person* and for this reason it is regarded as partaking of the *imago Dei* (e.g., by the Greek Fathers). The strong belief in the resurrection of *the body*, which goes back to the beginnings of Christianity, can make sense only in such an approach.[30]

Now, if the body is associated with the person as an organic part of the mode in which the person realizes the presence of man in the event of communion, it is evident that the presence-*in-absence* which is part of the predicament of creaturehood should be experienced in the body *par excellence*: the body becomes the existential reminder of our creaturehood in the double sense we observed in the example of art, that is, by being the mode by which man *is* as a *presence* through his *ekstasis* towards communion (hence the erotic movement of man is also a matter of the body), but at the same time by emphasizing the absence of being through death.

All this means that the overcoming of death represents a longing rooted in the *personhood* of man. It also means that this overcoming

---

[30] This may help us to see the connection between the various uses of the word 'body', for example in Paul: the body of the risen Christ which is the 'mode of existence' of true humanity is a 'presence', both in the sense of the 'Parousia' and in that of the Eucharist, *only in and through communion*, i.e., as community (Church). The four connotations of 'body' in Paul (Christological, anthropological, ecclesiological and eucharistic) meet and thus make sense because of the ultimate identity between 'presence' or life and communion.

is a matter of turning the presence-in-absence of being into presence-without-absence[31] and this is not a matter of inherent capabilities of a 'substantial' character but of *personal communion*. The agony of nothingness which accompanies existence calls basically for communion. Death shows created existence to be suspended in the void because communion which sustains existence seems to be exhausted or rather negated by the limits of creaturehood. Man was not created immortal, but by having his personhood he was made capable of communion with the immortal God. Death came to him not as a punishment in a juridical sense but as an existential consequence of the break of this communion; it came at the moment that man became introverted, and limited the ekstatic movement of his personhood to the created world.

Sin, therefore, entered as *idolatry*,[32] that is, as an *ekstasis* of communion with the created world alone. In this way, what sin did was of deep ontological significance: it made the limitation of creaturehood show itself in the existential contrast between being and nothingness. This contrast appeared inevitably as soon as created existence affirmed itself through communion within the created realm. The possibility of communion was thus preserved only in order to make the longing for communion even stronger and to emphasize the absence of Being in every presence, that is, the absence of God which ultimately means death. The *imago Dei*, that is, man's personhood, was both preserved and destroyed: the presence-in-absence structure of human existence testifies to this paradox. Man can pervert his personhood but he cannot eliminate it entirely. This possibility of perversion can be illustrated by some fundamental results of the Fall

---

[31] An ontology which does not ultimately overcome non-being is no ontology at all. What good is existence, argues St Athanasius in his *De Incarn.*, if death finally overcomes it? A 'dying being' is the greatest absurdity that can exist for ontology. It is, of course, a real absurdity and we must appreciate modern existentialist philosophy for waking us up from the dream of pure, positive ontology based on the world as it is (ontological or cosmological arguments, etc.). But the fact that a 'dying being' is still a *being*, for it is *there*, points, as I have already argued, to the possibility of ultimately overcoming the absurdity. Christian theology, by speaking of the Resurrection of Christ, fights simultaneously against two opposite schools of thought. It denies the possibility of pure ontology on the basis of the world as it is; and it affirms that there *is* a possibility of a pure ontology of this world, yet only on the basis of the fact that it *will* ultimately exist — of the fact, that is, that being is personal and depends on love. An uncritical acceptance of the 'being-into-death' ontology by Christian theology is impossible without finally a loss of 'the ontological content of the person'.

[32] Cf. J. Macquarrie, *Principles of Christian Theology*, 1966, p. 238f.

which have a direct relationship to man's capacity and incapacity as a person, while the inability to eliminate personhood entirely is to be seen in the existence of human freedom. We shall have to devote a few lines to each of these items as they represent basic aspects of our subject.

7.

If we try to understand the way in which human personhood becomes perverted through the fall, the following points may serve as illustrations:

(a) The *ekstasis* of personhood becomes, in the fallen situation, experienced as *apo-stasis* (distance) between person and nature. As was explained earlier, by being person man was meant to offer to creation the possibility of hypostatic catholicity, that is, the fulfilment of nature's ultimate reference to Being, a fulfilment which would take place as a unity respecting the integrity and diversity (*diaphora*) of beings. This would allow man the unique honour of being *the priest of creation*, that is, the one in and through whom creation would be *referred back* (*anaphora*) to the Creator. But the fall of man destroys this possibility precisely because man's ekstatic movement, by being limited to creation, does not allow for the catholicity of creation or nature to be ekstatic towards what is external to it in and through the human person, since the latter, by his introversion, has lost his true ekstatic movement towards 'outside' creation, that is towards the Creator. This not only explains why 'the whole created universe groans in all its parts' (Rom. 8.22) awaiting our salvation, but at the same time it throws light on the actuality of human existence itself. For the inability of human personhood to be ekstatic towards what is outside creation and thus to unite nature in personhood leads to the fragmentation of nature and hence to an *individualization* of beings: each being acquires its identity not through the hypostatic differentiation which emerges from communion, but through its affirmation *in contrast and opposition* to the other beings. Difference becomes division[33]

---

[33] I owe this distinction to the remarkable insight of St Maximus the Confessor. Apart from this distinction, the reader must have already noted the use I have been making here of derivatives of the Greek words *stasis* and *phora* for the ontology of the person. To recapitulate this usage, two basic Greek words for ontology, *stasis* and *phora*, are qualified through the notion of personhood as follows:

Stasis (being 'as it stands', as it is 'in itself') is realized in personhood both as *ek-stasis* (communion, relatedness) and as *hypo-stasis* (particularity, uniqueness). In the perverted state of personhood, these become *apo-stasis* and *dia-stasis* (sep-

and person becomes individual, that is, an entity affirmed by way of contrast to rather than of communion with other entities. Thus, 'the other' becomes an existential contrast to one's self, 'my hell' and 'my original sin' (Sartre). Human nature becomes through pro-creation individualized by bringing forth beings as individuals; its ekstatic movement does not produce diversity *in unity*, but *in division*. Fragmentation and individualization is the price that nature pays for man's introversion. It is also the very basis of death.

(b) A fundamental consequence of this is to be seen in man's capacity for knowledge. As was stressed earlier in this chapter, by being person man recognizes being as a 'presence' in an event of communion in which things are 'present' in their catholicity and integrity as beings. Knowing emerges in this way only out of loving: love and truth become identical. But this can be possible only if nature and person are not in a relation of opposition, that is, as long as the division into distanced individual beings has not taken place. But the fallen state of creation with its implication of individuality inevitably results in a distance of contrast between beings (cf. paragraph [a], above), which makes knowing receive temporal priority over loving: in order to relate in communion (= love), I must first relate by way of contrast, since 'the other' being poses its identity to me only as an individual, that is, a being defined by its contrast to myself. Knowing, therefore, begins, inevitably, in this situation, with a process of *gathering information* about the other being, that is, by subjecting it to my observation which will lead to a description (establishing characteristics) and evaluation (establishing qualities and value) of this being.[34] And since this can only happen by way of relating all this to what I

---

arateness and individuality). Similarly, *phora* (the movement of being towards outside itself) leads in personhood to *dia-phora* (difference, otherness) and to *ana-phora* (reference or movement towards outside creation). In terms of personhood, therefore, both *stasis* and *phora* are neutral categories, inconceivable in themselves. It is the way they are qualified through the above-mentioned composites that relates being to *beings*, i.e., to ontology as particularity and as life. Person-hood, rightly understood, is precisely about being as *particular living beings*.

[34] Aristotelian metaphysics can serve as an illustration of this. Aristotle strives through his notion of 'substance' to arrive at the very being of a particular thing beyond, so to say, the various qualities and characteristics that characterize the particularity of this thing. And yet even the notion of 'substance' remains for him part of his whole complex of categories. Hence the difficulties in understanding the exact role that 'substance' plays for metaphysics in Aristotle, as they are brought out in the discussion of the problem by Professor D.M. Mackinnon ('Aristotle's Concept of Substance'; cf. also his 'Substance in Christology — A Cross-bench View', in S.W. Sykes and J.P. Clayton (eds.), *Christ, Faith and History*, 1972, pp. 279-300).

already know through a rational process, my first step towards communion with the other being takes place in my *rational* capacity. One can love only what one knows, since love comes from knowledge, we are told by Thomas Aquinas[35] — except that this is our fallen situation and should not become part of our metaphysical anthropology, still less of our approach to Trinitarian theology, as was the case with Thomas. From all this, the step towards understanding man's capacity for knowledge in terms of 'com-prehension', 'con-ception', and so on, of reality (cf. section II, above) is as inevitable as its repercussions for human life, or even for the life of nature as a whole.

This dichotomy between love and knowledge implies a distance not only between person and nature but also between thought and action within the human being itself. Once the possibility of knowledge arises as independent of and prior to the act of communion (love) with the other being, it becomes possible for man to dissociate his thought from his act and thus falsify the event of truth. Thus man can become a hypocrite, and *it is indeed only the human being that is capable of hypocrisy.* This cannot be explained except through this perversion of personhood[36] which provides for the distance between thought and action. In the situation of fallen personhood, truth no longer appears as we described it earlier, namely as the outcome of an event of communion in which man takes part, but as a possession of the individual thinking agent who disposes of it as he wishes. Needless to say, Truth cannot really arise in such a situation; and yet the paradox is that man can, so to say, deep in himself, be aware of what the Truth is, but dissociate it from his act. The distance between thought and action helps hypocrisy to arise, and this is only part of the general state of individualization to which reference was made under (a), earlier. Since the 'other' becomes a threat to 'myself' (Sartre) in a fallen state of existence in which difference becomes division, 'myself' needs to be protected from the 'intruder' of my individuality. Hypocrisy serves as a perverted way out, when the *ekstasis* of personhood drives us towards communion as the event of truth.

---

[35] *Summa Theol.* Ia 2ae, 4. This, in fact, goes back to Augustine (*De Trin.* 10.1).

[36] It is interesting to note that *persona* or *prosopon* came to be associated in the classical Greco-Roman world with playing a role in the theatre. Hypocrisy is not unrelated to personhood; it is the state of existence in which the person becomes *persona* or *prosopon* in this 'theatrical' un-ontological sense. This observation may help us to appreciate further the significance for ontology and culture in general of identifying *prosopon* with *hypostasis* by the Greek Fathers (see my earlier remarks on this). Contrast that, however, with modern sociological theories of personhood which tend to remove personhood from ontology again and relate it to the idea of 'role'.

8.

Now all these examples show that personhood may appear to be perverted in a fallen state of existence but not entirely extinguished. The fact that the illustrations just given apply to the human being *par excellence*, if not exclusively, indicates this, for it is only the human being that possesses this perverted personhood in which the longing for real and full personal communion is tragically present. But the preservation of personhood in the most paradoxical form of its extreme self-denial is to be seen in human *freedom*.

Freedom is an essential part of the *imago Dei*, for without it man could not be in any way like God, since he would have to be governed by necessity (Gregory of Nyssa).[37] In the fallen state of existence which is characterized by the dialectic of good and evil,[38] freedom has come to signify the possibility of choice between two things, and thus it has acquired a rather ethical significance. But the primary and true meaning of freedom is to be found in its ontological content to which I referred in some detail earlier.

That freedom represents such an ultimate existential possibility is to be seen precisely in the fact that one is free not simply to choose between two things — there is nothing existentially ultimate about that — but *to refuse one's existence*: this is the proof of the fact of freedom. Man is thus free to refuse his personhood, that is, the difference between person and nature: he can choose to become a thing.[39]

That this is the main issue behind the fall of man is precisely what I have been trying to say in this chapter. Man, by his fall, chooses to sacrifice his personhood by individualizing his existence in the manner of the division and fragmentation of thinghood. Yet, in saying this, I have also noted that this individualization does not eliminate the personal dimension of longing for communion, and a similar thing is to be noted with regard to freedom. Freedom was given to man as a dimension of personhood, in order that the essential or natural difference between God and creation would not become distance

[37] 'For if necessity *in any way* was the master of the life of man, the image (of God) would have been falsified in that particular part' (*The Great Catech.* 5)

[38] As well as by the individualization and fragmentation of being which are inherent in it.

[39] One may argue that the possibility of refusing existence implies a choice between two things, thus leading us back to the moral concept of freedom. But the alternative to existence, although it may appear to imply a choice between two possibilities, is not in fact an alternative with an ontological content (since its 'content' is non-being); it is not like choosing to go to London or not to do so. Freedom puts to the test the very heart of ontology as a whole. See below, n. 41.

and division (*diairesis*), but, on the contrary, a *realization of communion* between the two. In creating man as a person, God had in mind communion, and freedom was the only way to this. With man's choice to introvert the ekstatic movement of his personhood towards himself and creation, the ontological difference between Creator and creatures was affirmed as a gap, that is, not as difference, but as division, and man became enslaved to nature. Freedom led to slavery, but paradoxically enough, like the ekstatic tendency of personhood to which I referred earlier, it did not disappear. How does this appear in human existence? This problem lies behind the very essence of the question of human capacity and incapacity, and I have not yet found anyone who grasped this in all its fulness and acuteness better than Dostoevsky. I should like, therefore, to refer to him rather extensively at this point.

In the writings of Dostoevsky, the problem of freedom is presented in the form of two extremes. On the one hand, man still, deep in his heart, wants to feel so independent that he wishes to be free not only to create but also to destroy. Reasonableness and harmony are not his ultimate goals in existence; those who assume this are rebuked bluntly by Dostoevsky: 'Where then have all these wiseacres found that man's will should primarily be normal and virtuous? Why have they imagined that man needs a will directed towards reason and his own benefit? All he needs is an independent will, whatever it may cost him, and wherever it may lead him...' (*Letters from the Underworld*). This is the moral that follows from the words of the hero of these *Letters* after describing the order which humanity could achieve through its culture and civilization: 'I should not be surprised if amidst all this order and regularity of the future there should suddenly arise some common-faced or rather cynical and sneering gentleman who, with his arms akimbo, will say to us: "Now then, you fellows, what about smashing all this order into bits, sending their logarithms to the devil and living according to our own silly will?" That might not be much, but the annoying thing is that he would immediately get plenty of followers'.[40] Dostoevsky did not live long enough to see this

---

[40] This tendency of man to destroy is to be seen against the background of his capacity to create as it were 'out of nothing', in a God-like fashion (cf. my discussion of this problem earlier). Thus, it becomes clear why the demonic or fallen existence is tied up not only with freedom but also with the quite legitimate desire of man to be God. It is obvious in this case that the categories of good and evil (moral judgements, etc.) are too posterior ontologically to what is at stake here to be of any applicability to the mystery of freedom.

very thing happen in the two World Wars which confirmed so tragically his insight into the human being.

But this is only the one extreme in which freedom survives in man.
The other is seen by Dostoevsky to exist in the form of man's deep
longing for suffering: 'I am sure that man will never renounce genuine suffering even if it brings him ruin and chaos'. The reason for
this is that 'suffering is the one and only source of true knowledge;
adversity is the mainspring of self-realization'. This interpretation of
freedom in terms of suffering, on which Dostoevsky insists throughout his works, reveals the mystery of freedom as the capacity of man
to embrace fully his incapacity, that is, as his ability to turn weakness
into strength or rather to realize his power in weakness. This paradox is nothing other than what Paul means when he writes in 2 Cor.
12.10 after mentioning his full acceptance of suffering: 'for when I
am weak, I am strong'. Human freedom, in its true meaning, abolishes the scheme 'capacity *versus* incapacity' and replaces it with the
paradox of 'capacity *in* incapacity'. In the light of this, the approach
to human capacity and incapacity as concrete endowments and possessions of human nature (cf. section II, above) is shown once more
to be wrong. Man in his freedom appears to deny any natural possession, any capacity — only by so doing he proves fully that he is free,
and thus shows himself to be capable of something that no impersonal creature has. It is this kind of freedom that the Grand Inquisitor in Dostoevsky's *Brothers Karamazov* cannot forgive to Christ who
stands before him having — and offering men — nothing, no worldly
or religious security, but 'freedom'.

Man's capacity willingly to embrace suffering to the utmost point
shows that even in the slavery of his fallen state he remains a person,
though an unhappy one. Just as by frankly facing absence man
becomes capable of faith in presence, in the same way by facing suffering and not turning away from it with the help of various 'securities',
man affirms his freedom in a negative way. This is no romanticizing
of suffering as there is no idealization of absence and death; these
are man's worst enemies. But the important thing in human existence is that the only way to abolish these things, the only way to conquer them, is freedom, and this implies freedom to undergo them.
The Cross is the only way to the Resurrection, and this does not take
away from the Cross its utter shame and repulsiveness.

Now, the most paradoxical thing that lies in the fact of freedom
is that man cannot 'free himself' from it — if he wanted to do so
— unless he extinguishes himself completely. This makes Sartre's

words, 'man is condemned to be free', sound quite true. For the alternative which freedom poses for man's existence lies between accepting existence as a whole as something of which man freely partakes, or making existence something which man controls himself. The world as it is given to us tempts man's personhood to disregard or even destroy it and in a God-like fashion create it, as it were, anew. This is inherent in personhood as part of the ontological ultimacy which, as we have seen, is implied in it. Indeed, if personhood is to be regarded as being *of* this world, it becomes *demonic*, tending towards the negation of the given world. Hence evil, which in its ultimacy aims at such a destructive negation of the given world *cannot but be personal*, for only a person, as we described personhood here, can move towards the annihilation of the existent. Art, for example, being a distinctive characteristic of human personhood, by denying or even destroying all forms of the given reality can also do that (as we can observe in many forms of modern art which, not insignificantly, have emerged at a time when personhood and freedom have become predominant notions in our culture). This is genuine, though demonic, personhood. Genuine because, as I said earlier, it is part of personhood to recognize beings not as compelling realities but as *idia thelēmata*, and demonic because in fact the world is not man's *idion thelēma* — it exists independently of his choice — and therefore human freedom can prove itself ultimately only through the annihilation of what exists. If personhood in all its ontological implications were to be extrapolated from this world as something belonging to it, so to say, 'naturally' or even 'analogically', then we could be sure that this world, that is, this *given* presence of being, would not exist — and man being himself 'given' would not exist either. Personhood, understood in its terrifying ontological ultimacy to which I have tried to point in this chapter, leads to God — or to non-existence. To recall the words of Kirilov in Dostoevsky's *The Possessed*, 'Every one who wants to attain complete freedom must be daring enough to kill himself... This is the final limit of freedom, that is all, there is nothing beyond it. Who dares to kill himself becomes God. Everyone can do this and thus cause God to cease to exist, and then nothing will exist at all'. But the world continues to exist in spite of man's ability to opt for non-existence. Freedom thus is shown to be ultimately not a matter of decision: its ontological content lies beyond the concept of choice, it is indeed incompatible with it.[41] As long, of course,

---

[41] This shows how ontologically irrelevant the notion of freedom becomes when understood primarily in terms of decision. If decision becomes an ultimate proof

as non-being appears to threaten being or even to condition it, non-existence will appear as a possibility, a sort of an alternative or choice (man, for example, may reach a point of destroying creation and signs of that are already filling us with horror). As long as death goes on, evil will tempt us to opt for the demonic, as if it were an ultimate possibility (as long as it is, for example, possible for someone to die the temptation for killing him will be there for us). If, therefore, ontology depends on the observation of *this* world, if our metaphysics is nothing but 'descriptive', being is ultimately just as much of a possibility as non-being. But will death go on for ever? This will depend on whether metaphysics is 'descriptive' or, in terms of what I have been saying here, 'ekstatic'. It will depend on whether being depends ultimately on its own nature or on love which is 'as strong as death'. The ontology of personhood is the key to the answer of the question whether being is in any sense ultimate or not.

Freedom, therefore, appears to present man with 'two' ultimate possibilities: either to annihilate the 'given' or to accept it as *idion thelēma*. But because *in fact* the world is *not* man's *thelēma*, if he is still to maintain his freedom in accepting the world, he can do this only by *identifying his own will with that of God*. Is that conceivable? Christianity throughout the centuries has tried to conceive this in terms of

---

of freedom, non-existence must be ultimately a possibility for being, since it represents an 'alternative' for decision. This would mean that freedom can ultimately be the negation of being. But the possibility of an ultimate negation of being amounts to the very impossibility of ontology: how can we speak of being, if non-being can ultimately overcome it? (cf. my argument earlier about the presence of the presence-in-absence paradox; also above, n. 31). By negating God as the affirmation of existence in spite of the possibility of the choice of nothingness which exists for man, atheistic existentialism is in fact denying existence altogether. In the same way, those who project into God the notion of choice (Anselm, Barth, and a long series of theologians, including especially modern Process Theology which has created a real monstrosity out of the idea of choice, which it calls 'God') imply inevitably that there are ontological possibilities which are confronting God himself, thus giving ultimate ontological content (in the form of a possibility presented to the ultimate Being, God) to being as well as to non-being. But the point emerging from our discussion of freedom here rules out such an ultimacy for choice and decision: if freedom is ultimately a matter of choice and decision, then, if it really is *ultimate*, there must be also a 'decision' or 'choice' against being, an ultimate possibility of non-being; but if there is an ultimate possibility of non-being, then being is ultimately negated and hence ontology itself is an impossibility. All this points to the conclusion that if we wish to speak of being in a serious way, to push, that is, the ontological question to the ultimacy which it deserves if it is to be ontology at all, we can only do that by making freedom a corollary of love and by regarding love (and its freedom) as the ultimate ontological notions.

obedience of man to God. It has failed because it has been unable to maintain freedom in and through this obedience. Man has felt like a slave and rejected the yoke of God. Atheism sprang out of the very heart of the Church and the notion of freedom became prominent again. There is more than 'obedience', or rather something quite different from it, that is needed to bring man to a state of existence in which freedom is not a choice among many possibilities but a movement of love. This state obviously can only be realized from outside human existence. The whole of Christian doctrine ought to be precisely about this.

III. PERSONHOOD IN THE LIGHT OF CHRISTOLOGY AND PNEUMATOLOGY

I have dealt rather extensively with the implications of personhood for understanding human capacity and incapacity, for my aim has been to show that only through a study of personhood could our subject be properly approached. I should now try to see what this means in terms of theological doctrine, and especially of Christology, since the mystery of man reveals itself fully only in the light of Christ.

1.

If what has already been said about human personhood is right, then the first observation to be made is that Christology should not be confined to redemption from sin but reaches beyond that, to man's destiny as the image of God in creation. There are, therefore, two aspects of Christology, one negative (redemption from the fallen state) and another positive (fulfilment of man's full communion with God; what the Greek Fathers have called *theōsis*).[42] Only if the two are taken together, can Christology reveal human destiny in its fulness.

If we recapture for a moment the existential content of the fall, to which reference was made earlier, sin reveals itself not in the form of a juridical relationship between God and man, but mainly as a perversion of personhood, leading through man's idolatrous introversion towards created being alone, to the opening up of the abyss of nothingness, that is, to the *division* between the two natures, divine and human, which were meant to be in communion, and hence to death because of the incapacity of nature to refer itself to God in its

---

[42] This 'beyond-redemption' kind of Christology is implied, for example, in Irenaeus' understanding of Adam as a child destined to grow up in communion with God, and it is explicitly stated for the first time by Maximus the Confessor who says that the Christ event would still be realized even if there had not been the Fall.

integrity. The absence of God was thus felt deeply in the person's ekstatic nature as the abyss of nothingness, and man could not fulfil his drive for presence except tragically in and through absence. The ultimate meaning of the Fall was, therefore, in the fact that by perverting personhood (personhood being *the only* way of communion with God) man turned the difference between uncreated and created natures into a *division* between the two, and thus ruined God's purpose in creating man: communion.

If we follow this point of division of natures and combine it with the introversion of human personhood, Christology acquires the significance of the event in which the division of natures (divine and human or created) becomes *difference*, and this happens *exactly as it was meant to happen* by the creation of man, namely through opening up personhood — and through it creation as a whole — to communion with God. This explains the sensitivity of the early Church to the question of the full *unity* of two natures in Christ as well as to the *integrity* of these natures. The anthropological significance of Christology, therefore, contains the following elements in connection with what has already been said about personhood.

(a) Human nature in Christ recovers its ekstatic movement towards God and thus it overcomes its individualization. In this sense, creaturehood becomes a 'new creation' in Christ, that is, a nature which can have a hypostatic catholicity in its reference to being. This leads to a full realization of the *priestly character of humanity*: humanity can now, in Christ, recapitulate and 'refer back' (*anaphora*) nature to its creator. Hence, the importance of Christ in this respect is that personhood is now objectively restored *not on the level of an individual* but *on the level of true personhood* which is capable of bearing *human nature in its catholicity*. Had Christ been another 'individual' among us, this catholicity of nature would not have been realized.[43] The exclusion of the extreme Antiochene view of an individual human subject in Christology appears to be essential in this respect.[44] The understanding of

---

[43] Can the biblical notion of Adam as the one, for example, in whom 'the many have died' or as 'the one man Jesus Christ' in whom the 'many' will live (cf. Romans 5–6 and above, n. 14) make any sense to *ontology* — and not just to homiletics? If so, I do not see how this can be done without so changing our ontology as to allow for the concept of the person as the bearer of the totality or 'catholicity' of its nature.

[44] The incapacity of human personhood to escape from individualism and become the bearer of human nature in its integrity is due to the antinomies which I discussed extensively in the previous section as inevitable parts of creaturehood. The real issue, therefore, between Antiochene and Alexandrian Christology in the early Church must be seen against the background of the question: can human person-

the mystery of Christology primarily in terms of personhood rather than 'nature' shows the importance of the classical notion of *hypostatic union* for the expression of this mystery. Unlike the notion of *communicatio idiomatum*, that of hypostatic union aims at giving ontological priority to the person rather than to the natures of Christ. Just as it is only this or that particular man that makes it possible for 'human nature' to be particular beings and thus to be at all, and just as it is the Father and the Son and the Spirit that make it possible for 'divine nature' to be at all (there is no nature 'in the nude'), the same is true about Christ's being: it is his *person* that makes divine and human natures to be that particular being called Christ. In accordance with what I have tried to say in this chapter about the ontological significance of personhood, the person, or hypostasis, is not generated by nature or derived from it (it would not be established in freedom and communion, if it were so). In other words, we cannot begin with the natures of Christ as though they were something ultimate or self-existent, and if that is the case, we avoid the question which has constantly bothered theologians, namely whether 'two natures' does not, in fact, mean 'two persons'. We also avoid the dilemma 'divine *or* human person' as well as the curious composition 'divine *and* human person', precisely because we cannot speak of the person as if it were an object — as we do about natures — but can understand it only as *schesis*: as that *schesis* (relation) which is *constitutive of a particular being* and in which or by virtue of which natures are such a particular being — or beings — and thus are at all.

The '*schesis*' which is constitutive of Christ's particular being is the filial relationship between the Father and the Son in the Holy Spirit in the Trinity, and in this sense Christ's person can be called 'divine person'. This may give the impression that by saying such a thing we have opted for a 'divine person' — versus a 'human person' — in Christ, thus adopting the dilemma 'divine *or* human person' which we had intended to avoid. But it is not quite so, because man 'in Christ' becomes a true person *not through another 'schesis'* but only in and through the one filial relationship which constituted Christ's being. In other words, 'human person' and 'divine person' cannot in this case be placed in apposition as though they were two parallel 'entities' of some kind: the dilemma 'divine or human person' as

hood be true personhood if taken *in itself?* The Alexandrians would reject an autonomous humanity in Christ precisely because they would not conceive of man — in his true humanity realized in Christ — apart from communion with God. The key issue, therefore, was personhood (as the capacity for communion).

well as the composite 'divine and human person' disappear in Christ by virtue of the fact that one and the same *schesis* is constitutive of Christ's being, both with regard to his humanity and with regard to his divinity. These problems appear *only outside Christ* when humanity establishes itself as being or beings not as a result of communion with God but in contrast with him: it is when we look at Christ from this angle that true and full humanity appears to be constituted as a being (or beings) by virtue of a *'schesis'* which is other than that of relation with God. This 'angle' is a result of man's fallen state of existence in which he tends to constitute himself as a being by relationships other than his relationship with God (e.g., by a sort of paganistic relation with creation or a humanistic self-affirmation and self-existence). It is precisely salvation from this kind of 'personhood' that Christology proclaims, and we can never do justice to it unless our ontology allows for the constitution of a human being through a relationship, a *'schesis'*, which is other than that of man with himself or with creation.

Faced with this sort of being, Christ, whose particularity is constituted by virtue of a *'schesis'* with God rather than with man or with creation alone, man fears that in this kind of Christology there is no room for a full *human* personhood. But because personhood is a *schesis* there is no such thing as 'human personhood' purely and simply except in the sense of 'man loving himself' in a sort of self-existence or loving creatures in a sort of idolatrous existence. Any other kind of personhood would imply a *schesis* with God and that would be precisely the kind of personhood I described a moment ago with regard to the hypostatic union of Christ. This kind of personhood does *not* imply the loss of human personhood; it simply offers to man the relation with God as the constitutive element of his being instead of leaving him with the only other possibilities that are left to him for being a person, namely relation with himself or with creation.

In Christ, therefore, every man acquires *his* particularity, *his* hypostasis, *his* personhood, precisely because, by being constituted as a being in and through the same relationship which constitutes Christ's being, he is as unique and unrepeatable and worthy of eternal survival as Christ is by virtue of his being constituted as a being through his filial relationship with the Father, which makes him so unique and so eternally loved as to be an eternally living being. In Christ, therefore, understood in the way in which I am trying to describe hypostatic union, man not only maintains his personhood but so fulfils it as to make it constitutive of his being in the ultimate ontological sense which, as we have seen, is implied in the notion of person-hood and which is to be found only in God. This is precisely what is implied in Baptism, which is *constitutive* of a 'new being' (note the term 'birth' applied to Baptism), of a being which is not subject to death and therefore *ontologically ultimate*, precisely because Baptism is essentially nothing other than the application to humanity of the very filial relationship which exists between the Father and the Son (note the narratives of Christ's baptism in the Bible and the baptis-mal rites of the early Church).[45]

Through such an understanding of the hypostatic union, we can thus throw light on another aspect of the Christological mystery: Christ as the 'catholic' man or as the 'one' who is at the same time 'many'. In view of what has just been said about Christ's personhood, Christ is 'one' in his own hypostasis, that is, as he relates eternally to the Father, but he is also at the same time 'many' in that the same *schesis* becomes now the constitutive element — the *hypostases* — of all those whose particularity and uniqueness and therefore ultimate being are constituted through the same filial relationship which con-stitutes Christ's being. The biblical notion of the 'body of Christ' acquires in this way its *ontological* significance in all the variations in which this notion appears in the Bible: the anthropological (Adam — first and last), eschatological, ecclesiological, eucharistic, and so on.

(b) Human nature now becomes able to turn God's absence in cre-ation into presence. Christology reveals its relevance for humanity only if what has been said here earlier about human capacity for presence-in-absence is made the context of the Incarnation. It is precisely because there is in man the longing for presence and the search for it in the realm of absence (cf. Acts 17.27 and Sartre, above) that the Incarnation acquires its *raison d'être*. According to Athana-sius,[46] God meets man 'from underneath' (*ek tōn katō*), that is, within, and not without, the space-time structure. The immense significance of this for space and time hardly needs to be stressed. By being bear-ers of presence and not absence, these creaturely conditions of space and time open up towards infinite capacity as they become bearers of the *ekstasis* of humanity in Christ; they are given 'a sort of tran-sworldly aspect in which they are open to the transcendent ground of

---

[45] That this is, in fact, how the result of Baptism was understood in the early Church, following St Paul (Gal. 3.27), see: Tertullian, *De Bapt.* 7-8; Theophilus of Antioch, *Ad Autol.* 1.12; Cyril of Jerusalem, *Catech.* 21.1; etc.

[46] *De Incarn.* 14.

the order they bear within nature'.[47] Human capacity, therefore, does not require a departure from creaturely conditions in order to exist. Communion with God is possible for humanity — and through it for the entire creation — only in and through creaturely existence. History is no longer, as it was for the Greek world, the obstacle to communion with God, but its ground.

(c) This meeting of God with man 'from below', that is, from within creaturehood, implies that the presence given in Christ had itself to go through the abyss of absence, for this, as we have seen, is what creaturehood taken in itself means. The Cross of Christ, and especially the idea of his descent into Hades, are the only way to communion with God. Only in utter incapacity can human capacity be realized. Christology as a pattern for anthropology rules out entirely, as titanic and demonic, any human capacity that does not deny itself in incapacity. It is no wonder, therefore, that the Church from the beginning required the sacramental death of each man in Baptism before any communion with God could be established in Christ.

(d) The overcoming of death as the acute ontological form of absence — in and through death alone — is, therefore, in the light of Christology, a capacity given to humanity in its incapacity. An anthropology which has eliminated from its vision the resurrection of the body is not Christologically inspired. No matter how difficult this idea may be for an anthropology which approaches man as a substance — and I suggest that the difficulty lies precisely *there* — this idea is inescapable when man is approached as a *person* in the way I have tried to describe personhood in this chapter. For all that personhood implies as *ekstasis* and *hypostasis* involves the body, and besides, what is the point in Christology as the realm of the realization of God's presence *in* creation, if the most acutely felt ontological problem of this absence, namely death, still remains? Christology would have nothing existentially important to offer to anthropology, if this were so.[48]

(e) Finally, and as an overall observation, it must be added that if Christ is taken as the Man *par excellence*, theology cannot help but develop a very high view of man. Man cannot be defined as *simul*

---

[47] T.F. Torrance, *Space, Time and Incarnation*, 1969, p. 18.

[48] It would eventually have nothing to offer to the ontology of this world which is subject to corruption, because the point (which is often forgotten) is that man dies because of and together with the dying of the rest of creation. It follows, therefore, that the resurrection of our bodies will be dependent on the transformation of the entire cosmos and vice-versa.

iustus et peccator, much as this might be true as a psychological experience. Anthropology in the light of Christology moves beyond the dialectic of the fallen human state. There is ultimately only one kind of dialectic possible, that of created and uncreated, and this in Christ is raised to the level of personhood so that it may, in an event of communion, become a dialectic of *difference* and not of division. Thus, man becomes truly man, that is, he acquires fully his natural identity in relation to God, only if he is united with God — the mystery of personhood is what makes this possible. *Theosis*, as a way of describing this unity in personhood, is, therefore, just the opposite of a divinization in which human nature ceases to be what it really is. Only if we lose the perspective of personhood and operate with 'nature' as such, can such a misunderstanding of *theosis* arise.[49]

2.

All this may be acceptable as far as Christ — the Man himself — is concerned. But the question that this raises is how all this may relate to each man in his particular existential situation, and here theology has, in my view, usually been of little help to anthropology. For to establish the existential link between Christ and each particular man is not easy without a courageous application of the notion of personhood to theology. This, in effect, means that Christology itself has to be conditioned in two ways, pneumatologically and ecclesiologically — something that theology is rather reluctant to do.

Dietrich Bonhoeffer in his *Christology* has gone remarkably far in this respect, given the fact that he does not seem to operate openly with pneumatology as a decisive condition for Christology. His idea of Christ *pro me*, combined with a stress on *community* as the focus of Christ's presence, opens up great possibilities for an appreciation of the anthropological significance of Christology. Taking my starting point from this Western theologian, I should like to relate all this to human capacity and human incapacity.

(a) Christ does not simply stand *vis-à-vis* each man, but constitutes the ontological ground of every man. This is what it means for anthropology that Christ does not represent an individualized and fragmented human nature, but man as a whole. The insistence of the Greek Fathers on this idea was a necessary corollary of their view of man, and my own insistence in this chapter on the understanding of

---

[49] This explains why the idea of *theosis* has never been really accepted without reservations in Western theology.

individuality as a perversion of personhood and, therefore, as a falsi-
fication of true humanity, is in accordance with this kind of Christology. Christology, therefore, does not offer Christ to anthropology as a
model for imitation, as an *imitatio Christi*, for this would be perhaps of
an ethical but certainly not of an ontological significance to anthropology. Neither could Christology be of any real help to anthropology
if it offered Christ as the victim for the sins of humanity in a substitu-
tionary manner which would not affect man's being ontologically. For
such a Christology may answer man's needs for forgiveness but not his
problem of death (unless death is deprived of its ontological content
and becomes a penalty imposed and removed according to the wish
of the Judge).[50] In order that Christology may be relevant to anthropology, it must 'de-individualize' Christ, so that every man may be 'de-
individualized' too, and personhood may be restored.[51]

(b) A 'de-individualization' of Christ requires a conditioning of
Christology by pneumatology, for it was *in the Spirit* that the de-individualization of Christ's humanity, too, became possible. The Spirit
is not to be brought into the picture *after* the figure of Christ has been
completed, for there is nothing more unbiblical than this.[52] Christology is pneumatologically conditioned in its very roots. But this is precisely why, in each man's relation to Christ, the Spirit is not simply
an assistant to the individual in reaching Christ, but the *in*, in which
he is participant in Christ. Baptism was from the beginning '*in* the
Spirit' and '*into* Christ'.

(c) Now, this is a dead doctrine enforced upon the people's minds
by dogmaticians as long as it is offered outside an anthropology of
personhood. For how an individual here can join another individual
there (in Palestine) with the help of another individual (the Spirit) no
man can sincerely conceive of or sense in any way.[53] As I have rather

---

[50] This juridical approach to death marks, in fact, the understanding of the relation between sin and death in most of Western theology since Augustine.

[51] The reader will have realized that 'de-individualization' does not mean the dissolution of personal particularity but, on the contrary, the condition for the emergence of true personal otherness and identity. See above, Chapter 1.

[52] This leads to the significance of the doctrine of the Virgin birth: a human
being establishing its identity and particularity through the process of procreation
is bound by individualization — no human being can be a bearer of the totality of
its nature (be, that is, a 'catholic' man), though this is what personhood drives it
towards. A birth 'of the Spirit' can secure for man the great mystery which characterizes the holy Trinity, in which each person is the bearer of the totality of divine
nature.

[53] No wonder, therefore, that the usual, though so obviously unsatisfactory, ways

extensively argued earlier, individualization is precisely the fact that accounts for the impossibility of real communion, because it implies distance and hence division instead of difference. It is impossible, therefore, to obtain any clue to the relation between each man and Christ in the Spirit unless the individual dies as such and rises as a person.[54]

(d) Personhood, as I have argued, is the mode in which nature exists in its ekstatic movement of communion in which it is hypostasized in its catholicity. This, I have also said, is what has been realized in Christ as the man *par excellence* through the hypostatic union. This, I must now add, is what should happen to every man in order that he himself may *become Christ* (according to the Fathers) or 'put on Christ' (according to Paul). And this is what makes Christ the head of a new humanity (or creation) in that he is the first one both chronologically and ontologically to open up this possibility of personhood in which the distance of individuals is turned into the communion of persons.

(e) But all this leads to an understanding of Christology in terms of ecclesiology. For, by being the initiator of personhood for humanity, Christ acquires *a body*, and not only that but he can only be spoken of in terms of this body (Acts 9.5; 1 Cor. 12.12; etc.). At the same time, man in relating to Christ in and through personhood affirms his existence only in communion, in the *koinonia* of the Spirit. The restoration of personhood in Christ thus leads inevitably to the community of the Church which, in its turn, offers impersonal nature the possibility of being 'referred' to God in its integrity through the personhood of man. This makes the Church *eucharistic* in its very nature, and man God by participation in God.

3.

Now, this is again a treasure given in 'earthen vessels' (2 Cor. 4.7). The capacity for *theosis* is given in the form of a constant struggle with the Devil. The Bible, in affirming the anthropological sig-

---

of handling this problem are mainly either of an ethical kind (relating to Christ through an imitation of his life, obedience to his teaching, etc.) or a sacramental kind (relating to him through media of grace). None of these, however, can make sense for the ontological significance of Baptism as participation in the very being of Christ, in his 'body'.

[54] Baptism relates to personhood in that through it man's person establishes its identity (a) as a relation in the communion of the Spirit, and (b) as the very filial relationship between the Son and the Father. The meaning of Baptism in the New Testament involves precisely these points, which we may call ecclesiological, Christological and Pneumatological.

nificance of Christology, has allowed for an extra-human factor to appear strongly in the whole picture: human capacity and human incapacity have to be viewed in the background of this extra-human factor, Satan, whose work makes God's *Parousia* in Christ call for a final Parousia yet to come. Satan, whatever one may wish to mean by that, points to the fact that quite independently of man's decision the possibility of non-existence appears to be an 'ultimate' alternative to existence. Everything, however, hangs upon whether this possibility is *ultimate*: is this alternative of non-existence ultimate? Will it be in the end overcome? I have tried to show why, in terms of philosophical thinking, the ultimacy of being is possible only if ontology is finally a matter of personhood, as I have described it here. In terms of doctrine, the answer to this question is given through *eschatology*. Eschatology can be described as ultimacy in terms of history or time (as distinct from an ultimacy in terms of the presence of being, of ontology). Christian eschatology invites us to look at the ultimacy of being from the angle of Parousia. But, as I said earlier, only if this Parousia points to the ultimacy of being in terms of ontology as well as history can it bring with it an answer to the question of the survival of being. Christian doctrine achieves this identification of the historical with the ontological ultimacy only if it operates through the following assertions:

(a) Christ, the 'last Adam' or the eschatological Man, is risen *from the dead*, which means that there is no ultimacy for death and non-existence. Freedom is ultimately not a 'decision', since it cannot opt in an ultimate way for non-existence and death. (Needless to say that without the Resurrection the Cross of Christ can have no relevance whatsoever for ontology, since to stop with the Cross would imply that death — and non-existence — continues to be an ultimate possibility for being.)

(b) If there is no option for non-being in an *ultimate* sense, though there is such an option in an *actual* sense, this means that a *second* coming of Christ is needed to make obvious the disappearance of the choice of non-being. This 'making obvious' of the ultimacy of being (and the non-ultimacy of non-being) will thus have to involve an 'epiphany', a *transfiguration* of the world, a 'new creation', 'new heavens and new earth' in which 'this corruptible body will be dressed with incorruptibility'. It will involve an ontology *which will mean the survival of our world* and thus will not amount to a denial of history and matter in a Gnostic or Neoplatonic sense. But it will be at the same time an ontology which will *not* be determined by individualism, decomposition and death. Because of that, it will be neither 'descriptive' in the logician's sense nor antinomical in the existentialistic sense, for in both of these senses ontology rests ultimately on the *actual* world as it is determined by individualization and not by communion.

(c) It is because eschatology is such a cosmic and ontological matter that it automatically implies the impossibility of freedom to exercise itself ultimately as a decision and a choice: how can you opt or decide for or against the annihilation of the existent (which is part of the ultimacy of freedom) if such an annihilation is shown to be no longer a possibility owing to the disappearance of death? The Parousia carries with it, therefore, the *final* judgement, that is, the end of all judgement, by its being *the* judgement: those who have opted for the demonic will realize that they have opted for the impossible, that Satan was in fact a 'liar' and has 'deceived' them by allowing for non-existence to appear as an ultimate possibility. History, therefore, the time of choice and decision, becomes crucial for eternity precisely because ultimately there is no history ('there will be no time any more') and hence no choice. This will mean that personhood as demonic will be eternally 'tortured' by the very ontological fact that the choice of annihilation, that is, of the rejection of the given world, will be unrealizable. This is the meaning of 'eternal condemnation' put in existential terms.

(d) This means ultimately that ontology — the ultimacy of being — is conceivable only in terms of personhood, as I have tried to describe it here. Eschatology implies that being will be shown to be in the end *personal* in the two ways of 'personal' mentioned in this chapter: hypostatically and ekstatically. Hypostatically, because it will become clear that each person is so *unique* that it was deemed to be worthy of survival. There will have to be, therefore, a resurrection of the *bodies* — these 'modes of existence' of ours — if that survival is to take place. And it will be also an ekstatic survival, because *only by virtue of our being so loved as to be regarded as unique* will we survive hypostatically, as 'particularities', as bodies. It will only then be possible for us to realize what it means that being is to be found ultimately in personal *communion* and not in the 'self-existent'. Now we only know 'through a mirror' — if, that is, that mirror is not so darkened as to be the darkness of this world. This mirror is the community, the Church, which in terms of 1 John reflects God's love in the world. *'Extra ecclesiam nulla salus'*. But what sort of *'ecclesia'*? The right kind of ecclesiology becomes in this context crucial for the notion of personhood.

CONCLUSION

If we now try to summarize the views presented in this chapter with particular reference to the classical theological debate concerning human capacity and human incapacity, the following points seem to emerge as the most basic ones.

(a) Methodologically, the issue under discussion cannot be decided on the basis of human nature as such. The phenomenon of man escapes all substantialist definitions. The borderline of human capacity and incapacity lies only in God himself. Hence, the issue can be decided on the level not of nature but of *relationship*, that is, of personhood. Human capacity and incapacity are revealed only in the way man *relates* to God and the rest of creation.

In speaking of the human nature, therefore, Chalcedonian Christology is not to be understood as implying that human nature *per se* is an indication of humanity. No, the humanity which is revealed in and through Christ is not a humanity which is ultimately defined in terms of its nature as such; it is true and real humanity only because it is constituted in and through personhood; it is 'hypostatic' in being 'ekstatic', that is, free from its 'natural' boundaries and united in communion with God. The anthropology of Chalcedon would be entirely misunderstood if humanity were to be defined *a priori*, outside the 'hypostatic union', as if the phenomenon of man could be conceived in itself. This misunderstanding has in fact occurred and continues to occur, accounting for the actual problematic of the Christological question. The anthropology of Chalcedon depends entirely on the notion of personhood as I have tried to describe it here: man emerges as truly man, as a category distinct both from God and the animals, only in relation to God. For Chalcedon, the equation 'man = man' is unacceptable; it is that of 'man = man-in-communion-with-God' that emerges from its Christology. The first equation corresponds to the ontology and the logic of the 'self-existent'; the second one is logically conceivable only if what has been said here about the ontology of personhood is accepted.

(b) The debate whether man is, in his nature, *capax Dei* (or *infiniti*) or not, in this way becomes irrelevant and extremely misleading. For it stabilizes the states of capacity and incapacity on the permanency of naturehood. Instead of this, an approach to man via personhood, with all that this implies, reveals that capacity and incapacity are not to be opposed to each other but to be included in each other. Only the scheme *capacity-in-incapacity* does justice to the mystery of man.

(c) The highest form of capacity for man is to be found in the notion of *imago Dei*. Yet, if this notion is put in the light of personhood rather than nature, it has to be modified, for what it in fact means is not that man can become God in his 'nature', but can be in communion with God. The word *Dei* in this expression implies not a Deistic view of God but a Trinitarian one: man can himself live the event of communion which is realized in divine life and he can do this with and for the entire creation; he is in fact made as *imago Trinitatis*, and this is possible for him only because of his ability to be a *person*.

(d) Looked upon from the angle of personhood, man reveals his creaturehood in a way of *difference* and not *division* from God. Only through personhood, which implies communion as well as the integrity of being, can God and man be clearly distinguished from each other, precisely by affirming their distinct identities in communion. Any *a priori* juxtaposition of divine and human natures is part of the individualization which results from the Fall and which is overcome in Christ, who *unites* God and man in a *communion* that poses clearly *the identity of each nature*.

(e) The division and individualization of natures, which results from the break of communion and the distortion of personhood in the Fall, poses the relation between man and God as one of presence-in-absence. Creaturehood, in this way, tragically reveals its natural limitations of space and time in the form of absence, especially through death, which signifies human incapacity *par excellence*. Christ as *the* man, by restoring the communion of natures in and through his *personhood*, turns the created realm into a presence of God. The world acquires thus its ekstatic catholicity as it is lifted up to communion with God through man.

(f) Thus, the overall relationship between God and the world ('two realities or one?') is determined by the distinction, suggested by Maximus the Confessor, between difference and division. This can make sense only through personhood as the *imago Dei* by means of which God has willed his world to relate to himself in communion. Juxtaposing *a priori* the world to God goes against the very heart of Christology, since Christ realizes the unity of God and the world, through man, in communion. The issue of human capacity and incapacity serves as a significant illustration of this when it ceases to represent a dilemma. In communion with God, man is capable of everything (Mk 9.23; Phil. 4.13; etc.) — though only in the incapacity of creaturehood, which poses itself clearly in such a communion. Thus, the conclusion brings with it the echo of Paul's words: 'when I am weak, then I am strong' (2 Cor. 12.10).

Chapter 7

'CREATED' AND 'UNCREATED':
The Existential Significance
of Chalcedonian Christology

1.

When the Gospel began to spread among the ancient Greeks and especially among those who had some philosophical education, the first serious problem which presented itself was that of the relationship between God and the world. In the whole of Greek thought, the world was considered as eternal. It was impossible to speak of any beginning of the world in the full sense of the term, in other words in the sense that the being of the world, its ontological 'substance', had a starting point, nor of whatever it was that would have allowed the statement that the world was created *ex nihilo*. Certainly, in the *Timaeus*, Plato proposes a creation of the world and a god who creates it 'by his own free will'. But to what extent is this demiurge-god of Plato 'free'? And to what extent is the creative act of the Platonic god ontologically absolute — with the meaning that we gave above to 'ontological beginning'? The answer is clear from the fact that, to create the world, this god used 'matter' which pre-existed eternally. The demiurge-god of Plato is in fact a decorator. He gave the world form, harmony, physical laws and everything that makes it *kosmos*, a harmonious, unified and gracious whole, but he did not give it existence in the full ontological sense, because something pre-existed for him to fashion (eternal 'matter', and even space).[1] So there can be

---

[1] It is clearly proposed in the *Timaeus* that Necessity firmly restricts the creative action of the demiurge-god. This limitation consists of two fundamental factors

no question of a *beginning* of the world, in the full sense of the term. In the mentality of the ancient Greek, there was no place for *nothing*, for ontologically absolute nothingness, for non-being. What we now call 'annihilation' the ancient Greek feared and drove instantly from his thoughts. There was always something, even if formless (at worst), as there is everywhere something: 'everything is full of gods'.[2] The ancient Greek certainly did not reject the concept of *non-being*, but he linked it inseparably to *being*, and *non-being* was so strictly linked to *being* that it lost its absolute specificity: *non-being* already contains in itself the possibility of being which can itself be said to *exist*. Thus, in one way or another, everything exists eternally, and the world has always existed in whatever way it might be. Simply recall the words of Aristotle in his *Metaphysics*: '[P]roduction would be impossible unless something already existed. Whence it is clear that some part of the final product must necessarily pre-exist; and that part is the matter, which is present throughout the process and ultimately becomes something'.[3]

Likewise, the ancient Greek hated chaos and veritably adored the 'Beautiful', which he identified in his mind with order and harmony, with *kosmos*. Behind the notion of creation, attraction is hidden, the *eros*-love that the *beautiful* arouses (and by extension the Good which

---

which, according to the *Timaeus*, the demiurge cannot refuse. The first is matter, possessing certain properties that dictate to the demiurge-god the way in which he will use it. The other is what we would call 'space' (*chora*, for Plato), which also possesses, of itself, movement and expansion (something that the intellect cannot grasp well, since it contains change, but that it must accept as a necessity in the act of creation). Creation, thus conceived, is not an act by which god sets the world in motion from the start — since movement already existed as a property of space which itself pre-existed creation. Creation is rather an act which sets this movement in the right direction and draws from it a world which is as good (beautiful) as it can be in such conditions. See especially, *Tim.* 48a, 50b-d, 49a, etc.

[2] Plato, *Epinomis* 991d. Aristotle, in his *Physics* (IV.4.212 a 21 and IV.6-9), insists that there is no such thing as the *void*.

[3] Aristotle, *Metaphysics*, Book Z, ch. 7 (ed. J. Warrington; London, 1961). In the *Metaphysics*, Aristotle raises the question of whether something that exists can proceed from its negation (e.g., 'the healthy man' following medical treatment can presuppose 'the sick man', that is, the negation of health), or from the idea that pre-existed (in the example, the idea of health), since everything always proceeds from something else. He prefers the second solution: everything, he says, proceeds from some element, and, he adds, it is not fitting that this element be its negation (e.g., the nothingness which precedes the 'Christian creation'); rather this element is matter (linked certainly with form). In such a philosophy, it is difficult, even impossible, to find the origin — the absolute origin — of whatever it might be, beginning with that of the world.

is synonymous with it): god creates because he abhors chaos and disorder; he is a god of order and beauty, a god of the *kosmos*; that is, in the final analysis, a *cosmic* god. Even if, in principle and by pure hypothesis, the god of Plato could just as well not fashion the world (to invoke, as in the *Timaeus*, the 'free will' of the demiurge), the Good, in that case, by leaving the chaos without form and by not fashioning the world, would not really be a god of the *beautiful*. In fact, the Beautiful exerts an irresistible attraction as much by means of love (*eros*) as in the creative act, while the ugly provokes aversion (the modern Greek term for the opposite of the beautiful characteristically means 'without shape, without form', *aschemos*). Loving an ugly man or, worse, a sinner (one who would oppose the harmony of the moral world) is just as inconceivable as resisting the attraction and the love of the beautiful and the good. The god of Plato has no freedom, in contrast to the God of Christians who loves sinners and the 'ugly' perhaps even more than those who are 'beautiful and good'.[4] So, the Christian God does not create because he loves the *beautiful* and wants to give form and beauty to the world. He creates because he wills something else to exist other than himself, 'something' with which to have dialogue and communion. He creates because he wants to give existence to something which in no way existed before (hence, creation from ontologically absolute nothingness). The creative act of the Christian God is essentially an ontological act, properly constituting another existence. The creative act of Plato's god is essentially an aesthetic act, the giving of form to pre-existent matter.

The consequence of these guiding principles of Greek thought was an organic and indissoluble bond between god and the world. The god of Plato was attained by way of observing the world, just as the Beautiful was attained by way of observing sensible beauty, for example, that of the human body. For the Stoics, reason, which is at once a divine and cosmic principle, maintains everything. For the Neoplatonists, the 'One', 'Intellect' and 'Being' constitute an indissoluble unity, thanks to which the world is 'beautiful' and worth living in.[5] However, if god and the world were to confront one another for a moment and their relationship was to be turned into what we call a *dialectic*, it follows, in the spirit of ancient Greece, that the universe

---

[4] Love of the beautiful is dictated by the attraction exerted by the beautiful. Love of someone ugly or of the sinner, on the contrary, is not dictated by any attraction, that is, by any necessity: it is an act of absolute freedom.

[5] See more on this in my *Being as Communion*, 1985, p. 29f.

would collapse. Antitheses can certainly be used, and Greek thought enjoyed this game, but on condition that the antitheses are not onto-logically absolute and that they do not give 'space' or 'time' to abso-lute *non-being (ouk einai)*. Hence, ascent and descent are the terms of an opposition that the pre-Socratic mind used, while immediately emphasizing their unity. Ultimately, it is a question, ontologically, of just one thing, which from above seems a descent and from below an ascent. There is no dialectical relationship, in an absolutely ontolog-ical sense. There is a mutual dependence, in which the phenomeno-logical opposition fades in favour of the unity of being.

In such a vision of things, the notions of created and uncreated cannot be appreciated dialectically, and in fact are completely devoid of meaning. 'Creation' is one thing, the 'world' *(kosmos)* is another. The *world* is a concept offered to history by the ancient Greek mind, precisely by ontologically linking god and being, thereby forming a harmonious and divine whole: the *kosmos*.

Creation as *ktisis* is a notion encountered for the first time in Christian writings with the apostle Paul and it clearly presupposes an *absolutely* ontological beginning; it is something like an event that happens for the first time (cf. Col. 1.16-17). As a result, in Christian theology, it is not proper to use the word 'cosmology' with reference to creation. Likewise the word 'world' *(kosmos,* in its Greek sense) when speaking dialectically of the God-world relationship, because without God the world ceases to be *kosmos*. (By being essentially cos-mological, ancient Greek thought was theological, *par excellence*.) The *world* has an obligatory link with God and presupposes the presence of God in it in order for it to be *kosmos*, whereas *creation* presupposes an act of God which brings into existence something other than and outside of himself, a 'creation' which is located not *in* him but *vis-à-vis* him. Hence, the schemas 'created-uncreated' and 'God-world' are fundamentally different. The first makes an absolutely dialectical link necessary, while the second does not permit one.

2.

Patristic theology sprang from the womb of ancient Greek thought (the Fathers of the Church in the first centuries were Greek in thought and education). That is why it showed a particular sensitivity with regard to the theme we are addressing. Christian theologians in the first centuries were almost obsessed with maintaining the dialectical relationship between the created and the uncreated. The Church was threatened so stubbornly by Gnosticism, Arianism and many other theological disputes precisely because of the difficulty of this question. From the outset, it was strongly insisted that God must not be ontologically tied to the world in our thinking. The epithet used of God in this regard was 'un-begotten' (*agennetos*), and 'not made' (*agenetos*), in other words, the one who is neither engendered by anyone else (*theogony*), nor 'produced' by someone else (creation). The world, on the other hand, was created from 'non-being' or *ex nihilo*. In order to emphasize the absolute and ontological aspect of the beginning of the world, and perhaps to avoid any Platonic interpretation of the dogma of creation *ex nihilo*, patristic terminology — unlike certain contemporary theologians — makes no distinction between the use of the terms '*mè einai*' and '*ouk einai*'. Without going into an analysis of the sources, we may simply remind those who do make such a distinction of some prayers from the Divine Liturgy which are written in a language both very patristic and very philosophical. Thus, in the Liturgy under the name of St John Chrysostom, we read: 'You who out of nothing (*ek tou mè ontos*) have brought all things to be…' (Prayer of the Trisagion), or 'Out of nothing (*ek tou mè ontos*), You have brought us to be…' (Prayer of the Oblation), but also: 'You who from the abundance of your mercy have brought everything to be out of nothing (*ex ouk onton*)' (Prayer at the inclination before Communion). Hence, the *nothing* from which the world has been drawn is ontologically absolute; it has no relationship whatever to being, it has no ontological content at all. When the Fathers speak of creation from nothing, they are not envisaging the decoration of the universe nor the production of the world from a formless clay, but a production from 'nothing' in the absolute sense.[6] It could indeed be said that the Greek Fathers were the first to introduce into Greek philosophy the absolute concept of *nothing*. At this point, an ancient Greek would immediately ask: What is this 'nothing'? And he would give it some ontological content (that is what Plato did with the *mè einai*), thereby satisfying the exigencies both of his reason (the *mè einai*, in some way or other, must 'be'; put another way, that which 'is not', what is it?) and of his ontology (there is neither space nor time for *nothing* in a world which is really *kosmos*).

So, why did the Greek Fathers abandon Greek ontology so as to advance towards the created-uncreated dialectic? What pushed them into this overturning, conversion and baptism of the Greek mind, into this radical Christianization of hellenism? The reasons were both historical and existential. We must examine them briefly.

---

[6] Thus, St Athanasius, *De Incarn.* 3.

3.

Historically, the Greek Fathers were grappling with two incompatible approaches to God, which led to two opposing ontologies; on the one hand, the god of the Greeks who was always linked to the world, submitted to the being of the world, and who remained the absolute being. Even when it went 'beyond essence' (*epekeina tes ousias*), Greek thought did not rupture the ontological union between god and the world. On the other hand, there was the God of the Bible, who was so independent of the world that he was 'conceivable' without relation to the world (something inconceivable for ancient hellenism) and could do what he wanted, free from any logical or ethical obligation: a shockingly arbitrary God, who has mercy 'on whom he has mercy' and who has compassion 'on whom he has compassion' (Rom. 9.15), a God who is unaccountable to any Reason or Ethic. (Such was the God of the Bible — notice that we have subsequently 'rationalized', 'moralized', and therefore 'hellenized' him!) In such an approach to God, it is not being that holds the decisive place in ontology, in absolute relationship with the truth of existence, but rather *freedom*. It is precisely the notion of *freedom* which imposes that of *nothing* as an absolute notion. Yes, this world might just as well not have existed at all (could an ancient Greek have said that?). The fact of existence, for an object, does not just follow of itself, but is something owing to the free will of someone. This *someone*, who according to biblical faith is God, is not dependent on the being of the world (nor on his own being) because he gives being to all that is. He is the cause not only of beings but also of being *qua* being — and even of his own being.

So we come to the existential reasons which led the Fathers to the *created-uncreated* dialectic. Let us set them out briefly.

II. THE EXISTENTIAL SIGNIFICANCE OF THE CREATED-UNCREATED DIALECTIC

1.

Existence is the fruit of freedom. The fact that the world is *created* and not eternal, having radically — in an ontologically absolute fashion — begun from 'nothing', means that it could just as well not have existed. This leads to the conclusion that the existence of the world and our own existence is not obligatory or self-explanatory, but the fruit of freedom. If the world was eternal, it would just exist; we would not ask why it exists. The only natural question in that case would be: 'Why does it exist in this way or that way, in this or that form?' It would be the scientific question of how to apply the different laws that regulate the universe. For science, the existence of the world, in its absolute sense, is axiomatic,[7] a presupposition that must necessarily be accepted in order to make progress in investigating the world. But this ontological obligation is removed and disappears from the very moment that the *created-uncreated* dialectic is introduced. To say that the world could just as well not exist means that existence is for us a gift of freedom, a grace. Creation and grace thus coincide.

Such a conception of the world gives a quite specific quality to our life. Accepting that my existence is a gift moves my heart to overflow with gratitude as soon as I become conscious of my existence. Thus, the awareness of being, and ontology, becomes *eucharistic* in the deepest sense of the term: an act of grace, of thanksgiving. What in the liturgical life of the Church was so quickly called the 'Eucharist' was linked from the start to the *created-uncreated* dialectic. Some ancient liturgies characteristically made no reference to thanksgiving for the gift of the coming and redemptive work of Christ (see, for example, the *Catecheses* of St Cyril of Jerusalem). On the other hand, there are no liturgical prayers that did not include, first and foremost, a thanksgiving celebrating existence itself, the fact that the world exists. The consequence of this is a very concrete attitude to life and a kind of human being who considers nothing of what he possesses as his own, but who relates everything to someone else, who is grateful for everything and does not think in terms of 'having rights'. The consequence is an attitude and a life of grace, overcoming the *ego*, individualism and all feelings of 'superiority' or concupiscence; being ready to *give thanks*, to give one's entire existence, to fight against death itself and to offer oneself in an exercise of freedom, analogous to the act which brought one's own existence into being. Knowing that our existence is a gift of freedom and not an 'eternal' and self-evident reality does not just deliver us philosophically and intellectually from the captivity of thinking in terms of obligatory 'axioms' and logical 'categories'; it frees us from enslavement in our very existence, an enslavement forged by biological necessity and its instincts. It makes us grateful for the gift of existence without enslaving us to it; we can value it while freely making a gift of it. Such is exactly the attitude of the martyrs and the saints, the attitude of the Church, flowing from the *created-uncreated* dialectic.

---

[7] Nowadays, however, science is more and more preoccupied with the question of the origin of the world.

2.

Existence is relentlessly threatened by death. This is the second consequence of the *created-uncreated* dialectic and it is just as essential as the first. To say that the world is *created*, in other words that 'there was a time when it was not', does not simply mean that it could just as well not exist. It equally means that the world could at any moment cease to exist. Absolute nothingness, 'non-being', which is a principle of the existence of creation, is not automatically suppressed by the fact of existence: on the contrary, it ceaselessly permeates and penetrates it. What is *created* is, *of its very nature*, mortal (St Athanasius).[8] It is therefore impossible to envisage an 'active and efficacious energy', a drive, a movement or any power or impulse instilled by God in the nature of creation such as to assure it eternally of existence. This poor quality Aristotelianism, frequently introduced by theologians when interpreting Fathers such as St Maximus the Confessor is, in essence, a negation of the *created-uncreated* dialectic and even a betrayal of the mind of the Fathers; it means, in effect, that what is *created* possesses in its nature — even if given by God — the possibility of existing by itself. The act of creation then appears in some way to have endowed the very nature of the world with a sort of 'created grace', an idea which prompted countless errors in medieval Western theology.

No, what is *created* naturally contains, at its heart, no power of survival; Heidegger so rightly called it 'being-unto-death'. Being *created* means for us that we are mortal and that we are under threat of total and absolute destruction. The threat of death is the threat of nothingness, of absolute nothingness and 'non-being', in other words of returning to the state of *pre*-creation. This threat, faced by anything *created*, cannot be escaped by an 'innate force' proper to the nature of what is *created*. Our nature means that we come into the world as mortal people, biologically we die at the very moment that we are born. The whole world — by the very fact that it is *created* — perishes while existing and exists while perishing: its life and ours are not 'true life'. What is *created* is, by nature, tragic, because its existence is determined by the paradoxical synthesis of two elements which exclude one another absolutely, namely life and death, being and nothingness, all because its being had a beginning, a 'starting point'. All the beings which make up the being of *creation* are determined by a *beginning*, a fact which inevitably creates distances in the relation-

---

[8] St Athanasius, *De Incarn.* 4.4-6.

ship between beings and leads to the possibility of composition and decomposition, of absolute separation and also of absolute division of beings, which is precisely what we call *death*. Space and time, which exclusively characterize what is *created*, are the very expression of this paradox. By time and space, we all commune with one another in weaving together the thread of life; but it is also by time and space that we are divided from one another by the cutting edge of death. How will the *creation* surmount this, its very own tragedy; how will it conquer death?

The *created-uncreated* dialectic already excludes in advance some solutions that have appeared in the history of theology and philosophy. For example, we cannot say that death is overcome thanks to the immortality of the soul, even supposing that this immortality is a God-given gift to humanity. Whatever gives to the *created* the possibility of existing in a durable, 'natural' way breaks the dialectical relationship between the created and the uncreated, makes the created something 'divine' by nature, and leads to an obligatory immortality. Christian theology has frequently fallen into the snare of such a 'solution' which does not correspond to the authentic mind of the Fathers.

Neither can the 'moral' or 'juridical' solution lead to the overcoming of death. This is the solution that came out of Western realism and was adopted by modern pietism, something foreign to Orthodox tradition but nevertheless dangerously infiltrating the Orthodox world. This solution supposes that the created can improve itself, become better, even perfect, 'perfect itself' in the terminology of pietism, by cultivating the virtues and by practising natural or divine law. No, death is not conquered like that. The only thing conquered is preoccupation with the problem of death; awareness of the tragic reality and inadmissible character of death is what vanishes. Pietism creates people who neither protest nor rage at the existence of death because they take refuge in their belief in the immortality of the soul to console themselves and others, and because they absolutize morality to such a point that they believe that immortality is won by virtue.

Death is natural to creation and it is not overcome by any effort or faculty of the created itself. By morality creation improves itself but it does not save itself from death; while the idea of the immortality of the soul, setting aside the fact that it makes existence obligatory, simply mitigates the tragic aspect of the death of the body, of the very form of creation, which is threatened by death with sinking into non-existence. The more humanity rages at death — and woe to us if we cease to rage at it — the more we shall seek to overcome creation, far from Plato and all forms of pietism. The *created-uncreated* dialectic keeps this rage alive in human consciousness, because it considers existence as a gift evoking gratitude and consent, a gift which, precisely because it is grace and freedom, cannot of itself exist eternally. The world is so *created* that it cannot exist by itself, but it is so loved by God that it must live. Death, the 'final enemy' of existence, must be overcome.

III. TRANSFORMING THE CREATED-UNCREATED DIALECTIC BY CHRISTOLOGY

1.

The teaching of the fourth ecumenical council on the person of Jesus Christ, like the whole of patristic Christology, loses all meaning if it is not related to the problem of the *created* and the overcoming of death. If Christ is presented there as saviour of the world, it is not because he brought a model of morality or a teaching for humanity; it is because he himself incarnates the overcoming of death, because, in his own person, the *created* from now on lives eternally. How is it so? The Council of Chalcedon uses two adverbs that seem contradictory and mean nothing unless they are brought into the light of the *created-uncreated* dialectic. These adverbs are, on one hand, *adiairétôs* (without division) and, on the other hand, *asynchytôs* (without confusion). In the person of Christ, the *created* and the *uncreated* have been united 'without division', in a way that admits no division, but equally 'without confusion', that is to say without losing their identity and their own particularity.

The first of these adverbs, 'without division', means that between the *created* and the *uncreated* there must not exist any distance or separation. Time and space, which as we saw above act on the nature of creation as paradoxes which unite and divide at the same time, thus causing it at the same time both existence and non-existence (death), must become bearers of union alone and not of division. Death cannot be conquered if this 'without division' is not fulfilled. The more creation makes itself autonomous and exists by itself, the more it is threatened by death, since as we have seen death is due to the possibility of division and separation of beings that is caused by the 'beginning' which governs creation. In other words, in order to live, the *created* must be in a lasting and uninterrupted (indivisible) relationship with something *uncreated*, in order to cover thereby the distance which has its inescapable source in createdness, and in order to communicate lastingly with something outside itself. Every created being that does not go out of itself and unite without division to something other is annihilated and dies.

However, if what it unites with to overcome death is itself *created*, as happens in biological love, it does not escape death. *Created* being can only survive when united with something *uncreated*. That is why love, which is precisely the flight of beings outside themselves in order to overcome the limitations of creatureliness and death, is an essential aspect of the resolution of the problem of creation. Anyone who does not love, in other words who is not united 'without division' to something outside themselves, dies. Only love, in other words union 'without division' with the uncreated God, assures immortality, because everything created is destined to perish.

Christ incarnates precisely this free union of the *created* and the *uncreated* as the way of transcending death. If the *created-uncreated* relationship is not indivisible, death is not overcome. Every 'distance' between God and man brings death, says Chrysostom.[9] Overcoming death presupposes union between the *created* and the *uncreated*. That is the meaning of 'without division'.

'Without confusion', on the other hand, means that this union, while being perfect and absolute, does not suppress what we have called the created-uncreated dialectic. Why? And how are we to understand such a paradox in existence?

First of all, the why. It is clear from what has been said up to now that the *created-uncreated* relationship must always remain dialectical, if existence is indeed a gift of freedom. The moment this dialectic is suppressed, the world and God are indissolubly united, the being of God as much as that of the world becomes the 'product' of necessity and not of freedom. Christology does not abolish the dialectic. The person of Christ does not forge a unique and inevitable union of the divine and the human, of the *created* and the *uncreated*. 'Without division' does not signify necessity and suppression of the dialectic, that is, of freedom. 'Without confusion' safeguards the *created-uncreated* dialectic; in other words, it safeguards freedom, just as 'without division' safeguards love. These two adverbs are thus, in the language of existence, terms defining the two critical and limit points of existence: freedom and love. Without love, that is, without going out from the self-centredness and self-sufficiency of being in

---

[9] John Chrysostom, *Hom. in Eph.* 3 (PG 62, 26). Cf. Irenaeus, *Adv. Haer.* V.27.2.

a movement of unity with the 'other' and finally with the 'Other' *par excellence* (the Uncreated), there is no immortality. However, without freedom, that is without maintaining diversity and the particular identity of the lover and the loved, immortality is still impossible.

By uniting *created* and *uncreated* 'without confusion' and 'without division', Christ has conquered death, in a victory which is not an 'obligatory' event for existence, but a possibility won only by freedom and love.

This victory is achieved in the Resurrection, without which there can be no talk of salvation, because death is the problem of creation. 'If Christ has not been raised', says St Paul, 'your faith is in vain' (1 Cor. 15.14). Christ is 'the Saviour of the world' not because he sacrificed himself on the Cross, thereby wiping away the sins of the world, but because 'he is risen from the dead having trampled death by death'. The West (Catholic and Protestant) has viewed the problem of the world as a moral problem (transgression of a commandment and punishment) and has made of the Cross of Christ the epicentre of faith and worship. However, Orthodoxy continues to insist upon the Resurrection as the centre of its whole life precisely because it sees that the problem of the created is not moral but ontological; it is the problem of the existence (and not of the beauty) of the world, the problem of death. And the Resurrection of Christ was made powerful thanks to the union 'without division' but also 'without confusion' of the *created* and the *uncreated*; in other words, thanks to the love that makes the *created* and the *uncreated* surpass their limits and unite 'without division', and thanks to the freedom which means that the *created* and the *uncreated* do not lose their diversity by going beyond their limits in this union, but on the contrary preserve it, and so maintain their dialectical relationship.

2.

So we arrive at the heart of Christology. Christology will remain a 'dogma' devoid of existential meaning unless and until it is translated and lived in an ecclesial way. What do those terms 'without division' and 'without confusion' mean outside the experience of the Church? A 'dogma', a logical (or rather 'metalogical' for believers and absurd for unbelievers) proposition which, at most, is acceptable with regard to Jesus Christ himself, who was man and God, but not for each of us. In its ecclesiological meaning, however, this dogma expresses a way of being. Most of all when it gathers for the Eucharist, the Church reveals the great Christological paradox: the *created* and the *uncreated* are perfectly united without their specificities being abolished; and it does so when each member of the Church, freed from the yoke of his or her biological hypostasis, is united with the other members in a relationship of indissoluble communion from which springs the specificity of each person, in other words, the true identity of each one. All contradiction between 'without division' and 'without separation' vanishes. The dogma becomes more 'understandable' in the language of existence, while remaining forever beyond reason and concepts in the language of a logic based on the experience of unredeemed creation.

The experience of the Church is the only way in which the existential meaning of Christology becomes a reality. Outside the experience of the Church, love and freedom ('without division' and 'without confusion') divide and annihilate one another. *Erotic* love in its biological form begins with physical attraction, that is, with necessity, and ends in biological death, that is, in the destruction of specificity, of the 'without confusion'. Nothing is more 'confused' and destructive of specificity than the body becoming earth and scattered bones. Even in its aesthetic form (the attraction of the good and the beautiful, the classical '*kalos kagathos*'), erotic love is also a love which destroys freedom and specificity, the 'without confusion', because it springs from the attraction of the *good* (and so from necessity) and ends in the *idea* of the *good* (and not in the concrete person), thereby allying itself with the ruin and ugliness of death that destroys the specificity and identity of the loved one.

If we rely upon biological love and sentimental love, we end up losing freedom and specificity, 'without confusion' sinks into 'without division' and all is swallowed up in death. If, on the other hand, we want to preserve the 'without confusion', our freedom, on the basis of our biological existence, then we lose love, the 'without division', and sadly end up once more in death. In order to preserve diversity, we separate ourselves from others, in our effort to free ourselves from the other who constitutes the biggest challenge to our freedom. The more we unite two beings, reaching the point of 'without division', the more we run the risk of creating *confusion* between them. In our biological existence, union 'without division' conflicts with our diversity in relation to others, which is the 'without confusion', with the result that we search for freedom in the individualism that cuts us off from others and promises to safeguard our identity. However, is this separation from others, this very 'without confusion', again not ultimately death? Death is not just the dissolution of beings into a single, confused 'substance', in other words the suppression of 'without confusion', as we saw above. It is also the final separation of beings, in other words the affirmation of 'without confusion'. 'Without confusion' is just as deadly as 'without division' as long as they remain apart and are not absolutely identified with each other. Freedom without love leads to death, as does love without freedom. That, unfortunately, is an essential element of creation.

For the *created* to escape this *destiny*, it needs a new birth, that is, a new way of being, a new *hypostasis*. It is not without reason that the Christology of Chalcedon insists on the fact that the hypostasis of Christ is that of the eternal Son in the holy Trinity; in other words, in the uncreated God, and not a human, that is, created, hypostasis. If the hypostasis of Christ had been created, death would have been just as fatal for him and victory over death impossible. The same goes for each human being. If our hypostasis is the one taken from our biological birth, then, as shown above, freedom and love — those two constituents of existence — remain apart from one another and death follows. However, if only we can acquire a new hypostasis; in other words, if our personal identity, that which makes us persons, can spring from free relations which are loving and loving relations which are free, then our created nature, united without division and without confusion to the uncreated God, will be saved from its destiny of death. By means of Baptism, followed by the Eucharist, the Church offers us that possibility, because it gives us a new identity deeply rooted in a network of relationships[10] which are not obligatory, like those which create the family and society, but free.

In order for the world to live and for each of us to do likewise, as unique and particular persons, love and freedom, the 'without division' and 'without confusion' of Christology, must be identified with one another. That means, with regard to our existence, that they must be 'ecclesialized', so as to nourish a new and true life in the body of the Church and in the body of the Eucharist, where love springs from freedom and freedom expresses itself in love.

IV. SOME PROBLEMS FOR FURTHER DISCUSSION

1. *The Meaning of Death*

I have maintained that precisely because Christian faith regards the nothing from which the world came forth as absolute 'non-being', creatureliness implies that death is a return to the nothingness of

---

[10] All personal identities originate in a network of relationships: biological identity in the family, social identity in society, and so on.

'non-being'. Consequently, by definition, death is essentially nothing other than the threat of a return to nothingness, to the 'non-being' of the *pre*-creative state. It is something written into the very nature of what is *created* — no sooner created than mortal.

I should like, at this point, to invoke the witness of St Athanasius. The following passage, one of many, explicitly shows that death, on one hand, *belongs to the nature of what is created*, and, on the other hand, leads to the 'non-being' of the *pre*-creative state.

> For the transgression of the commandment turned them back to the state in accordance with their nature;[11] so that just as they had come into being out of non-being, so were they now deservedly on the way to returning, through corruption, to non-being again. For if men who by nature once were not were called into being by the presence and loving-kindness of the Word, it follows that, deprived of the knowledge of God and turned towards things which do not exist...they should be deprived of the benefit of existing forever; in other words, that they should be disintegrated and abide in death and corruption.[12] Man is mortal by nature, since he is made out of nothing (ἐξ οὐκ ὄντων).[13]

The position of St Athanasius, which also rests upon various biblical passages that explicitly evoke death as 'corruption' (*phthora*), 'destruction' and 'perdition',[14] must be understood in relation to the definition of life, which is the opposite of death. The biblical and patristic concept of life is never concerned with the power and energy and movement of creatures considered in themselves. Life is always understood as relationship and as communion.[15] Even for God himself life is a matter of relationship, of the communion of the persons of the holy Trinity. This is even truer in the case of what is created, which receives its existence from someone else. The world cannot live except in relation, in communion with God. Death is the severing of that relationship and, conversely, the severing of that relationship means the loss of life. This amounts to saying that death — as the opposite of life — means the severing of relationship with God. Therefore, wherever there is a rupture of communion with God, there is death, and wherever there is death, there is the loss of life, in other words, non-existence (unless someone believes in an existence without life).

[11] Note the fact that sin is a fall into a state not against nature but 'in accordance with nature'.
[12] So death means: being 'deprived of the benefit of existing forever'.
[13] St Athanasius of Alexandria, *De Incarn.* 4.4-6 (PG 25b, 104B-C).
[14] Cf. 2 Thess. 1.9; 1 Thess. 5.3; Rom. 9.22; Phil. 3.10; Heb. 10.39; Mt. 7.13.
[15] See my *Being as Communion*, p. 78f.

2. The Question of the Immortality of the Soul

The above view, which, as I have shown, is not my own invention, gives rise to many problems. These problems essentially derive either from a belief, latent in many Christians, in the immortality of the soul, whereby death no longer constitutes a return to non-being since the soul, of its nature, lives eternally, or from a belief that God does not create mortal beings, and consequently that what is created cannot but live. With regard to the first belief, namely in the immortality of the soul, I have said enough above about the soul not being immortal by nature, since it is not eternal but created. Consequently, it too is subject to the destiny of creation *if left to itself*. We can certainly speak of an immortality of the soul that is not 'natural' but 'by grace', but that is possible only by means of a logical contradiction. The fact that the soul can be immortal *by grace* does not logically permit us to say that it *is* immortal, since the fact that it is created means that it is not immortal in its nature.[16] In fact, if we accept that the soul can be immortal by grace, we implicitly accept that it is not so by nature. Indeed, immortality by grace is conceivable, as we shall see, but why limit it just to the soul? Immortality by grace, when and where it prevails, concerns the body and the material world in general just as much as the soul. To speak of immortality only with regard to the soul — and only for the soul — even by grace, is a distraction: it involved specially attributing to the soul qualities (i.e., natural qualities) of immortality. But God does not want only souls to be saved — maybe *this* is what lies behind the immortality of the soul idea — he wants also the salvation and survival of bodies and of the world as a whole. If there is, therefore, an immortality by grace — and there is — let us not restrict it to the soul, because deification concerns the whole of creation, including the material world.[17]

3. The Salvation of the World by Christ

Let us now address the following question: Having created it, can God allow the world to be lost? The question is relevant and the answer is certainly No; but that does not mean that, in order to be saved, the world must have acquired, at the time of its creation, an immortality

---

[16] Only God 'has immortality' (1 Tim. 6.15-16). If, therefore, a creature is *by nature* immortal, it is God. For an excellent discussion of this matter with reference to the patristic sources of the first two centuries, see J. Romanides, *The Ancestral Sin*, 1989², pp. 124-28 (in Greek).

[17] St Athanasius, *Ad Serap.* I.25.

by nature. If such a thing had happened, there would have been no necessity for the Incarnation of the Word, as St Athanasius deduced; having been endowed with immortality at the time of its creation, according to this hypothesis, created reality would not have been lost whatever happened (fall, sin, etc.). Why, in that case, go to all the trouble of the Incarnation? If it was not the danger of creation's perdition that made the Word take flesh, what was it? The remission of sins? But repentance would have sufficed for that: 'Certainly, if it was only a question of offence, and not of the corruption which ensued, repentance would have sufficed. But if...men were in the power of corruption *owing to their nature*...what else could be done',[18] except the Incarnation? The Word became man, according to St Athanasius, because of the 'threat of perdition' (that is how I characterized death above). If death was not a return to 'non-being', everything could have been resolved without recourse to the Incarnation.

God is not going to allow death to destroy creation. But his way of acting to secure that is not by instilling immortality, from the moment of creation, into the nature of what is created; that would make death into an ultimately harmless decomposition and the Incarnation of the Word would be a useless luxury, from an ontological point of view. In such a case, would we be able to say that 'God is love' and that he never abandons his creature? The threat of total and absolute destruction, of which I spoke above, cannot prevail, but for that to be the case it is necessary either for the love of God to deprive man completely of his freedom or for man to use his God-given freedom to choose Christ. With regard to the former case, it must be said that when someone loves you without you wanting to be loved and when he stubbornly persists in keeping you close to him, he is exercising a selfish restraint: such is not the attitude of God. It is precisely for this reason that Father Florovsky writes: 'The way of dis-union is not closed to creatures, the way of destruction and death'. 'There is no irresistible grace, creatures can and may lose themselves, are capable, as it were, of "metaphysical suicide"'.[19] We cannot, therefore, even in the name of the love of God, create a permanent, natural and neces-

---

[18] St Athanasius, *De Incarn.* 7. That death is a return to *kata physin* is expressed vividly by Athanasius (*De Incarn.* 4): 'the transgression of the commandment turned them back to the state in accordance with their nature; so that just as they had come into being out of non-being, so were they now deservedly on the way to returning, through corruption, to non-being again...'

[19] G. Florovsky, 'Creation and Creaturehood', in *Creation and Redemption*, Collected works of Georges Florovsky, vol. 3 (1976), pp. 43-78, here at p. 49.

sary bond between the created and the uncreated that would annul the 'threat of annihilation' which is death. Being and non-being, life and death, are by definition absolute distinctions.

Given these conditions, how is the world to live? I would say that the answer lies in a Christology which puts emphasis on the Resurrection. It is not by chance that that is the Christology of Orthodoxy. I have insisted on this point above. I shall try to say a little more here even though a correct analysis of the subject would need much more space. I wish only to make some suggestions here, without taking refuge in quotations, because the theme has not been discussed in detail in the past. Nevertheless, in the spirit of the tradition, we have the right — and perhaps the duty — to interpret the faith of the Fathers.

Death is the opposite and the negation of life. It is a step towards *pre*-creative 'non-existence'. This is our starting point, and our course is determined by an understanding of creation as created out of absolute 'non-being', and also by an assurance of the freedom of God, who, as I emphasized above, makes existence a grace and a free gift. If we do not start from this point, we shall inevitably conclude — if our thought is coherent — that the existence of God and the world is absolutely necessary. The conflict between St Athanasius and Plato with regard to the dogma of creation is precisely due to these very profound reasons. The same reasons drove St Athanasius to persevere in his understanding of death as a return to 'non-being' and as a natural state for what is created.

Starting from this point, St Athanasius proceeds to the solution of the problem:

> Seeing the reasonable race...wasting out of existence, and death reigning over all in corruption... [the Word] took to himself a body... This he did that he might turn again to incorruption men who had turned back to corruption, and call them back from death to life by the body he would take to himself and by the grace of the resurrection. Thus he would make death to disappear from them as utterly as straw from fire.[20]

As a result, that is, of the Incarnation and Resurrection of the Word, 'we now no longer die as people condemned; but as those who are rising from the dead we await the general resurrection of all'.[21]

Therefore the key to the solution of the problem: 'How can we escape death understood as destruction?', lies not in the nature of

[20] St Athanasius, *De Incarn.* 8.
[21] *De Incarn.* 10.

what is created, nor in creation itself, but in the Resurrection of Christ. The Resurrection has drawn from death the sting of destruction. Thanks to the Resurrection, we know henceforth that creation will survive.

The fact that the solution lies in the Resurrection and not within creation safeguards certain fundamental principles of Christian faith; one of these principles is freedom. In Christ, creation survives not by necessity, as it would if immortality was natural for what is created and particularly for the soul. Christ as man freely unites the created and the uncreated. Likewise, after the Ascension and Pentecost, the Holy Spirit unites the saints with the body of Christ by appealing to their freedom. Immortality is thus the fruit of freedom from beginning to end. Union with the body of the risen Christ makes the holy Eucharist 'the medicine of immortality and an antidote to death' (St Ignatius). But this union constantly presupposes freedom.

The other principle safeguarded by the Resurrection is the survival of the *material world*. The fact that the Lord is risen shows that freedom cannot destroy the world; but, for all that, free creatures are not deprived of the tendency towards nothingness, which they may opt to follow. The Devil, who represents this option *par excellence*, does not lose, after the Resurrection, his freedom to act with a view to destroying creation and destroying himself as a created being. The same goes for each personal creature who wishes to imitate the Devil. However, the news that a single being, namely Christ, is risen, bearing within him created nature, proves in an even more decisive way that the drive to destruction for creation is unfulfilled and a failure. To the question: 'If death is annihilation, destruction, and so on, what then happens to the man who seeks or accepts death as such?', the answer is that this man remains eternally free to aspire after the destruction of himself and others. However, being unable to attain it, simply because of the existence of *one* human being — namely Christ — and above all because this one has assumed the created world in his body, the Church, he will be eternally tormented by the non-accomplishment of his freedom. In this way, the words of the Gospel take on an existential (and not simply a juridical) meaning: 'and they will go away into eternal punishment, but the just into eternal life' (cf. Mt. 25.46). Hell is the existential space where all those who desire the loss of others — and cannot obtain it, because of the Resurrection — are held. Hatred is, *par excellence*, the foretaste of hell. However, and I wish to insist on this point, all of this does not mean that death is not, by definition, destruction. It follows, rather, from the fact that the Resurrection of this *one* has removed death's target, its object, which is creation. If one was to define death after the Resurrection of Christ, it would have to be called: 'the unfulfilled threat of destruction'. The Resurrection has rendered death inoperative. 'O death, where is your sting?' (1 Cor. 15.55): this cry is incomprehensible without the feast of the Resurrection. It would be a multiple mistake to transfer it to the very nature of creation. That is the mistake that I have tried to highlight above.

The mistake becomes particularly dangerous, moreover, for us who live in the time before the Second Coming, because if we rely on the solution of the immortality of the soul, which removes from death the notion of non-being, we risk rendering useless the resurrection *of the body*. If we accept the idea that death is not the threat of 'destruction' (as I have called it here), but that it is simply an episode in the course of life, then not only will we not understand the reason for the Incarnation, but we will be blind to the way in which human beings — including Christians — 'live' death; because death — even to the Christian — appears to be aimed at our destruction. If it did not always retain that purpose in the eyes of all, it would be unnecessary for us to ask God to keep our departed ones eternally in his memory. Being kept in the memory of God is a question of survival, and not just of happiness or 'repose'. If death did not aspire to the destruction of creation, it would no longer be necessary for us to participate in the divine Eucharist, which is not simply 'for the remission of sins', but also 'for eternal life', the 'medicine of immortality'.

In conclusion, if we would truly understand and assess what Christ has saved us from — which has been my main concern throughout — we must realize that he saves us from pre-creative 'non-being', nothing less. But we shall never understand this unless we link the notion of death to destruction; because if Christ saves us from anything, it is from death.[22]

---

[22] This at least is what St Athanasius insists upon in his *De Incarnatione*, as is clear from the passages quoted above: the Incarnation did not aim at forgiveness or the satisfaction of divine justice, for that could have been achieved otherwise; the only reason that necessitated it was the overcoming of death, the granting to man of the 'ever-being' that belongs by nature only to God.

APPENDIX:
A Dialogue with Philip Sherrard

THE LETTER OF DR SHERRARD

Dear Dr Nellas,[23]

I recently read the article by Dr Zizioulas, 'Christology and Existence', published in the second issue of the periodical *Synaxi*, together
with his letter in the third issue. The purpose of the article and the
letter was to determine the existential significance of the terms 'without division' and 'without confusion' in Orthodox Christology. At
the same time, Dr Zizioulas gives us an interpretation of patristic
thought which I think needs clarification at some points. The following deals with a few of these.

1.

Fundamental to Dr Zizioulas is the idea that God created the world
from nothing, *ex ouk ontōn, ex nihilo*. For Dr Zizioulas, 'nothing' has
an absolutely privative or negative character. It is the 'ontological
absolute nothing'. 'It has no relationship whatever to being, it has
no ontological content at all'. And as if wishing to put an end to any
further discussion of this matter, he adds: 'an ancient Greek would
immediately ask: What is this "nothing"?'

Personally, I do not understand why only an ancient Greek should
have asked such a question. When we propose an idea or a concept,
either it refers to some reality or it does not. If it does not refer to
any reality, then it is not worth even proposing it. If, however, it does
refer to some reality, then we are justified in asking what this reality
is. In the matter we are discussing here, it appears that the concept
of the idea of nothing refers, for Dr Zizioulas, to some reality. At least
he assures us that it has an absolute character: it is the 'ontological
absolute', an absolute 'non-being'.

But if God creates from nothing, and if, as Dr Zizioulas maintains, nothingness has an utterly privative and negative character,
this means that in eternity, prior to any act of creation or created

---

[23] The late P. Nellas was the editor of the periodical, *Synaxi*, in which the article,
'Christology and Existence', which is the basis of the present chapter on 'Created
and Uncreated', appeared for the first time in Greek. The correspondence published in this Appendix appeared in Greek in the above periodical in 1983.

world, we must acknowledge two absolute realities: the reality of God and the reality of nothingness, which is something outside God. That is to say, creation presupposes a creative principle (God) and nothingness. Without nothingness, which is something outside God, God could not have created. In other words, God is not absolute and his freedom is not unlimited: God himself and his freedom are limited up to a point by the 'ontological absolute nothingness', or absolute 'non-being'. How, then, can we avoid the conclusion that there exists in the nature of things a radical dichotomy, a dichotomy which destroys the idea that God is not only absolute, but is also absolutely free: or is it that the interpretation which Dr Zizioulas gives of the idea of nothingness — that is, it is absolute non-being with an utterly privative and negative character — is not correct? Indeed, how can the privation of a relationship exist before the relationship itself, or the negation of existence before existence itself?

2.

Dr Zizioulas writes: 'the fact that the world is *created*...means that it could just as well not have existed'. If this observation is correct, why does the world exist? Because, Dr Zizioulas tells us, God 'wills something else to exist other than himself, "something" with which to have dialogue and communion', 'he wants to give existence to something which in no way existed before'. Leaving aside the purely anthropomorphic character of this assertion — for how else can Dr Zizioulas have such an intimate knowledge about what God wills and what he does not will — would it not have been contradictory if God had willed something and did not realize it? Thus, if indeed God wills to have communion with something other than himself, and this 'something' is the world, then the world must exist of necessity. Or should we say that God sometimes wills it and sometimes does not? And besides, what kind of God would the Christian God have been, if he had not manifested his creative power? God could have a creative power which he does not manifest and still continue to be God.

3.

According to Dr Zizioulas, man as a created being is totally bereft of any quality or property which is not also created, and consequently condemned to death and annihilation. For this reason, in order to escape death and annihilation and live, man 'must be in a lasting and uninterrupted (indivisible) relationship with something *uncreated*', with 'something outside' himself. And Dr Zizioulas adds: 'every created being that does not go out of itself and unite without division to something other is annihilated and dies'. Thus '*created* being can only survive when united with something *uncreated*'.

That which allows created being to come out of itself and be united with uncreated being, Dr Zizioulas tells us, is love. But how is it possible for a created being to come out of itself — that is to say, to transcend its created nature — if this property, love, which permits it to do so, is itself created? A person cannot pull himself up by his own shoe-strings. Unless man has within him, from his nature, some property which transcends his created properties, he has no possibility of coming out of his created self. To say that a human being can come out of his created self without having within him, arising out of his nature, some property which transcends his created properties and powers, is completely without meaning. How then can a person escape from death and annihilation if his nature is bereft of any property and power which is uncreated?

4.

Dr Zizioulas insists that the idea of the immortality of the soul is a mistaken idea because the soul is 'not eternal but created', and everything that is created is subject to death. This implies that God cannot create something which is immortal. But in that case, what can we say about the angels? The angels are certainly created. Are they therefore mortal? And if God can create an angel, which is immortal, why can he not create a human soul that is immortal?

These are a few points which, I think, call for some clarification. Yours etc.

    Philip Sherrard

THE RESPONSE OF DR ZIZIOULAS

Dear Synaxi,

Philip Sherrard's letter, published in issue five, invites me to clarify a number of basic points in my article, 'Christology and Existence', which appeared in issue two of the periodical, and also in my letter which was published in issue three. I thank Dr Sherrard for paying me the compliment of an attentive reading. Although many of the points he raises seem to me sufficiently well explained in the article and letter which have already been published, I shall try to make a few additional comments in the hope that the subject broached by my article will be illuminated still further — at least for those who

are able and willing to understand what I was attempting to say —
so as to make any further discussion from me unnecessary. The main
points raised by Dr Sherrard and my own replies are summarized in
the following paragraphs.

1. *The Meaning of Nothingness*

(i) I begin first by correcting a fundamental error which Dr Sherrard makes in his reading of my article, and which forms the basis
of a large part of his argumentation. Where I write that nothingness
in the doctrine of the creation of the world is 'ontologically absolute'
(*ontologika apolyto*), Dr Sherrard reads and transcribes as 'ontological
absolute' (*ontologiko apolyto*). The difference is enormous. In my article I write that, in interpreting the doctrine of creation from nothing, we must understand nothingness as 'ontologically absolute'. In
his letter, Dr Sherrard represents me as regarding nothingness as an
'ontological absolute', and thus easily concludes that 'the concept or
the idea of nothing refers, for Dr Zizioulas, to some reality. At least
he assures us that it has an absolute character: it is the "ontological
absolute", an absolute "non-being"'. Thus, on the basis of this mistaken reading of my text, Dr Sherrard represents me as accepting
the opposite to that which is the core assertion of my article, namely,
that nothingness represents a reality alongside God, a point of view
at odds with the entire thrust of my article.

If Dr Sherrard had read my article correctly ('ontologically absolute' rather than an 'ontological absolute'), he would perhaps have
taken a different line. When I write that nothingness is 'ontologically
absolute', this means that, regarded from an ontological point of
view (i.e., ontologically), nothingness is an absolute, that is to say, it
has absolutely no relation to being; it is not an existent thing. Therefore, since it has no ontological content, nothingness cannot constitute a reality alongside God — it does not constitute a reality in any
sense at all; it has no being (*ouk einai*).

(ii) Led astray, perhaps, by this misreading, Dr Sherrard arrives at
the following conclusion: 'For Dr Zizioulas, "nothing" has an absolutely privative or negative character'. But where in the article do I
speak of the 'privative or negative' character of nothing? Nowhere.
And this is because for someone who maintains, as I do in my article,
that nothing has absolutely no ontological content, such a statement
would be impossible. 'Privation' and 'negation' only exist if there is
something from which the subtraction (privation) may be made or
which may be rejected (negation). But if nothingness does not rep-

resent any reality, its non-being is 'ontologic*ally* absolute' and cannot have a privative or (in this sense) negative character. The language which we should use includes such phrases as 'not by lack', 'nor by privation' to remind ourselves of the expressions of the Dionysian corpus.

(iii) But if nothingness is absolutely unrepresentative of any reality, as I maintain, how can we say anything about it? At this point a vital question arises, which Dr Sherrard poses in his letter: 'When we propose an idea or a concept', he writes, 'either it refers to some reality or it does not. If it does not refer to any reality, then it is not worth even proposing it'. It follows that, if nothingness does not refer to any reality, we are wrong to use it in our formulation of the doctrine of creation and the Fathers were wrong to use it and should be rejected ('it is not worth even proposing it'). On the other hand, if nothingness does represent a reality of some kind, we should still not use it, because then it would signify that there is another reality alongside God, which would limit the freedom of God. What then should be done?

I do not know which solution Dr Sherrard would prefer: should we make no use at all of the concept of nothingness in the doctrine of creation or should we use it in accordance with the principle which he himself proposes (every concept should refer to some reality), in which case we would limit the freedom of God? Dr Sherrard does not appear to give us the solution to the dilemma which he himself poses.

Indeed, if we were to accept the principle that 'every concept must correspond to some reality', then we could not make any theological use at all of the concept of nothingness. But the Fathers did use it and we continue to do so. And since it is impossible either for the Fathers or for us to use it as a concept indicating some reality (because we would imply that some reality existed alongside God before creation), it follows that the principle that Dr Sherrard proposes, that every concept must refer to some reality, is not acceptable either to the Fathers or to dogmatic theology.

This of course poses an enormous problem, for philosophy as well as for theology. The principle that every concept refers to some reality led Plato to hold that even nothingness has some existence — otherwise we should not be able to speak about it. But biblical faith, by holding that God and his freedom are presupposed by any ontology, liberates ontology from epistemology. Being is free and transcends the concepts. Concepts do not limit being and truth. There is always an apophatic element with regard to concepts, with regard to knowledge: the knowledge of being and being in itself are different things. Epistemology is connected with ontology but is not identified with it.

All this implies a new ontology in which freedom plays the primary role. We cannot investigate this vast theme in a letter. In relation to nothingness in particular, I repeat that if every concept is necessarily identified with some reality, then the Fathers were wrong to speak of creation 'from nothing'. If they used this language, it was because for them the concept of nothingness could express something that did not exist. Unlike their pagan contemporaries who believed that existence was a given, and therefore a necessary reality, they believed that existence and reality are a consequence of freedom. But such an idea would have been unintelligible if there had not been some such concept as that of nothingness which neither presupposed nor referred to any absolutely existing reality. Otherwise reality would have been something that limited the freedom even of God himself, as indeed it does in Platonism. Our consideration of the theme consequently returns to the main argument of my article: do we accept the world as a gift of freedom in the absolute sense which the term freedom has, or do we not? If the answer is yes, then nothingness is a word worth using even though it does not refer to any reality.

2. *God as Creator by Necessity*

In his second observation, Dr Sherrard raises the question of the independence of the existence of the world from the will of God. Doubting my view that the world exists because God 'wills something else to exist other than himself', that is to say, that the world exists only because of the will of God, he raises three objections:

(i) That my position implies 'anthropomorphism' since how else do I know 'what God wills and what he does not will'. But the fact that God wills the world to exist does not depend on anything other than the loving relationship which God freely creates with the world in Christ. If Christ had not existed, we should not have known what God wills or does not will with regard to the existence or not of the world. It is precisely this that excludes anthropomorphism from this matter, since our knowledge is based on a free act of God which reveals what he wills.

(ii) That 'if indeed God wills to have communion with something other than himself' — as I maintain — 'and this "something" is the world, then the world must exist of necessity'. And this is because, as

Dr Sherrard maintains, God cannot sometimes will something and sometimes not will it. From this argument only one conclusion can follow: since the will of God is immutable and eternal it is therefore necessary for him. But this conclusion is not one with which I concur. Under the stimulus of Arianism, it was clarified in patristic thought by St Athanasius the Great that the 'nature' of God is one thing, and the 'will' of God another. The will of God, on which the existence of the world depends (as opposed to his nature, on which the existence of the Son depends — see 'homoousios'), even though immutable differs in that it could have had no existence at all and this without consequences for the being of God. That is to say, God could have never willed the existence of the world and still have remained himself. The existence of the world does not constitute a necessary presupposition for the existence of God, although the existence of the Son constitutes the way in which God exists. This subtle distinction (the Son as God's mode of existence, the world not as his mode of existence) constitutes the difference between will (even when immutable and irrevocable) and nature.

(iii) 'What kind of a God would the Christian God have been, if he had not manifested his creative power? God could have a creative power of such a kind that he does not manifest it yet still continues to be God'. These words of Dr Sherrard are clearly reminiscent of Origen (*De Princ.* I.4.3). One could reply by reversing the question: 'What kind of God would the Christian God have been if he could not but be a creator?' For a God who can not but be a creator has creation as a presupposition of his existence. If he ceases to be God because he is not creating, then creation limits his existence. Where then is his freedom, which elsewhere (see above) Dr Sherrard emphasizes so strongly? Indeed I cannot understand how we can reconcile the idea that God is absolutely free with the idea that he cannot but be a creator.

3. *Misunderstandings of the Concept of 'Nature'*

(i) In the third point of his letter Dr Sherrard raises a vast problem. This problem would not have existed if many of our theologians had not used the term 'nature' in a sense different from that customary in the Greek language, which was also the sense in which it was used in theological discourse.

How can man love God, asks Dr Sherrard, if he does not have 'within his nature' the power of love? Dr Sherrard indeed wants this to be not a created power (since he writes: 'a person cannot pull himself up by his own shoe-strings') but an uncreated one.

It is precisely at this point that the misunderstanding of the terms occurs. To say that the properties of the uncreated can become a part of the *'nature'* of the created is equivalent to stating the greatest possible contradiction. The term 'nature' both in ancient Greek thought and in patristic usage always means the boundaries which differentiate one thing from another, just as according to Herodotus the 'nature' of a crocodile is one thing and that of an elephant is another. The divine nature has properties which on the one hand can be bestowed on creatures, but on the other cannot become part of the *nature* of creatures. The natural properties of the divine nature, for example, in Christology, can never become *natural* properties of human nature — because then the distinction between the natures would be abolished. When people commonly say, then, that at the time of creation God inserted uncreated properties into the 'nature' of creatures, either they do not know the meaning of 'nature' or without realizing it they are 'confusing' the natures. The natures of the created and the uncreated even in Christology (not to mention creation) are united 'without confusion', which means that the properties of one nature never become *natural* properties of the other. Consequently, we cannot say that divine (uncreated) properties are granted *to the nature* of creatures.

How then have we come to unite created and uncreated in Christology? The answer is *through the person* ('by hypostasis' or 'hypostatically'). St Cyril of Alexandria took great pains to emphasize this and his position was never fully understood by the West (hence, too, the suspicion felt by the anti-Chalcedonians for the Definition of the council and the Tome of Pope Leo I). The properties of each of the natures are exchanged by means of the person of the Word, a fact which enables the natures to remain unconfused. Conclusion: the created takes on the properties of the uncreated, not as part of its nature but as part of a relationship which is created by the person. But the person belongs to an entirely different category from the nature — it belongs to the realm of freedom and is in no way a natural category, or a part of the nature. Thus and only thus can we have two natures and one person in the same being (namely, Christ). Otherwise, if the person were based on the nature, we would have had two persons, since we have two natures. Consequently, Dr Sherrard cannot have the love with which human beings love God simultaneously both uncreated and part of the *nature* of creatures.

(ii) The love with which human beings love God really is uncreated, as Dr Sherrard would have it, but precisely for that reason, as I have shown above, it is not part of their nature. ('Not that we should love God, but that He loved us', 1 Jn 4.10). And human beings as natures can of course love, but this love is always connected with some necessity (the biological, moral or aesthetic attraction of the good). Nature entails necessity by definition and for this reason, although fundamentally good, it is not free, it cannot transcend the givenness of its existence and rise above itself by its own powers. The way in which the true uncreated (i.e., free) love also becomes the love of human beings, of creatures, is not through its becoming part of their nature, part of the nature of the creature (this would have abolished the difference between the natures of the created and the uncreated) but through its entering into relationship with God, through its becoming enhypostasized in the relationship between the Father and the Son. This is done by the hypostasis-person of the Son of God, who by his Incarnation and subsequently through baptism in the Holy Spirit brings human beings freely into this relationship, giving them in this way a new identity different from that which nature gives them through their biological birth. For anyone to love God, then, is a matter of relationship (of personhood) and not of nature. Even God's love does not spill from him like the overflowing of a cup, as Plato sees it. This view was rejected by the Cappadocian Fathers[24] (with a clear reference to Plato) in order to counter the dangers of Eunomianism. Thus God loves us not through our nature (or through His nature)[25] but through a person ([that of] Christ) and only in this way — through this person — can we love him in turn. If anyone should say that personhood has nature within it and therefore the love of God becomes a natural property of man, he not only overlooks the difference between nature and person, but also confuses the natures, the properties of which naturally remain unconfused and are only united in a *communicatio idiomatum* hypostatically (i.e., personally). If the uncreated properties could have become part of the nature of the creature (and especially, as some say, in creation), then we would not have needed the person of Christ. But these lead us to the final theme arising from Dr Sherrard's letter.

---

[24] St Gregory Naz., *Or. theol.* III.2.

[25] The fact that love is a property common to all three persons of the Trinity does not contradict the truth that all the properties or 'energies' of God's nature exist and operate only *hypostatically*, i.e., in a personal way. This must be emphasized particularly with regard to St Gregory Palamas who, contrary to the way he is usually presented, insists on the *enhypostatic* character of divine energies; see S. Yagazoglou, *Communion of Theosis*, 2001 (in Greek), pp. 155ff.

4. The Theme of the Immortality of the Soul

In the final point of his letter, Dr Sherrard proceeds again to make an idiosyncratic interpretation of my article. He says that I insist 'that the idea of the immortality of the soul is a mistaken idea, because the soul is not eternal, but created, and everything that is created is subject to death'. Thus, he concludes that in my view: 'God cannot create something which is immortal'. But nowhere in my article or in my letter do I say that the soul is not or cannot be immortal. Indeed considerable imagination is needed in order to find in my article the idea of a mortal soul. I say something quite different in these texts and I am sorry that instead of that which constitutes the main idea of my article, conclusions are drawn about ideas which I do not maintain. For this reason I am grateful to Dr Sherrard for giving me the opportunity to clarify the following matters once and for all.

(i) Even though the idea of the immortality of the soul is not of Christian origin, it has passed into the tradition of our Church, inspiring even our liturgical hymns. Nobody can deny it without finding himself alienated from the very worship of the Church.

(ii) For every student of the history of the first centuries it is abundantly clear that the Church did not accept this Platonic idea without certain limitations and presuppositions. These presuppositions include among other matters three basic things. One is that souls are not eternal but created. The other is that the soul should in no way be identified with the human being. And the third — and most important — is that the immortality of the person is not based on the immortality of the soul but on the Resurrection of Christ and on the future resurrection of the body. Of these three statements the first needs no discussion. The idea of the eternal pre-existence of the soul, which had been accepted even by Origen, was officially condemned by the Fifth Ecumenical Council (Constantinople, 553 CE). The other two statements, however, have an immediate relevance to my article and for this reason I shall attempt to analyse them in the two points which now follow.

(iii) *The human soul is not the essential human being.* The soul is one thing and the human being is another. As all the Fathers from the Apologists and Irenaeus to Athanasius and Maximus believed, the soul is part of the human being but is not itself the human being, who is a psychosomatic entity. When this is taken seriously, then its implications with regard to the immortality of the human being are vast. In my article I argued that the idea of the immortality of the soul cannot constitute the basis of the idea of the immortality of the human being. And this is not because the soul is not immortal but because the soul is not the human being. For the concept of the human being to exist, the body is also needed, but the body dissolves upon death. That is why in the passages which I quoted from St Athanasius the Great in my article above, death was clearly — most clearly, and even to the point of giving scandal to some, not of course by my words but by those of the holy Father — regarded as a return to the pre-creationary 'non-being', although the same Father in other passages accepts the immortality of the soul. Accustomed as we are to identifying the soul with the human being, we cannot understand why there is no contradiction in the thought of St Athanasius. Athanasius is interested in the immortality of man — not just of the soul. And in death he sees the dissolution of the being which is called man (cf. the words of Justin Martyr: 'When this harmony is dissolved, the soul leaves the body *and the man no longer exists*'; *Dial.* 6). That is why, even though Athanasius accepts the idea of the immortality of the soul, he is not satisfied with it as a solution to the problem of death. Since if the concept of man is to exist it must necessarily include the human body, Athanasius seeks for the solution to the problem in areas other than those of the immortality of the soul: in the Incarnation of the Logos and in the Resurrection, both of which include the human body. One would have to be perverse to read the *De Incarnatione* and not see that although its main theme is death and deliverance from it, there is no mention anywhere of the idea of the immortality of the soul as the answer to the problem of death, only of the Incarnation and the Resurrection of the Logos.

The conclusion that follows is precisely that which I maintain in my article. The immortality of the soul is rejected neither by St Athanasius nor by anything I have written. That which is rejected is the belief that since the soul is immortal the problem of death as the threat of the annihilation of man has been solved. This would have been the case, naturally enough, if the soul had been identified with the human being. That is the view of Platonism which did not regard the body as an essential constitutive element of human identity. This unfortunately is the view that has prevailed amongst many Christians who in one way or another tend to identify the human being with the soul. But if this were to be accepted: (a) it would make any expectation of the resurrection of the body superfluous (if the essential self is located in the soul and the soul is immortal, why should we look forward to the resurrection of the body? — simply that human existence should be improved or that the concept, the ontological reality, of man should exist?); and (b) it would make Christ himself, his Incarnation and his Resurrection superfluous (since the immortality of the soul would guarantee us immortality, I do not see anything fundamental — of vital concern to human existence — that Christ offers us). This is what I wished to emphasize in my article: to persuade my readers to base their hope of immortality not on a natural property of the soul but on a person, on Christ and his Resurrection. Can there be any room for misunderstanding?

(iv) But there are also deeper reasons for this viewpoint. The immortality of the soul cannot provide the solution to the problem of death, not only because man in the fulness of his meaning and reality does not exist without the body, but also because the immortality of the soul constitutes a *natural* immortality and consequently one which is *necessary* for man. Even the damned exist for ever on the basis of the immortality of the soul, but their existence, precisely because it is natural and necessary, is a kind of 'death'. This has nothing to do with pain and punishment. Hell is the place of the dead precisely because what is absent is the personal identity which personhood gives, the positive relationship with God, our being recognized as beings by God. It is the condition of 'I do not know you' (Mt. 25.12), not of punished children who are paying the penalty of their wrongdoing. The sufferings of the damned are described in holy Scripture and in the Fathers in words which not only are to do with the emotions (sorrow, groaning, gnashing of teeth, etc.) but also have an ontological significance (perdition, destruction, corruption, etc.). It is precisely for this reason that the Church also prays to God through its bishops 'that Thou mayest not allow Thy creature to be swallowed up by perdition'.[26] The terms 'perdition', 'destruction' and so on are biblical (see Mt. 7.13; Rom. 9.2; Phil. 1.28; 3.19; 1 Tim. 6.9; 2 Tim. 1.10; 2 Pet. 2.1; etc.). These terms are not metaphorical, as they are often interpreted by preachers, but ontological. They refer to the personal identity which is bestowed by God 'in the Son'. It is significant that in our memorial services for the dead the Church prays repeatedly that their memory should be eternal. Why so? Because for a person to be held in the memory of God is equivalent to his or her existing: if God forgets us, if he says 'I do not know you', we fall into oblivion and non-existence. It is the relationship and not nature itself which endows man with hypostatic reality (we should note how ontological, i.e., hypostatic, a thing is the relation-

---

[26] Prayer by the bishop for the dead, in *Euchologion* of the Orthodox Church.

ship of personhood). It is this which makes human nature a concrete reality ('enhypostasizes' it) as it does also with the very nature of God himself, whose nature would have been without existence or hypostasis without the Trinitarian relationship. It is in this sense that 'souls' are commemorated in the Church as *names*, that is to say, as identities which are bestowed within the context of a relationship (there are no names where there is not a relationship). Names are given not on the level of nature (at our biological birth) but at Baptism, in the filial relationship (adoption) which is created in freedom.

Thus we also arrive at the meaning of the phrase 'save our souls', which is often repeated in the worship of the Church. Many see the salvation of the soul simply in terms of the avoidance of eternal punishment, not as something with an ontological significance. Because we have lost the sense of a personal ontology we do not understand that a personal relationship, love, endows our nature with being, with existence, and does not just make us happy or better people. But the soul, even though essentially immortal, has a need, in order for it to exist, to be enhypostasized in a relationship, in a person, to assume an eternal identity different from that which has through simply being. This identity is given by God within the context of a relationship which a person freely (i.e., through exercising freedom as love and vice versa) acquires within the Church — the very place of freedom and love. The soul's natural immortality is therefore of no benefit to it. If it is not 'saved' by acquiring this new identity on the level now of personhood — not of nature — it will fall away from the memory of God, it will fall into the 'I do not know you', and for this reason — in spite of its natural immortality — it will not exist in God's eyes. This is the so-called 'spiritual death' which acquired its name precisely because it constitutes annihilation with regard to the memory of God, a fall into an essential anonymity, an 'identity' which derives not from the hypostasis-relationship with God, but from nature. As St Irenaeus puts it: 'separation from God is death'.[27]

(v) It is in this way that we can conceive of Christ as saviour even of the angels themselves, to whom Dr Sherrard also refers in his letter. The angels are immortal by nature (even if they are not entirely incorporeal).[28] Consequently, since they live for ever on account of their nature, one could perhaps have said that ontologically they do not need Christ. But apart from the fact that even they are not

---

[27] Irenaeus, *Adv. Haer.* V.27.2.
[28] John Damascene, *De Fide Orth.* 2.3.

entirely incorporeal (this is not strictly relevant here, because the body of Christ is exclusively a *human* body, not an angelic one), that which counts for their immortality is not their natural but their personal immortality. If they too do not desire freely, like human beings, to participate in the relationship which Christ as a person creates between created and uncreated, their natural immortality is of no benefit to them — they too will fall into the anonymity of the place of the dead. Christ is saviour of the whole of creation (including the angels)[29] because for anything created to exist eternally is a matter concerning a relationship with God which is free and loving and this is given — is enhypostasized — only by Christ not by means of a natural, necessary immortality but by means of a free relationship within the context of the relationships of the Church in which the angels also participate. Thus for the angels and for humankind and for all the worlds that exist (as the late Father Justin Popovitch used to say) nature will have no reality (hypostasis), whatever forms of immortality it may have, unless it finds its reality (is enhypostasized) in the relationship of the Father and the Son and the Holy Spirit. As to how and why nature cannot exist in itself but only as a relationship-person, this is difficult for us to understand without accepting that relationship (= freedom and love) creates beings, *hypostases*, even from nothing. Consequently we have an undeniable need for an ontology of love as freedom, not as nature.

5. *Epilogue to the Discussion*

May I be permitted before closing the discussion which was occasioned by my article to express a few general thoughts. Why have all the arguments which I developed above needed so much clarification and comment? Is it just insufficient clarity on my part and the lack of a philosophy which would give ontological priority to freedom? Or are there perhaps deeper reasons which make such profound truths a problem even for Orthodox sensibilities? I fear that the latter is the case. And this ought to worry every responsible person, at least within the Orthodox world.

Modern Orthodox thought is going through a period of theological confusion. On the one hand Western scholastic theology, with its undoubted influence on modern Orthodox dogmatics, created a sterile dogmatism from which today even Western theology is liber-

---

[29] Cf. Ignatius of Antioch, *Smyrn.* 6.1: 'if they [the angels] will not believe in the blood of Christ, to them also there will be judgement [κρίσις]'.

ating itself. This dogmatism is expressed in formulas which we learn by heart without ever searching out their existential meaning. Thus if someone attempts to unite dogmatic teaching with existence, he comes under suspicion as an innovator, or an 'existentialist'. But there is also something else which intensifies the confusion. I am speaking of the corrosive effect on modern Orthodoxy of a kind of 'spirituality' which finds the message of freedom and love a hard one and seeks the existential experiences of faith in ideas which 'comfort' the soul and give it security and assurance. Within this context not only are sermons on doctrinal themes avoided, but even when they are given, they do not reveal the whole dynamic power of the doctrine which is interwoven with love and freedom, with the audacity of personal identity. Nature gives assurance, while personhood as freedom is fraught with danger.

Within this atmosphere we have learned to find comfort in ideas such as that of the immortality of the soul and not to long for (this is the real meaning of the expression *prosdokān* in the Creed) the resurrection of the body. How many believers live in a state of joyful longing for the resurrection which is to come? How many have been taught that that is how they should spend their lives? How many are comforted by the idea of the immortality of the soul to such an extent that if one were to ask them what essential thing the resurrection of the body would contribute to their happiness (which means what essential thing would the last enemy, which is called death, take away from them), they would not reply simply and clearly — if they were frank — that they possess everything as things stand at present (provided they are living, of course, the sacramental life of the Church) and consequently the resurrection of the body would not make the slightest difference to their happiness? Thus death does not bother them, nor does the delay in the resurrection of the dead (a delay which made the early Christians long for the resurrection anxiously) dominate their lives as a vital concern and not simply as a doctrine which must be accepted as a sacred expression of truth with no consequences for our existence.

I once attended a funeral at which the priest delivering the homily claimed how 'beautiful' was death, this 'rung on the ladder to eternity', in words closely reminiscent of the description of the death of Socrates in Plato's *Phaedon*. Not only was this in stark contrast with the way those present at the funeral were experiencing the tragic reality of death, not only did it disagree thoroughly with the view of death as 'the last enemy' of God expressed by the Apostle Paul and by the Lord himself in the agony in Gethsemane, but it came into sharp conflict with the *troparia* of St John Damascene which could be heard coming from within the church at the funeral service. The phrase in the *troparia*, 'I bewail and lament [these are harsh words] when I conceive of death', had no relation, of course, to Plato's *Phae-don*. Neither had it any relation to the cleric's sermon. It seemed to come from another world, a world so forgotten that if one had said to this cleric that he was 'Platonizing' in his homily, he would have reacted with great surprise if not vehement protest.

If this is not theological confusion, then what is it? When, of course, the facing of death without sorrow and fear ('that you should not be sorrowful like those who have no hope', 1 Thess. 4.13) takes place with reference to the Resurrection of Christ in the hope of the resurrection of the dead, as is the case in the passage from Paul which is read at funerals, and in the Fathers, then this facing of death takes on its proper meaning. When, however, it takes place on the basis of the idea of the immortality of the soul, which is *not* the case in Paul, then indeed, for the reasons I have discussed here, the confusion becomes dangerous.

It is to this situation that I address the argument which I develop in my article. It marks an attempt to render unto Plato the things of Plato and unto Christ the things of Christ.

With thanks for the hospitality of your columns.

John D. Zizioulas

Chapter 8

THE CHURCH AS THE 'MYSTICAL' BODY OF CHRIST:
Towards an Ecclesial Mysticism

INTRODUCTION

Ecclesiology is the area of theology which appears at first sight to have very little to do with the subject of mystical experience. The Church is commonly understood as an *institution*, an organization determined by fixed laws of government (Canon Law) and loaded with notions of *potestas*, *divino iure* or not, in which everything moves according to *order*. Is it possible to speak of mystical experience in such a case? Do not order, institution, and so on, rule out automatically that which is commonly called 'mystical experience'?

The fact that there is indeed such an incompatibility in the minds of many people is evident from the various 'either/or's or antithetical schemes which have become current terminology among theologians. It would suffice to think, for example, of the scheme *Amt und Geist* introduced by A. Harnack and R. Sohm[1] and, implicitly or explicitly, omnipresent ever since in modern ecclesiologies: hierarchy, ministry, and so on, are incompatible with *Geist*, that is, with the Spirit of liberty that 'blows wherever it wills' (Jn 3.8).[2] Other artificial schemes, such as that of institution versus event,[3] point in the same direction. And it is not simply a matter of theoretical construction and schematization:

---

[1] Cf. K.H. Neufeld, *Adolf Harnacks Konflikt mit der Kirche*, 1979, *passim* and pp. 156ff., 202ff.

[2] Cf. the views of A. Sabatier, *Les Religions d'autorité et la Religion de l'esprit*, 1903, and other liberal theologians of the nineteenth century. Also A. Loisy, *L'Evangile et l'Eglise*, 1902.

[3] Cf. J. Leuba, *L'Institution et l'événement*, 1950.

the entire history of the Church seems to show that charisma and institution are quite often in conflict with each other. Monasticism in the ancient Church posed a real threat to episcopal authority,[4] and the struggle between the two 'powers' does not seem to have been fully resolved up to now. The mystics tend to isolate themselves from the ordinary body of the Church. Mystical experience is identified with the *extraordinary* and the unusual,[5] often with the *individual* as distinct from or even opposed to the common mass of Christians that make up the Church.[6] If mystical experience is to be understood in such terms (as the extraordinary and the subjective and individualistic), then it presents real problems to ecclesiology. It either conflicts with the idea of the Church fundamentally, or has to be somehow accommodated to the institutional aspect of the Church. And this latter requires real creativity on the part of theology so as to make the extraordinary and unusual organically united with the ordinary and common in the life of the Church.

But does mystical experience have to be related only or primarily to the extraordinary and the subjective? If the term μυστικὸς is understood in the way it was originally used in the early Church then it not only becomes possible but it appears to be imperative to dissociate its meaning from the extraordinary or the unusual and relate it to the experience of the *whole* body of the Church. For the

---

[4] This was particularly noticeable at the time of St Photius in the ninth century CE.

[5] A. Deblaere, 'Mystique: Le phénomène mystique', *Dictionnaire de Spiritualité*, X, 1980, col. 1893, defines mysticism precisely as that which 'exceeds the schemes of ordinary experience'. 'The word itself (*mysterion, mystikos*) signifies something "hidden", "secret", outside the expectations of knowledge and experience proper. The mystical phenomenon designates in the first place a movement...in the direction of a particular object, not simply profane, nor eternal, but situated beyond the limits of normal, empirical experience...' For fuller discussions of the subject see the classical works of W. James, *The Varieties of Religious Experience*, 1902; E. Underhill, *Mysticism*, 1911; W.R. Inge, *Christian Mysticism*, 1899, who listed 25 definitions of the word 'mysticism'.

[6] This was the meaning given to mysticism especially in the West, which 'mostly under Augustine's impact, eventually came to understand the mystical as related to a subjective state of mind... Here we witness the formulation of the modern usage of a state of consciousness that surpasses ordinary experience through the union with a transcendental reality', L. Dupré, 'Mysticism', in M. Eliade (ed.), *The Encyclopedia of Religion*, 1987, vol. 10, p. 246. B. McGinn, *The Foundations of Mysticism*, 1991, p. 249f., takes a different view on the later St Augustine, who, according to him, 'spoke of union in terms of the bond that knits all believers into the one Body of Christ, not the union of the individual soul with God'. This distinguishes him, according to this author, from the mysticism of Plotinus.

term μυστικὸς derives from the verb μύω,[7] and this verb is at the root of *mysterion* (μυστήριον) with which the early Church indicated experiences common to all its members, such as Baptism and the Eucharist, without which no one could be called a member of the Church. It is precisely this sense that allows St Cyril of Jerusalem to use the term μυστήριον for the sacraments,[8] and Maximus the Confessor to call his interpretation of the eucharistic liturgy *Mystagogia* (Μυσταγωγία). Μύστις or μεμυημένος is *every* member of the Church — not some members only. And mystical theology (μυστικὴ θεολογία) is never used in the early Church to denote the extraordinary and the unusual but the institutional itself. Thus, the Dionysian writings use the term μυσταγωγὸς for the bishop, who is part of what the same writings call 'hierarchy'.[9] The early Church did not know of any opposition between *Amt* and *Geist*, or institution and mystical experience. Ecclesiology, including the institutional aspect of it, was not only compatible with mystical experience; it was even the place *par excellence* of true *mystagogia*.

All this implies that in ecclesiology the term 'mystical' acquires a meaning of its own. Ecclesial mysticism, as we may call it from now on, is a mysticism which has special characteristics. In this chapter we shall attempt to point out these characteristics and also to place them in the context of theology as a whole. We shall do this by taking our starting point from the idea of the Church as the *Body of Christ* (although one could start from other ideas), an idea that needs to be clarified before it is properly used for such a purpose. After that we shall try to isolate certain types or forms of mystical experience which pertain to ecclesiology. In this connection I propose to deal with some of the fundamental components of ecclesiology and try to see in what way we can speak of mystical experience in relation to them. Such components include the sacraments, particularly Baptism and the Eucharist, as well as the 'word' and its relation to sacrament. Another component is the ministry, both ordinary and extraordinary, which should not be ruled out *a priori* as irrelevant for the subject of mysticism. Finally, a particular place must be reserved in our consideration, at least from an Orthodox point of view, to asceticism and monasticism and the idea of the 'holy man' in general.

[7] Originally the word designated 'to remain silent', as in the case of the ancient Greek cults. In Neoplatonism it acquired the meaning of wordless contemplation.
[8] Cyril Jerus., *Catech.* 18.32 (PG 33, 1053f.); 23.22 (PG 33, 1125B); etc.
[9] Cf. R. Roques, *L'univers dionysien*, 1954, esp. pp. 232f., 296f.

In all this it is evident that we shall constantly be operating with the vicious circle of assuming that we have a conception of the 'mystical' while aiming at defining its content. Mysticism is not simply presupposed here as a given; it is also expected to emerge as a conclusion. This is why in concluding this chapter we shall ask the question again of what Christian mysticism is and what it implies — seen now from the angle of ecclesiology. Thus it is hoped that some of the central issues will come into focus in the particular context of a systematic treatment of ecclesiology.

I. THE 'BODY OF CHRIST' AS A 'MYSTICAL' NOTION

1.

The application of the image of the 'body', and more specifically of the 'body of Christ', to the Church goes back to St Paul, as is well known. It is not our purpose here to enter into a detailed discussion of the meaning given by Paul to this image. The subject has become controversial among biblical scholars and has been dealt with quite extensively in modern bibliography. What I think we ought to recall here is that this image has gone through a long and revealing history in relation to the adjective 'mystical' attached to it. Let me outline the main phases in this history.

The first phase is that of the Pauline use of the term 'body of Christ'. What characterizes this phase is the simultaneous use of it for (a) Christological purposes (Christ's personal body, especially in its risen state), (b) ecclesiological purposes (the Church as the body of Christ) and (c) eucharistic purposes (the body of Christ as it is broken, shared, and communicated in the Eucharist). All these uses appear in Paul's writings in such a way as to imply no need for further explanations: Paul switches from one use to another as if it were the most natural thing to do.[10]

This implicit identification of all these three uses of the term 'body of Christ' continues throughout the patristic period and at least up to the twelfth or even the thirteenth century. Henri de Lubac, in his classical study, *Corpus Mysticum*,[11] examines in detail the history of this concept in order to conclude with an observation that bears directly on our subject. He notes (and this is confirmed by other studies such as those of Fr Yves Congar)[12] that from the thirteenth

[10] Thus, in 1 Cor. 6.15-20; 10.16-17; 11.1-27; etc.
[11] H. de Lubac, *Corpus Mysticum: L'Eucharistie et l'Eglise au Moyen Age*, 1944.
[12] Y. Congar, *L'Eglise de s.Augustin à l'époque moderne*, 1970, p. 168. Cf. his *L'ecclésiologie du haut Moyen-Age*, 1968, pp. 86ff.

century onwards these three uses of the term 'body of Christ' (the Christological, the ecclesiological and the eucharistic) are carefully distinguished by the scholastics so as to acquire entirely different and indeed *independent* meanings. It is in this context that the term 'mystical body of Christ' would be attached exclusively to the Church and would acquire a very specific meaning.

The consequences of this development have been quite serious in the course of history. This development was accompanied by the tendency of scholastic theology to treat the sacraments (including the Eucharist) as an autonomous subject in relation to both Christology and ecclesiology.[13] This meant that we could now speak of the 'mystical body of Christ', the Church, without necessarily referring automatically to the Eucharist — or even to the historical and risen personal body of Christ — as was the case in Paul and in the early Church. *Corpus mysticum* was to be used for the Church alone,[14] and mainly for the Church in its heavenly, ideal and invisible existence, for the 'communion of saints', which transcends and escapes our everyday experience. It is clear from this that the term 'mystical body' takes shape in close relationship with the fate which awaited the very term 'mystical' since that time, namely its identification with that which lies beyond the ordinary and the historical and surpasses all understanding.

A correction of this development, albeit only partial, took place in the twentieth century. We may call this a new phase in the history of the term 'mystical body'. This made its appearance in the 1930s with the monumental work of Emile Mersch, *Le Corps mystique du Christ*, which tried to connect again the idea of the 'mystical body' with its Christological roots, making use of all the biblical and patristic material that refers to Christ as a corporate entity. Almost at the same time, or just a few years later, biblical scholars led by H. Wheeler Robinson[15] put forward the theory of 'corporate personality' as a fundamental biblical concept and thus further enhanced Mersch's stress on the collective character of Christology, which has played a central role in theology ever since.

---

[13] Cf. Y. Congar, *L' Eglise de s.Augustin*, pp. 173ff.

[14] This allowed the possibility of speaking of the pope as a *caput* of the mystical body, which would have been impossible if the term 'mystical body' had retained its earlier association with the Eucharist. Cf. Y. Congar, *L'Eglise de s.Augustin*, p. 168f.

[15] *The Hebrew Conception of Corporate Personality* (1936), followed by A.R. Johnson, *The One and the Many in the Israelite Conception of God* (1942), and J. de Fraine, *Adam et son lignage* (1959).

Now, I have called this development a 'partial correction' because, although it connects again the ecclesial with the Christological use of 'body of Christ', it does very little to connect it with the third use, namely the Eucharist.[16] This use was left out of ecclesiology almost entirely until an Orthodox theologian, the late Fr N. Afanassieff, brought it to the fore with his 'eucharistic ecclesiology', without of course entering into any serious systematic theological reflection on the matter. Works such as those already mentioned of de Lubac and Congar, and also of G. Dix[17] and the Lutheran Werner Elert,[18] though primarily historical in nature, did a great deal to relate the idea of 'body of Christ' to the Eucharist and thus implicitly or explicitly to ecclesiology. It now seems that we are at a point in the history of scholarship where we can no longer operate with the idea of 'body of Christ' in ecclesiology without simultaneously taking into account the original synthesis of the Christological, the ecclesiological and the eucharistic. We shall try to take this into consideration throughout this chapter.

But what of the adjective 'mystical' in such a synthetic approach? History has bequeathed to us only the sense in which the scholastics and, later on, Mersch have used it. If we are to apply it to the synthetic use of 'body of Christ', it is obvious that we have to give it a new meaning. It must be made to include also the historical as well as the eucharistic understanding of the 'body of Christ' simultaneously. What sense are we then to give to 'mystical'?

2.

It is obvious that in order to do this we have to go outside the strict ecclesiological field and consider some broader philosophical and theological areas, leading in the first instance to Christology. In order to make a rather difficult task somehow easier, let me propose as a basic working hypothesis a definition of the term 'mystical' along the following very general lines.

All forms of mysticism seem to have to do with man's desire, and indeed deep existential need, to bridge the gap between what he in fact is or experiences and what transcends him. In religion this means bridging the gap between being human and the divine[19] —

---

[16] This seems to apply also to the papal encyclical, *Mystici corporis* (1943), which owed its inspiration to the work of Mersch.
[17] Mainly his *The Shape of the Liturgy* (1945).
[18] *Abendmahl und Kirchengemeinschaft in der alten Kirche hauptsächlich des Ostens* (1954).
[19] I. Marcoulesco, 'Mystical Union', in Mircea Eliade (ed.), *The Encyclopedia of Reli-*

whatever this may imply: a personal being or a state of existence which lies beyond the actual. Mysticism thus always has something to do with soteriology and is the aspect of a relationship which could be called 'positive', that is, a relationship stressing *unity* rather than distance and otherness.

This stress on unity rather than on distance, inherent in all mystical experience, can easily lead to *monism* in philosophy and religious thought. Biblical 'religion', if we may call it that, appears to be particularly sensitive to monistic views of existence and by implication also to mysticism.[20] I maintain that such monism was always present in classical Greek thought from the pre-Socratics to the Neoplatonists, and that patristic theology had to wrestle with this issue as the most crucial one — perhaps the only one — in its relation with pagan Greek philosophy. It is against this background of the struggle to maintain the dialectic between 'created' and 'uncreated' existence in the Greek thinking culture of the patristic period[21] that we must place and try to understand the application of the 'body of Christ' idea to Christology in that period.

A careful study of the Christology of the Council of Chalcedon would reveal to us that the deeper concern of the Fathers was how to arrive at the unity between the divine and the human in Christ without falling into mystical monism. There is no doubt that Chalcedon wants to make sure that the gap between the 'created' and the 'uncreated' is fully bridged. This is a soteriological demand which can be called 'mystical' in that it is inspired by the desire to bring about a total and unbreakable unity between divine and human. This demand is met with the insistence of the Council that in Christ divine and human natures are united ἀδιαιρέτως (indivisibly). And yet the need is felt immediately to qualify this by another adverb pointing in the opposite direction: ἀσυγχύτως (without confusion). Thus Christology bridges the gap between created and uncreated in a way that avoids monism and maintains the created-uncreated dialectic. In orthodox Chalcedonian Christology it is impossible to utter such mystical phrases as 'I am Thou and Thou art me'[22] and the like. Following and

gion, vol. X, 1987, p. 239: 'The experience of union between the subject and its divine object is considered the supreme stage of mystical experience and of contemplative life'.

[20] On this ground certain Protestant theologians (E. Brunner, R. Niebuhr) hold mysticism to be essentially anti-Christian, linked more with Neoplatonism and paganism than with the Gospel.

[21] See Chapter 7, above.

[22] Such expressions are to be found mainly in Islamic Sufism (which seems also to

marvellously explaining Chalcedon, St Maximus the Confessor later worked out philosophically a set of distinctions which, in my view, express the orthodox patristic position on mysticism in a perfect way. These distinctions are expressed with the pair διαίρεσις (distance) versus διαφορά (difference).[23] If Chalcedonian Christology were to be expressed philosophically, it would be absolutely necessary to work out an ontology whereby distance (διαίρεσις) is not an inevitable corollary of otherness (διαφορά), and unity does not destroy but — and this is important — *affirms and realizes otherness*.

In the body of Christ, therefore, understood Christologically, mystical union results not in fusion but, on the contrary, in otherness. The 'one' does not *fall* — as is the case with Neoplatonism — when it becomes 'many'; it is enhanced and made real through the many. We shall see later how important this notion of the 'one' and the 'many' is for ecclesiology. At the moment we simply note its importance for mystical union in the case of Christology. The body of Christ involves a unity which makes the otherness between God and man emerge even more clearly. The biblical concern for absolute divine transcendence is thus maintained in 'body of Christ' Christology. Philosophically, this is done with the help of a radical distinction between 'division' and 'difference' (διαίρεσις and διαφορά), as well as with the help of the distinction between 'nature' and 'person', which allows for unity to emerge as something due to *person* and not to nature (*hypostatic* — not natural — unity).[24] These lessons from the Christology of Chalcedon apply also to the ecclesiological and eucharistic uses of the 'body of Christ' image, since these uses were at that time identical (note, for example, how the Nestorian or the Monophysitic controversies automatically affected the understanding of the Eucharist).[25] We must, therefore, reflect now on the ecclesiological signifi-

have influenced Christian mystics in the late Middle Ages): 'Between me and Thee lingers an "it is I" that torments me. Ah, of Thy grace, take this "I" from between us'. And 'I am He whom I love, and He whom I love is I'. Al-Hallaj in R.A. Nicholson, *Legacy of Islam*, 1939, p. 218. For the relation between Christian and Sufi mysticism, see M. Smith, *Way of the Mystics: The Early Christian Mystics and the Rise of the Sufis*, 1976.

[23] Maximus, *Ep.* 12 (PG 91, 469); *Th. Pol.* 14 (PG 91, 149); etc. For an excellent discussion of this matter see L. Thunberg, *Microcosm and Mediator*, 1995², pp. 51ff.

[24] The idea of 'hypostatic union' is central to the Christology of St Cyril of Alexandria (4th anathema; see Alberigo *et al.*, *Conciliorum Oecumenicorum Decreta*, 1962, p. 91) and is fully adopted by St Maximus the Confessor (*Ep.* 12 and 18; PG 91, 481 and 588). This is an important concept, for it indicates that the ground and centre of Christ's unity is a *person*, a *hypostasis* (the Logos).

[25] Cf. H. Chadwick, 'Eucharist and Christology in the Nestorian Controversy', *Journal of Theological Studies* 2 (1951), pp. 145-64.

cance of the 'body of Christ' idea, as it emerges on the ground of the Christological use just stated.

3.

If the mystical union implied in 'body of Christ' Christology is one in which unity amounts to otherness and vice-versa, the understanding of the Church as the body of Christ cannot but be based on the same principle. Here the matter becomes rather more delicate and it is necessary to make subtle distinctions in order to clarify an extremely complex idea. The application of the image of the 'body of Christ' to the Church has resulted in the course of history in certain misunderstandings of ecclesiology which could be called 'Christomonistic'. That this can affect the subject of mystical experience may be illustrated by the following remarks.

By making the Church the body of Christ in an exclusively Christological sense, it became possible to develop an ecclesiology in which the 'one' — Christ — acquired priority or independence over the 'many'. Union between God and man in the body of Christ was realized and canalized primarily through a relationship with Christ understood as an individual. The result of this was either a mysticism of some kind of erotic union with Christ the individual, or a sacramental-eucharistic mysticism centred on the objectified eucharistic body. In any case, the body of Christ did not automatically imply the community of the 'many' in the realization of man's unity with God. It is to this aspect that we must now turn our attention.

In order to apply the 'body of Christ' image to ecclesiology in a way that would do justice to the well-balanced mysticism of Chalcedonian Christology, we must condition it Pneumatologically right from the beginning. Pneumatology involves, among other things, two fundamental dimensions. One is the dimension of communion and the other is that of freedom.[26] Applied to ecclesiology these dimensions mean the following.

(a) The body of Christ is conditioned from the beginning by the 'many', that is, unity is *constituted* by otherness (the ἀδιαιρέτως does not precede the ἀσυγχύτως but coincides with it).[27] In more concrete terms it means that any form of unity with God in Christ, any 'mystical experience', *must necessarily pass through the communion of the 'many'*.

---

[26] See my *Being as Communion*, 1985, pp. 110ff. and 123ff.
[27] See above, Chapter 7.

In order to illustrate this point I should like to refer to the way Paul uses the 'body of Christ' image in 1 Corinthians, especially in ch. 12. There Paul insists that there is no charisma which can be conceived independently of the other charismata and that however impressive the extraordinary gifts that certain members of the Church possess, they are 'nothing' (οὐδέν εἰμι) without *love*. Here we must note that 'love' is nothing other than the 'communion of the Spirit' in the one body;[28] not a feeling or an act of the individual. By being a 'spiritual body' Christ's body is by definition a communion and therefore all spiritual gifts or 'mystical experiences' have to pass through the community and to edify it (οἰκοδομὴ) — this is the meaning of 'but have not love' (ἀγάπην δὲ μὴ ἔχω; 1 Cor. 13.1) — in order to be authentic. Mystical experience without love is inconceivable in the body of Christ, but love (ἀγάπη), it must be underlined, is the communion of the community. 1 John applies the same principle to the knowledge of God.[29] Spiritual mysticism is always ecclesial and passes through the community; it is never an individual possession.[30]

(b) The dimension of freedom is also crucial in the following ways. In the first place, it has to do with the freedom of God. No spiritual gift derives from natural or ethical qualities of man, but comes always from 'above' or outside nature and history. There is no room for 'natural' gifts in the Spirit.[31] Every gift is every time a new *event*. The body of Christ is thus built up through a convergence of new events and not through a preservation or transmission of historical realities. True, there is the one historical body of Christ extended and transmitted through the centuries. Charismata are thus transmitted by way of succession. And yet, all this happens every time as a new event,[32] *as if it did not have to happen.*[33] The freedom of the Spirit transcends

[28] This is evident from the context in which the 'hymn to love' appears in 1 Corinthians 13. Its purpose is to stress the interdependence of the charismata in the one body of Christ.

[29] 1 Jn 2.4, 8, 11, 20, etc.

[30] Note that even for Dionysius the Areopagite 'mystical insight belonged essentially to the Christian community, not to private speculation or subjective experience', L. Dupré, 'Mysticism', p. 246.

[31] This view is implied in the insistence of St Gregory Palamas and the Hesychasts on the *uncreated* character of the divine energies: 'since the gift which the saints receive and by which they are deified is none other than God Himself, how can you say that that too is a created grace?', Gregory Palamas, *Against Akindynos*, III.8.

[32] See further, my *Being as Communion*, p. 185f.

[33] This is particularly evident in the eucharistic *epiclesis*: although the words of institution offer the historic 'guarantee' of Christ's real presence, the invocation

historical causality, because causality in history and nature implies necessity. Being is conditioned by event, and mystical experience is not simply *a participation in an objectively given reality, but an implication in a set of new events.* The body of Christ *is* by *becoming* again and again what it is as if it were not at all that which it is. The Spirit brings the charismata from the future, from the eschata, as new events; he does not elicit them out of history as out of a deposit of grace. Mystical experience is thus a participation as *anticipation*, a coming of the Kingdom into history not 'by observation'[34] but as a 'thief in the night'.[35] Spiritual mysticism is thus *eschatological* in nature.

With these observations in mind, we can understand better why the Eucharist is the most 'mystical' of all acts of the Church and Prophecy is one of the highest ministries. But on these we must say a few more words immediately.

II. EUCHARISTIC MYSTICISM

The most striking feature of the eucharistic liturgy in the early Church is that from the very beginning it was conceived in terms of *vision.* The Prologue of the fourth Gospel in speaking of the Logos made flesh uses visionary language (ἐθεασάμεθα τὴν δόξαν αὐτοῦ — 'we beheld his glory'; Jn 1.14),[36] reminding us of the visions of Moses, Isaiah, and so on. The book of the Apocalypse is also situated in a visionary context and is undoubtedly related to eucharistic experience.[37] Ignatius of Antioch sees the Eucharist as a τύπος of the eschatological reality with the bishop seated on the throne of God.[38] All ancient liturgies borrow the vision of Isaiah with the τρισάγιον as their basis,[39] while the Byzantine liturgy does its best to make out of the Eucharist a vision of the Kingdom.[40]

This connection of the Eucharist with vision is the most convincing proof that the Eucharist is the mystical experience of the Church *par*

---

of the Spirit is necessary for this presence to happen, as if the historical assurance were not enough.

[34] Lk. 17.20.

[35] 1 Thess. 5.2.

[36] Jn 1.14.

[37] See P. Prigent, *Apocalypse et liturgie*, 1964.

[38] Ignatius, *Magn.* 6.1.

[39] Cf. G. Kretschmar, *Studien zur frühchristlichen Trinitätstheologie*, 1956.

[40] See my article, 'The Eucharist and the Kingdom of God', three parts in *Sourozh* no. 58 (November, 1994), pp. 1-12; no. 59 (February, 1995), pp. 22-38; and no. 60 (May, 1995), pp. 32-46.

excellence.[41] It is so by applying all the dimensions of 'body of Christ' ecclesiology, which we have just outlined. It is 'spiritual' by being communion and *epiclesis*, that is, love and freedom at the same time. It is eschatological by presenting us with an *event* constituted anew every time, in which the new heaven and new earth of the Kingdom are anticipated. By partaking of the eucharistic body we enter into the new aeon, the new earth and new heaven. It is this that makes us cry at the end of the liturgy: 'we have *seen* [note, vision] the true light; we have received the heavenly Spirit'.

It has been unfortunate that in the course of history sacramental theology somehow lost the visionary character of the Eucharist. This led to a noteworthy shift in eucharistic mysticism. The accent has fallen on a mysticism of the historical ἀνάμνησις in the sense of a psychological retrospection involving the re-enactment of a past event, rather than the anticipation of a future one. No wonder, then, that eucharistic mysticism acquired similarities with the pagan hellenistic mysteries utterly foreign to the patristic understanding of μυστήριον. As a corollary to this, eucharistic mysticism was deprived also of its communal character and became a matter of the psychological experience of the individual. All this has led the Church away from the original understanding of the Eucharist as the mystical experience of the Church *par excellence*. Eucharistic experience was thus 'spiritualized' in the wrong sense, that is, it became a matter of unity with God through the human mind or 'spirit'. The 'body of Christ' lost its 'bodiness' both in the sense of corporateness or community and in the sense of materiality. From a vision of the glory of a transfigured creation it became a means of escaping from matter and the senses.[42] In short, the eucharistic mystical experience needs to be united again with the Judaeo-Christian apocalyptic tradition going back to Hebrew prophecy. It is this that will make it biblical in the most profound sense. 'Φάρμακον ἀθανασίας' (medicine of immortality) must be seen in the context of the eucharistic *community* embodying the eschatological community. This is the Ignatian context.

At this point it appears necessary to clarify the role of symbolism in the liturgy. It is often thought that eucharistic mysticism especially in the Orthodox tradition employs symbolic language, gesture, and so

---

[41] Hence the traditional description of the Eucharist as 'the mystical supper'.

[42] It should not be forgotten that Christ's Transfiguration on Mount Tabor was a transfiguration of his human *body*. Orthodox tradition, including the Hesychasts, never deviated to an anti-body or anti-matter mysticism. See J. Meyendorff, *A Study of Gregory Palamas*, 1964, p. 173, with quotations from Palamas on p. 150f.

on, as ways of signifying 'spiritual' realities through material means. I personally think that this way of thinking, going back to Origen and ultimately to a Greek and Platonic mentality, is essentially foreign to the Orthodox liturgy.[43] All gestures, colours, and so on, employed in the liturgy are used *typologically*. Typological mysticism seeks to connect past or present *events* with the eschaton;[44] it does not induce the mind to higher intelligible realities by means of the senses. Typological mysticism does not operate with a scale of values in which matter is only the starting point of the ascent to an ideal world, like a beautiful human body in the Platonic meaning of participation in the world of ideas. In the liturgy, matter is not a window to higher things. It is the very substance of a transformed cosmos.

This typological mysticism of the liturgy is tied up with biblical prophecy in such a deep way that it becomes inevitable to speak of another aspect of ecclesial mysticism, namely *the word* and especially its prophetic utterance.

III. PROPHETIC OR WORD MYSTICISM

Prophétisme sacramentel is the title of a well-known study by the late Professor J.J. von Allmen. The thesis is developed further in his later book, *Célébrer le salut*: sacrament and word have to be brought together in an organic synthesis. This is, in any case, a demand stemming from the encounter between the Roman Catholic, Orthodox and Protestant Churches in the Ecumenical Movement. Is there a mystical experience that can be applied to the word?

The problem seems to be entirely absent in the early Church and for the following reason: it was still at that time inconceivable to dissociate the eucharistic mystical experience from the prophetic, just as it was impossible to dissociate prophecy from vision, of God and of the future Kingdom. The word *heard* was at the same time *seen*: φωτισμός (enlightenment) came both aurally and visually. There was no incompatibility between word and mystical experience at that time.

One of the reasons why this incompatibility arose in the course of history is related to the fact that it was gradually forgotten that the word of God in the Church is prophetic and not didactic. Of course, there is also the didactic word in the Church: teaching (διδαχή) and

[43] A. Schmemann, *The Eucharist*, 1987, makes this point very forcefully.
[44] Cf. J. Daniélou, *The Bible and the Liturgy*, 1956.

reading the scriptures as narrating events of the past. But the original purpose of Scripture and of the word of God was to announce
eschatological realities to the people, to proclaim the Kingdom. This
is the essence of prophecy. In this case, the word comes to us not from
the past but from the future; it is an echo of things to come. Hearing the word of God is entering into the same mystery or mysteries
that the Eucharist portrays. That is why the prophets in the primitive
Church (cf. *Didache* and also the Apocalypse) were allowed to preside
and speak at the Eucharist, and the bishops were in this sense nothing but successors of the prophets (cf. *Martyrium Polycarpi*). Equally, it
is for the same reason that there has never been in the Church sacramental action without words, especially words from the Bible,[45] since
all sacraments, and especially the Eucharist, are proclamations of the
Kingdom. But in saying this we must make sure that we do not confuse the prophetic with the didactic word. The sermon is not always
or necessarily a mystical experience. It is so when it allows for the
eschatological reality to visit us in history. Hearing about the Kingdom must be accompanied by seeing the light of the Kingdom. It is
only then that the word becomes a mystical experience. The same
is true of reading the Scriptures. If the word of God comes from the
future and not from the past, its proper place is the eucharistic context. It is there that prophetic utterance and prophetic vision are
made into one reality. Then οὐκέτι περιηχῆ ἀλλὰ ἐνηχῆ (you no longer
hear about, but you hear from within), to use a significant distinction
made by St Cyril of Jerusalem in contrasting the state of the catechumen with that of a baptized person.[46] The latter, by participating
in the sacraments, does not hear *about* the Kingdom but hears from
within it. 'Hearing about' (περιηχεῖν) and 'hearing in' (ἐνηχεῖν) have
to be united, and the latter must embrace and transform the former.
When the word is 'heard in', it is not something that man grasps,
seizes and con-ceives (all the aggressiveness of the human intellect)
but something that embraces him and makes him its own. The preposition ἐν, as contrasted with περὶ, points precisely to the communion of the community as a *sine qua non conditio* for a mysticism of the
word.

[45] Cyril Jerus, *Procatechesis* 9 (PG 33, 349A): the exorcisms at Baptism are 'divine'
because they are 'collected from the divine scriptures'.
[46] *Procatechesis* 6 (PG 33, 344A-B): 'Thou wert called a Catechumen, which means
hearing about the sacraments (*mysteria*) from outside... Thou no longer hearest
about [them] but thou hearest from within; for the indwelling of the Spirit henceforth fashions thy mind into a house of God'.

IV. MINISTERIAL MYSTICISM

Ministry, *Amt* or Church order, is the aspect of ecclesiology that seems to have least to do with mystical experience. Yet it would be inconceivable to leave this aspect, which is to be found in the very heart of ecclesiology, out of our consideration.

What makes it possible to see with Ignatius of Antioch a τύπος of God in a ministry such as that of the bishop, or the τύπος of the apostles in the college of the presbyterium, and so on? Is it a peculiarity of someone inclined to mysticism, or can it be interpreted with reference to fundamental ecclesiological principles?

The answer to this question depends on the extent to which we are ready to apply to ecclesiology what we may call *iconic ontology*. In a cultural tradition which is dominated by objectification and individualism in ontology, it is impossible to convey the idea that a certain minister is acting as an *icon* of Christ or of the apostles. 'Icon' in this case has to be understood in a way fundamentally different from both the classical Greek (mainly Platonic) and the current Western understandings of 'image'. In the Platonic sense of εἰκών the image participates in something *already there*. Truth is always pre-existent. In the iconic ontology of the Greek Fathers, an εἰκών is normally an 'image' of things to come.[47] Truth here lies in the future. This is expressed in a concise way by St Maximus the Confessor when he writes: 'the things of the Old Testament are shadow; those of the New Testament are εἰκών; truth is the state of the future things'.[48] This is a reversal of the Platonic view 'image' and represents an ontology worked out on purely biblical grounds, borrowed from the prophetism and apocalypticism to which we referred earlier (cf. the vision of Isaiah). The ministry, by being iconic in this particular sense, is itself a mystical event which allows us to partake of future realities, of the Kingdom, without transforming the minister either into a sign empty of ontological content or into an individual possessing in himself a *character indelibilis*. Both functionalism and 'character' theology of the minis-

---

[47] Clement Alex., *Strom.* 4.22 (PG 8, 1352); Origen, *In Jo.* 10.16 (PG 14, 333); 10.38 (PG 14, 380); Eusebius, *Hist. Eccl.* I.3.4 (PG 20, 69); I.3.15 (PG 20, 73): the Old Testament is an εἰκών of the New. For other fathers, however, the OT is not even an εἰκών, but σκιά (shadow): Methodius Olymp., *Symposium* 5.7 (PG 18, 109); John Damasc., *Imag.* 1.15 (PG 94, 1244); etc.

[48] Maximus, *Schol. in eccl. hier.* 3.3.2 (PG 4, 137). The question of authorship is essentially irrelevant, since these ideas are to be found in other works of Maximus.

try deprive the ministry of the Church of any mystical content. Iconic ontology, on the contrary, operating with a view of participation as *anticipation*, introduces into the ministry a mystical dimension faithful to the demands of the Bible.

Now, this iconic mysticism of the ministry requires the event of communion in order to happen. This is part of the *charismatic* character that all ministry possesses in the Church. I have already referred to 1 Corinthians 12–13 and the meaning that charisma possesses there. The whole concept is relational. The Spirit realizes the body of Christ here and now as a complex of ministries, all of which are interdependent. Participation in the ministry of Christ takes the form of a convergence of all the charismata in a community which portrays in history the Kingdom to come. The ministers are thus μυσταγωγοί in that they introduce the faithful into this community that offers a vision and a foretaste of the Kingdom.[49] The iconic, the relational and the charismatic explain each other. The equation of ministries with charismata by Paul in the above mentioned passage involves a mysticism of the 'body of Christ' which is basically biblical.

V. Ascetic or Monastic Mysticism

In the context of the variety of charismata making up the body of Christ, history has known a certain type of charisma which is called the monk or the ascetic. Because this type of charisma has established itself firmly in tradition, and above all because it has been commonly associated with mysticism, we must devote some special consideration to it.

The first remark to be made is that in the light of our thesis here it is wrong to associate asceticism with mysticism in an exclusive way. The ascetic Fathers are wrongly called the mystical theologians *par excellence*, especially in the East. Nowhere in the patristic tradition is the term 'mystic' associated with the desert Fathers, whereas it is normally used in connection with ordained ministers, especially bishops,[50] and this for reasons that we have already discussed.

---

[49] It is not accidental that St Maximus calls his work on the Eucharist Μυσταγωγία, while presenting the Liturgy as an icon of the future Kingdom. It is equally significant that the technical term he uses to name the Eucharist is *Synaxis*, i.e., the assembly of the community. There can be no icon of the Kingdom without the community.

[50] See esp. Dionysius Areop. and Maximus.

However, although the ascetic is not normally called 'mystic' in the early Church, this represents a way of mystical experience which bears its own characteristics and which has to be brought into relationship with ecclesial mysticism as a whole, as we have described it here. What are these characteristics?

If we look at the phenomenon of Christian asceticism from the point of view of its historical origins and its development in the patristic period, we note that this phenomenon made its appearance in history as a form of emphasizing the eschatological nature of the Church in its extreme demands of biblical apocalypticism. The monk was the member of the Church who took so seriously the biblical claim that the Kingdom will break into history, judging it and bringing this world to an end, that he undertook to break all ties with this world and live as a citizen of the Kingdom to come.[51] The belief that we have no μένουσαν πόλιν (abiding city) here but τὴν μέλλουσαν ἐπιζητοῦμεν (we seek the one which is to come)[52] formed the starting point of asceticism in history. Eschatology, the expectation and vision of the Kingdom,[53] lies in the background of monasticism, and this should never be forgotten as we try to understand its 'mysticism'.

Because of this break with the world and history, the monk had to experience not only a 'historical' death, as a 'departure from the world', but also a death of his 'self'. Here the model was Christ and his Cross, a reality already present in the experience of Baptism. This implied a kind of mystical experience which can be called *kenotic* and which consists of the following elements.

(a) The breaking of one's own will. Just as the Son in his *kenosis* obeyed the Father and emptied himself of whatever was properly regarded as his own (Phil. 2) reaching the crucial decision at Gethsemane of saying 'not as I will but as Thou willest', in the same way the monk had to find a γέρων, a spiritual father, to whom he would offer his full obedience.[54] It is interesting to note that all this involved a

---

[51] For a discussion of the biblical origins of early monasticism, its association with the idea of the 'renunciation of the world system' and its connection with Christ's proclamation of the Kingdom, see G. Florovsky, *The Byzantine Ascetic and Spiritual Fathers*, vol. X of his *Collected Works*, 1987, esp. pp. 17-107.

[52] Heb. 13.14; cf. Phil. 3.20.

[53] Cf. Gregory Palamas, *Triad.* I.1.4: St John the Baptist was a precursor of monasticism because, like him, the monastic community announces the imminence of the *Parousia*.

[54] The importance of the ascetic's attachment to an 'elder' or γέρων, as his spiritual guide, is emphasized by monastic authorities such as St John Cassian, 'On the Holy Fathers at Sketis and on Discrimination', in *The Philokalia* I (trans. and

horizontal relationship and not an individual relationship with God. The event of communion that characterizes all charismatic life lies at the heart of asceticism. There is no devaluation of the body or any kind of Manichaean dualism that can explain the original intention of monasticism. There is basically an application of the kenotic model of Christology to charismatic existence, taking place through a *relationship* with others and not as an individual experience.[55]

(b) This breaking of one's own will signified the achievement of *freedom, par excellence*. Freedom from one's own will is the highest form of freedom, for the passion of self-preservation is the strongest of all necessities binding man. In the context of acquiring this freedom, the monk experiences death and reaches the abyss of nothingness.[56] This makes him a mystical communicant with the very depths of the human or created condition, with its fall and the consequences it has had for existence. The mysticism of the ascetic is thus in the first instance a descent into Hades, a participation in the anxiety, the fears and the death of all men. None, therefore, knows better what it means to be human; none has a deeper communion with humanity

---

ed. G.E.H. Palmer, Philip Sherrard and Kallistos Ware, 1979), pp. 95-108, esp. p. 103; St Symeon the New Theologian, on whom see H.J.M. Turner, *St Symeon the New Theologian and Spiritual Fatherhood* (1990), *passim*; St John Climacus, *The Ladder of Divine Ascent*, chs. 52-53 (ed. Holy Transfiguration Monastery, Brookline, MA, 1978); and others. This tradition reaches Russia mainly through St Paisius Velickovsky, the Athonite, and is dominant in Eastern Orthodox monasticism up to this day. See more on this in Bishop Kallistos Ware, 'The Spiritual Father in Orthodox Christianity', *Cross Currents* 24 (1974), pp. 296-313.

[55] It is true that solitude is the state sought after by the early monks, especially those who chose to be hermits. Yet even in this state the monk is supposed not to isolate himself existentially from his fellow men, but to be concerned with them in his prayers. 'If a man will say in his heart — "I am alone with God in this world" — he will find no peace', according to an 'apophthegma' of abbot Alonius (quoted by G. Florovsky, *The Byzantine Ascetic and Spiritual Fathers*, p. 107). St Basil goes as far as to insist on community life as the ideal monasticism (*Reg. Fusius tract.* 7; PG 31, 928-933).

[56] Cf. the 'saying' of St Silouan the Athonite, 'keep thy mind in hell and despair not', quoted and profoundly commented upon by the late Fr Sophrony (Sakharov), *The Monk of Mount Athos*, 1975, pp. 115-18: 'Man's consciousness that he is unworthy of God, and his condemnation of himself for every sin, in strange fashion makes him kin with the Spirit of Truth, and sets his heart free for divine love. And with the increase in love and the light of truth comes revelation of the mystery of the redeeming descent into hell of the Son of God. Man himself becomes more fully like Christ; and through this likeness to Christ in the "impoverishment" (κένωσις) of His earthly being he becomes like to Him also in the fulness of eternal life. God embraces all things, even the bottomless abysses of hell...'

and with creation as a whole, than the ascetic.[57] If eucharistic mysticism offers a taste of the Kingdom, ascetic mysticism begins by offering a taste of Hell. The desert Fathers are described as the most sensitive beings in history, those who weep even when they see a bird dying, those who understand all forms of human sin and weakness, for whom there is no sinner that cannot be forgiven or at least loved. This mysticism of participation in the fallen human predicament realizes the Church as the mystical body of the *crucified* Christ. But it must be noted that this is not an individualistic experience; it is based on freedom from the self.

(c) This freedom from the self leads to a movement of finding one's identity not through self-affirmation, but through the *other*. This makes mysticism *agapetic* or *erotic* in a way, however, that distinguishes it sharply from the Platonic eros of Antiquity, for in the latter case love is not free; it is bound by the law of attraction exercised by the beautiful and the good. One cannot love the ugly or the sinner for one cannot be attracted except by the Good. In the ascetic experience, based on kenotic Christology, one loves precisely what is debased and ugly[58] and this means that one loves free from all rational or moral necessity and causality. Mysticism here is so different from forms which imply an irresistible attraction of the soul by God as the highest Good. The ascetic loves first of all and above all the sinner, not out of condescension and compassion but out of a free existential involvement in the fallen human condition. Ascetic mysticism is not grounded on attraction, for attraction implies necessity; it is grounded on free *kenosis* from whatever is attractive[59] through a descent into the boundaries of creatureliness to which the fall has brought us all.

[57] Important in this respect is the idea of the *hypostatic principle*, proposed by the late Archimandrite Sophrony (Sakharov). See especially his, *We Shall See Him as He Is*, 1988, esp. ch. 13, pp. 190-220. All of Fr Sophrony's works are centred on this idea, according to which the axis of Christian life is the *person* or *hypostasis*, just as God is the 'One Who Is' as person or persons. This principle is realized through the communion of love, through obedience and self-emptying for the sake of love for the other. This makes one regard one's being as identical with that of the 'whole Adam' (*Words of Life*, 1996, pp. 16, 40). Prayer reaches out this way to embrace all humanity, not in a general and vague way but in and through each concrete human hypostasis or person: 'in learning to live with one person, we learn to live with the millions of people who are like him. In this way, we enter progressively into deep suffering for all humanity' (*Words of Life*, p. 47). See also his book, *On Prayer*, 1998.

[58] This makes the love of one's enemies essential to the ascetic experience, as St Silouan the Athonite insists. See Archim. Sophrony, *The Monk of Athos*, p. 69f.

[59] The ascetic abstains from natural attractions not out of a negative attitude to nature but in order that he may be free to love all, even the unattractive ones.

(d) It is only through this free *kenosis* that the ascetic is led to the light of the Resurrection. The light of Mount Tabor, the light of the Transfiguration, which the Hesychasts claimed to see, was given as a result of participation in the sufferings, the *kenosis* of Christ.[60] The narrative of the Transfiguration contains this reference to suffering (Mt. 16.24; 17.12). Seeing the uncreated light of God is a mystical experience which presupposes participation in the *kenosis* of Christ. It is not, as is often thought, a matter of praying and exercising techniques of the yoga type.[61] It is a matter of participation in the mystical body of Christ in its crucified form, a communion in the sufferings of Christ,[62] which the ascetics experience through their struggle against the passions, above all of φιλαυτία (love of self).[63]

This leads to a final remark which concerns the epistemological aspect of ascetic mysticism. We know from history that Origenism, which exercised a strong influence on Eastern (and Western) monasticism, operated with the view that what man needs in order to obtain divine knowledge is the purification of the mind from all sensible things and concentration on itself or on God by way of ascending contemplation. This is essentially Neoplatonic mysticism and as such it was rejected by the patristic tradition. But what is interesting is the way in which this rejection took place. Maximus the Confessor seems to be the decisive figure in this case, too.[64] By adapting principles already present in a trend of monasticism known as the 'Macarian' type, Eastern monasticism up to and including the Hesychasts[65] corrected Evagrianism, which was responsible for the spread of the above mentioned Origenistic views. The correction involved the adoption of the Macarian principle that the organ of knowledge and the centre of the human being is the *heart* (a biblical idea — καρδία) and not the νοῦς, and that therefore the νοῦς had to come down to the heart and unite with it. This principle was applied later by the

---

[60] See Cyril of Alex., *Homil. diver.* 9 (PG 77, 1009-1016), who clearly relates the glory of the Transfiguration to Christ's sufferings.

[61] There is much profit to be had from reading the relevant chapter ('The Jesus Prayer–Method') of the late Fr Sophrony's book, *On Prayer*, 1998.

[62] 1 Pet. 4.13; cf. Phil. 3.10; Heb. 2.9-10.

[63] See I. Hausherr, *Philautie: De la tendresse pour soi à la charité selon S. Maxime le Confesseur*, 1952.

[64] See I.H. Dalmais, 'Le doctrine ascétique de Maxime le Confesseur d'après le *Liber Asceticus*', *Irénikon* 26 (1953), pp. 17-39.

[65] See J. Meyendorff, *A Study of Gregory Palamas*, pp. 135ff. Cf. my 'The Early Christian Community', in B. McGinn, J. Meyendorff and J. Leclerq (eds.), *Christian Spirituality*, 1986, vol. 1, pp. 23-43.

Hesychasts of Mount Athos through the well-known controversial technique.[66] Seen in the light of this background, all this amounts in the final analysis to a mystical experience based on *love*. We know God only as we purify the heart (οἱ καθαροὶ τῇ καρδίᾳ τὸν θεὸν ὄψονται — the pure in heart shall see God)[67] because the heart is *not the source of feeling*, but the locus of obedience to the will of the 'other' and ultimately the 'Other' *par excellence*, God. Love as the epistemological principle of ascetic mysticism is again a matter of emptying oneself from one's own self-centredness, an ek-static movement which has nothing to do with human self-consciousness but with communion and relationship.

CONCLUSIONS

Ecclesial mysticism implies an experience which takes us away from what is normally called mysticism. Here union with God does not take place on the level of *consciousness*. The problematic of mysticism operates normally with the assumption that the organ (centre) of spirituality is consciousness. Hence it opposes to *knowledge, ignorance*. However, this presupposes or leads to *individualism* in mystical experience. The crucial thing is not what happens *in me*, in my consciousness, but what happens *between me and someone else*. Knowledge emerges from love, and mystical experience is not preoccupied with what I feel or am conscious of. Ecclesial mysticism turns one's attention outside oneself. Introspection and self-consciousness have nothing to do with ecclesial mysticism. Thus, to know God as he knows himself is not to enter the mechanism of divine self-consciousness, but to enter by grace into the sonship (υἱοθεσία) which is conveyed to us by the loving relationship between the Father, the Son and the Spirit, a relationship which allows each of these persons to emerge as utterly *other* while being utterly *one*. The knowledge that God the Father has of himself *is the Son and the Spirit*: the Son is the ἀλήθεια of God, the mirror in which he sees himself.[68] Such an ontology of personhood *not* conceived as consciousness[69] but as relationship (σχέσις)

[66] "The heart directs the whole organism and when grace receives the heart as its share it rules over all the thoughts and all the members; for the intelligence and all the thoughts of the soul reside there', Macarius of Egypt, *Spiritual Homilies* 15.20 (PG 34, 589). Gregory Palamas, *Triad.* I.2.3; II.2; etc., defends Nicephorus the Hesychast on the basis of this Macarian anthropology.

[67] Mt. 5.8.

[68] Athanasius, *Contra Arian.* I.20-21 (PG 26, 54-57).

[69] Cf. above, Chapters 1 and 6.

forms the basis of mystical union in the Church. The Church as the body of Christ points to a mysticism of communion and relationship through which one is so united with the 'other' (God and our fellow man) as to form one indivisible unity through which otherness emerges clearly, and the partners of the relationship are distinct and particular not as individuals but as persons.

This kind of mystical union presupposes the Christological ground laid down by Chalcedon, according to which union between man and God is realized in Christ without division but at the same time without confusion, that is, a perfect unity which does not destroy but affirms otherness. The Church as the 'mystical body' of Christ is the place where this Christologically understood 'mystical union' is realized.

LIST OF SOURCES

All material previously published is reproduced here with the kind permission of the original publisher(s).

The Introduction was first published in English in *Sobornost* 16 (1994), and in *St Vladimir's Seminary Quarterly* 38 (1994), www.svspress.com.

Chapter 1 is published for the first time in the present volume.

Chapter 2 was first published in Christoph Schwöbel and Colin E. Gunton (eds.), *Persons, Divine and Human* (Edinburgh: T&T Clark, 1991).

Chapter 3 appears for the first time in the present volume.

Chapter 4 was first published in Christoph Schwöbel (ed.), *Trinitarian Theology Today* (Edinburgh: T&T Clark, 1995), under the title 'The Doctrine of the Holy Trinity: The Significance of the Cappadocian Contribution'. The Appendix is published for the first time here.

Chapter 5 was first published as 'The Teaching of the 2nd Ecumenical Council on the Holy Spirit in Historical and Ecumenical Perspective' in the volume, *Credo in Spiritum Sanctum*. Atti del Congresso Teologico Internazionale di Pneumatologia (Vatican City: Libreria Editrice Vaticana, 1983), vol. 1.

Chapter 6 was first published in the *Scottish Journal of Theology* 28 (1975).

Chapter 7 appeared first in Greek in the periodical *Synaxi* (1982), and then in French in the review *Contacts* 36 (1984) and 37 (1985), under the title 'Christologie et existence: la dialectique créé-incréé et le dogme de Chalcédoine'. The present text is a translation from the French by Paul McPartlan. The Appendix is a translation from the Greek by Norman Russell.

Chapter 8 is published for the first time here.

INDEX OF NAMES

Index kindly produced by Mr Dionysios Skliris.